Praise for *A Haunted History of Invisible Women*

"Delightfully harrowing and full of spine-tingling horrors, *A Haunted History of Invisible Women* is not your average book of ghost stories. Hieber and Janes go far beyond the obvious thrills and chills, providing fascinating context and lavish detail in this incredibly empathetic book as they gently remind us not only of what we are but what we may become. You'll be thinking about this one long after you finish. Read it with the lights on!" —**Deanna Raybourn**, *New York Times* and *USA Today* bestselling author

"Thought-provoking and deliciously eerie, this intriguing study of phantom females not only delves into the history behind the legendary hauntings that chill our blood, but also gives detailed descriptions of real-life ghost encounters." —**Leslie Rule**, bestselling author

"This book accomplishes the impossible—to tell true stories of abuse, murder, horror, and the plight of women, and somehow make that an elegant and compelling piece of writing. This should not only be read . . . but taught. Brava!" —**Jonathan Maberry**, *New York Times* bestselling author of *Relentless* and *Ink*

"An absolute must-buy for the spooky people of the world. Hieber and Janes lead the reader on a guided tour of America's most fascinating and noteworthy female ghosts that is utterly brilliant and deeply compelling. The authors examine these stories with a keen feminist lens and resurrect the real women behind them with respect they were seldom afforded in life. It's extraordinary to find a book that is so chilling, yet so full of heart. You'll find yourself haunted by these stories." —**Mallory O'Meara**, bestselling author of *The Lady from the Black Lagoon* and *Girly Drinks*

"*A Haunted History of Invisible Women* is a beautifully researched and well-written observation of women's ghosts across time. From the famous to the not-so-famous, their stories and the history surrounding them both fascinate and mesmerize. If this book doesn't leave with you a sense of wonder and a healthy dose of goosebumps, check your pulse—you may already be among the spirits." —**Marc Hartzman**, author of *Chasing Ghosts: A Tour of Our Fascination with Spirits and the Supernatural*

"This is the book I have always wanted to read. Expert storytellers Hieber and Janes take us on tour through the lives of real women who would become legendary ghosts, adding depth to stories I thought I knew and introducing me to characters I've never met before. With wit and empathy, *A Haunted History* brings the spirit of these women to life. Their stories are touching, shocking, inspiring, and intimately relatable. They tell the ways women have learned to navigate their world, to thrive, and live authentically against the odds. They reveal the ways society objectifies and classifies women who defy norms and challenge the expectations of their time. These ghosts still have something to say and have much to teach." —**Leila Taylor**, author of *Darkly: Black History and America's Gothic Soul*

"Deeply researched and lovingly written, *A Haunted History of Invisible Women* is the ultimate paranormal compendium on female ghosts of America. Not only is this a compulsively readable book, it'll send a chill down your spine while illuminating the dark shadows of a nation." —**Kris Waldherr**, author of *The Lost History of Dreams* and *Unnatural Women: A Novel of the Frankenstein Women*

"*A Haunted History of Invisible Women* looks beyond the legends of maligned female ghosts and gives us their real histories. It is both a meditation on the misogyny of a ghost-hunting culture that capitalizes on false narratives of sex and death, and a fascinating look at the flesh-and-blood women behind the ghost stories. This book is a long-overdue search for historic truth, yet it recognizes that 'When it comes to ghosts, truth is as elusive as the spirits themselves.'" —**Chris Woodyard**, author of *The Victorian Book of the Dead*

"The things which truly frighten us are the things which are real. That is why women love horror: it allows us a healthy exploration of our real-life terrors. There is a sisterhood of haunted women throughout history, both actual people and fictional characters. I was thrilled to learn more about them all through the eyes of two women who are members of that sisterhood." —*Ohioana Library* **Magazine**

AMERICA'S MOST GOTHIC

HAUNTED HISTORY STRANGER THAN FICTION

LEANNA RENEE HIEBER & ANDREA JANES

CITADEL PRESS
Kensington Publishing Corp.
kensingtonbooks.com

CITADEL PRESS BOOKS are published by

Kensington Publishing Corp.
900 Third Avenue
New York, NY 10022

All Kensington titles, imprints, and distributed lines are available at special quantity discounts for bulk purchases for sales promotions, premiums, fund-raising, educational, or institutional use. Special book excerpts or customized printings can also be created to fit specific needs. For details, write or phone the office of the Kensington sales manager: Kensington Publishing Corp., 900 Third Avenue, New York, NY 10022, attn: Sales Department; phone 1-800-221-2647.

CITADEL PRESS and the Citadel logo are Reg. U.S. Pat. & TM Off.

Library of Congress Control Number: 2025936285

First hardcover printing: October 2025
ISBN: 978-0-8065-4374-1

ISBN: 978-0-8065-4375-8 (e-book)

10 9 8 7 6 5 4 3 2 1

Printed in the United States of America

The authorized representative in the EU for product safety and compliance
is eucomply OU, Parnu mnt 139b-14, Apt 123
Tallin, Berlin 11317, hello2@eucompliancepartner.com

Contents

CONTENTS

Introduction

Leanna and Andrea

Fog clings to the contours of a decaying manse. One jaundiced light illuminates an upstairs window. Is there a figure at a bay window with a hand on tattered curtains? On second glance, no; there is no one that you can see in that turret. But you feel you are being watched. The air is too close and leaves an acrid taste on the tongue. Sounds are strange to your ear; the bird calls are shrill and the light casts shadows at longer angles than it should. Each sense strains and you haven't even taken your first step toward your inevitable destination.

You've guessed it: You've stumbled into a Gothic tale. And no, as you suspected, it won't let you go unless you willfully escape it, one way or another. It will haunt you like a ghost. The Gothic, as a genre, is designed to be an alluring, mesmerizing phantasm. Raising the hairs on the back of your neck. Making you question your reality, your sanity, and perhaps teaching you something of the perilous precipice between life and death. And you willingly subject yourself to the psychological journey.

The Gothic is popularly understood to contain immutable core elements: isolation, gloomy weather, an old house, a woman in peril and a brooding or menacing man, a forbidding land-scape, an element of madness or instability, the supernatural. The uncanny breaks through the veil of rationality; powered by the mind of the subject, the eye of the viewer, the body of the living who encounters something inexplicable. Anna Letitia Aikin, early Gothic author of "Sir Bertrand," said of the genre: "A strange and unexpected event awakens the mind, and keeps it on the stretch; and where the agency of invisible beings is introduced . . . our imagination, darting forth, explores with rapture the new world which is laid open to its view, [and] rejoices in the expansion of its powers."

Leanna has spent a lifetime in the Gothic, as a classically trained actress performing extensively in Gothic dramas like *Dracula*, as an author of fifteen Gothic-informed novels, as a goth (not to be generally conflated, but in her case, a subculture and style parallel to her life in Gothic literature) and as a lecturer on the topic of Gothic settings. She has a personal shorthand for the top tenets of the Gothic:

1. Dread is the engine of the Gothic. You know something odd, dangerous, questionable, life-threatening, startling, or horrifying will happen, it's just a matter of when. The Gothic often employs a long, slow, sanity-questioning burn (see Henry James's *The Turn of the Screw*).

2. Psychological focus has to be at the forefront. We have to be in the mindset of the protagonist as they figure out their situation and seek to maintain their autonomy and agency in an oft-confining environment, whether we believe them as the narrator or not (again, *The Turn of the Screw*).

3. *Setting is* character. It doesn't have to be a castle like in Horace Walpole's 1764 inception point, *The Castle of Otranto*, but the setting has to be larger than life and as much a force of nature exerting influence on the story as any other person or circumstance, be it Du Maurier's

Manderley, Shirley Jackson's Hill House, Charlotte Brontë's Thornfield Hall, or, to give Henry James this trifecta here, Bly Manor. Each of those named buildings radiates its own character. Setting need not even involve a house; a Gothic tale can involve a wilderness, a ship, or any other extreme, unpredictable, dangerous external environment that somehow threatens or confines the protagonist. Whether the paranormal in a Gothic is explained as mundane (Arthur Conan Doyle's *Hound of the Baskervilles,* Shirley Jackson's *We Have Always Lived in the Castle*) or offered as factually haunted (Hill House), the possibility of the paranormal is generally present. To start *The Castle of Otranto* off, an enormous helmet falls from the heavens to kill a family member, so realism is questionable from the jump.

Shake these ingredients and make sure this strong cocktail is topped off with *loads* of atmosphere—there literally cannot be too much. This is a genre meant, as Aikin reminds us, to expand senses as if they are magical powers, encouraging engagement with another world in which the "agency of invisible beings" is hard at work.

Yet the Gothic resists firm boundaries. When researching for this book, we were variously told that the Gothic is more of a mode than a genre, or even an aesthetic: It is a series of "traveling tropes," adaptable and malleable, generously encompassing, slippery, shape-shifting, amorphous; the Gothic is "vibes, all vibes." It was architecture, it was history, it was literature, it was culture. It was European, it was American, it was cosmic. It was postcolonial, it was queer; it was about race, it was about capitalism, it was about gender. It was Us and it was the Others. The Gothic does not deal in clarity. It is obscure and multi-foliate, an overgrown "garden of forking paths" that lead only to endless threading branches in an infinite forest surrounded by a foggy wasteland, a craggy mountain, an endless ocean, and boundless space. It resists easy definitions, and though there are some helpful signposts along the way, it seems to not want to be mapped. Questions beget questions, and research opens up still more rabbit holes and labyrinthine pathways.

All this sounds pretty dramatic, but the Gothic really *is* all around us, especially in America, where we are haunted by our foundational violence. Our bloody history directly informs the American Gothic as an aesthetic and a genre, and its tropes are an ideal vocabulary for talking about history. They are particularly apt right now.

Angela Carter famously stated in 1974 that "we live in Gothic times," which feels even more appropriate and true in our specific moment in history. The first wave of the Gothic novel coincided nearly exactly with the beginnings of the Industrial Revolution, from roughly the 1760s to the 1840s. Its second wave crested during the Victorian era, alongside a renewed spurt of industrial expansion and rapid urbanization. In both periods, whiplash-quick technological changes accompanied a disruption in long-held patterns of human habitation and migration, while slavery, colonialism, and an utter disregard for the natural environment concentrated wealth in the hands of the few while annihilating the ecological balance of our planet, and everything resulted in intense social upheaval. Sound familiar? Humanity is arguably currently riding another historic wave of precedent-shattering foundational change, as AI upends a reality that has already been warped by social media and the throttling of journalism as our news sources are replaced by for-profit internet algorithms. We are unsure of what's real and what's not real, and unable to keep pace emotionally with dizzying changes. Entire industries are crumbling, others building up faster than we can comprehend them. Climate change and conflict augment existing patterns of human migration, and wealth accrues to the most morally reprehensible humans on earth. Is it any wonder that the Gothic, which can be, as Nick Groom wrote, "a metaphor for the less tangible anxieties and traumas of the human condition," is thriving and more relevant than ever?

This is what makes applying a Gothic lens to "true" stories—in our case, ghost stories—a provocative idea. People often think of the Gothic in terms of fiction, of literature and film. The term is only rarely applied to the realm of nonfiction, which is what ghost stories and folklore are. But ghost stories and folklore are also cultural production, straddling the line between fantasy and reality, metaphor and history, real and unreal. The boundaries between art and life have been blurred since the very beginning: Horace Walpole not only wrote the first Gothic novel, *The Castle of Otranto*, but he lived it too, in a Gothic Revival mansion he called Strawberry Hill. Walpole struggled with some complicated issues of inheritance and property during time he was writing *Otranto*, stressors that informed and inspired the book's obsession with ownership and heirs. From Horace Walpole to your friendly neighborhood goth, life is art and vice versa. What's more, the language of the Gothic, and of ghost stories, is the perfect vehicle for us to work out the fears and anxieties of our lived experiences: A woman running from a house has the entire patriarchy pursuing her, with all of its threats of murder and sexual violence. This breaks beyond all boundaries of genre.

And so, while this book offers stories that may seem idiosyncratic and surprising at first, you will assuredly find Gothic elements in each tale that might be reasonably recognizable: isolation and entrapment, hidden chambers, haunted houses, a woman in peril and a brooding or menacing man, forbidding weather and landscapes, madness, family curses, and, of course, ghosts. All are true to the fluid, atmospheric, untraceable quality of the Gothic.

These stories evoke feelings of dread, foreboding, mystery, fear, and suspense; the tales of the hidden places and people in this country that remain in the shadows, histories just waiting to impinge upon the current day and unleash their wild horrors. They hold up a mirror to our terrors, our guilt and our trauma, our nation's ghosts, our cities' specters.

A few words of warning: This is not a travel guide, nor is it intended to be a complete or comprehensive state-by-state guide to haunted places. Neither is it an academic or authoritative guide to the Gothic; for that there are many wonderful books already in existence, and we have listed some at the end of the book, along with a list of talented modern authors of fiction working in the genre today. We are not professors or historians; we are storytellers, and we share these tales in the same spirit of wonder with which we encountered them.

We'll be focusing mostly on women's stories, because when one takes a look at Gothic literature, a theme is readily apparent: Women Running from Houses. Because setting is character and the domestic sphere has been so entwined with women's expectations and societally enforced rules and roles through history, it's inevitable that the Gothic, full of heroines in various states of peril and mental strain, becomes a way to examine tales of agency and self-reliance as a tool for survival. This agency in the face of existential threat is also fundamental to the Gothic, and also very much one of the reasons for the genre's current appeal.

Another word of warning: If you are not familiar with the Gothic yet, please be advised that the threats and dreadful things so prevalent in this genre may be triggering. Some of these stories deal with topics such as suicide and sexual trauma, and while we are always mindful to approach these topics sensitively and respectfully, the Gothic is by definition a rather dark and scary place. Please proceed with caution, but take heart.

The Gothic heroine runs; she outwits her potential captor, she survives. We may live in an era of tumult, torment and existential threat, but we will not be annihilated. These stories are, like our current reality, bleak and full of dread, but the characters in them will live to see another day.

Much like in *A Haunted History of Invisible Women*, we're choosing stories that truly call to us, speak to us, haunt us, get under our skin and make us think. Examples of tropes and archetypes will abound, but so will their subversions, an aspect that often leads to a ghost story's lasting impact. This book won't be a comprehensive list of every ghost story that seems plucked from a Gothic tale—we can't attend to every one—but we hope you'll be just as intrigued by fascinating local histories and ready to pick up wild literature it puts us in mind of.

As wild as some of the stories may be, we'll try to get to the heart of them, to separate fact from fiction while lifting up the truly uncanny aspects that can't be denied. But do remember, as your senses strain, that the Gothic was created as a construct to question the world around the reader; to safely examine the psychology of an era and its confines and cruelties. Ghost stories tend to provide the very same bellwether.

Walk with us through the fog. The destination may not be readily apparent. But you'll know when to run.

New York
December 4, 2024

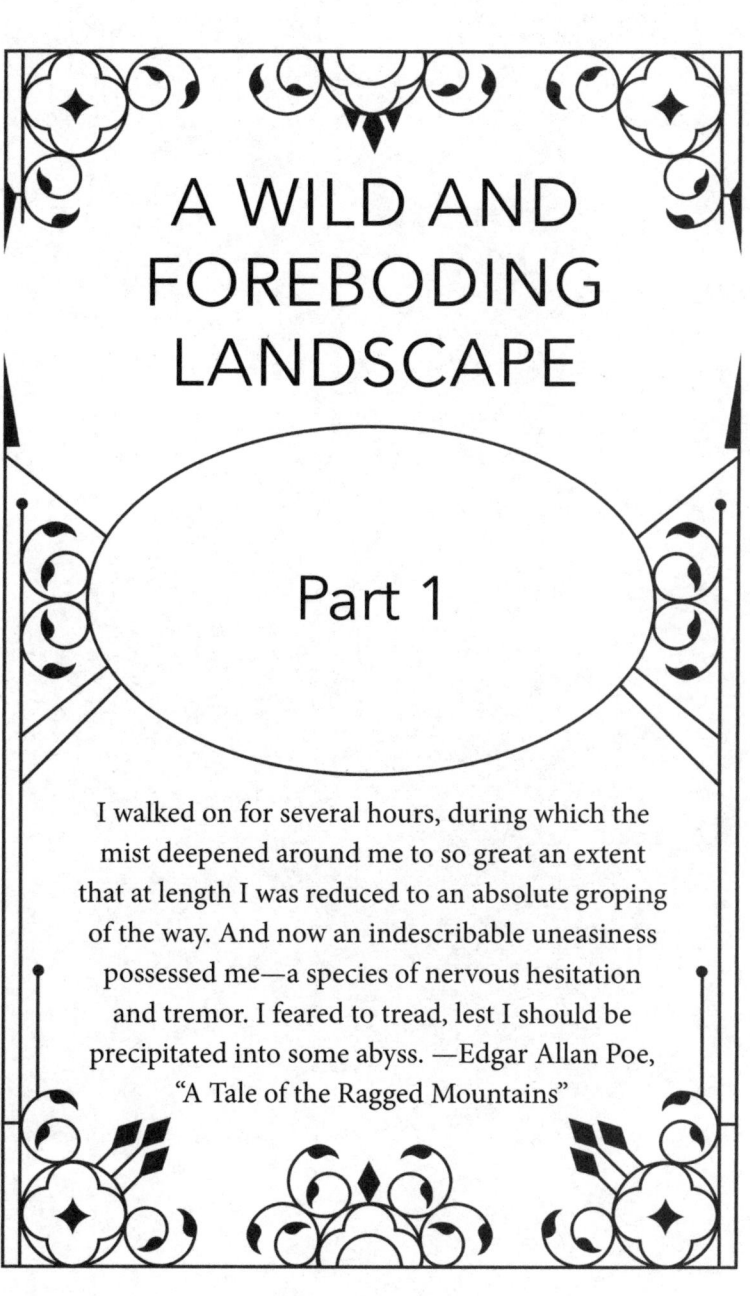

A WILD AND FOREBODING LANDSCAPE

Part 1

I walked on for several hours, during which the mist deepened around me to so great an extent that at length I was reduced to an absolute groping of the way. And now an indescribable uneasiness possessed me—a species of nervous hesitation and tremor. I feared to tread, lest I should be precipitated into some abyss. —Edgar Allan Poe, "A Tale of the Ragged Mountains"

Canadian Gothic: Bear Woman

Andrea

Bear Woman lived in a cave.

Her real name, so they say, was Marguerite de la Rocque de Roberval. She was a French noblewoman who traveled to Canada in 1542, on an expedition of colonization. She sailed aboard a ship commanded by her guardian, Jean-François de la Rocque de Roberval, a powerful man appointed viceroy to Canada by the king of France. At some point along the voyage, it came to his attention that Marguerite was having an affair with a man aboard the ship. As punishment for her indiscretion, Roberval marooned her on an isolated island in the frigid waters of the Gulf of Saint Lawrence. He left her in this freezing, hostile wilderness with her maidservant, a sixty-year-old nurse named Damienne. In some versions of her story, Marguerite's lover commandeered a lifeboat and rowed it to the island to be with her; in others he was also marooned by Roberval. The castaways survived their first winter by huddling for warmth in a cave. In this cave, Marguerite gave birth to what some consider to be the first European baby born on the North American continent.

The unforgiving climate and lack of provisions were too much for the little family: the lover died before spring, and

Damienne perished as the second winter dawned. The baby followed soon after. Marguerite, driven to the brink of insanity by her grief and isolation, tortured by near-starvation and hallucinations of fearsome supernatural beings—spirits, phantoms, and demons—survived through fervent prayer and by hunting wild animals on the island, learning to shoot and kill, most memorably a bear with fur "as white as an egg." After two years in the wilderness, she was rescued by a fishing boat and returned to France.

After her return, Marguerite lived quietly and worked as a private tutor to the daughters of the nobility. Her story struck a chord with the French queen, Marguerite de Navarre, who apparently knew Marguerite de la Rocque personally and may have assisted her with procuring some of these jobs. The queen wrote up the tale in her *Heptameron*, a collection of short stories meant to be France's answer to the *Decameron* (and one of the few prominent books authored by women at the time). The narratives in the *Heptameron* were sometimes bawdy or erotic, often dealing with interpersonal intrigue and romance, and de Navarre applied this decidedly sexy approach to Bear Woman's ordeal. She focused on the religious and romantic aspects of the experience—her lover, her faith in God that sustained her during her ordeal; a specifically Protestant faith.

Another contemporary chronicler adopted a Catholic viewpoint. André Thevet was a priest, and primarily was interested in Marguerite's story because it dealt with his pet subject: demons. Thevet was a friend of Roberval's, and after hearing his version of events, traveled to the city of Nontron in the South of France, to interview Marguerite herself. He was intrigued by her tales of demons and spirits, which he seemed to take literally. Thevet wrote his own account of Marguerite's story, in which he "devotes many paragraphs to the evil spirits on the island: how they took on the form of wild animals, or manifested as horrifying visions that tormented her."[1] Thevet's is the most detailed version of events on historical record, and, other than Marguerite de Navarre's account, one of our few primary sources of the event.

But both accounts reveal their biases. Thevet was Catholic; de Navarre was Protestant. In sixteenth-century France, these were life-or-death distinctions, as the country was roiled by years of violence and religious warfare amid the tumultuous introduction of the Protestant faith. The two chroniclers have different faiths, genders, experiences, and aims in writing their works, and each has a different relationship to the participants. And here's where Bear Woman becomes so much more than a colorful tale: To read her story is an object lesson in the impossibility of perfect history, which is, as most of us know, as full of unreliable narrators as any Gothic fiction.

Accurate histories of women's lives, which were so often unrecorded, are doubly difficult to ascertain. The real Marguerite de la Rocque is hard to pin down; we don't know exactly who she really was. There were a dozen or so sixteenth-century French noblewomen named Marguerite de la Rocque, or, as it is variously spelled, de la Roque; she could have been any one of them. The best researchers cannot find her because the historic records simply aren't there: most women weren't considered important enough to keep track of. We have no definite records of her birth, death, title, or surname, or even anything that proves the precise nature of her connection to Roberval, so her true identity remains a mystery.

"Marguerite" was one of the most common female names in France at the time, and "de la Rocque" one of the most common surnames in the South of France, where she was very likely from. Certain things about her can be ascertained: that she had some sort of familial relationship with Jean-François de la Rocque de Roberval. She may have been his cousin once removed, and she was very likely his ward. It is probable that she was an orphan, and had not reached the age of majority by the time of their voyage to Canada, as she was probably about nineteen or twenty years old at the time. We know that she was nobility, as she is referred to as *Damoiselle*, "the lady," an appellation that would not have been applied to a commoner. Beyond that, unless some avid scholar unearths a previously undiscovered original sixteenth-century French legal document, everything is conjecture.

But it is unlikely such a document will ever be unearthed. Years of occlusion, much of it deliberate, some of it accidental, have muddled her story even more. Roberval took pains to deliberately strip a lot of identifying information from the official record, such as the name of Marguerite's lover. We don't even know his first name. The reasons for Roberval's cover-up are fairly obvious: it's one thing to maroon your young, female ward, another to abandon a nobleman to certain death.

We can be fairly certain that the lover *was* a noble, given that he brought to the island, among his other supplies, his own arquebus and a small musical instrument called a *citre*.[2] An arquebus, an antiquated proto-rifle, was a costly piece of equipment that required military training to use. An arquebus weighs twenty pounds, requires nineteen steps to load, and is notoriously finicky; in battle, it usually required two men to load, stabilize, and fire the weapon, and it was not something that could be easily or cheaply obtained by a commoner. And a *citre*, similar to a lyre, was something only a gentleman could afford to possess and have the leisure to learn to play.

Had the lover's name come to light, his family would surely have demanded reparations for their loss, an expense Roberval could ill-afford. Roberval had been "[a] kind of playboy who . . . lived a rakish life at court, amassing large debts while allowing the king and everyone else to believe his fortune was intact. He had borrowed money against several of his assets . . ." and was very likely extremely cash-poor.[3] In fact, there are many who believe that his marooning of Marguerite was motivated less by morals and more by the fact that legally, as his ward, her assets would pass to him in the event of her death—a near-certainty, when one considers the conditions of her abandonment on that remote, frigid, inhospitable island. We can fairly safely assume that acquiring Marguerite's property was very likely at least partial motivation for the marooning, particularly when one considers that all the important documents relating to Marguerite's land holdings—wills, deeds, tax, or land transfer records—have conveniently, mysteriously vanished from the Roberval family archives.

Revealing the lover's identity could also have caused a scandal at court, threatening Roberval's status as a favorite of the king. In the fraught atmosphere of courtier politics, reputation and popularity were vital. To reveal the lover's identity would risk Roberval's social as well as literal capital, and it was not a risk he would have been willing to take. Better to keep things quiet. A nobleman, unlike a woman or a servant, would be missed.

There is an alluring element of gallantry to the way Marguerite's lover joined her on the island. It is said that he refused to abandon her, commandeered supplies and a small boat, possibly at gunpoint, and forced Roberval's crew to let him join her. Once on the island, he taught Marguerite to handle the arquebus and helped her to fashion a rudimentary sort of shelter.

The lovers attempted to build a *logette*, a log cabin, but of course they were woefully unprepared and inadequately supplied. The wind-whipped island with its thin, peaty soil would have been nearly bare of trees. Perhaps they cut up the small boat the man sailed over in, and also utilized the canvas he brought with him. They may have used branches, or even the island's peat itself. It was late July when they were marooned, and they managed to survive that summer and early fall by killing the abundant wild game, possibly fishing the remarkably rich waters (early European explorers noted that cod and other fish thrived in such abundance in Canada's coastal waters that one could simply scoop them out of the ocean with a net), and foraging among the various "edible wild fruits" that grew on the island.

At some point, the lovers were married in a simple handfasting ceremony with Damienne as witness; in all recorded accounts of the event, Marguerite refers to her gentleman as her "husband." It is almost a scene of bucolic domesticity, tinged with shades of high romance. For a man to maroon himself with you, build you a cabin with his bare hands, all while serenading you on his *citre*—well, this is fairly irresistible stuff.

But the *logette* that love built proved useless against the shockingly cold Canadian winter. The three of them moved into a cave to survive, as it would have been much warmer, if not as comfortable. The cave was said to have been very small, with hardly enough room for three adults, and certainly no standing room. They would essentially have had to squat or crawl at all times. In this dark, narrow cave, her lover died. He had lived on the island for about nine months before he perished. While he was no doubt weakened by the incredible exertion it must have taken to survive in the wilderness all this time, his spirit by this point was also broken—he seems to have imagined someone would come along to rescue them, and then when it sunk in that nobody was coming, he lost the will to live.

Shortly after her husband died in the cramped, squalid cave, Marguerite gave birth. She had only Damienne to assist her in her labor. It was February. That child passed the earliest days of his life huddled in near-total darkness, surrounded by cascades of snow and howling, knife-sharp winds. (Actually, the close quarters, warmth, and darkness of a cave would be familiar conditions for a newborn baby. For the mother it might be less than ideal, but the baby would experience an almost seamless transition from womb to world.)

Roberval, meanwhile, was huddled and shivering with the rest of the ship's crew and passengers in a poorly heated, hastily constructed fort downriver in what would later become Montreal. In that first winter of late 1542 and early 1543, our villain and his crew were starving, rotting inside and out from scurvy. It was no wonder they were not faring well: Roberval was not cut out for life in Canada and lacked the survivalist skills it entailed. He'd never wanted to go to Canada, the place Jacques Cartier called a "land of stone and fearsome cliffs," and had only accepted the commission for the Crown in desperation, hoping that it might solve financial problems.[4] It is not hard to picture him sniveling and shaking with cold that first winter in Quebec—the man is clearly no hero. He is certainly not remembered with fondness, or at all, in Canadian history. In fact, I'd never even heard of him before reading Marguerite's story. Growing up in Canada, I was thoroughly schooled in the history of New France. We were taught of Jacques Cartier in abundant detail; we learned all about Samuel de Champlain; we literally re-created the battle of Wolfe and Montcalm at the Plains of Abraham on a class trip to Quebec City in eighth grade, or grade eight, as we say at home. But at no point, ever, were we taught the name of Robert, Sieur de Roberval. When I read of him as an adult, I was surprised to learn this man I'd never heard of had once been viceroy of Canada. He got away with his cowardly crime, I suppose, but was certainly swept under the rug of history. To this day, his sole namesake in the entire country of Canada is one small suburban neighborhood on the outskirts of Quebec City.

The villainous Roberval fits in neatly with that most Gothic of tropes: the evil nobleman who imperils the innocence of his younger kinswoman. While our Canadian Gothic involves a forbidding island instead of a crumbling castle, the power dynamics are the same. This antagonist threatens our heroine's bodily safety as well as her assets and property; he abuses his power over her to imprison or even kill her. These villains are everywhere in Gothic fiction; most of all, Roberval and Marguerite make me think of Signor Montoni and Emily St. Aubert in *The Mysteries of Udolpho*. Marguerite actually has a lot in common with the heroine of Ann Radcliffe's novel: both are Frenchwomen, orphans from noble families in reduced circumstances whose stories take place in the sixteenth century, and both of these heroines will be imprisoned in isolated places by their villainous relations. Roberval, her captor in the guise of protector, is so like a mustache-twirling, cape-flinging, cackling, sneering, leering cliché from a storybook that he, despite being an amply documented (if somewhat obscure) historical figure, seems somehow even less like a real human being than the shadowy and mysterious Marguerite.

There is also a faint but odious whiff of incestuous desire here, the cornerstone of any properly Gothic family. As repellent as it is to contemplate, the entire story with the "lover" may have been a cover-up, the poor boy a fall guy for Roberval's misdeed, Damienne a deliberate choice of midwife, the baby a double Roberval. Or perhaps the lover wasn't so innocent either— as writer Edmée Lepercq has noted, in the sixteenth century, rape was considered a form of seduction. We don't know the precise nature of love and desire, as it was portrayed back then.[5] As horrifying as it is to contemplate, that could mean that Marguerite was actually marooned on an island with her own rapist. If either of these scenarios were true, it's no wonder she didn't press charges upon her return to France, as rape wasn't technically considered a crime in most circumstances. While there's no evidence for, or even suggestion of, rape in any of the accounts, an aura of sexual threat and corruption floats over the whole mess of it. Of course, I'm reading this as a scholar of the Gothic, so I'm going to make these interpretations; André Thevet had his demons, I've got mine.

As Swedish feminist Karolina Ramqvist points out, there is a delicate balance between redressing Marguerite's historic invisibility and contributing to it by making her a blank slate onto which we project our own fantasies and interpretations. In any case, with or without actual incest or sexual violence, the power dynamics in this story remain imbalanced, threatening, heavily weighted in favor of the malevolent nobleman over the innocent and imperiled young ward. She was quite literally helpless, as evidenced by the fact that she went to Canada in the first place: Nobody in their right mind would leave France for Canada in the sixteenth century unless forced to, unless they were convicts sentenced to exile in the frozen wasteland of the north, or desperate cash-strapped nobles, or . . . young wards legally incapable of saying no.

Most of Roberval's passengers were, actually, convicts. Almost all were men; besides Marguerite and Damienne, there were only four other women aboard ship: Mariette de la Tappye, forty, convicted of murdering her son-in-law; Cassette Chapu, forty, convicted of abuse and fornication; Antoinette de Paradis, twenty-five, convicted of theft; Jehanne de la Veerye, thirty, convicted of having sold her daughter. On one of the other ships, there was an eighteen-year-old, Mondyne Boispie, who was accompanying a former convict.[6] These women were to serve as broodmares and drudges to populate, feed, and scrub New France. We can imagine they were all traveling reluctantly. Nor were the male convicts aboard ship eager to go; they had to be forced to leave their cozy dungeons in France to embark for this terrible, unknown wilderness. It was not a treat, in other words, to go to Canada.

The Gulf of Saint Lawrence, where Marguerite was marooned, is a vast, cold body of water between the province of Quebec on the mainland of Canada and the remote, scattered islands and peninsulas of the Maritime Provinces to the east. These islands are jagged, rugged, and forbidding, and Roberval would have passed one after another as his crew navigated the Strait of Belle Isle on his way down the river to the colony at what would become Montreal. There are dozens of such islands, and Roberval failed to note the precise one on which he marooned Marguerite. He did, however, leave us with its name: according to him, the place is called "the Isle of Demons."

For centuries, tall tales have been told about the Isle of Demons, which was supposedly avoided by the First Nations people dwelling nearby, so haunted was it by malevolent spirits of every kind. Even today, ghost stories circulate of Marguerite and her phantom lover, sometimes accompanied by Damienne (and sometimes not, because ghost stories shift with retelling), glimpsed by lone hikers on rocky outcroppings. But we don't know exactly where this island might be located, or if in fact it ever existed. The Isle of Demons appeared on several navigational maps . . . until it didn't. In sixteenth-century maps, it appears in the locality near what is now called Quirpon Island, off the coast of Newfoundland, but subsequent explorations failed to find it. Its existence became much disputed, and it was deemed to be imaginary, perhaps an invention, a mistake, a fanciful metaphor, or a nautical version of a "trap street," a cartographic bit of misdirection wherein false landmarks are deliberately included in order to identify would-be plagiarists.

The region of Quirpon is famous, incidentally, as the UNESCO World Heritage Site L'Anse aux Meadows, an ancient vestigial Viking village marking the area of first European settlement a thousand years ago. The Vikings didn't remain, however, as the climate was too unforgiving, even for them. Newfoundland itself is referred to colloquially as "the Rock," which should give you some idea of the nature of its terrain—notably harsh, even for the Canadian Maritimes. The explorer Jacques Cartier himself remarked that there was "not one good barrelful of earth" along the whole coast of it.

Though Roberval went on record as saying he marooned Marguerite on the Isle of Demons, leading many to believe Quirpon Island was the site of her ordeal, one amateur historian adamantly disputes this.

Elizabeth Boyer was an American lawyer, law professor, and feminist who lived in Ohio in the 1970s, and she was a devoted biographer of Marguerite de la Rocque. Boyer unequivocally places Marguerite on an island in Harrington Harbor, Quebec, some 280 kilometers (174 miles) to the west of Newfoundland. When Marguerite was marooned there in the 1540s, the little cluster of islands in Harrington Harbor were known as the Islands of St. Martha. They were named by Jacques Cartier, who first explored the area some ten years before. Because he first saw the archipelago on that particular saint's day, July 29, he named them after her, as any good Catholic boy would do. Later, Roberval's ship's pilot, perhaps in sympathy with Marguerite, called the archipelago "Les Iles de Damoiselle," and that name stuck for quite a while.

The pilot's careful navigations, mappings, and observations were collected in a cherished document called a *routier*, which would have been carefully handed down to subsequent generations of explorers. This pilot, one Jean Alfonse, served directly under Roberval and thus could not defy his orders to maroon the young woman—but he could lodge his protest the one way he knew how. His naming of the islands is a quiet act of sympathy and defiance that speaks volumes. (By contrast, a later biographer friendly toward the viceroy attempted to make the name "Roberval Island" happen, but it never quite caught on.) Roberval was a tricky one; he likely told people Marguerite was on the so-called Isle of Demons to discourage them from going to rescue her, or as a bit of misdirection.

Because of Roberval's general untrustworthiness, and Boyer's scholarly assiduousness, my money's on Harrington Harbor. Boyer even found a cave there during her research trips that seems to fit the bill. The cave is visible on maps and findable on the island in Harrington Harbor to this day, and locals tell tales of shards of pottery and pieces of an old shoe found in what they call "Margaret's Cave." Alfonses's name choice of "Ile de Damoiselle" also seems like a pretty broad clue. But, as with so much of this story, there's no way to know for sure.

Like Marguerite herself, the Isle of Demons is impossible to know with any certainty. But I like it this way. These imaginary islands subvert the rational, Enlightenment-era world of navigation and knowability, with its maps and boundaries, operating, as Angela Carter would say, "against the perennial human desire to believe the world as fact." The Isle of Demons is, like the Gothic itself, "endlessly transitive, aways moving, shifting and changing as it goes."[7] So we have here an unknowable woman on an unknowable island: This is not only very Gothic, but also very Canadian. In the "Conclusion to the *Literary History of Canada*," literary critic Northrop Frye wrote "that Canadian sensibility . . . is less perplexed by the question 'Who am I?' than by some such riddle as 'Where is here?'" In a country where our identity seems so often defined by what we are not (namely, not American), this strange little island that resists a definite name and location seems characteristically appropriate. "To enter Canada," Frye writes, "is a matter of being silently swallowed by an alien continent."

One thing we can say with certainty: Whether the island was in Quebec or Newfoundland, it would have been as cold as all the clichés of Canada would have you believe.

Even having grown up in Canada, I couldn't—and still can't—handle the relentless chilliness of the country, the scanty summers, the brief, cold springs, the dryness of winter with static sparking off my hair, the interminable, miserable gray slush of Toronto's streets for weeks, months, at a time; shivering and wearing two winter coats layered over one another in Montreal. Once, while sailing off the coast of St. John's in July, I wore a parka. I remember, as a child, waiting in vain for spring to come and it still snowing in late April. I cannot fathom how a woman from the relatively mild climate of France withstood a Canadian winter.

But somehow, she did.

While Roberval and his crew sailed back to France as soon as the ice melted, defeated and stymied in their attempt to found a permanent French colony—Montreal would not officially come into being until nearly a hundred years later, in 1642—Marguerite, Damienne, and the infant held on. Marguerite spent that spring and summer fighting off wild animals, newborn strapped to her chest, she and Damienne wielding sword and arquebus, killing bears to survive.

It all sounds so unrealistic and improbable, but Elizabeth Boyer has an intriguing theory about Marguerite's true identity that makes her survival more plausible: that she was the daughter of a minor noble, who would have grown up in financial constraints, as many of the nobility did in France at the time. Because of the way land was inherited, sons (and sometimes daughters) would receive holdings of decreasing size and value through the generations as inheritances were parceled off into smaller and smaller portions. This, added to the fact that the nobility were legally forbidden to become artisans or tradesmen, led to a lot of secretly impoverished nobles putting on a bold front while shamefacedly living in drafty, leaking castles, and having to work alongside their own peasants on their farms. A girl born into such a family would have, ironically, been in a stronger position to survive being marooned on an inhospitable island: It's possible she would have known how to kill, skin, and prepare animals, cook them over a fire; to mend and sew, to plant; to be hardy. There is one person, Marguerite de la Roque of Etouars, who is a strong contender for the "real Marguerite." Etouars is located in the South of France, not too far from Nontron, where Marguerite settled upon her return. This Marguerite of Etouars was also an orphan and about the right age to have been Roberval's unwilling ward, subject to his whims, and with no say in whether or not she went to Canada. She still would have had some property to her name—not much, but enough to make her disappearance convenient, financially, for Roberval. Her family was not as rich as it had once been, and the circumstances of her upbringing were fairly humble and hardy stuff.

This theory of Marguerite's true identity makes sense to me. Only a girl who'd had a somewhat challenging life would have what it took to survive not one, but *two* Canadian winters. The feat of her survival is staggering. Remember, the climate in this part of the world is so lousy, even the *Vikings* couldn't hack it. Yet this woman was out there slaughtering bears single-handedly with an arquebus, a weapon whose gunpowder has a shelf life of about a year—less in cold weather—with a newborn baby in tow, no less.

She fought for survival and she fought for her son. She guarded him against bears and wolves and wolverines and she did it all in unfathomable conditions in a frigid wasteland. She became fierce, protective, and wild. In André Thevet's account of Marguerite's violent showdowns with the local wildlife, he claims that she killed three bears in one day, including the afore-mentioned creature with fur "as white as an egg." Assuming this last beast is indeed a polar bear, as most assume it was, that would make her a remarkable warrior indeed, as the *Ursus maritimus* is one of our planet's most fearsome predators. She is now no longer Marguerite, but a mythical archetypal goddess figure: here, having battled the beasts of the Canadian wastes, she transforms into the Bear Woman, unleashing an atavistic inner wildness and awakening her dormant strength.

The symbolic relationship between women and bears has a long history across many cultures. In ancient Greece, there was a shrine to Artemis, where prepubescent girls danced in imitation of bears in a ritual to prepare for womanhood, for bears were sacred to that goddess. Followers of Artemis were expected to remain virgins, though, and in one myth the nymph Calisto was turned into a bear as punishment after she was "seduced" by Zeus and became pregnant. Later, when she was about to be shot by a hunter—her own son, in fact—she was saved when Zeus took pity on her, intervened, and set her among the stars as the constellation Ursa Major. Her son later became Ursa Minor: Little Bear.

There are many more examples of such foundational myths that describe the bear's feminine and matriarchal archetypes. It is no accident that the term *mama bear* is part of our lexicon. Our subconscious symbolic kinship with the bear has worked its way not only into our language and culture, but persists even in internet memes: While we all had a good laugh at the "man or bear" debate of 2024, there was also something deeply resonant about it. The internet meme circulated in the summer of that year, a viral question on social media that posed the conundrum, "Women, who would you rather encounter while alone and unarmed in the woods: a man or a bear?" Nearly every single woman chose the bear. It was a silly social media diversion that ended up inadvertently profoundly illustrating that women feel so unsafe at the hands of men that they'd rather be stuck in the woods with a wild bear. Marguerite would no doubt agree. In Celtic mythology, Artio is a bear goddess associated with fertility, motherhood, and initiation into womanhood. And a Korean foundational myth attributes the creation of the world to the bear mother Ungnyeo. Finally, the Blackfoot story of the Woman Who Married a Bear demonstrates what happens when a woman unleashes her wild side upon her neighbors.

The Blackfoot story in turn loosely inspired Canada's weirdest novel, *Bear* (1976), by Marian Engel. In the novel, Engel seems to be trying to out-Carter Angela—whose short story "The Tiger's Bride" contains one of the "most memorable sex acts in twentieth century fiction"—by penning this Canadian classic of a lonely archivist who enters into a sexual relationship with a bear. The book's current critical reception has been summed up, succinctly, as "What the actual fuck, Canada?" Canada's essential weirdness is often overlooked or forgotten, but it's there if you know where to look for it, from the unhinged horror of David Cronenberg to the hallucinatory surrealism of Guy Maddin, which novelist Douglas Anthony Cooper has called Canada's most "flamboyant demonstrations of the grotesque." Cooper in turn quotes famed Canadian scribe Robertson Davies, noting that "Canada is in fact a mystical northern race, though it prefers to 'present itself to the world as a Scottish banker.'"[8] Even beloved Canadian icon L.M. Montgomery, best known for penning the whimsical kid-lit masterpiece *Anne of Green Gables*, threaded ribbons of darkness through her work, which is taut with family scandal, unloved orphans, ghostly encounters, murder, accidental poisoning, premature burial, and "a family legend that Satan appeared at a dance party."[9] We are not nearly as bland as people think we are; like most isolated people who live in the woods, we're a tad strange.

As a second winter dawned, Damienne fell, or jumped, to her death. We can't quite be sure which—all we know is that she died, and that local legends tell of an elderly woman who fell from a cliff. She too may have given up hope of rescue and couldn't bear the thought of living through a second winter in the cave; after all, as Elizabeth Boyer writes, "Old ladies dread the cold."

Not long after Damienne died, the baby perished.

After their deaths, Marguerite lived alone on the island for another winter. In her isolation and terror, she suffered dreadful, horrific hallucinations and was tormented by terrible visions of phantoms and apparitions on the hellish, haunting Isle of Demons. The months when no one else was with her were the worst. Throughout the year's darkest months— December, January, February—she was "embattled with monsters . . . They haunted her as strange hallucinations in the light of night; demons found their way into the cave and [she] lay there, repeating her prayers, in the hope they'd disappear."[10]

Now Bear Woman is really alone, and her story takes on the nightmarish hue of Gothic horror, in which isolation so often plays a central part. Enforced solitude highlights our human vulnerability; it also forces us to sound the depths of our own dark recesses. Being alone with your own thoughts is the true terror of isolation. To do so in the wilderness is doubly terrifying. In the Gothic, the wilderness is the place that defies boundaries of "civilized" society. These are the spaces where we revert to our own wild natures, the places that are unmanageable, where fear erupts and humans perish. The wilderness, from the Old English *wild-deor*, the "place of wild animals," is "unknown, inhuman, unruly, untamed, uncultivated . . . a place of terror, where you lose your way, get turned around, become lost and be*wild*ered."[11]

Bear Woman was tortured by wild animals and supernatural entities at once. Or they may have been one and the same. It is Thevet's account that provides the most evocative descriptions of the spirits, demons, and visions that haunted Marguerite, giving us dozens of phrases like:

"She constantly saw the most strange visions which man can imagine . . ."

"I heard her tell of these frightful things, these evil spirits . . ."

"These evil spirits did [ravage] around them [and] went about to throw down their little cabin, presenting themselves as species and shapes of horrible animals . . ."

"Often during the night they heard cries so loud that it seemed to them as though they were made by more than a hundred thousand men. . . ."

It's significant that Thevet conflates evil spirits with savage animals, a motif that would come into play repeatedly throughout the colonization of the New World: the wild-beast-as-supernatural-menace returns again and again in New World Gothic. Modern commentators have come up with loads of natural explanations for these supernatural sounds, everything from moose to ptarmigans to loons. But most intriguing to me is this remark of Thevet's:

The demons "never approached their lodge, nor showed themselves visibly until she was alone [and] under the stress of her sorrows."

Solitude and stress? Aside from the polar bears, this sounds very much like postpartum life.

Karolina Ramqvist, in her book *The Bear Woman*, acknowledges the parallels between Marguerite's story and a new mother's postpartum feeling of isolation. Ramqvist's book is a work of autofiction that explores both the unknowability of Marguerite de la Rocque as a historic figure and the shifting identities and feelings of isolation that visit a person in early motherhood, which I can only imagine must feel doubly intense in the perpetual cold and dark of a Swedish winter.

Throughout the book, Ramqvist's narrator increasingly overidentifies with Bear Woman; she too knows how it feels to be utterly alone-with-an-infant and fighting off the demons of solitude. And yet, by the point in the story in which Bear Woman is living in pure isolation, having visions, praying constantly, and fully divested of all trappings of the human race, including other humans, Ramqvist's narrator begins to feel almost an undercurrent of envy at Marguerite's isolation. This might be because, not long after the isolation of early postpartum ends, the slow realization of your *lack* of solitude begins. Suddenly, you are not only no longer alone, you are *never* alone. As infants become toddlers, their need for closeness intensifies. Suddenly you become aware of your lack of "me time," you are touched out, you cannot poop or shower alone. If you have a second child, a third, the feeling exacerbates. There are no weekends or holidays, and there is no end in sight. No ship is coming to rescue you.

During the pandemic, I also began to envy anyone who had time alone, including Bear Woman. I was exhausted at never having a single minute without another person in my apartment. I hated my husband for snoring and twitching and triggering my insomnia, resented my child for being the thing that stood between me and getting my work done. I *did* want to live on a rock. I longed to be alone so badly. Recently, a woman in Spain made the news after she lived alone in a cave for several months. When she emerged, and was asked how it was, she said it was the most relaxing time she'd ever had in her life. I dreamed about this.

I became obsessed with the idea of female hermits, and wanted to write a book about them. There was one, Sarah Bishop, who lived in a cave in Connecticut's West Mountain in the late 1700s; there was another who lived on a beach near Lake Michigan; one who lived in the Florida Everglades in the 1940s; another, Anne LaBastille, who built herself a cabin in the Adirondacks in the 1960s.[12] Wild women, women who ran with the wolves. I envied them. I did not feel like a social creature just then. I'd had too much time with my family, no time alone, ever. I needed space, solitude, wildness, freedom, and time to write. I eagerly clicked on articles with headlines like, "Is Becoming a Hermit the Ultimate Feminist Statement?" Then I learned that most of these female hermits I'd idealized had been more or less forced into isolation, often raped or traumatized in some way, driven to the wilds by men who had broken their minds and spirits. They weren't free, they were fleeing.

The idealization of isolation wasn't the answer I'd imagined it was, and like motherhood itself, brought with it a host of complicated, often contradictory and ambiguous feelings. Now that the pandemic is "over" and time has passed, the nature of my relationship with my child has changed too. The clingy four-year-old who always wanted to play with me has become a Roblox-obsessed third grader who only wants to be left alone with her iPad. At eight years old, my daughter still loves to be with Mom, but inevitably she will grow up and become a teenager and want to be away from me. I think of this sometimes when she asks me to hold her as she falls asleep; I take her in my arms as I did when she was small and she is so large now that we resemble the Pietà. I kiss her forehead and whisper the nickname I gave to her as a baby: "Good night, Little Bear." When I say this, I picture Bear Woman tenderly wrapping up her infant in a bear-fur blanket, singing softly to the snug little bundle. I realize that they must have worn bear-fur cloaks, slept under bear-fur blankets, to survive. Every animal that attacked her husband's shallow grave, or tried to kill her baby, ultimately ended up giving her life. Survival and motherhood have their own paradoxes. The children who seemed underfoot during the day will be tenderly missed once night has fallen. Having a child is a process of being incredibly lonely, then never being alone for several years, followed by being more alone than ever. My great-grandmother used to say, "Your children are only on loan to you."

In November 1544, after two years and five months, Bear Woman was picked up by a fishing boat and she returned to France. Marguerite de Navarre wrote, "She told me that when she embarked on to the Breton boat to return to France, she was overwhelmed by a certain wish not to leave there, to die in that solitary place, like her husband, her child, and her servant, and that she desired to remain there, torn by sorrow as she was."

Elizabeth Boyer writes of the "strange and almost mystical hold" Bear Woman had over her. Boyer's *A Colony of One: The History of a Brave Woman*, self-published in 1983, is the only book-length history of Marguerite, and it is out of print. The book is an astonishing work of scholarship. It took Boyer over ten years, was entirely self-directed and (presumably) self-funded; it involved hours of tireless research in French archives, travel not only to France but also to an extremely remote area of Canada; an understanding of law and inheritance; extensive knowledge of French such that she was able to decipher handwritten documents written in arcane sixteenth-century French, and to interpret their nuances; and intensive archival research. Boyer's understanding of Marguerite's ordeal is threaded through with empathy and imagination, and with a devotion to its physical and sensory details: the strength and dexterity required to fire an arquebus, the vast reserves of mental fortitude and sheer strength of will required for survival, a firsthand understanding of the land and topography, and a vivid comprehension of the frigid cold of the Canadian winter. Boyer traveled to the furthest reaches of Quebec to discover more about Marguerite, driving over twenty hours from the nearest city with an international airport, then to an island reachable only by ferry boat or seaplane—and even then only in summer, for the sea ice freezes over in the winter—to speak with several present-day inhabitants of Harrington Harbor, the ones who told her of the existence of Margaret's Cave on the island, and about the shards of old pottery and pieces of an old shoe that had been found there.

It's odd that she doesn't say what, exactly, drove her to go tumbling down this particular rabbit hole, to write passionately, and with what great detail, about every aspect of Marguerite's life. Reading Boyer's book, I wished she had been more personal and intimate with her reader and let us know the source and fuel of her obsession. Beyond the allusion to the "mystical hold," the author gives us no more clues as to why she spent a decade of her life writing first a novel and then a history of Marguerite de la Rocque. Boyer, it seems, wants to maintain an enigmatic air, a cloak of dignified mystery that she refuses to remove.

For clues, I look online, where I discover Boyer was a member of a second-wave feminist group with an antiabortion stance—an intriguing fact, given the centrality of motherhood to Bear Woman's story. (Boyer herself had no children that we know of.) I look at the dust jacket of *A Colony of One*, which says, "Few authors could have researched and written this book. As a lawyer, Elizabeth Boyer has the access and expertise to find and evaluate early legal documents. As a student of the French language, she had the ability to scan and compile massive amounts of early French records. As a sailor she comprehended the navigational and logistical aspects of early voyages under sail. And as an outdoorswoman she understood the survival aspects. Moreover, as an American of Huguenot descent, and a feminist, the author felt a sense of duty toward this long-neglected heroine." I suppose I must take her at her word, then. Because the book was self-published, I realize, it is likely the dust jacket copy was written by Boyer herself, in the third person. Her pleasure in independent scholarship seems to demonstrate an affinity for isolation, for working outside the world of traditional academia, which is utterly fitting for the biographer of Bear Woman. In her author photo, Boyer portages a canoe triumphantly, smiling proudly. There is joy on her face.

We don't have to be mothers or Huguenot descendants, Swedish feminists or outdoorswomen, to feel this same mystical hold over us when we read Bear Woman's story. We too are endlessly shifting and changing, ultimately unknowable people on imaginary islands, at one moment utterly alone, the next moment envious of women who live in caves; at one moment tortured by our demons; the next, finding that the visions that come to us in solitude are actually gifts. We love our children, our families; we long to be away from them, we miss them when we are gone. Our most secret lives are unfathomable, our histories obscure even to ourselves. We are at times imperiled, but we do not roll over and die. We emerge from caves, battle demons, draw on our secret wild natures. Like Bear Woman, we are tortured, but we live. We survive trials of unimaginable loneliness.

Had circumstances been different, Bear Woman might have taken her place alongside the likes of Ernest Shackleton in the annals of Great Feats of Human Endurance in Very Cold Climates, or at least be given the respect she deserves. But I don't think Marguerite will ever be a hero in that sense. Her story is at once too large and too small, too complex and too vague; the nature of her survival is too granular to play out on a large scale. It is too messy, too female, too similar, in its own

way, to the thousand small feats of endurance that women perform every day. And it is too Gothic, a genre often characterized
merely as having a "gentlewoman in distress" by those who miss
the point of what it means for women to "run from houses." It
not only means escape—it means survival. It takes a lot of guts
to claw our way out of gloomy castles and dark caves. To face
the starkness of our own minds when they are finally stripped
of the things we have been taught to fill them with since we
were children—namely the needs and approval and authority
of others—and to sit with whatever of us is left.

The ancient Greeks had a word for an ideal life; they called
it *eudaimonia*. It can be translated as "well-demoned." A person
who had a good relationship with their demons lived a good
life. Maybe this is the kind of solitude we need right now. Did
Bear Woman, by surviving her demons, learn the secret of life?
Can learning to live with our demons save us?

Dead Ships and Dark Dreams: Ghost Ships of Southern Maine

Leanna

Standing on the jagged, striated claws of land that reach out into the inlets, eddies, and bays of Wolfe's Neck Preserve in southern Maine, I heard ghosts.

At least, that's what I thought at first, and it's easy to see how one could be convinced of disembodied, paranormal experiences. I stared out across the placid water, thick forest to my back, a small, rugged island just ahead of me and to my sides, a curving, rocky shoreline. One thin isthmus of land stretched out past a cove where it pointed like a long, accusing finger toward the ocean beyond. The acoustics of this coastal precipice startled me.

I heard voices ahead of me, as if they were standing a few feet before me. But there was only water there. Further still, along that forested isthmus, no one stood along the bank. I heard an entire family talking. A child screaming. I whirled around and saw no one. Only when I went back the way I came, around a large boulder, did I see the family I'd been hearing, an excited child eager to scramble onto the plateau of rock. I don't know much about the science of acoustics, but I'd never in my life experienced such a disorienting bounce of sound as on that stretch of rocky coast.

So, it was easy to imagine how easily one could become convinced of a haunting; disembodied voices clattering against the ear. If the fog was thick and the sounds were close, imagining a blackened, battered prow piercing through the mist like a knife would seem inevitable; a cursed, phantasmagorical ship that sails forever, doomed to keep trying to dock along the perilous coastline to which it never returned.

It must be noted that in English-language reference, and in general Romance language tradition, ships have been gendered as *she* for centuries. A mother-goddess who shields her crew and is loved by her workers and leaders. *She* is boarded, she sails, she holds, she carries, she travels, she harbors. But yes, she is often endangered; at the mercy of unpredictable weather. Sometimes she sinks. Sometimes she sails again. Sometimes she may be spectral; an eternal harbinger piercing through the murk, floating over the water. She is a home for her passengers, she seeks a port in which to rest.

The legend of the Flying Dutchman, a cursed ship powered by a spectral crew, was the first ghost ship I encountered as a child who loved folklore and ghost stories. While accounts of the legend differ, whether driven by misfortune, a criminal wickedness, or simply bad weather, this cursed ship and its spectral crew can never dock. Wagner's operatic version may be the most compelling and the most famous. It does, however, perpetuate a woman's death as the core plot point, a reliance on which classical opera is relentlessly guilty. Wagner's version posits that the doomed captain can return to land once every seven years to search for a love that will break his wandering, eternal curse. A young woman named Senta, who had long dreamed of being the one the infamous Dutchman might seek, meets him during one of these seven-year moments and the two fall for one another. They are later thwarted by misunderstanding. Senta sacrifices her own life by throwing herself into the sea. The final tableau sees her and the folkloric hero she adored in a spectral reunion; the curse broken and their spirits joined in death. An unsettling theme of art and ghostlore revisited: that a woman has to die in order to be believed or found worthy.

The first print appearance of the Flying Dutchman dates back to 1790 when John MacDonald notes the superstition of the spectral ship had already been well-established by the time he included it in *Travels in various part of Europe, Asia, and Africa, during a series of thirty years and upwards*. The tale gained traction in sailor superstition, particularly around bad weather, perhaps emboldened by optical illusions on water like a superior mirage, a fata morgana or *looming*, in which rays of light are bent, refracting at various indices, to appear as if an object is airborne.

The Flying Dutchman was born of Dutch maritime and colonial power. One inspiration may have been Dutch captain Bernard Fokke, who made trips from the Netherlands to the island of Java, Indonesia in what seemed like preternatural speed. His contemporaries insisted he was in league with the Devil for his swift travels. If I were going to curse a ship of that time and off that route, I'd have tied it to the inhuman Dutch colonial practice of forbidding native Indonesian farmers from growing anything but spices for export. Indigenous Indonesians across the archipelago starved while cultivating crops for European plates.

Dutch ghostlore and folktales weave their way into American culture thanks to Washington Irving and his fascination with the "quaint," if sometimes (in his opinion) backward, customs he observed while escaping epidemics in Manhattan for Sleepy Hollow in New York's Hudson Valley, where traditional lore inspired Rip Van Winkle, the character of Diedrich

Knickerbocker and of course, the Headless Horseman; a figure in all these local tales.

Another classic, fantastically Gothic doomed ship stars in Samuel Taylor Coleridge's epic poem *The Rime of the Ancient Mariner*, published in *Lyrical Ballads* in 1798. Often hailed as the beginning of British Romantic poetry, this tale is presented by a mariner forever bound to tell his tale of cruelty and the woe that followed after he killed an innocent albatross at sea when the bird soared over his ship. Gustave Doré's haunting, stirring engravings of the mariner's ship float through my mind as I consider this topic; invoking the ship as if it were an Acherontic vessel floating across purgatorial waters. The sacrifice of something innocent flows through these cursed narratives.

But what happens when the idea of a doomed, cursed ship becomes actualized, given the name and history of a real ship? What moves a tale out of the annals of classic prose and into actual, lived folklore? The sightings of cursed ghost ships are most certainly amplified by those famous literary vessels as templates, but many have striking, uniquely strange details of their very own.

I've made a habit of standing on as many points along the New England coastline as possible and one can simply inhabit, in a moment, the moody, treacherous, rocky Gothic settings that gave rise to Lovecraftian imagery and weird, witchy, haunted tales. The atmosphere of a Gothic novel creeps over you; encroaching mist along the outcroppings. Nowhere felt as immersive to me as the coast I've described in southern Maine. Into that atmosphere, a ghost ship was born after it never came home.

Along Casco Bay and around the Harpswell-Freeport region, repeated, spectral sightings of a schooner named the *Dash* have been seen along the irregular, rocky coastlines for over two centuries.

The *Dash*, at any moment, may try in vain to dock again to change her fate. She might be an omen of inclement weather or she may appear to collect the spirit of a relative of a former crew member. A harbinger of death, the ship has repeatedly appeared to startle the living and carry the souls of the dead like Charon's boat across the river Styx in Greek myth.

A wooden-hulled privateering vessel, a schooner built in the Harpswell-Freeport region in 1813, amid the ongoing War of 1812, to scout for (and plunder with full license of the United States) enemy British ships, the *Dash* was successful on what had been reportedly fifteen notable, valiant runs. But on her sixteenth, she disappeared. All her Freeport-based crew were lost.

Poet John Greenleaf Whitter wrote his own homage to the Flying Dutchman as reinterpreted for the *Dash*. "The Dead Ship of Harpswell" eternally seeks a peaceful port and is forever foiled in safe passage.

> What flecks the outer gray beyond
> The sundown's golden trail?
> The white flash of a sea-bird's wing,
> Or gleam of slanting sail?
> Let young eyes watch from Neck and Point,
> And sea-worn elders pray,—
> The ghost of what was once a ship
> Is sailing up the bay.
> From gray sea-fog, from icy drift,
> From peril and from pain,
> The home-bound fisher greets thy lights,
> O hundred-harbored Maine!
> But many a keel shall seaward turn,
> And many a sail outstand,
> When, tall and white, the Dead Ship looms
> Against the dusk of land.

Published in *The Atlantic* magazine in June 1866, Whittier's poem gave the real-life tragedy of the *Dash* and her crew additional immortal power.

Author Robert P. Tristram Coffin, forever drawn to his native Maine lore, wrote his own homage to ghost ships in his 1936 novel *John Dawn*, additionally pulling from the ongoing lore of the *Dash*. Incidentally, this very writer is the reason why it's nearly impossible to kill the "Witch's Curse of Bucksport Maine" myth we've written about before. (While there were no witch trials in Maine and the "curse" is, in fact, an admittedly curious flaw in a gravestone and not a spell, Coffin's poem cemented a curse in the American imagination as if it were a real event.) When people want to see something as haunted or want a more interesting explanation for a curious but otherwise mundane thing, something paranormal *is* created, for better or worse.

But the *Dash* does have an outsized history that shifts it out of the realm of poetry and folklore alone. During her run as a privateering vessel, the *Dash* and other ships like her were regarded as a sort of sea militia working for the United States against a stifling British blockade of New England ports. The *Dash* was armed with several working cannon and several model ones (to make her appear more armed than she was; these were known as "Quaker" guns, noting the pacifism of the Society of Friends). The *Dash* was particularly successful and considered uniquely lucky. But perhaps that in itself tempted fate.

In January 1815, her luck ran out when Captain John Porter is said to have lingered too long saying goodbye to his newly wedded wife and it took two signal-gun firings from the ship to bring him back aboard. Perhaps reluctance founded in a dread premonition? Accounts say that once the *Dash* left Freeport for the Gulf of Maine, she did so racing another American privateering vessel, the *Chamberlain*, and her swift, impressive speed launched her headfirst into a winter storm. She was never seen again. At least, not whole. And not with a living crew.

A few months after the *Dash's* disappearance, fishermen began spotting her prow piercing through thick fog, silently heading toward Freeport at a fierce clip even when no wind was driving the sails. Her name was legible; *Dash* floating along at eye level, and the silent crew stood aboard, staring toward the port they never got back to. Reports of the ship would come in batches from locals, fishermen and other sailors; the fog evidently the perfect atmosphere to draw this ghost ship back home. The legend of the *Dash* expanded from mere omen and ill weather, taking on greater importance as an usher of souls; coming to collect descendants of the lost crew and fold them into the fog of the great unknown.

She's even drawn fire.

An entertaining though incredulous account repeated again and again in books, articles and blogs written throughout the last sixty years, claims that in the early days of World War II—when Allied forces monitored harbor strongholds and ports of interest—during a patrol around the Casco Bay area a British ship noted as the HMS *Moidore* fired on the *Dash* as it pierced through an oppressive fog. The anachronistic, startling tall ship and black mast, the word *Dash* clearly visible upon her prow, supposedly took the blasts and disappeared again.

The only problem is there hasn't *been* an HMS *Moidore*—or even a USS *Moidore*—to have fired on the *Dash*. *Moidore* doesn't appear on any log of ships deployed by either country. It's possible the term *Moidore* for a ship goes back to privateering at a time when the US and Britain were not allies, but on opposing ends of a revolution. A *moidore* is a coin of Portuguese currency that was commonly found in England and her colonies. A currency mentioned in classic adventure stories like *Robinson Crusoe* and *Gulliver's Travels*, moidores could easily have been captured loot during the *Dash*'s days of privateering. Perhaps the idea of a British ship firing again on an American ship along the Maine coast was just an echo of the War of 1812, when Maine was particularly vulnerable, coming back to haunt the former rivals-turned-allies at a time when the whole world was fraying at the seams.

It's quite possible that in the thick murk of fog and in the immense anxiety of World War II, an unknown, unregistered ship was fired upon by a patrolling vessel, and it's possible the ship they saw disappeared again, but the truth of it wasn't pinned to an actual vessel or verifiable military record. So it's easy to think it all part of the ghost lore.

What *is* frighteningly true, however, is that Nazis reached Maine. On April 23, 1945, the USS *Eagle 56* was fired upon and sunk by a German U-boat 853 in Casco Bay. Only thirteen of the sixty-two crew members survived. Because the attack came at the end of the war, and the U-boat had not received orders of any surrender, the sinking of the *Eagle* was reported as an engineering and boiler failure rather than an escalatory attack from a foreign adversary. It wasn't until 2001 that the full truth came out and the US Navy finally awarded Purple Hearts to survivors and family members that had been denied them under the guise of an accident rather than an attack. Perhaps there's a haunting to be had in this injustice; perhaps these war dead, with the truth of their deaths hidden and covered up at the time, have left their own ghostly imprint upon the bay, drawing forth further inexplicable sights, sounds, and activity.

The *Dash* is also a harbinger of death. Journalist and Maine native Sam Smith, who covered Washington under nine presidents, was the editor of the *Progressive Review* for fifty years and the founder of the national Green Party, among other movements, has his own *Dash* tale to tell. In an essay compiled in the "memoirs" section of his site, he notes that folklore became deeply personal one day as his mother gazed out to sea over lunch in 1975 and exclaimed that she saw the ghost ship of Harpswell, adding her own uncanny sighting to the generational tale Whittier evokes in his poem.

My reaction was to think, there she goes again. And then to think no more about it. A few hours later, down on the shore, my father had a heart attack and died. As we returned from the hospital and parked the car, my mother suddenly cried, 'The ghost ship of Harpswell' . . . We went inside and pulled out a volume of John Greenleaf Whittier's poems and found it. The ghost ship of Harpswell had been the privateer *Dash*, which had been lost at sea after compiling its remarkable record. It would be later said that women saw the vessel just before their husbands died, but would make nothing of it.[1]

I read these accounts and then stood on the exact coastal edges at Wolfe's Neck Preserve noted in some of the *Dash* sightings, imagining a scene of deep fog, old ships piercing through as if parting the veil between worlds. I felt like I could see it unfold before my eyes, the peculiar acoustics rattling around my ears in a confounding manner. It sets the mind to spinning. The day I visited this coastal curiosity I was taken under by the muse herself. Immediately, as if I'd channeled it, I wrote a fictional story about a ghost ship and her vengeful female captain. Additionally, I've pinned the setting of a forthcoming Gothic novel to this very spot. The curious rocky coast of this bay continues haunting me in the most visceral ways.

Is all of this merely tall tales for tall ships? Well, if one isn't easily convinced, there is the verifiably doomed *Isidore* to consider.

For the past ten years I've been a part of the Southern Maine Steampunk Fair at the Brick Store Museum, a lovely little historic outpost founded by Edith Cleaves Barry, who wanted to celebrate local industry, lore, and history. When discussing the topic of this book with the staff, noting my interest in local ghost ships, director Cynthia Walker immediately gave me access to a script the museum uses for the museum's All Souls' Walk through the cemetery, where local historical figures speak at their gravestones about their lives.

The daughter of the ship owner, the woman the fated ship was named for, Isadore Smith, speaks about the wreck at her grave site, describing the day of the *Isadore*'s launch in 1842 as ominously gray. The ship had a halting stop to its launch, unable to fully reach the water, a fact considered by sailors to be an extraordinarily ill omen: "as *no one wanted to be aboard a ship that doesn't want to go into the water!* The next day another attempt was made to launch the *Isadore*, and she tipped so badly that some feared she would capsize."[2]

Finally, the boat sails at the very end of November, its first night out very still. But the following day, a freak early winter storm whipped up winds and ice, freezing sails and making the ship impossible to control. During the All Souls' Walk, Isadore explains that everyone on board was lost to icy waves and that hardly any bodies could be recovered. Describing how *every* crew member's family came forward to recount how, to a man, each sailor had experienced nightmares and troubled premonitions prior to the voyage, she continues in the script:

"One sailor had envisioned seven coffins on the shore . . . and it was just seven bodies that washed ashore! There have even been reports of the ghost ship *Isadore* off Bald Head Cliff. People have spotted the ghostly crew with gazes fixed straight ahead; the ship vanishes when other boats try to approach."

The immediate reporting surrounding the dashed and sunken *Isidore* (Isadore and Isidore spelling differences persist in these historical documents) whose sinking prompted discussion of another ill-fated vessel the year prior, was just as grim. An article in the *Bangor Daily Whig and Courier* on December 5, 1842, notes, under the heading "Most Melancholy Disaster," with capital letters and italics as presented, declares:

"It becomes our duty to record one of the most distressing disasters by sea that has ever taken place in our vicinity. On Wednesday night last, the barque Isidore, Capt. Leander Foss, from Kennebunk-port for New Orleans, was driven ashore in the gale, on Cape Neddick Rocks, a few miles south of Wells village, and totally wrecked, and, melancholy to relate, every person on board, consisting of FIFTEEN MEN, including the crew, *perished!*" The article goes on to relate: "This was her first voyage, she was driven ashore on the same point of rocks on which the Wm. Fales was wrecked last March." And the article closes with the harrowing: "during the gale a body, without head or arms, was washed ashore in the same place, supposed to be one of the unfortunates who perished on the wreck of the Wm. Fales. It cannot be identified."

The capacity to focus on the grisly aspects, even in the immediate, seems to be a common human impulse across time. And right away, there was a helpless examination of the nightmare premonitions experienced by so many of the crew. Believing their concerns only after their deaths certainly didn't do the crew any good. Instead, the living are left to lament.

"Lines Composed on the Loss of the Barque Isidore of Kennebunkport," written in 1842 to commemorate the ship's loss, is another document shared with me by Cynthia at the Brick Store Museum. Originally published as a Broadside and archived without authorial attribution, the poem is "to be sung to the tune of "Young People All Attention Give," and it notes the ignored premonitions of the crew:

But when they left, a secret fear
Possessed the minds of kindred dear,
That a sad fate would them befall,
Proving destructive to them all.
Those fears were not an idle dream,
They hasted to the dismal scene,
Where all was in confusion hurl'd
And friends had left the present world.

The haunting remains for the living to examine: Why weren't they believed? Why couldn't that have been enough to delay the sailing for a day? Would it have helped, or was it doomed regardless? Hauntings float side by side with uncertainty. Like a voice one hears right in front of them, but there's nothing and no one to be seen, a trick of the bay, an odd, acoustic quirk of these jagged inlets.

The sailors were right to be frightened; their premonitions came true. Like the plight of so many victims who had an intuitive fear of what lay ahead, their warnings were not heeded and they were forced into their own unfortunate prophecy. This sort of dread knowledge haunts a great deal of history and its resulting ghostlore; workers who are afraid their working conditions will end up killing them. Perhaps ghost ships simply honor, and remind all those tied to its industry, the grimly alluring dangers of the sea. The unfathomable deep; the sea as cosmic void. It is another world. It is a siren call and a cruel mistress.

May she sail forever, be she the *Dash*, the *Isidore*, or more; a warning, an omen, a harbinger, a remnant of the past and a present haunt. May she pierce through the fog of our perception and jar us into listening to our own instincts. Perhaps in doing so, she can haunt a person into taking better care of themselves and advocate for those around them. After all, aren't we all just looking for safe harbor and peaceful rest?

Swamp Goth: Southern Gothic in the Sunshine State

Andrea

Can the Southern Gothic be said to exist in Florida? Some say yes. If you've ever been to, or seen images of, a Floridian hardwood hammock of trees, with spreading live oaks dripping Spanish moss, you might be inclined to agree. Live oak trees plus Spanish moss equals Southern Gothic. That's just math. The essential weirdness of Florida beckons with imaginative possibilities—surely there is something mysterious in the water, something even more menacing than gators and snakes. Then there's that sultry, stultifying heat, the vaporous humidity. But is it Gothic? Is it even Southern?

In Florida, they say, "The further north you go, the more south you get." As you hover near the Georgia border, this feels true: Visit Jacksonville or Tallahassee, and the vibe is distinctly different from your Miami Beach or Fort Myers cohort. Despite all the Jimmy Buffett clichés people throw around, Florida is not a cultural monolith.

The Sunshine State is nothing if not unique, a cavalcade of sheer, unremitting absurdity of every possible variation from the Panhandle to the Keys, and I love it because there is nothing that delights me as much as the utterly bizarre. In this sense, I hold Florida to be a generous dispenser of gifts, bringing me great joy with places like Gatorland, whose slogan is, "You know what y'all need? Y'all need Gatorland." What does that even mean? It's like jazz: If you have to ask, you'll never know, and if you don't know, y'all need Gatorland. Florida is inarguably a paradise of the strange.

Florida "contains multitudes," says photographer Anastasia Samoylova, evoking Walt Whitman's famous phrase. She describes it as "a harbinger of complex political, demographic, and environmental shifts in the rest of the country; or it contains nothing at all, a bizarre oddity whose sole purpose is to provide fodder for clickbait headlines," a reference to the #FloridaMan and #FloridaWoman internet memes of recent years. It is a mythical place, otherworldly, looming large in the American consciousness and rife with all manner of symbolism; an enclave of strange beauty and legend, a place to warm your old bones, a punch line, a slough of despond for history teachers, a Taylor Swift song. I believe that your opinions and referents vis-à-vis Florida say a lot about you—meet me on the lanai and we'll talk about it.

But is it Southern Gothic? I visit Florida a lot, as moms with young kids and retired parents tend to do, and I've become increasingly fascinated by it the more time I spend there. The unusual flora and fauna alone captivate my imagination, but I also have become more and more intrigued by its many wonderful historic oddities. For example, did you know that the first embalmers in the country were located in Orlando? And that Cassadaga is home to one of the nation's two Spiritualist communities? (The other is in Lily Dale, New York.) Even Disney World, for heaven's sake, is a bastion of darkness: from the Gothic motifs of thorn-girt castles and sleeping beauties, to Walt's own well-documented obsession with death (Bambi's mother, anyone?) and the fact that Disney theme parks remain popular destinations for Americans to scatter their loved ones' cremains. And let's not forget their little Haunted Mansion. There's so much more to this state than sunshine and oranges.

All of my instincts compelled me to say that Florida *felt* Gothic as hell, but did it really meet a strict definition of Southern Gothic per se? Southern Gothic is the purview of New Orleans and Mississippi, William Faulkner and Tennessee Williams, not Gatorland . . . right? I was ready to admit that maybe the Southern Gothic didn't actually exist in Florida, except in my imagination, until one day, as we were driving south of St. Augustine on the I-95, I noticed something on Google maps, located off a little back road called the Old Dixie Highway.

"What are the . . . Dummett Plantation and Sugar Mill Ruins?" I asked out loud.

The Old Dixie Highway, as its name indicates, is a remnant of the past. Once an inviting stretch of two-lane blacktop, now gray and cracked, it signifies an earlier, bygone era of Florida tourism. And off-road, an even earlier and more obscure era of Florida's history languishes: Between Jacksonville and Daytona Beach along the northeast coast of Florida lies an entire stretch of landscape dotted with ruined sugar plantations. I felt astonished to discover this, but I'm not naive enough to wonder why I, a frequent visitor to Florida, had never once heard of any of these places. If it was up to me, ruins would be one of the *first* things I'd show any visitor to my state, because the full picture of any place only becomes clear when every aspect of its history is able to be told. The tourism board of Florida feels differently, for obvious reasons. Deep, heavy, difficult histories are by and large not what people come here for.

Sugar plantations in northeast Florida include: the Cruger-dePeyster Plantation and Dunlawton Sugar Mill Gardens (both near Daytona Beach), Dummett Plantation and Sugar Mill Ruins, and the Bulow Plantation Ruins, both about forty minutes south of St. Augustine. (There are more ruins in Florida than just these, including one on the west coast north of Tampa and another one near Tallahassee.) As I saw these dots on the maps unfurl before me, I realized that, for better or worse, there was incontrovertible evidence of the Southern Gothic in Florida.

The Dummett Plantation and Sugar Mill Ruins are now nothing more than a small cluster of broken-down coquina walls assembled inauspiciously off the side of the highway. *Coquina* is a type of stone quarried in Florida that is made up of millions of tiny shells all compressed together. It is Spanish for "little shell." The walls of the Castillo de San Marcos fortress in St. Augustine are made of coquina, as are the factories and refineries of these sugar plantations. As sugarcane was picked, so was coquina quarried by slave labor.

A few desultory signs explain with more brevity than insight that this was once the 2,000-acre sugarcane plantation and refinery of Colonel Thomas H. Dummett, who bought the plantation in 1804 and named it Carrikfergus. Dummett made a fortune refining sugar and molasses to be distilled into rum, all processed using the unpaid labor of two hundred enslaved people.

In 1825, Dummett hired an Irish engineer to build a steam-powered sugarcane crusher, which quadrupled his productivity compared to his old water-powered cane crusher, thus making his plantation the site of the largest and most profitable refinery in the state. In 1835, during the Second Seminole War, the plantation was raided and burned to the ground. Dummett and his family sought refuge in the city of St. Augustine while the Seminoles proceeded to destroy every other plantation in the area, and the war raged on.

A historic sign on the premises states merely that, *These ruins are the remains of the sugar and rum processing factory built in 1825 and owned by Thomas H. Dummitt.* It is not clear why his name is spelled differently on the informational sign here. The sign says nothing about the plantation's destruction, nor does it provide any context for the Seminoles destroying a building on the land that had been stolen from them.

Since there was no further information or interpretation available at this historic site, I had to rely on the internet. The following entry on the *Atlas Obscura* website gave me more context:

> The mill ceased running in 1835 when the plantation was raided by local Seminoles, during a time when the American government was forcefully relocating Native Americans under the Indian Removal Act. The tribes refused to leave, prompting the Second Seminole War. The Dummett family fled to St. Augustine while Seminoles raided and burned the plantations that occupied the land that was once theirs.

Nor does the sign at the plantation provide any information about the enslaved people who labored here, where they come from, or what happened to them.

The state of Florida is currently working hard to erase Black history from the educational curriculum, from denying the existence of the Civil Rights movement in Florida to whitewashing the history of slavery. As of this writing, educators in the state where Zora Neale Hurston wrote *Their Eyes Were Watching God* are now required by law to say that slavery provided vital job training and skills to enslaved people. This mandate was part of Governor Ron DeSantis's 2022 Stop WOKE Act, which is still being contested in courts (part of it was struck down in July 2024). "Florida's current educational mandates are unfortunate," said Ashlie Pounds, a paranormal researcher who grew up in the state and shares footage of her historically informed investigations online. Ashlie told me that, "Growing up in Ft. Lauderdale, we did not learn about slavery or Native American history," despite the fact that the history of slavery is "embedded in Florida roots," and that, while she had heard of the sugar mill ruins, "the way they are usually discovered in Florida is 'Take your family to brunch at the old Sugar Mull ruins.' That's pretty much all that's advertised. General family and dog time."[1] A quick survey of Trip Advisor reviews confirms this: only four of the Cruger-dePeyster's 196 reviews mention the enslaved people who actually worked on the plantations. This abridged and glossed-over version of the past is a result of the state's general approach to historic site interpretation.

On the website for the nearby Bulow plantation, a reenactor earnestly intones that the enslaved people were "given a certain amount of work to do each day," and when they finished that work they were allowed to go fishing or work on their own gardens. His eyes shift slightly to the right as he notes that the overseer he portrays was not only "benevolent" toward the enslaved, but also on good terms with the Seminoles, and even had "drinking parties" with them. He seems uncomfortable, and I wonder how constrained the rangers and interpreters are at these historic sites, where government funding and mandates dictate what they can and cannot say.

Nowhere at any of these aforementioned sugar plantations, or on their websites, is any specific mention made of individual enslaved people, their names, or their lives, other than to note that there are accounts of Colonel Dummett's daughter Anna "playing with slave [sic] children and teaching them to read." The same website notes that Colonel Dummett's plantation "produced sugar and rum *with the help* of roughly 40 local Indians and 100 slaves" (emphasis mine).[2] One notable exception to this apparent code of silence is the Kingsley Plantation in Jacksonville. Their website, maintained by the National Park Service, goes into specific details, including the lives, names, and histories of as many enslaved persons as they have historic records for. It is distinctly different from the smaller, state-run historic sites, and even provides a list of resources for further reading about the topic of slavery at the plantation (as of this writing in early 2025).[3]

The state of Florida in general, however, was slow to acknowledge its role in the history of American slavery and clearly, as we have seen, still avoids doing so whenever possible. This may be the reason why we don't tend to think of Florida at first when we think of the "peculiar institution," as slavery was once called, even though it was one of the eleven Confederate states. It's not really part of our national shorthand for "the South." But slavery is most emphatically a part of the state's history. Back when Florida was a Spanish colony, from the 1500s through the early 1800s, slavery was legal, but enslaved persons could be manumitted, marriage was encouraged, and children were born free. Of course, this was only if you consented to Catholic baptism, as the Spanish colony had a twofold directive: one, to secure resources for Spain, and two, to propagate more Catholics. Under Spanish rule, the colony, particularly near St. Augustine, developed one of America's largest populations of free Black people. Enslaved persons from nearby English-ruled colonies often escaped to Florida, the first of whom arrived from Carolina (as it was then called) in a stolen canoe in 1687. They were granted freedom there if they agreed to convert to Catholicism and serve in the military.

Then in 1819, long after the British colonies had become American states, Spain ceded Florida to the United States, and the handover was official by 1821, at which point Florida ceased to be a colony where Black people could, potentially, find freedom, and became a slaveholding state. Planters from the Old South migrated to central Florida and established large plantations, growing a variety of crops, including cotton and, along the northeast coast, sugar. The majority of Florida's free Black population emigrated to Cuba at this time. Some enslaved Black people fled into Florida's deepest hinterlands, aided by the Seminoles. Florida would remain a slaveholding state until after the end of the Civil War.

Florida, it is worth noting, is not the only state that downplays its history of slavery. New York state, where I live, was an active participant in the transatlantic slave trade, but official New York state historic sites tend to emphasize our role in the Underground Railroad instead, which is fair enough, but adds to an inaccurate "us vs. them" dichotomy. To be clear, New York, especially New York City, is very much complicit in the history of American slavery. In the eighteenth century, New York City was the largest slave-owning port city in the English colonies, second only to Charleston, South Carolina, and New York did not fully outlaw slavery until 1827. Demonstrating the close ties between Northern capital and Southern agriculture, one of the Florida plantations I researched, the Cruger-dePeyster plantation, shares part of its name with a wealthy New York family (see my chapter on Melrose Hall for more about the dePeysters) and the machinery for the Cruger-dePeyster sugar mill was financed by investors from the city.

The history of the Gothic aligns almost uncannily with the history of the transatlantic slave trade. As Leila Taylor points out in her book *Darkly: Black History and America's Gothic Soul*, "Thomas Jefferson inherited his first thirty slaves from his father (he would own 607 over his lifetime) the same year Walpole published *The Castle of Otranto*. That same year, 1764, [America] and England were still about forty years away from ending the slave trade." And she reminds us that in 1818, the year that brought us Mary Shelley's *Frankenstein*, Frederick Douglass was born into slavery. "The narratives that inform our language of terror," Taylor notes, "were beginning to take shape while the seeds of a home-grown American gothic were starting to take root."[4]

This homegrown Gothic notably includes the Southern Gothic. Originally a pejorative term, Southern Gothic is used to describe work by writers of the American South that reimagine Gothic tropes for the specific geography and cultural contexts of the American South. Southern Gothic may feature images of the grotesque and macabre, of decay and decline, of violence and horror. Such explorations are usually tied to social issues specific to the American South, including the aftermath of slavery.

Toni Morrison's *Beloved* exemplifies the American Southern Gothic, with its manifestations of the ghosts of American slavery made real. So central are the horrors of racism and slavery to our history, and hence our literature, that critics such as Leslie Fiedler have declared that all of American literature is "bewilderingly and embarrassingly, a gothic fiction."[5] Toni Morrison herself pointed out how the specter of whiteness hovers over all American literature in her own work of criticism, *Playing in the Dark*. There is no American Gothic without the Southern Gothic, and there is no Southern Gothic without the history of slavery.

In contemporary fiction, Tananarive Due is currently writing Florida-set masterworks of contemporary horror that, I would argue, have Gothic elements to them. Due, the daughter of a Civil Rights Activist—her mother, Patricia Stephens Due, was jailed for forty days after a sit-in at a Jacksonville Woolworth's lunch counter—set both her short story cycle *Ghost Summer* and her novel *The Reformatory* in the fictional Panhandle town of Gracetown. In the story "Ghost Summer," the sins of the past come to bear on the present in a terrifying way. I read it late at night about three years ago—in Florida, as a matter of fact—and it gave me literal nightmares. In the story, pursued children are running through a swampy landscape, its mud and brackish waters oozing around them as they flee deep into its unforgiving obscurity. In *The Reformatory*, the Gracetown School for Boys stands in for the real-life Dozier School for Boys, an infamous reformatory where Due's own great-uncle died in 1937.

There are some who would argue that the Gothic is not inherently political. But it most emphatically is and always has been. You cannot have the Gothic without politics, for such a thing does not exist. Agatha Andrews, host of the influential podcast *She Wore Black*, interviewed Gothic scholar Neil McRobert (who also has his own horror podcast, *Talking Scared*). McRobert declares, "If you don't understand the raw politics [of the Gothic], you haven't understood the story in its most fundamental form."

From its inception in England, the aesthetics and literature of the Gothic have been inextricable from the political. The American Gothic would be no less political. There's a price to pay if you want to experience the pleasures of the Gothic, and acknowledging the political aspect of the genre is the price of admission. Or as Agatha Andrews put it, you can't just be "here for the vibes."

Ruins, of course, are quintessentially Gothic, and surprisingly political as well. During the first wave of the Gothic aesthetic in England in the eighteenth century, ruins were celebrated as a link to the long-forgotten past—itself a highly politicized and problematic category. (See, for example, the appropriation of the term "Anglo-Saxon" by far-right groups.) The predominance of ruins in the English landscape was a consequence of the Dissolution of the Monasteries, a wholesale destruction of all Catholic religious sites and iconography during the reign of

Henry VIII. Two hundred years later, the destruction of all that precious old art and architecture was deemed lamentable, and visits to ruined abbeys (most famously, Tintern Abbey) were among the first forms of "dark tourism" practiced in the modern era.

Englishmen weren't entirely satisfied with genuine ruins, though. It seemed there weren't enough to go around, and so they built them. Faux ruins, neo-Gothic houses, and follies became all the rage in the late eighteenth century, some deliberately aged with acid to make them look older. Follies were decorative architectural flourishes, relatively small, nonfunctional buildings often designed to look like ruins or castles, that served no other purposes but to delight the eye and supply a nostalgic bit of whimsy on the grounds and in the gardens of those who could afford to build such things purely for aesthetic pleasure. The term comes from the French *folie*, meaning nonsense, silliness, or foolishness. *The Castle of Otranto* author Horace Walpole's own home, Strawberry Hill, is perhaps the most famous example of this practice. His contemporary William Beckford, author of the Gothic fever dream of a novel *Vathek* (1786) used his "massive fortune derived from slavery, [colonial trade], and the Industrial Revolution," to build a similarly lavish mansion called Fonthill Abbey.[6] Fonthill eventually collapsed and became a real ruin.

The sugar plantations in Florida are the genuine ruins that link to this same economic system that provided Walpole and Beckford the inherited wealth to finance these places.

When you're standing at a site of excruciating human suffering, you quickly realize that nostalgia is kind of bullshit. The Gothic has always been about looking to the past, but not necessarily uncritically. Neil McRobert says that the Gothic, by pointing out the traumas that live in the past, is "one of the few storytelling modes that doesn't say, 'Wasn't the past *great*?'"

Setting a story in a "fictious yesteryear," as so many Gothic novels do, draws awareness to how much nostalgia is actually manufactured. The aestheticized "past" of the Gothic is one of excess; its highly stylized language and labyrinthine plots, richly suffused with dreamlike symbolism, are deliberately signaling to us that maybe we should be questioning the way things are presented. The Gothic asks "questions about reality, about epistemology, what we know and how we know things . . . who's in charge here, who is the authority in this text? They're saying you have to question authority." If the Gothic is all about secrets coming to light—and it is—then this is more important than ever now, he says. "True Gothic is almost always about questioning power structures." People in power have secrets, McRobert says, and it's our job to ask questions—hard questions. "Gothic always interrogates."

Walking amid the ruins of a sugar plantation in a state that is currently erasing these histories, it feels like a question worth asking. If you pause by the ruins and listen for a moment, if you notice the absence of any historic interpretation that accurately portrays the lives of the enslaved, then you are now part of that process of interrogation. There are some who frown upon the concept of dark tourism, turned off by things like tourists taking selfies in front of sites of mass death and destruction. I do think there is a place for dark tourism. But it shouldn't be about voyeurism or aestheticized thrills packaged for entertainment and profit. One travel website I came across calls the Cruger-dePeyster Plantation the "perfect spot to take those Goth pose pictures!" This is exactly the kind of cringeworthy stuff that a more robust program of historic interpretation at these sites could prevent. This goes without saying, but the places where enslaved people suffered should not be a backdrop for fun "goth poses."

In 2014, artist Kara Walker installed a 35-foot-tall statue made of sugar, an exhibit called *A Subtlety, or the Marvelous Sugar Baby* in the soon-to-be-demolished former Domino sugar factory in New York City. The groundbreaking exhibition was a searing commentary on the legacy of sugar production and its reliance on slave labor. Art critic Roberta Smith, reviewing the show for the *New York Times*, was quick to point out that, like racism, sugar's ill effects are not confined to the past:

> Which brings us to our own self-destructing present, where sugar is something of a scourge, its excessive consumption linked to diseases like obesity and diabetes that disproportionately affect the poor. The circle of exploitation and degradation is in many ways unbroken. No longer a luxury, sugar has become a birthright and the opiate of the masses. We look on it like money, with greed. Heavily promoted, it keeps millions of Americans of all races from fulfilling their potential — an inestimable loss in terms of talent, health and happiness.

In Florida, these ironies are embedded into the landscape in these coquina ruins amid their encroaching hammocks of hardwood. The erasure, lack of knowledge, and misrepresentation of Black history in schools and interpretive sites cannot lie by omission any longer, when one hears and reads about them in front of these crumbling walls and dried-out wells that dot the landscape. The stones remember and the stones do not lie.

In the Southern heat and humidity, forests grow around the ruins, the land taking back what was stolen, "but the eerie structures remain silent relics of the area's troubled past."[7] It's hard to think of these ruins as a fun place for a stroll when they are so haunted by the energy of what happened here. The ruins interrogate us right back, if we take a moment to pause and feel the stones communicating, wordlessly. It's palpable, another layer of feeling amid the eerie emptiness and stillness and the heat and the quiet. It's a hum amid the trees, the landscape still resolutely beautiful, its loveliness unvanquished amid the horror. All that history, death, exploitation, it lingers like the cloying, too-sweet remnants of a sugar cube on your tongue. It is a nauseating aftertaste of the excesses of the past carried into the present, a taste you want to wash away. But you cannot wash the past away. The past is not even past, as Faulkner reminded us. They can change the curriculum, but the crumbling coquina walls retain the heat of the sun, the stain of blood, the memory of sugar, the weight of a hogshead of rum.

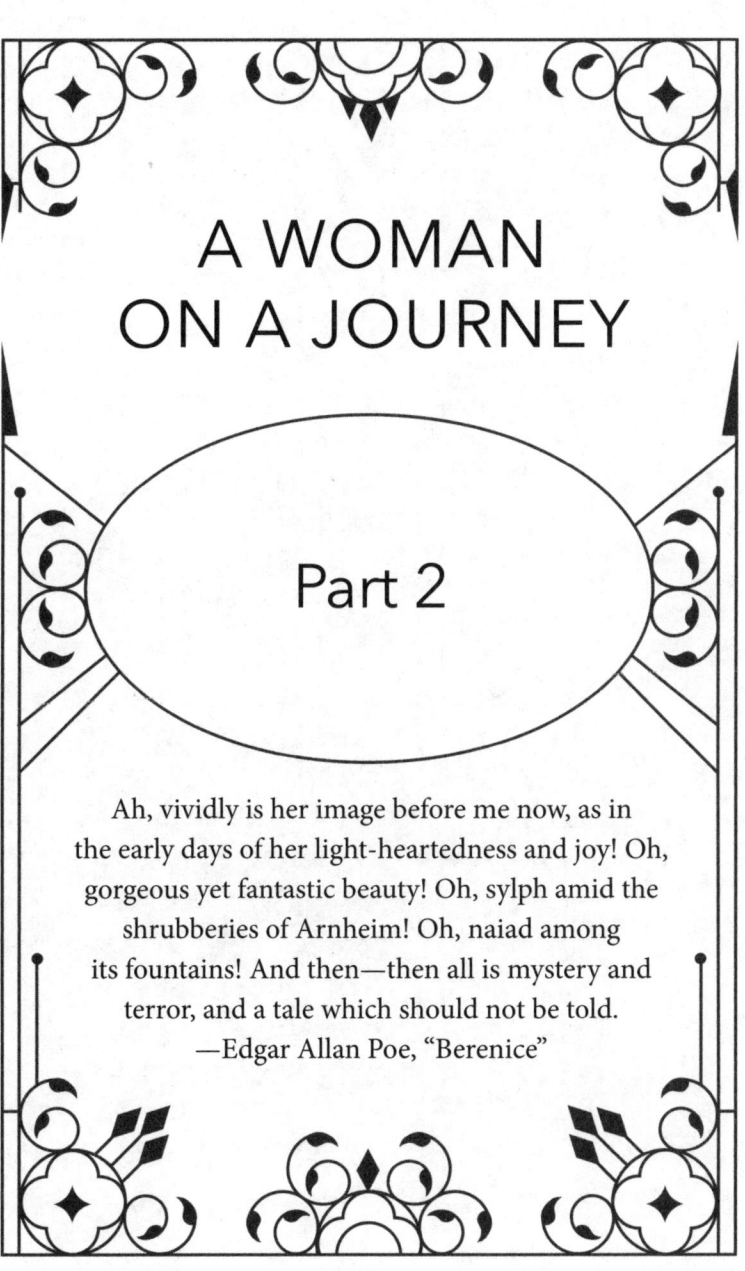

A WOMAN ON A JOURNEY

Part 2

Ah, vividly is her image before me now, as in
the early days of her light-heartedness and joy! Oh,
gorgeous yet fantastic beauty! Oh, sylph amid the
shrubberies of Arnheim! Oh, naiad among
its fountains! And then—then all is mystery and
terror, and a tale which should not be told.
—Edgar Allan Poe, "Berenice"

Portrait of a Lady:
Marian "Clover" Adams

Leanna

A once-celebrated socialite and talented photographer lies nameless below a striking statue. There, sorrow takes on a distinct presence of its own. Experiences vary when standing before the six-foot, seated, shrouded figure surrounded by a brooding grove of evergreens at Rock Creek Cemetery in Washington, DC. Whether one feels a sense of oppressive spectral weight or an otherworldly unease, no one can forget being in the statue's awe-inspiring presence. When I sat on the large, wide, angled, polished stone bench that surrounds this hexagonal plot, I wept. In part because I knew enough about the woman it commemorates to make visiting her grave an intensely emotional experience, in part because the statue is one of August Saint-Gaudens's finest works of art.

Though her name remains absent from the monument, the woman in whose honor the statue was erected evoked just as many strong emotions during her life as a pillar of capital society.

Marian "Clover" Hooper Adams once lived and died approximately a thousand feet from the White House. Her home on H Street was a magnet for great minds of the nineteenth century. A witty, well-loved figure in both Massachusetts and DC intellectual and political spheres, her untimely death cast a great shadow over many notable people. Not only was Marian a talented artist herself, a gifted photographer, she was a muse of the highest caliber.

The Portrait of a Lady by Henry James was first serialized from 1880 to 1881 in *The Atlantic Monthly* and *Macmillan's* magazine, then printed in novel form in 1881, considered by critics to be one of James's finest works. The inspiration for his heroine, Isabel Archer, was known in part to be taken from Clover Hooper. The same would be said of another James creation, his titular heroine, *Daisy Miller*. A witty Boston socialite, Clover had grown up with James and remained his lifelong friend. James wrote to his brother William in early March 1870 about a quality he particularly admired and found inspiring: "Clover Hooper has it—intellectual grace . . ."

Henry James, in the annals of ghost lore, is most famous for *The Turn of the Screw*, in what might be the textbook example of an unreliable narrator: a governess unsure if the haunting she's experiencing is legitimate paranormal phenomena or her own untrustworthy senses. James leaves us, the reader, to consider for ourselves what to think.

The Portrait of a Lady follows the spirited Isabel Archer, a New Yorker who finds herself the recipient of a large inheritance. Rejecting various suitors, as she feels they'll be a threat to her independence, she eventually accepts a proposal from an American expatriate in Italy. Proving to have no real affection for her, her husband had schemed with an accomplished, but nefarious woman, Madame Merle, for Isabel's money. As the marriage sours, James pits the Old World of Europe against the American New, a friction core to Gothic literature and to folk horror: that old ways are threatened by new or outside ideas, like that of a freethinking woman, and vice versa. The fiercely independent Isabel finds herself trapped; a prime Gothic heroine beset by a greedy, arrogant man, a scheming matron, and a host of lies. She flees to the bedside of her dying cousin in England, the man responsible for her fortune. There, Isabel expresses her unhappiness and her relative suggests that since she is still young, she could regain her freedom if she chooses to.

In another act of handing the reader their own conclusion, the ending of *The Portrait of a Lady* is ambiguous, whether Isabel returned to her unhappy marriage or whether she embraced the independence she'd cherished and had been so afraid of losing at the beginning of the novel remains unresolved. Does she hollow out and fade in a loveless marriage or does she leave and forge her own way in the world as she'd wanted to do from the start? It is another mystery of the age. Similarly, history leaves us to ponder what exactly happened to the woman who inspired great literature, but remained a sidenote in life.

Four years after the publication of *The Portrait of a Lady*, Marian "Clover" Hooper Adams's story would take a dark and irrevocable turn when she took her own life. Her body was found in front of her bedroom fireplace in her H Street residence.

Not only would Clover be oddly memorialized by the evocative statue in Rock Creek Cemetery, she would be omitted entirely from her husband's autobiography. It seems that her taking her own life made her unmentionable, due in no small part to her husband's grief, but also the significant stigmas and unresolved trauma surrounding suicide.

I first wrote about Clover for the fourth volume of Amanda Woomer's *Feminine Macabre* journal series in an essay, "An Unnamed Sorrow Where Marian Adams Should Be." I was so stunned by the fact that such a beautiful memorial sculpture, such a haunting piece, would bear no name attached. I had to find out why.

Born into a wealthy Boston family in 1843, "Clover" as she was known to everyone, was no stranger to tragedy. Her mother,

Ellen Hooper, had given her daughter the nickname Clover as she was a "lucky" child, born to a woman whose bouts with tuberculosis had made additional children a precarious prospect. As a child, Clover would sign her letters "Clover leaf" or draw a four-leaf clover with pride, but she may have wondered, at times, if her moniker was ironic. Ellen Hooper died of tuberculosis when Clover was young. Her maternal grandmother became a recluse and shunned her family after losing her son in an accidental drowning. Clover's Aunt Sue, who had stepped in as a mother figure after Ellen Hooper's death, took her own life by drinking arsenic after her marriage failed. Thankfully, Clover's close relationship to her father gave her an anchor to life and a steady, loving hand.

Coming of age in the Civil War, Clover volunteered for relief and aid commissions, with family members either serving or deeply embedded in the Union cause. Being part of such meaningful work, for a woman who'd lost so many parental figures, was a comfort. She was well-educated, curious, observant and smart. In the mid-nineteenth century, Boston was referred to as the "hub of the universe" and Clover's life there and later in Washington would intersect with countless influential people. Her Aunt Caroline was a dear friend of reformer Margaret Fuller, also mentioned in this book, and her family was close with the entire Transcendentalist set, especially Ralph Waldo Emerson. Clover would become friends with the infamous "Mrs. Jack," Isabella Stewart Gardner, another woman living boldly on her own terms. But Clover was caught in the middle of the rise of the "new woman" and a more reserved, domestic, and traditional place in society; that same friction Henry James pens in *Portrait of a Lady*.

Clover married writer and professor Henry Adams (grandson of John Quincy Adams and great-grandson of John Adams) in 1872, two years after author Henry James had written to his brother about Clover's unmatched "intellectual grace." Their union was seen as advantageous; the Hooper family was wealthy and the Adams name was a famous cornerstone of the country, though it carried a great weight of responsibility. An Adams was supposed to make something of himself and Henry worked tirelessly as a professor at Harvard and then in Washington as an author of notable tomes on American history and government.

From all accounts, the marriage seemed to be companionable and mostly compatible, even if Henry's views on women remained conservative. While derisive of the suffrage movement, he did believe in the cultivation of mutual respect between husband and wife. Depending on Clover as a peer and confidante, Henry consistently praised his wife's intelligence and was known to let her shine at parties as a luminous wit, sitting back and appreciating her as a flame that brought famous moths close for repartee and intense conversation. He treasured her keen ability to manage a household and their complex social obligations. The couple enjoyed one another's minds, sharing a deep love of history and art. Both spoke more than one language and Clover often helped Henry sift through historical archives. During their travels abroad, she provided critical aid in his authorial process by researching government correspondence of previous administrations.

That they were not able to conceive any children seemed to be a quiet, but profound disappointment. Having children certainly was expected of prominent couples and the blame, if doled out, fell reliably on women. Clover doted on nieces and nephews and *pointedly* avoided the subject of her own lack of children.

Photography was a fond pursuit that had been in her life for some time, Henry having bought an elaborate setup for their honeymoon trip down the Nile. Clover helped with the staging, process, and development of the images. One of the photographs taken of Henry on their hired boat the *Isis* may have been her work, but her own penchant and talent for photography wasn't set in motion at this stage. Later on, her photographs would serve as a direct window into her inner life; images that remain prosaic, personal, revealing, and intimate.

The zenith of her photography spanned 1883 to 1885. But in that short time, she managed to capture remarkable slices of life, vibrant portraits that truly evoked the soul of the sitter or staging compositions that displayed haunting insights. Around the same time, Alice Austen began documenting a swiftly changing New York City from her home on Staten Island that she shared with her lifelong partner Gertrude Tate. Alice's home, nicknamed Clear Comfort, is now a federally recognized historical landmark of LGBTQ+ history. There is no indication that the two gifted women photographers ever met, but their female subjects navigate their own place in a rapidly transforming world. Alice and Clover were deemed hobbyists rather than professionals. Professional pursuits for women of their class and status were reserved for the men in their lives.

In the nineteenth century, the increasingly simplified processes of photography were considered an acceptable form of diversion and entertainment for women of means. It was a way to document the family; their expected purview. Obtaining an art education was becoming more widely accessible for women across all classes, as another way to train the eye for decoration and domesticity (and for the working classes, a way to make supplementary income), but a line was drawn in what would be considered *professional* work and *who* would be considered a professional in doing so. Another *new* thing threatening to unseat old ways. Photography would not be considered a "true" art form until Alfred Stieglitz made it so in the twentieth century, and women photographers along the way continued to be designated merely hobbyists well into those decades.

When *Century* magazine requested permission to use Clover's photographic portrait of writer George Bancroft as a cover feature, Henry Adams declined the invitation for her. He didn't want to be seen as advocating for an author whose style he wasn't fond of and didn't want undue attention being drawn to his family as the influential people they were. While all of that was true, it was likely an excuse, as Adams simply didn't approve of an upper-class woman being noted for something outside the home, as is clear in his fiction. His mostly unknown novel *Esther*, whose heroine borrows heavily from Clover, gives up on her artistic ambitions as hopeless; that she can never be anything more than an amateur. Adams did not believe a woman could have her own goal, art, or ambition *and* fulfill her duties as a wife. The novel ends without easement or resolution and some parts of it prove almost prophetic. I can't imagine what it must have felt like for Clover reading those drafts.

As a couple, they drifted apart, Henry increasingly solitary with his massive sequence of historical volumes, Clover feeling (I think understandably) listless.

But they found a fresh source of joy in planning a new home on H Street in Washington, one designed by Henry Hobson Richardson, for whom the popular Richardson Romanesque style was named. Sharing a love of architecture and aesthetics, they enjoyed the process together and came to consider Richardson a true friend. Clover took a truly vibrant and arresting portrait of him during the proceedings. Clover and Henry lived next door to the new home as it was being built. But Clover would never end up living in it.

Despite the societal and interpersonal limitations Clover was all too aware of, she had been diligently keeping photography journals since 1883, noting her processes and documenting successes and failures. The albums made in the last year of her life include less and less details as they go on, as if she couldn't find the heart or the words. And the subjects shift from people to abandoned and dilapidated buildings, mirroring a growing darkness that had taken ahold of her.

Many ghostlore accounts of Clover haunting the hotel that stands on the site where she died sensationalize the dynamic between her and her husband as volatile, insinuating that his being interested in young, pretty women drove her to unhealthy depths. There's no evidence that there were any physical affairs or indiscretions, Henry being of a somewhat puritanical bent, but emotional infidelity seems clear.

Henry Adams had become increasingly enamored with Elizabeth "Lizzie" Cameron, the young and pretty wife of politician Donald Cameron, having written in December 1884: "I shall dedicate my next poem to you. I shall have you carved over the arch of my stone doorway. I shall publish your volume of extracts with your portrait on the title page. None of these methods can fully express the extent to which I am yours." Both Henry and Lizzie guarded their social position and Lizzie did not indulge Henry further in these sentiments, nor did the two commence an affair, though they would maintain correspondence and friendship for decades. His letter to another woman declaring "I am yours" was sent a year before Clover's death.

Clover was too keen to have been unaware of her husband's enthusiasm for Mrs. Cameron's company and while it may have worried or unsettled her, Clover continued to retain Lizzie as a friend. Perhaps this strategy was to keep a rival close, but the fear of the dissolution of her marriage doesn't seem to have been, as some more lurid online ghost story accounts have suggested, the predominant factor in her suicide. It would seem the loss of Clover's father, as Adams had somewhat predicted in *Esther*, would prove too much to bear.

Having lovingly written to her father through every travel and adventure of her life, through every period of change, having spent most of her days either living nearby or spending summers together, the true anchor of Clover's life died in the summer of 1885. After the loss of so many formative figures, this loss in particular sent her drifting into a particularly deep depression. She wrote to friends about her husband's patience with her during this period, but she couldn't seem to find her way out of it. Her close-knit circle of family and friends were deeply worried about the couple's notable withdrawal from society.

On December 6, 1885, Clover swallowed potassium cyanide and died alone in front of her hearth. That a chemical used to reveal her photographic images would be the one to end her life is an irony lost on no one who learns about her. She was forty-two years old. The cause of death noted by the coroner was "paralysis of the heart." Such wording was more of a kindness and a distinct effort to maintain the respectable status of the family. Suicide has never been an easy thing to discuss or navigate, no matter the time period.

In Natalie Dykstra's deeply thoughtful and detailed biography, *Clover Adams: A Gilded and Heartbreaking Life*, she notes the position of Clover's subjects:

"The people in her images are often separate from each other, they rarely look directly at the camera, and they are often disconnected from or turned away from the viewer. And though Clover transformed what saddened her into something beautiful and something she could share, this transformation of loss—did not and could not save her. In the end, she seemed no more than a ghost."

A distressing photographic self-portrait of Clover haunts me, and it's showcased in Dykstra's biography. Her eyes, after the development of the photograph was complete, have been scratched out.

After Clover's passing, gossip and speculation swirled around the Adams home. Ghost stories circulated immediately.

Accounts of the H Street house becoming haunted appeared contemporaneous with her tragic death; the prominence of her family providing all the more grist to the mill of lurid tales. Passersby were said to feel uneasy in front of the house, where they heard wretched sobs or sighs from within. Another spectral account declared that the house was never warm again, no matter how many fires had been set, especially in front of the hearth where Clover's body had been found.

If people didn't know what to think about Clover's death, they most certainly didn't know what to do with the statue that Henry Adams put in place as a memorial. He commissioned the famed Augustus Saint-Gaudens to create a looming, hooded figure that he insisted would remain untitled, but who visitors would dub *Grief* or *Sorrow*.

In my "Unnamed Sorrow" essay about Clover for *The Feminine Macabre*, I discuss the monument as follows:

> The untitled sculpture at an unnamed grave is, in and of itself, an unanswered question. It is an active query, which gives it a certain life-force. It is animate in that it remains such a curious choice for a loved-one to leave behind. To this day no one really knows what to think about it. In a 1908 letter Adams wrote to Saint-Gaudens' son Homer, Henry demanded: "Do not allow the world to tag my figure with a name! Every magazine writer wants to label it as some American patent medicine for popular consumption . . . Your father meant it to ask a question, not to give an answer; and the man who answers will be damned to eternity like the men who answered the Sphinx." It is noted in this letter as *his* figure and he only mentions men asking questions. Of his wife's monument. She remains absent from the conversation, even in the hypothetical and philosophical.

In Greek myth, the Sphinx learned her riddle from the Muses. The inspiration of poetry, art, song, and science, the Muses are also keepers of knowledge and memory. We might consider the Muses folklorists. As metaphor and embodiment of art and tradition, they're of critical importance.

This is the beauty that ghost stories can offer us: a way to keep telling the stories of lived experiences, but only if we ask who the ghost really *is*. Beyond her thought-form as a muse, demanding more of them than just a Lady in White or an unknown, voiceless specter. What can their lives say about them now; the origin that then became icon? We must ask why their names were left off, why they were not credited, or why they became amalgams and absorbed into a new identity and cultural touchstone that erased their personhood in the process. Sometimes, that erasure was committed by the ones who supposedly loved them best.

Mystery surrounding Clover and her passing was only heightened by Henry destroying all of her letters. He never named her once in his autobiography, entirely omitting the thirteen years of their marriage from the core of his story. Henry never remarried and died in 1918 at the age of eighty. After his death, a relative found the half-empty bottle of potassium cyanide in the top drawer of his writing desk. He had been out of the house when Clover died, but he always kept a reminder of the tool of her death nearby, even though he'd hardly ever speak her name again.

I realize this detail may make the modern true crime enthusiast wonder if he'd killed her, but it just doesn't track. A supposition of his guilt wasn't pursued then, no such suggestion was made in Clover's biography, and it doesn't align with Henry Adams's character. He was self-absorbed, often cowardly, and coveted his status. He didn't have a motive. If he wanted to cheat on Clover, he, like every other man of the time, simply would have, while maintaining the domestic solidity he had always treasured with Clover. I believe she took that stability from him, rather than the other way around.

Clover should be named and celebrated as her own woman. I want her to be part of her own story again, even if the journey is painful. Loss, sorrow, depression, and the act of taking her own life does not erase the fact that there was a figure of great intelligence and talent at the center of the narrative. *That's* who I thanked and honored when visiting her grave.

The Gothic heroine is sometimes a figure of tragedy, yes, because she is often a victim of circumstance, but she is also a core pillar of storytelling. It is through her struggles that we try to understand our own agency in a broken world or our culpability in creating those circumstances in a society in which tragedy seems to be the only available outcome.

The H Street homes that Clover and Henry lived in no longer stand. The area was razed in 1927 to make way for the still-extant Hay-Adams Hotel, where reports of hauntings still circulate. Ghost tours of DC note that Clover Adams's full-body apparition has been seen at the hotel and that at times, the chandeliers would begin to sway in a mysterious, unnerving manner. Most notably, the curious, distinct scent of almonds has been detected wafting on the air with no discernable source. Potassium cyanide smells of almonds.

I admit, knowing all this, when I visited the lush, historic, wood-paneled Hay-Adams Hotel lobby, fully on intake while drafting this chapter, I was *convinced* I smelled almonds. It was likely just the enormous, mountainous bouquet of white roses and lilies and other fresh flowers that dominated a fine table near the elevators. But as I wandered the first-floor meeting rooms, dining rooms, and ballroom, the smell followed me. While I'm a believer in the paranormal, I don't think a clairolfactory (a paranormal occurrence involving the sense of smell) haunting was in play here. The human mind is so easily able to create a haunting and I think my mind was evoking Clover, wanting to be close to her, as I wish for all the subjects I write about. I was all too aware the ghost of her house existed in the foundations of the hotel I wandered.

Clover's photographs outlive her, vibrantly surviving as a window into her talents. Extant letters to her family and friends offer proof of her skill in capturing the tumult of the DC political landscape with incisive humor. The Massachusetts Historical Society in Boston houses Clover's photography collection and contemporary critics regard her as a gifted contributor to the history of the medium.

When visiting DC, take a stroll through Rock Creek Cemetery. Sit at one of the benches Henry installed for meditative contemplation and ponder the enigma he would also be buried under. Consider what the statue evokes. Moving past the initial thoughts of sorrow or grief, one might find resilience. I find the statue deeply stirring. Eerie, yes; frightening, no. Entering into that copse of tall evergreen shrubs, fully hidden from the rest of the cemetery, I felt like I was entering the cave of the Oracle of Delphi in Greek lore; drawn there to ask questions of the divine mystery.

Eleanor Roosevelt felt much the same way. After a particularly fraught time in her own life and marriage, she remarked to a friend that sitting before this statue surrounded by evergreen boughs made her feel better, stronger. Perhaps the spirit of two beleaguered political women could find solace decades apart, a spiritual kinship, a weary understanding of their tenuous place in the world.

Whether in the end she considered herself lucky or unlucky, Clover inspired others while she lived and her resting place can, if one allows for it, transform sorrow into strength. When I visit the statue, I say Clover's name, both her real name and this beloved nickname. And I will continue to do so. I realize saying her name won't etch letters into her monument, but let's not countenance the idea that she's a footnote, merely the wife of an Adams, or an unanswered question. She is a muse and we should name her. Thank you, Marian. Thank you, Clover.

Ghost Brides

Andrea

> And so, all the night-tide, I lie down by the side
> Of my darling—my darling—my life and my bride,
> In her sepulchre there by the sea—
> In her tomb by the sounding sea.
>
> —*Edgar Allan Poe, "Annabel Lee"*

We've all heard her story. She was killed, hit by a car on the way to the ceremony. She was trapped in a trunk on her wedding day. She was jilted and threw herself into the sea. And now she haunts this cliff, this car, this attic, this hotel, her snow-white veil floating eternally and ethereally.

Why are ghost brides such a classic trope? Is it the Poe-esque juxtaposition of death with youth and beauty? Is it the fact that a woman clad in a white gown is already appropriately dressed for the afterlife, her diaphanous white veil ready-made for her shade in the most symbolically neat packaging of all ghosts? Is it because, though we have all been socially conditioned to desire it, we secretly fear marriage?

With her deep origins in fairy tales and folklore, and her many expressions in ghost stories and Gothic literature, the ghost bride is an archetypal figure that is deeply embedded in popular consciousness. She has existed for centuries in folklore as an apparition who warns the bride- (or groom-) to-be of the dangers that lie ahead, dangers of an excess of passion, or a lack of it, dangers of trusting your heart to someone you maybe don't fully know yet. There's a narrative arc to a wedding that is tinged with fear, which we brush off as wedding-day jitters. The bride is the radiant focal point of the day, and at the precise moment of the fatal kiss, as maiden morphs into wife-and-mother, her fate is sealed. I hope, for your sake, your husband is a benevolent overlord and not a murderous Bluebeard, dear lady.

In pop culture, the ghost bride trope is evergreen, from Constance Hatchaway the animatronic ghost bride of Disney's Haunted Mansion, to the unforgettable image of Geena Davis in her *Beetlejuice* wedding dress—the wedding is in fact that movie's moment of greatest visceral horror, jarring amid the comedy. The ghost bride as a fictional and folkloric device is so rich and instantly readable at once that she is already accepted as a ready-made symbol of wasted potential, innocence and purity cut down in her prime, a commentary on the transient and fleeting nature of youth, ad infinitum. It's a trope that's spent a long time wrapped in tissue paper in Grandma's trunk (next to a bride's corpse, presumably). It's Miss Havisham in her wedding dress, forever a bride manqué. What can one say about her that isn't already said and announced up-front? As I write this, Constance Hatchaway waves and smiles at me in my mind's eye, saying, "I am already axiom, darling, don't try to unpack my trousseau." But there's still something compelling about the concept of the ghost bride, so much deep-seated anxiety about power and status and vulnerability and trust, that it bears looking into.

Lydia Carver is the ghost bride of Maine, haunting a charming resort in Cape Elizabeth's Crescent Beach near Portland, called the Inn by the Sea. She died in a shipwreck on the schooner

Charles in 1807 while returning from a shopping trip to Boston to buy her wedding dress, and her body was found and buried in a local cemetery in Cape Elizabeth.

After reading the story of Lydia Carver on a road trip through Maine, I convinced my family to detour at the Inn by the Sea. Our car—resplendent with its NYC street parking scratches and vomit-encrusted car seat—stood out in the parking lot, let me tell you. My husband was nervous the whole time. He has a lot of class-based anxiety and was certain we'd trigger some kind of "plebe alarm." I get a thrill out of sneaking around hotels I can't afford to stay at, and thoroughly enjoyed myself. I meandered through the dining room and around the grounds with ease, so much so that I had to be physically stopped from trying to take a dip in the pool ("We'll get caught!" my terrified spouse assured me). Instead of taking an illegal dip, I contented myself with strolling down toward the little cemetery in the garden, which I found completely charming. A little country graveyard by the sea? Irresistible. And there, thrillingly, was Lydia's grave just as the guidebook said. I snapped about a dozen photos, then strolled back into the hotel. I only dared to ask one person about the ghost and received such a penetrating stare that I fled, my husband's voice ringing in my head. Walking down to Crescent Beach, I let my imagination wander.

According to locals, as well as staff and guests at the inn, Lydia's ghost has been spotted wearing her wedding dress not only around the inn, but on the nearby highway. One woman saw her by the side of the road with her hand resting lightly on a deer, like Cate Blanchett in *The Lord of the Rings*. Cleaners in the hotel have seen her early in the morning in supposedly empty rooms; front desk clerks have witnessed the elevator stop and open on the lobby floor, completely empty, all the buttons lit. Brides-to-be have had strange dreams before their wedding nights, wherein their dresses move and float around the room, which actually sounds rather lovely, and they wake up to find their gowns have moved during the night. Presentiments are strange things! To me this sounds like an omen, yet as far as I know, nobody to date has called off their wedding after such a portentous dream. They probably assume it's a classic anxiety dream. There goes our modern therapized society sucking all the fun out of the Gothic again.

I do wonder what the guests think of the little graveyard on the property. Obviously, to a weird little gremlin like me it's an added attraction, but some guests are unpleasantly surprised when they discover their room is in view of it. When I finally worked up the nerve to talk to another employee at the hotel, they off-record confirmed that at least one guest has asked to move to a different room when they realized they can see a cemetery outside their window.

The putative portrait of Lydia that hangs in the hotel demonstrates why such guests are in the minority, though: She is not spooky or hideous or in any way the least bit threatening. She's a traditionally lovely, sweetly smiling woman pictured in a silky white gown that shows a faint, but decorous hint of nipple. She wears a wedding ring on her left hand, prominently displayed. The painting has no provenance, so nobody can be quite sure if it is indeed supposed to be Lydia Carver, but the hotel has sort of adopted it as her unofficial portrait. The dress, in any case, is accurate to the period in which she died, so it's easy to imagine she at least may have looked like that from the neck down, if she was fashionable. (Ironically, though modern visitors to the hotel will read the white gown as a wedding dress, it was very likely just a regular day-dress, since white gowns didn't become fashionable bridal wear until after Queen Victoria popularized it in her 1840 wedding to Prince Albert.) Once the hotel claimed this as Lydia's image, it was frequently used as the go-to illustration of her, found online and in most media coverage of her story, and so it has become her. So it goes in the way of ghostlore.

Another print in the hotel literally shows a shipwreck, a black-and-white etching of a smashed mast with a broken, listed vessel in the background. In the foreground, a fisherman cradles a lifeless woman washed up on the beach, one hand still clinging to a ship's rope. Again, there is no artist or date on the print, but it is extremely evocative of the wreck of the *Charles*, and the discovery of Lydia's body washed up on the beach. It was while standing before this etching that a certain New England trance medium attested to feeling Lydia's presence during a paranormal investigation around 2009. The medium, who does a brisk business in ghost hunting and other psychic services, including, among other things, "Russian Gypsy Angel Readings," felt Lydia all around the hotel the night of the investigation. It was a fruitful search. Her partner's EMF meters went missing, then were suddenly found. In the cemetery, malfunctioning cameras, drained batteries, and a plethora of orbs completed the experience, to the satisfaction of all paying guests. Lydia is not only a pretty ghost, but an obliging one too.

I like nautical ghosts and shipwrecks and can't resist the tragic poetry of a romantic bride, but according to a local historian, Charles Lagerbom, there's no evidence at all that Lydia was on her way to be married; the first time that was mentioned was in a poem written by a man named Ebenezer Robbins. "An Elegy on the Distressing Scene of the Schooner *Charles*" was published in 1807, and this is the first instance of Lydia being described as an "intended bride." That trip to Boston could have been for anything, but Robbins decided the only reason for a woman to go to a big city was, naturally, to shop. He decided her story would be more poignant if she was an unconsummated bride, and it totally worked.

I looked for something to explain our eternal fascination with the ghost bride, and it turns out this trope goes back quite a long way. In her book *The Once and Future Sex*, medievalist Eleanor Janega talks about that notorious old chestnut, the concept of medical "humors." Women were cold and wet, whereas men were hot and dry. Children, like men, were hot and dry. Only the act of aging would turn girl-children into women, and thus transmute them into cold, wet beings. According to Janega, "Advancing age, and death itself, were both associated with wetness." Maidens were considered the perfect age because they were "women enough to be distinguishable from men, but not so cold and wet that they became deathly." They had "all the attractive qualities of femininity but were free of the faults."[1] This was the "optimum age for women."[2] "The moment that they lived up to the promise of their maidenhood and became wives and mothers . . . they would lose the status that made them desirable in the first place." Bound up in that desirability was their availability: you could—potentially, at least—have the beautiful maiden you desired, as she was by definition not already taken. A beautiful married woman, however, lost that luster: "Married beauties could never be ideal because they were already owned."[3] A ghost bride who dies just on the brink of marriage has the luxury of remaining attractive and will never lose that status. But don't worry if you're already married. Janega notes that when the Apocalypse comes, all women will be returned to their ideal stage: a maiden just at the brink of marriageable age. Something to look forward to, ladies!

The ghost bride as a figure of horror has been most exquisitely expressed in Gothic fiction by Edgar Allan Poe. Poe knew that the true terror of the ghost bride lies in her cognitive dissonance, in the contrast between beauty and decay. I particularly think of "Berenice" here, wherein the young bride's wasting disease causes her face to turn into a skeletal rictus made all the more disturbing by the resilience of her strong white teeth, which refuse to decay at the same rate as the rest of her face. Witnessing this incongruity drives the story's narrator to madness; this is the same effect we experience when the lovely flesh-bride becomes the decayed and frightening ghost, corpse, or skeleton bride. Many of Poe's other female characters are also defined by their status as brides or, more accurately wives, namely Morella and Ligeia (and Rowena) and all of them have strong visual components: striking features, effulgent eyes, hideous teeth. Spectacle and the sensory are vital components to the experience of reading these stories, as befits the theme of the spectral bride: just as weddings contain an element of spectacle, so too does the ghost bride retain her visual allure—or repulsiveness, depending on your point of view.

The ghost bride exists in a liminal state. She is temporary, a wedding lasting only a few hours, or seasons if you count the run-up and prep. The bride is like one of those flowers that only blooms for a day. That's probably why the ghost bride is such an imaginatively compelling and arresting figure: Nobody is meant to be a bride forever. The bride marks a transition between two worlds, on the cusp between two states of being. Similarly, the ghost is stuck between two states of being, life and afterlife. The ghost bride, then, is trapped in a state of double liminality.

The Driskill Hotel in Austin, Texas, has a ghost bride story that also happens to be twice-told. It goes like this: In the olden times, like the 1900s, way back before recorded human history existed, a bride-to-be died by suicide in a certain hotel room. Then, in the 1990s, another bride-to-be did the exact same thing . . . in the exact same room. Oddly, the 1990s-era bride also leaves no recorded trace of her existence in any of the usual sources: newspapers, obituaries, Find A Grave.com, the entire internet. Possibly the 1990s is also too far back to find any existing sources? If you feel my skepticism oozing off the page, you get the point. This is a completely invented story, and I'm pretty sure I know who invented it, but for legal purposes I am not allowed to say. The ghostly bride of the Driskill Hotel has worked its way into Austin folklore and is a prominent feature on many of that city's ghost tours. Most people taking a ghost tour who hear this story won't question it, but they won't necessarily believe it either; the social compact of the ghost tour includes an element of willing suspension of disbelief, after all.

It's actually a rather elegantly structured story, filled with the kind of uncanny doublings that are so prevalent in Gothic fiction, which happens to be one of my favorite aspects of the genre. I love any narrative with doubles, doppelgängers, twins, two Kim Novaks. . . . Incidentally, the 1990s bride in the Driskill story also allegedly visited Austin to do some shopping before her wedding day, an echo of Lydia Carver that also appeals to me. Are the ghost brides of the Driskill Hotel fakelore? Probably. But it's an alluring story, so I'd just caution any ghost tour guide who's tempted to tell it to frame it as urban legend, to put it in context. And hey, it might be a good opportunity to discuss the appeal of the ghost bride archetype, and maybe buy a copy of this book (a win for all)!

The ghost bride is part of the dark tourism industry's inventory of stock characters, along with baby buried under floorboards and giggling ghost of a child who died on their own birthday. The Driskill Hotel encourages the story, since our society is currently in a current "ghosts = good business" wave. *So* many ghost bride stories I came across in my research took place at hotels, and no wonder. Besides the practical associations of brides with hotels as wedding venues and locations for honeymoons, the symbolism feels significant and resonant. Hotels too are liminal spaces—interstitial, temporary, not-quite-home—which might perhaps be one reason why ghost brides appear there so often.

In addition to the Driskill, the Dauphine Orleans Hotel in New Orleans, the Hotel Conneaut in Pennsylvania, and the Grand Galvez, also in Texas, all contain ghost brides. So does Yellowstone Park's Old Faithful Inn (an ironic name in this context!) and the Fairmont Banff Springs Hotel in Alberta, Canada. The Conneaut is said to be haunted by the ghost of Elizabeth, who died in a fire while on her honeymoon; the Old Faithful has a story about a headless bride who wanders the halls; and Banff Springs is said to be haunted by the ghost of a 1930s-era bride who tripped on her own wedding dress, which then caught fire on a wall sconce as she tumbled down a grand staircase.

The ghost bride of Galveston's Grand Galvez is known as Audra; she is said to have ended her life in room 501, or the West Bell Tower, depending on who's telling the story, after she heard her groom-to-be's ship went down in a storm. Galveston is a coastal city, so it follows that there's a connection to the seafaring trades. Ghost ships and ghost brides go hand in hand. Rather sweetly, the hotel threw a big bash in October 2023 to "give Audra the wedding reception she never had."[4]

The Dauphine has a most intriguing haunting connected to May Baily, a famed New Orleans bordello madam who operated her establishment in what is now the hotel. She's a notable historic figure and Big Easy personality, and the ghost story apparently involves her own sister. According to the hotel's website, Millie Baily's betrothed was killed during a gambling brawl, on her wedding day: "The ghost of Baily and her fiancée [sic], a Civil War soldier, frequently haunt the [hotel] grounds—Baily in her wedding dress and her fiancée [sic] in his uniform." There's a double dose of symbolism in this story, as the gallant young soldier ghost may be seen as a type of ghost bride equivalent: youth cut down in its flower, tragically.

Like the ghost brides of the Driskill, almost none of these hotel ghost brides have any provable connection to reality except Millie Baily of the Dauphine (I couldn't turn up any archival sources verifying the identity of Audra of the Galvez). In fact, the former assistant manager of the Old Faithful, George Bornemann, admitted to making up the headless bride ghost story in 1991. [5] But when one considers how freely fact and fiction mix in the Gothic, maybe it doesn't matter all that much. What matters more is how these ghost stories are told, interpreted, shared, and monetized (and who they benefit). If telling a ghost bride story teaches us who May Baily was, or stirs up conversation about folklore, or results in throwing a wedding party for a ghost, it's all good. Though the Banff Springs ghost bride story has never been proven, the Canadian government still went ahead and put her image on both a collectible coin and a stamp in 2014 (I am a proud possessor of the aforementioned stamp). In a press release, Canada Post employee Mike Shearon proudly noted that "bringing intriguing Canadian tales out of the shadows is what stamps continue to do."[6]

Locating ghost brides in their honeymoon suites is a pretty on-the-nose symbol, but effective. Traditionally, the wedding night is where you cross the Rubicon and there is no going back. The prevalence of hotel ghost brides may also speak to an undercurrent of anxiety about just what that wedding night entails, and what it bodes for the rest of your life until death do you part. The threat of sexual dissatisfaction, dominance, or even violence, manifests as fear and cautionary tale here. "Innocence under threat" is at the core of every good Gothic story, and it's also at the center of these "real-life" and folkloric ghost brides. I spoke with Anna Biller, director of *The Love Witch* and author of *Bluebeard's Castle*, about the idea of the female Gothic, and the gender dynamics at play.

"In any culture," Anna told me, "the most persistent ghosts have to do with the most troubling aspects of society. This is why women, who have traditionally struggled to be heard and to have freedom of movement, are so often at the center of ghost stories, both as ghosts and people persistently haunted by ghosts."

What about the idea of the Gothic heroine as a lady in peril? I asked. So much criticism of the Gothic is leveled at the "helpless" heroine, who is in constant danger. Anna's own book, *Bluebeard's Castle,* presents a female main character who is menaced by her abusive sociopathic husband, newly married and just beginning to reveal his true nature, as the novel's name implies.

"I believe good writing is writing that talks about what is, not about what should be. Women are still oppressed around the world (in this country if not legally, then socially and domestically), and real literature should reflect that," she replied. "I adore Ann Radcliffe, the Brontës, Mary Shelley, and Daphne du Maurier, the most famous examples the female Gothic, and I also love Angela Carter and Shirley Jackson. [Stories] about women in peril can absolutely be feminist, and [all] of these writers were essentially proto-feminist or feminist writers, because they go into female experience in such a detailed, psychologically astute, and personal way."

Another contemporary writer working in the realm of the Gothic is Margaret Atwood, who has drawn on the symbolism of folk and fairy tale motifs such as the ghost bride who literally suffocates in her trunk, and the bride whose very pores suffocate in her wedding dress. Atwood famously commented on the suffocating and dangerous aspects of marriage in *The Edible Woman* and *The Robber Bride.* I remember reading the book jacket copy of *The Edible Woman*, a story about a woman's mental dissolution following a marriage proposal, when I was young enough to be highly impressionable, and the words were burned indelibly into me: "She was supposed to feel consumed by love. Instead, she just feels consumed." *The Robber Bride* builds off the Grimm fairy tale "The Robber Bridegroom," which involves a woman threatened with death by her betrothed.

In the folklore motif of the menacing bridegroom, the specter bridegroom, the robber bridegroom, and Bluebeard are the inverse of the ghost bride, but they speak to the same threats and fears: the fear that sexual encounters will lead to death. Sex is supposed to give life, so the idea that it brings death creates the horror, much in the same way violence at a wedding is more horrifying by the contrast of what that event is supposed to be. Spectral bridegrooms, demon lovers, and death and the maiden stories warn not only of the potential death-bringing properties of sex (death by venereal disease, social death in the case of sex out of wedlock, death by botched abortion, in childbirth, or by marital violence, etc.) but also warn of the dangers of clinging to the past. Often, the spectral brides and bridegrooms in the folktales realize too late that their lover is dead. These types of tales can be found throughout the world and throughout history, as in the folktale of "Sweet William," the Gothic German story "Lenore," and Pawnee legends of the ghostly bride. And all of this is not to be confused with the corpse bride, a Jewish folktale that also warns of what happens when one fails to let go of the past . . . or, perhaps, when one blindly follows traditional expectations without knowing quite why they're doing so. I can't tell you how many divorced people I've spoken to who said they just got married because everyone else seemed to be doing it.

In nearly all of these stories it is always the bride at the center, even when the spectral bridegroom is supposedly the story's subject. The women are foregrounded in these tales, the men shunted off into anonymity. Who was Lydia Carver's husband-to-be? Nobody knows and nobody has ever bothered to find out. Like a Ken doll, the bridegroom is just so much background amid the lace and tulle. The bride is foregrounded in these tales because they speak to feminine fears. This is only natural, as marriage is much more treacherous ground for women. Writers of the Gothic have always been aware of this, and commented on it quite overtly.

From Madame Montoni in Ann Radcliffe's *The Mysteries of Udolpho* to poor Aunt Patience in Daphne DuMaurier's *Jamaica Inn*, married women in the Gothic tend to be cautionary tales of misplaced trust and unbalanced power. Radcliffe could not have been clearer when she put the following words into the mouth of her nefarious character Signor Montoni as he imprisoned his new wife in the forbidding castle's east turret: "There, perhaps, you may understand the danger of offending a man, who has unlimited power over you." In *Jamaica Inn*, du Maurier's depiction of domestic abuse is horrifying in both its accuracy and its casualness, in her searingly honest depiction of an abusive marriage and the offhanded references to beating wives "once a week," or "until they couldn't stand." In that novel, Aunt Patience is transformed from a vivacious young woman to a ghost of her former self through years of her husband Joss Merlyn's abuse, while the novel's astute protagonist Mary Yellan observes the thin line between attraction and repulsion, making Patience's deterioration heartbreakingly relatable. One minute you're being love-bombed by a charmer with bright eyes and strong, graceful hands, the next minute you find yourself shackled to a sociopath until death do you part.

Even in our more modern version of domesticity, marriage itself is actually detrimental to women's physical and mental health. In heterosexual couplings, married men are healthier and live longer than single men, while the inverse is true of married women.[7] Married women continue to perform *double* the unpaid housework of married men, leaving them with less free time to relax or pursue outside hobbies and interests, and this inequality deepens if children enter the equation. This is true regardless of whether or not that woman also works outside the home. If all this makes staying single sound appealing, according to the Gender Equity Policy Institute, single women still have 17 percent less free time than single men.[8]

It's also worth remembering that in many ghost bride stories, singlehood is literally portrayed as a fate worse than, or at least as equivalent to, death—hence the prevalence in these tales of jilted would-be brides throwing themselves from hotel windows, hanging themselves, or otherwise dying by suicide. In the folklore, both scenarios—marriage, *and* singledom—speak to the same essential anxiety.

And the primal anxiety at the heart of it all isn't literally a fear of marriage's potential side effects of inequality, or a terror of being single. At the heart of it is the fear of placing your heart into the hands of another flawed human. Trusting another person takes strength. And whether you're single or partnered, there is a potential for the kind of aloneness that *isn't* desirable, not a pleasant, solitary enjoyment of one's own company—no, *real* loneliness: the aching kind, the awful kind, the heartbreaking kind. The kind you can feel while eating dinner alone, or with a spouse who won't look up from their phone.

So while the ghost bride might seem, at first blush, retrograde or sexist, she is actually a fascinating figure, and a helpful one. When she appears as a spectral warning from beyond the grave as a cautionary tale to real brides-to-be, she is actually performing a boldly feminist act of provocation. Though our social expectations of what marriage should be have changed considerably since the days of Lydia Carver, to say the least, there is still an anxiety lodged in the substrata of our collective unconscious that marriage might not be the happily-ever-after you want it to be (shout-out to my fellow Gen X children of divorce). I think the ghost bride is here to help us work through *these* fears.

My mind wanders back to the brides who choose to get married in the Inn by the Sea, the ones who have nightmares about floating wedding dresses before their big day.

In the fairy tale "The Robber Bridegroom," the titular bridegroom asks his bride-to-be for a story to entertain him and his friends. Having been fully apprised of his murderous ways the night before by a friendly local crone whose advice she was wise enough to heed, the young bride-to-be cunningly frames his crimes as a fiction. She tells the story as though it were all safely made up, repeating the soothing refrain, "My dear, it was only a dream."

With each repetition of the refrain, she introduces a new accusatory detail that brings his wrongdoings to light: "I heard the screams."

"My dear, it was only a dream."

(I think of these brides-to-be slumbering near Lydia Carver's grave, consumed with anxiety. *My dear, it was only a dream.*)

"I saw the bodies."

The husband-to-be becomes unsettled, shifting in his seat, as our heroine continues.

"My dear, it was only a dream."

(Their wedding dresses rise and float around the room. *My dear, it was only a dream.*)

The young woman leaps from her chair and declaims, "Then I found this severed finger with a wedding ring still attached!"

Our heroine shouts her final accusation.

"My dear, that was no dream!"

The robber bridegroom trembles. Cue the guards and the robber bridegroom's arrest!

Our storyteller escapes with her life.

The Eternal Headmistress: Helen Peabody and Western College for Women

Leanna

The stern matron holds her vise grip on the haunted house. She looms large and exacting. Helen Peabody embodies the Gothic archetype of the domineering spinster headmistress ruling her queendom with an iron fist. With a purview far wider than that of the dour, controlling and manipulative Mrs. Danvers of Daphne du Maurier's classic *Rebecca*, Helen Peabody was a fierce leader above all else. She wanted the best for her charges, demanding nothing less of them or herself than shrewd, consistent excellence. Her portrait, hung prominently in the entrance foyer of Peabody Hall, arrests you in a steadfast stare. You'd better be on your best behavior.

Helen Peabody often sounded possessive when discussing her charges at Western Female Seminary, where she was principal for thirty-three years, her campus now part of picturesque Miami University in Oxford, Ohio. My alma mater. And the way the hauntings of Peabody Hall have been described through the years, her possessiveness and sharp discipline was taken out on male students once the college became coed. This is what I'd always been told as a student. Everyone regarded this as simple fact: You did not dare cross the unforgiving headmistress, or she would make your nights sleepless.

The day I moved into my first dorm in 1997, the bumper sticker on the car ahead of me read: *Founded 1809: Miami Was a College Before Florida Was a State.* Clarifying *Miami University,* not *University of Miami,* I quoted that bumper sticker whenever folks assumed I was going to school in Florida. Since I was particularly devoted to Victorian-era studies, I was proud that the state of Ohio had been such a prominent leader in women's education initiatives and that layers of nineteenth-century history surrounded every turn around the grand "public Ivy" (Miami liked to note itself as a public school with Ivy League prestige). Western College for Women was one of the first Protestant schools in the country to confer a Bachelor of Arts degree to women. Here I was, a century and a half later, enrolled as a Bachelor of Fine Arts theater major. I moved into Tappan Hall, an all-women's dorm that faced the gorgeous, sloping land known simply as "Western."

Picturesque tracts rolled away from the main campus in dramatic turns and steep hills. Laid out by noted landscape architects Vaux and Olmsted (of Central Park fame) in 1853, the name changed to Western College when the institution became coeducational in 1971, joining with Miami officially in 1974 while retaining unique interdisciplinary studies. Merging the campuses into one fully coeducational institution had people remarking that former President Peabody would be rolling over in her grave. Helen Peabody had a continuous, contentious relationship with "Miami men," as noted in her papers.

Ghost stories were part of orientation week, told by upperclassmen to thrill newcomers. Having spent my childhood making up ghost stories to scare my fellow Girl Scouts in the same part of southwestern Ohio, I knew the formula. Most of the campus stories seemed inventive stretches, many conflated different historical events, two different buildings, and three different time periods. Peabody Hall, though, whose interior had just undergone a multimillion-dollar renovation the year I started school, named for the stern president that had lived and worked for so many years under its eaves . . . *that* story, *her* building; *that* I believed was legitimately haunted. Workers during the renovation repeatedly claimed they saw Helen Peabody's ghost. But even before the renovations, she'd been haunting the premises as though she'd never left. Peabody Hall has a vast backlog of historic, anecdotal evidence while still remaining actively haunted to this day. Attending Miami alumni gatherings in New York, it inevitably comes up that I write about ghosts. Without fail, fellow alumni immediately exclaim, "Oh, Peabody Hall!" with matter-of-fact certainty. And Helen Peabody has her reasons.

Tall and imposing, Peabody Hall sits at the back of Western campus like it's lying in wait, crouched on large haunches at the crest of a hill. A large, redbrick Georgian-style building with prominent steps and wide windows, its wings stretch out impressively and its main hall is long and ponderous. A brass marker to the side of the large front doors notes the hall's namesake.

Western Female Seminary, later Western College for Women, was a daughter school to Mount Holyoke College in Massachusetts, where Helen Peabody was an alumna. The star protégée of Holyoke President Mary Lyon, education was Helen Peabody's sole mission and life's work. A pious, righteous woman, Helen would never marry and would give everything she owned to Presbyterian charities, in honor of Christ. As she said to her board of directors in one year's summary: "Work is ours. Results are His." Peabody wasn't running a convent, but I wonder if she'd have been better understood if she had.

A self-styled "Victorian goth," I *loved* our theater building; historic Presser Hall, a gray, castle-like fortress with Gothic arches and parapets, right at the edge of Western, as if we stood at the borderlands of some other realm. Every time I went out the back way, toward Western's grounds, I felt time operate differently. Light took on a different quality, as if the landscape knew it was something special, idyllic yet secretive. Western remains a place that if you aren't careful, it's easy to get lost in: rolling hills, surrounded by forested slopes with no clear view of paths back to the center of campus. Helen Peabody very much wanted a separation for her girls from the rest of the Miami setting and students.

A small cemetery a few blocks from the edges of Western proved a frequent haunt for me and a couple of melancholy friends (goths visiting graveyards; a stereotype that proves true). Every time my friend Jason and I took an evening saunter through that always-open gate, the two streetlights above the wrought iron fence would sputter and go dark. Every time. As if on cue, the minute we turned the corner, walking over from the theater building, they'd flicker and die, only to do it all over again the next time we decided to respectfully wander among nineteenth-century plots and wonder about the people buried there. It wasn't that a streetlight timer had gone off at a certain hour or that car headlights affected them—we went at different evening hours and the road was usually quiet. They guttered repeatedly, one then the next, the moment we started our approach. While I can't explain the behavior of the streetlights, it does track with the common motif of haunted areas—and sometimes haunted people—having an effect on electric lights.

Jason and I shared any ghost story that crossed our path. After the tall tales at orientation, he brought up Peabody Hall. He'd spent semesters there and attested to the hauntings himself, and those encountered by friends and colleagues. I dearly wish I could ask him again to recount his hair-raising tales of objects moving in poltergeist style and the hall's uncanny lights and noises. Sadly, Jason is no longer with us on this earthly plane. But I'd like to think he'd enjoy being brought up in a book of haunted history. Here's to you, Jason, I hope your spirit is having fun learning all the esoteric, mystical things we'd chat about until dawn. You are missed.

The most curious thing about Jason's insistence that Western campus was haunted was the red fox who would accompany him to class. An actual animal. A red fox would appear, regularly stepping out from bushes under a stone bridge on Western campus, and would trot along below, as if accompanying him from one side of the bridge to the other. It happened many times. A few days after he told me this, hoping I'd believe him, I was sitting with a costume-designer friend at the edge of the aforementioned cemetery. While I was contemplating a difficult personal decision, a red fox came out from the forested margin and trotted directly toward me, sat down, looked up at me, and cocked its head. My friend sputtered a murmured question: *Are you seeing this red fox? What is it doing?* When I said a startled hello, not knowing what else to say or do, the fox turned its head again. After examining me for a few breathless moments, it turned tail and slowly retreated right back into the woods it had come from. Stunned, this moment represented a shift for me, from a darker part of my life to a more determined one. When I shared this with Jason, we didn't know what to make of the fox, other than to deem it a cosmic encouragement to keep asking questions of the unknown, to keep embracing the paranormal as our normal. It's a promise I've kept every day since; to always maintain an open mind when it comes to the utterly inexplicable.

I'm not attempting to correlate the strange behavior of a red fox with Helen Peabody. In this case, it may speak to something far older. The red fox is a clever, symbolic figure in many different cultures, and the folklore of the Myaamia people, from which

Miami derives its name, is no exception. The Myaamia people ceded land the Miami campus and surrounding areas occupy in the 1795 Treaty of Greenville, but forcible removal took place in areas beyond the campus in 1846. The Miami Nation maintains a vibrant coeducational relationship with the university through the Myaamia Center on campus, founded to teach and share Myaamia culture, and the school has helped revitalize the native language. David J. Costa, a key figure in helping create Myaamia dictionaries, compiled historic interviews with native speakers in *As Long as the Earth Endures: Annotated Miami-Illinois Texts*, in which Paapankamwa Aalhsoohkaakani, "Fox Stories," feature a trickster red fox out to tease and outwit his older brother, Wolf. If encountering this character, be ready to adapt and think quickly.

The sight of that fox, seen by not just me but by a close friend, jarred me into a better place and a sharper mindset, reminding me that it was all right not to know what lay ahead: the important thing was to keep going with a good head on your shoulders. To stay sharp. And that ties directly back to Helen Peabody and what she tried to instill in her charges.

In every haunted story concerning Helen Peabody her ghost demands what she did in life: respect. Respect for her, respect for her students and for everyone's education. You can see it in her portrait; her visage exudes strength and fortitude and she wants you to step up and embody the same.

In 2018, Miami theater students presented *Echoes of Miami*, an entirely unique, immersive theatrical experience where audiences were split into three groups and led around the Center for Performing Arts building as if it were a haunted house. Gradually, some of the school's best ghost stories would unfold, the lion's share going to Helen Peabody. Three actresses channeled three different spectral incarnations of Helen Peabody, representing divergent aspects of her life and personality, one noted as "Defender Helen," another as "Man-Hating Helen," and finally "Historic Helen."

All of these identities do seem to be part of her real story. She was a fierce defender of women's education. She was a historic leader. She is quoted as saying in an address to students, "Miami men were always troublesome." Keeping the then-all-male Miami students off her all-female Western campus was a full-time job in and of itself. It's unsurprising that the now-coed Peabody Hall might garner her distinct spectral pushback. There's no evidence, however, that she actually *hated* men. While it's true she never married, she had close male colleagues, boards of directors and clergy that were very dear to her. She wrote about the delight of playing matchmaker between suitable teachers. What she did hate was anyone trying to distract her girls from their degree; she demanded an undisturbed period of respect and autonomy.

Before my library appointment with a few archival boxes of papers, I went to Peabody Hall to pay Helen a visit. I walked up the wide stairs, crossed the open porch, heaved open the great front doors and stepped inside with a thrill of excitement to be back in this building after many years away. I crossed the wide entrance foyer to the intersection of the first-floor wings, drawn in by the visage of the striking woman in the frame ahead of me.

I stared long and hard at Helen's portrait. She stared long and hard back at me. I asked her, as I do with any of the subjects I write about, to help me tell her story. The energy of that historic, first-floor hallway felt electric. To my ear, the building always had a sort of hum and it positively buzzed this time. Yes, it had been renovated since the days of Helen's management, but the historic character of the building still shines through, as does Helen's ease in presiding over it still, effortlessly exuding command.

Poring over the few boxes of papers concerning Peabody that are held in Miami's Havighurst Special Collections library,

I noticed a theme: Helen Peabody shared a sincere, loving warmth with those who were committed to good behavior and the ideals of higher education. Conversely, she had only dismissive contempt for those who didn't follow the rules her institution set forth. Helen Peabody was filled with an unflappable, righteous, zealous purpose. She's a spirit who seeks control.

That's what makes Helen Peabody so potent in this collegiate setting, where young people are testing the waters of autonomy and adulthood for the first time. Authority figures can become contentious when one is spreading their wings; a magnet for conflict. But for Helen, at a time when women could control so very little in their lives, and were relegated to so few spheres economically, socially, bodily and vocationally, she sought to give her charges confidence, self-ownership and accountability, to be strong, self-sustaining and intelligent in the face of a society that did not allow them their rights.

Helen's style of structural, holistic control was clearly evidenced in a typed transcription, tucked in amid all the Peabody papers, taken "From the notebook of Nattie Mills, class of 1862" titled the "76 Wishes of Miss Peabody." The document lists seventy-six rather strict rules, beginning with bathing in cold water each morning and continuing with demands, such as never sticking one's head out the window ("very impolite") and to never go outside without a bonnet.

What exactly *made* Helen Peabody this strict figure isn't entirely clear. Losing her father at a young age seems to have affected her, as did being in a large family while seeking some kind of purpose and focus. Helen truly found that clarity at Mount Holyoke, and it seems evident that her ability to assert control over herself, her environment, and others made her President Lyon's favorite. The most natural, handpicked figurehead to take up Western Seminary leadership, Helen Peabody held a torch aloft for others to find their way to order.

In an invitation for her girls to return for the seminary's twenty-fifth anniversary, Helen Peabody wrote: "Has the anchor held in the storm? Has the shield proved sufficient for all the fiery darts of the wicked? Has any part of the armor failed in the day of battle?" She sought to cultivate women warriors who could prove resilient in a world that did not consider them equals, holding them to high standards before society would expect them to become second-class citizens again. The language she uses is one of withstanding repeated assault. Contemporaries wrote that Miss Peabody was as interested in cultivating soul and character as she was in training intellects. A woman who felt that there was always a war to be won on more than one front, she could not afford leniency.

Notes on the history of the school, compiled by an alumna and typed on loose-leaf pages in the special collections library declared: "Sometimes there were serious enough infractions of rules to occasion private conference with Miss Peabody, which gave rise to the ominous expression of 'going to sit on the green stool.' In Miss Peabody's room was an octagonal stool covered with green rep, which she would ask the offender to pull up. Though our first principal was not versed in modern psychology, her niece says, 'the girls would melt under her and tell her everything they had done.'"

Control, and who wields it, is at the center of most Gothic narratives, particularly when it comes to women's agency and futures. What makes Helen Peabody notable is that she wasn't leveraging her own power over others for personal gain as is found in many a Gothic villain. Her quest for control was in order to lift other women up.

Peabody's disciplinarian nature, however, would prove her downfall. In June 1887, the headmistress denied graduation papers to Lottie Castner on the grounds of misbehavior. Once Castner pleadingly appealed the decision and was still denied, in a move that board members and officials deemed too drastic a punishment for a few pranks and mild infractions, Peabody's competence and strict methods came into question. Affronted by this lack of faith in her leadership, with her health deteriorating, she took a leave of absence that year. Returning for a final 1888 commencement, she then resigned, traveled overseas and later moved to California, where she died in 1905. A simple grave marker bears her name and reads *Nothing in my hand I bring*—a modest line from the Christian hymn "Rock of Ages." Her cremated remains were returned to Western by former alumnae and scattered on the grounds she'd worked so hard to maintain.

The youngest child of fourteen siblings, aunt to many nieces and nephews, Helen Peabody's last will and testament left all real estate and holdings of any monetary substance in her estate entirely to Presbyterian mission work, a move that would be legally questioned by relatives. But she maintained control to the end, and beyond. Despite countless setbacks and difficulties, Helen Peabody had created and maintained a legacy against all odds.

Western was a school that kept costs affordable, so that stellar education wasn't just the privilege of wealthy girls. The school survived disease outbreaks and more than one devastating fire. It persevered through the contentious times of the Civil War; Ohio was steadfastly a Union state, but a school in southern Ohio was particularly vulnerable.

In 1964, Freedom Summer volunteers trained hundreds of student activists at Western College for Women, putting lives on the line in the Civil Rights movement. Three Freedom Summer leaders left Oxford after training and went missing. James Chaney, Michael Schwerner, and Andrew Goodman were later found murdered by a conspiracy of Ku Klux Klan members that included local police. The activists' bodies were found buried in an earthen dam in Philadelphia, Mississippi. Just outside Peabody Hall sits a stone amphitheater memorial dedicated to their activism, their sacrifice, and a historical Civil Rights marker notes their deaths as changing the course of the movement.

Notable Western College for Women alumnae include Margaret Caroline Anderson, founder of *The Little Review*, United Nations Under–Secretary General Ameerah Haq, politician and eighteenth Secretary of Health and Human Services Donna Shalala, as well as numerous writers, suffragists, reporters, and ambassadors.

Helen Peabody couldn't have known all this would come to pass in her first lean years in the 1850s, but I'm sure she'd have hoped such world-changing people would be proud to call Western home.

Helen Peabody demands respect, or she *will* haunt you. Because this is now codified Miami lore, it also means that students will test it. Particularly male residents of Peabody Hall. What has become my favorite ghost story goes as follows:

Two male Peabody Hall roommates had heard the stories of Helen Peabody haunting their dorm and had already been advised by their RA not to speak disparagingly of the headmistress, especially not in front of her portrait. Evidently taking this as a challenge, the two students proceeded to do exactly that. Once rude diatribes in front of the president's picture had been dispatched, the two men went back to studying, as finals were looming. Over the course of the night, books crashed to the floor. Their lamp crashed to the floor. A thumping sound came from their wardrobe. And the message light on their dorm-room landline phone began flashing. Getting increasingly freaked out, the students checked their messages: nothing. They unplugged their phones from the landline and tried to focus. The lamp crashed off the desk again when no one had touched it. They turned on their phones, only to find that the message light was flashing again. After being *unplugged*.

Truly unnerved, the roommates brought their situation to their RA, the one that warned them not to rile the headmistress in the first place. The RA called the telecommunication office to see if calls had been made to the dorm phone. Yes. Two hundred of them. They were able to access a message. *It was a playback of the conversation they'd had in front of Helen Peabody's portrait.*

As if this wasn't enough, to truly make her point, there was another loud thud from the wardrobe as the students tried to get some sleep. Freaked out again, the smaller of the two roommates tried to wake the larger one, a Miami football player who was normally a light sleeper. He wouldn't budge. The other roommate fled down the hall to a less troubled room. In the morning, the football player said he dreamed that he was being held down, pinned by a fierce woman relentlessly scolding him.

Only when the two sincerely apologized to Helen Peabody's portrait did things settle down again.

Through the years, I've heard several iterations of such stories that all boil down to the same result: any disrespect in front of that portrait means she's going to mess with your mind— and your stuff—until you apologize.

According to a *Mysteries* subheading tab on Miami's website (which pops up as a top search result when inputting *Helen Peabody* and *Western Female Seminary*), Helen Peabody gets her own page, replete with historic black-and-white photographs of Peabody Hall. The page states: "In fact, it appears that Ms. Peabody may have done far more than merely turn over in her grave. According to some witnesses, her spirit leaves the tomb occasionally to watch over the women of Peabody Hall and to haunt the men who now dare to walk its corridors. Those who have seen her claim that Helen Peabody remains in death, as she was in life, a very formidable woman."

Throughout the process of researching and writing this chapter, I've found myself waxing nostalgic for the company of friends who have passed on. And I'm still filled with curious wonder at all the odd things I experienced during my Miami years. I remain drawn to Helen Peabody's steadfast spirit, one that paved the way for women's increasing capacities and achievements, a soul who walked the same grounds as I wandered so many years after her leadership, where I became inspired to tell stories about women like her, the reason why I chose a focus study in the Victorian era.

At that time in my life, Helen's controlling energy felt welcome when I was feeling out of control myself. A stalwart comfort, I felt like I could ask for her protection. Staring at her picture, I felt encouraged by her confident expression; as if through her, I could work my way through her rules and make something of myself after all. If her confidence never wavered, why should mine?

Long live the formidable President still watching over her charges, a trope eternal, alive to this day through the tales told of her, still hoping young women will receive what they need from all that she tried to give. And scaring anyone who dares to be "troublesome" in the process.

Alma mater, Latin for "nourishing mother," could not be more apt in this context . . . provided you respect her authority.

The Heroine Hero:
Charlotte Cushman

Leanna

A ghost light stands on a darkened stage. This long-held theater tradition, beyond its spectral name, is a practicality. An untrimmed, unshaded bulb sits center stage, lit when the theater is closed and all other lights are dark. Without the ghost light, if anyone crossed downstage, a fall into a lowered orchestra pit could prove fatal. But a ghost light does create its own legends; lighting the ghosts who wish to perform during their witching hours. After the doors close, it is *their* stage to command as they please.

I want to be a ghost light for Charlotte Cushman. Actress. Superstar. An icon of icons. Titan of Shakespearean performance. Transgressor of gender roles. Adored by politicians, artists, actors, poets, authors, and luminaries we consider historically famous in their own right. The level of her mid-nineteenth-century celebrity strains credulity, hence her inclusion in a book with the subtitle *stranger than fiction*. She was *mobbed* in her day. No other American stage actor compares to the absolute *fervor* she garnered.

I've come to resurrect this forgotten hero, a woman that once caused riots in the streets any time she left a theater for her next engagement. It's hard to imagine that level of hysteria for stagecraft in our modern world; thronged, paparazzi treatment seems solely reserved for Hollywood superstars. But Charlotte Cushman was, according to biographer Tana Wojczuk, America's first celebrity. Charlotte also happened to love women. Over the course of her life, in addition to the women she called her wives, Charlotte helped support, assist, and network an entire crowd of sapphic, lesbian, and queer identities. Yet she's largely forgotten today.

A theatrical foremother of sorts, Charlotte is fascinating to me. I debuted professionally with the Cincinnati Shakespeare Festival after receiving a degree in theater performance with a focus study in the Victorian era exploring women's gender roles and restrictions.

The first words of this chapter were drafted the week I moved to Charlotte's hometown of Boston for a month to rehearse and perform in the world premiere of a brand-new play, *Let's Misbehave* by Lawrence Gullo, a Jazz Age romp of a show about finding—and protecting—queer community in 1930s London. Debuting the role of "The Countess," an eccentric woman who protects marginalized youth, I can't help but think Charlotte would have loved the character I played in her old stomping grounds.

Tracing Charlotte's footsteps, I began at the end. I first visited her grave before I followed to places where she'd lived and passed away.

Charlotte Cushman's funereal monument is an enormous, towering obelisk, dominating her little plateau of eternity in the lush, atmospheric, expansive and immersive Mount Auburn cemetery, filled with Gothic architecture. An ironically phallic needle that rivals any of the wealthy family plots around her, a giant middle finger to those who would have resented that her impoverished roots, through her diligence, dogged determination, and unmatched skill, gave way to international fame.

Herself a whirlwind of Gothic tropes in a unique, inimitable manner, Charlotte was heroine and hero, matron and rake. To some, she could have been considered an antagonist, to others perhaps a heartbreaking villain, to many more, a patron saint of art and possibility. One of the most driven women of her age, she realized very early on in her life that she was the only person upon whom she could rely. The young America she was born into had only known peace (from the end of its second war with England) for six months.

The eldest child, born July 23, 1816, Charlotte defied convention from the first, an adventurous girl who liked to climb trees and cut dolls' heads open "to see what they were thinking." Her inexhaustible creative energy was encouraged in particular by her uncle Augustus. She took charge of amateur theatricals among siblings and friends, casting herself forever as the hero. A born performer, not only was she uncannily adept at recalling a play she only read once, her sense of character was in-depth and sophisticated from the start.

Elkanah Cushman, Charlotte's father, worked long hours as a seemingly prosperous merchant along Boston's Long Wharf. One night, in a game of jumping between ship decks with her brother Charles, en route to visit her father, Charlotte fell into the filthy water of Boston Harbor and almost died. Soon after, in an act that would never receive an explanation, Elkanah disappeared, leaving Charlotte's mother, Mary Eliza, with nothing but his accumulated debts. Mary Eliza tried to evade collectors but soon, all the family belongings were gone, every heirloom taken. Still, she refused to break up her family or send her children to relatives in New York. Instead, she scraped funds together to open a boarding house. Charlotte left school, where she'd been an accomplished student, to work full-time for her mother at age thirteen.

As 41 Brattle Street was near the Boston Common and the Tremont Theatre, actors became some of the Cushmans' best clients. Determined to lift her family out of the sudden poverty they'd been cast into, Charlotte listened intently to the performers and asked Uncle Augustus to take her to the theater the next time his ship returned to port. Charlotte's world was changed when she saw the famed William Charles Macready, acclaimed British actor, star in Shakespeare's *Coriolanus* at the Tremont Theatre.

For my part, it was a thrill to be rehearsing on Tremont Street around the same historic district, over a century later, realizing just how much I owe a woman like Charlotte, who lifted every actress up by her own success and dedication to her craft. I wandered the blocks around the Boston Center for the Arts, wishing the theaters Charlotte performed in still stood to carry her echoes.

During Charlotte's early career, in the mid-1800s, unless one could rise to particular artistic notice, actresses were considered one step above sex workers. The idea of the theater as an art form was its own controversy. English Puritans tore down Shakespeare's Globe and the same Puritans had come to America to hold witch trials that Charles W. Upham, future mayor of Salem, Massachusetts, noted were of such a wildly overwrought nature that the trials "have never been surpassed on the boards of any theatre."[1]

Drawn to heroic roles in classical pieces, Charlotte was well aware how few of them were women and that any stage actress was expected to be traditionally beautiful. Tall and strong, wide-shouldered and square-jawed, with a voice that spanned two registers, she knew her looks and talents might be better appreciated in opera, and into that field she threw herself fully. She'd already begun singing in the choir of a Unitarian church whose pastor was a gifted young prodigy named Ralph Waldo Emerson.

Emerson had been preaching a radical theology of individualism that he felt rose above the hierarchy of the church;

the core tenets of his Transcendentalism showing its roots. When Emerson left the church after the death of his young wife revealed faith offered no comfort, he turned to poetry and the elevation of the natural world. It isn't known whether his individualism directly influenced Charlotte, but her determination to carve her own path for herself was cast from a similar mold.

When Mary Ann Wood, famed opera singer of the day, came to Boston to perform in Mozart's *Marriage of Figaro*, she and her husband, also a singer, cast roles from local talent and Charlotte managed a big break. Well-reviewed by the papers, her tireless work ethic earning her the respect of her employers and peers, Charlotte was on her way. While working onstage in New Orleans, the sudden death of a leading actress in another company provided Charlotte's next fateful role, and into that void she stepped confidently, taking on the mother of all dramatic roles: Lady Macbeth. She *commanded* the stage; took it by the throat. Critics agreed that she was fierce, vivid, and meant for great things.

A life on the stage is unstable and that hasn't changed since the nineteenth century. A wildly unpredictable business, Charlotte's first years onstage were marked by chaos. Her run in New York City began with Thomas Hamblin at the "people's theatre" the Bowery, nicknamed "the Slaughterhouse" for its penchant for nativist-leaning, bloody melodrama. Hungry for American talent, Hamblin found it in Charlotte, who became his star. When the Bowery Theatre burned to the ground after one of Hamblin's pyrotechnic effects blazed out of control, Charlotte started over at the Pearl Street Theatre in New York's capital city, Albany, where her performances, so the joke went, gathered more politicians under one roof than the capitol building itself.

In October 1836, Charlotte was asked to perform Lady Macbeth to legendary actor Junius Brutus Booth's Macbeth.

Charlotte would later recall that while she was deeply fond of Booth's talented son Edwin, she couldn't say the same for Edwin's brother, John Wilkes. Rubbing her wrong from the very first, Charlotte had nothing but disdain for John Wilkes, calling him a drunken, reckless daredevil.

The following year, Charlotte stepped into the leading role of Meg Merrilies in a theatrical adaptation of Sir Walter Scott's *Guy Mannering* for the National Theatre in New York. Her interpretation of Meg as a fierce, harrowing, otherworldly but ultimately sacrificial old woman was wholly her invention, a personal challenge to craft a mind-blowing transformation for the audience. Just before curtain call, she wiped off the heavy lines of makeup that made her appear a weathered crone onstage, returning her physicality to neutral and stepping back onstage as the fresh, twenty-year-old actress she was. Her portrayal garnered the awe of critics such as a young Walt Whitman, who praised her in the *Brooklyn Eagle* and who would remain a devoted fan. Catapulted toward celebrity status, Meg's lines toward the beginning of the show prophesy Charlotte's future as a notable haunt: "If the dead come back among the living, I'll be seen in the glen many a-night after these crazed bones are whitened in the mouldering grave."

The responsibility of being the sole breadwinner for her entire family in the fickle profession of the theater meant stress was a constant battle. Charlotte's younger sister Susan had been abandoned by a conman of a husband while pregnant at fifteen, so a nephew was added to the family plate. But Charlotte rose above, managing to leverage the supporting role of Nancy in Charles Dickens's *Oliver Twist*, the final serialization of which had only just come out in America, into another starring centerpiece. Walt Whitman, who couldn't help but "marvel at the towering grandeur of her genius," editorialized in his column for the *Brooklyn Eagle* that Charlotte's theatrical prowess was proof America was ready to be a cultural competitor on the world stage.

When she asked for a raise from her managers, she was refused. Furious, she quit, accepting a yearlong contract as theatrical manager of the Walnut Theatre in Philadelphia. Then William Macready came calling; the actor she'd seen on her first foray into a theater. He invited her to act with him during his own theatrical run in New York. But as she could not relinquish her contract in Philadelphia, she took on both; commuting weekly by train, shifting from manager to costar. Exhausted but doggedly committed, she and Macready became friends. When she confided in him that she wanted, like him, to be able to set her own schedule, choose her own plays and costars, and demand a cut of ticket sales, he said she had to conquer England to be taken seriously back home.

The trouble with leaving for London was that by 1843, she'd fallen in love. Rosalie Sully was the daughter of popular portrait artist Thomas Sully and was an artist herself. Charlotte spent any time away from the stage she could with her secret sweetheart in her art studio or enjoying Rosalie's close-knit family. In turn, the Sullys enjoyed Charlotte's company, deeming her an eccentric but entertaining new friend.

During this first flush of love, Charlotte dared to take on the role of Hamlet, making a clear distinction that she would *not* take on a "breeches role" for titillation, camp, or comedic effect, as had been the standard approach by other women playing breeches roles prior. She would play a man's role as she did any part: with truth, depth, and voracious commitment. "Some critics who came to see her Hamlet said she was more convincing playing a man onstage than playing a woman in life."[2]

Her critical success in *Hamlet* made London the inevitable next step and in this, Rosalie was supportive. The couple committed to one another in what ways they could. Charlotte bought Rose a ring, they had a private ceremony and were intimate, as Charlotte happily recorded in her diary, with the addendum *Married*. By the end of the month, the actress was on a boat to England.

Upon arrival in London, Charlotte had to overcome British hesitancy to accept American talent. But she convinced John Medex Maddox, manager of the Princess's Theatre, that she could be his Lady Macbeth to American costar Edwin Forrest (five years before the Astor Place riots would erupt in Manhattan in his honor, an escalatory conflagration that would pit working-class Americans against upper-class Anglophiles and leave between 20 to 30 dead and 120 injured). Forrest's Macbeth was considered milquetoast while Charlotte's Lady Macbeth was electric, and audiences loved her. Walt Whitman was frustrated that American audiences had been slower to realize her greatness, again writing in his column for the *Brooklyn Eagle* that Cushman was "ahead of any player that ever yet trod the stage," going so far as to list famous actors of the century before he crowns her: "Miss Cushman assuredly bears away the palm from them all, men and women."

The success of her Lady Macbeth set the stage for her next move: playing Romeo in *Romeo and Juliet*.

Much like the ill-fated hero she was preparing to play, Charlotte's first marriage did not last long. Gossip about the romantic truth of Charlotte and Rose's relationship had gotten to Thomas Sully. The *particulars* of their passionate bond would have only been revealed in letters that Charlotte insisted Rosalie burn as she went about burning hers, but the truth of their marriage was found out regardless.

Sully forbade his daughter from having anything to do with the actress ever again, and Rose did not argue. Heartbroken and receiving nothing but ungrateful admonishment from her own mother, Charlotte did what she did best: threw herself into her craft.

Writing to her sister Susan, Charlotte demanded that her pretty sibling join her in London to play Juliet opposite her Romeo. This was a brilliant move, as it allowed for understandable fondness onstage between costars without the salacious gossip Charlotte was trying to avoid in her personal life.

Utterly transcendent, Cushman's Romeo was received effusively by audiences and critics alike. Men wanted to be her, women wanted to be wooed by her, and all of them brought flowers to her stage door. Her portrayal was heartfelt, reminding men that they too could feel emotion deeply, and her confidence, swagger, and magnetism were a revelation. What more could be possible if women were allowed such agency? Cushman's unerring devotion to and mastery of Shakespeare's text was deeply appreciated by English audiences, and she was soon touring the country with her sister, making very good money while doing so. Licensing her image for further profit, porcelain figures of sturdy Charlotte as Romeo with a dainty Susan as Juliet decorated mantels across England. Her role continued offstage as Charlotte assuaged her own personal heartbreak by wooing other women.

By the time Charlotte met Matilda Hays, who went by "Max," the accomplished English translator for famed French novelist George Sand, Charlotte was well-and-truly famous and had begun planning a triumphant return to America. The two went everywhere together and functioned as a married couple, referring to one another as wives, though they had to be careful about how passionate their connection appeared publicly. Friendly, close, and cohabitating relationships between two women weren't uncommon, but the idea of them being sexual or romantic remained unwelcome in broad society. Max put her acclaimed translation career on hold to accompany Charlotte back home, a tension set to boil over.

Charlotte toured the States in an arduous victory lap. Her return to her native Boston was particularly triumphant; she was celebrated as a decorated hero. Privately, however, her relations were tumultuous as she struggled to maintain peace between her and Max, whose writing needed more stationary stability.

Fame drained Charlotte even as she sought it, so when her time in Boston brought her into the circle of like-minded women like writer Grace Greenwood (nom de plume of Sarah Jane Clarke, the first female reporter for the *New York Times*) and gifted sculptor Harriet Hosmer, the four "Jolly Bachelors" decided to move to Italy to live out a dream of personal and artistic freedom in Rome. Max, as a translator, needed peace, quiet, and rest for her work, a life that was antithetical while on the road with Charlotte, and so Charlotte "retiring" to Rome, for Max, had been the hopeful ideal.

Charlotte's wealth and fame provided for her little Italian enclave, and while she may have initially found the idea of rest appealing, Charlotte's retirement from the stage was short-lived. She truly couldn't stay away, and it would seem her first and foremost spouse was the stage. Max left Charlotte acrimoniously, sending the actress a bill for wages and opportunity lost. There was no legal recourse for Max, as there had been no legal marriage, but Charlotte quietly paid in full.

A slight tempering effect happened when Charlotte met sculptor Emma Stebbins. Stebbins had come to Rome to study the great masters. Cushman's community had garnered quite the reputation for hosting charming dinners, encouraging intellectual rigor and, of course, championing women's freedoms. Emma Stebbins fit right in. The daughter of a prosperous Boston family, Charlotte found Emma to be noble, generous, talented, and self-possessed. She and Charlotte were the same age, forty-one, and friends remarked that Emma had a calming, more "ladylike" effect on Charlotte. The two were peacefully happy together through much of 1857.

This same year marked another of Charlotte's returns to the American stage, and like her others, this proved a raging success. But now, her tour was buoyed by the increasing discussion of women's rights. Women were looking up to Charlotte as an idol, a symbol of strength and liberation. Papers were ablaze with her triumphant performances as more women writers and journalists penned pieces on her. In Boston, young Louisa May Alcott wrote in her diary: "Saw Charlotte Cushman and had a stage-struck fit."

During this tour, Emma Stebbins stayed behind on the East Coast while Cushman went West. In Missouri, Charlotte met nineteen-year-old Emma Crow, daughter of her financial manager, Wayland Crow. The two became besotted. Much of what we know of this period in Charlotte's life is because Emma Crow refused to burn Charlotte's love letters. This is where Charlotte truly lives into her status as a nineteenth-century rake, a Byronesque, Gothic antihero, letting her charm, presence, artistic prowess, and fame do what it would; capture some young women in starry-eyed thrall. This was common for famous men of the time—attracting the attentions of adoring younger women, that was expected. Charlotte simply flipped the script. And while the relationship between Crow and Charlotte was entirely consensual, the power dynamics remained in Charlotte's court. She, in all aspects of her personal sphere, called the shots; the dominant force.

Charlotte later encouraged Emma Crow to marry her nephew Ned, who Charlotte had legally adopted years prior, giving him the name Cushman. Emma Crow Cushman became part of the family in hopes of remaining close to Charlotte. Initially, she and Charlotte quietly spoke of the first child she had with Ned as her and *Charlotte's* child. This, of course, drove an irreversible wedge between Emma Stebbins and Charlotte. But Emma Stebbins remained committed to Charlotte as a companion, and Charlotte's fame, connections, and impressive sphere of influence aided Emma in garnering her most famous commission: a statue for the great Bethesda Terrace in New York's Central Park. *Angel of the Waters* would celebrate the anniversary of the Croton Aqueduct bringing fresh water into the city. The bold, sturdy, broad-shouldered, and steadfast angel was modeled in part on Charlotte.

After briefly returning to Rome with Stebbins, Charlotte went back to America again in July 1861 and stayed with William Seward in Washington, who took her to meet the freshly elected President Lincoln. The two spoke passionately about Shakespeare. Lincoln made Charlotte promise not to retire until he'd seen her in his favorite play, *Macbeth*.

By 1863, war was underway. Charlotte returned to America to raise money for the Union cause, specifically for the Union Army's new Sanitary Commission, led by Frederick Law Olmsted, co-designer of Central Park. Committed to her promise to Lincoln, Charlotte wrote to her old friend and former costar Edwin Booth to request he play Macbeth opposite her Lady Macbeth. Lincoln came to dine with Charlotte and the Sewards nearly every night, eager to see her performance on October 17.

In an ominous bit of foreshadowing even Shakespeare couldn't have wrought, Charlotte toured the brand-new Ford's Theatre ahead of her and Edwin Booth's performance at the nearby Grover's Theatre. Lincoln was mesmerized by Charlotte's performance, as Shakespeare remained one of his tonics and guides in turbulent times. Charlotte noted in her own letters how drawn and haunted the president was after having been so full of good humor on her first visit.

When Edwin Booth's brother John Wilkes assassinated Lincoln at Ford's Theatre on April 14, 1865, he jumped onto the stage, shouting "sic semper tyrannis," *thus always to tyrants*, the motto thought to be Brutus's words after killing Julius Caesar. John Wilkes himself had acted in Shakespeare's *Julius Caesar* with his brothers not long before the assassination, in a fund-raising event for a statue of Shakespeare in Central Park. In Rome at the time, Charlotte heard the news of Lincoln's death a week later. Distraught, she grieved for the man she admired deeply, all while worried for her friend Edwin, who feared his entire family would be hunted down, damned by his brother's actions. Rallying from deep depression, Edwin Booth published a letter on behalf of the remaining Booth family emphatically supporting the Union and mourning Lincoln's death.

All this heartache made Charlotte homesick. With a diagnosis of breast cancer in 1869, she returned to America for good, moving her, Emma Stebbins, Ned and Emma Crow Cushman and their children, along with a revolving door of friends, into "Villa Cushman" in Newport.

Health failing, Charlotte couldn't help herself—she still wanted to work. Too weak for full performances, she managed excellent staged readings. Novelist Henry James recalled seeing Cushman channel Queen Katherine in *Henry VIII* from a lone chair on an empty stage. The way she brought Shakespeare to life entirely transformed his understanding of the text he had thought he knew well; he was transported. The term "Boston marriage" is one attributed to James, from his 1886 novel *The Bostonians*, denoting female life-partnerships, romantic or not. The term could be retroactively applied to women like Charlotte and her wives, but wouldn't have been a turn of phrase they'd have used.

In the end, Charlotte spent her final days in Boston, at the grand Parker House hotel, tended to by Emma Stebbins and, in the final hours, by everyone she held close.

After Charlotte's death on February 18, 1876, the nation went into intense mourning. In Boston, her viewing service overflowed beyond capacity, thousands poured into the streets, reporters from around the world attended the funeral. Thousands more came into Boston, waiting for hours just to glimpse her coffin. In New York, some ten thousand people gathered for a candlelight vigil in the streets. Every newspaper carried her obituary. She was compared to Beethoven, Napoleon, the best male actors ever to trod the stage, and every kind of genius or leader.

Emma Stebbins compiled letters and memories and published Charlotte's first biography, titled *Charlotte Cushman: Her Letters and Memories of Her Life*. The authorial attribution adds "Edited by Her Friend, Emma Stebbins." Stebbins's dedication page states: "To the dramatic profession, which Miss Cushman loved and honored, to which she gave the study of her life and the loyal devotion of her great powers, to which she has left in her example a noble and imperishable remembrance, this volume is respectfully dedicated."[3]

At the point of Charlotte's death, she and Emma Stebbins were no longer the wives they very much had been to one another at an earlier point, and so Emma's use of "friend" in the subtitle isn't misplaced, nor is it entirely closeted. The Close Friends Collective tour group in New York City, a group founded to tell queer history, draws its name from the fact that a lot of historic couples, however they may have identified privately in their own historic terms, were referred to publicly as "close friends" in life and in death, even if they were or had been much more.

While it's important to not erase queer history, it's equally important to avoid putting modern words or presumptions into historic mouths. As Daniel Walber, a Close Friends Collective cofounder and guide, said in our conversation about Stebbins and Cushman: a couple like them would not have used the term "lesbian"; the "language of being 'out' and 'not out' is less relevant historically." Couples would have had to consider if there was "a usefulness in announcing themselves." He stressed that remaining in community was often more important than a label, finding it more important that queer history not be erased than to get hung up on precise language. The question of "were they or weren't they together" can distract from the fullness of queer community that Charlotte was a part of.

Walber noted that Charlotte Cushman's uncommon celebrity was extremely useful, affording a way out of societal expectations. She could extend protection and freedom to her circle as they navigated their own "queer possibilities" (to quote the title of a Margaret Middleton article on historic queer representation).

The Close Friends Collective created a tour called *Gay Gothic: Love, Loss, and the Hereafter* through Brooklyn's massive (and heavily Gothic) Green-Wood Cemetery, where Emma Stebbins is buried. The tour notes queer people buried in Green-Wood and how their deaths, memorialization, and discussions of relationships have been navigated historically and presently. History changes, as does our perception of it, as do the narratives around those loved and those lost. The Close Friends Collective is interested in lifting up what was once buried or thought monstrous, inviting the queer dead to haunt their present celebrations.

As with Charlotte, I also paid my respects at Emma Stebbins's small, worn grave in a nondescript part of Green-Wood's vast premises, her resting place such a startling contrast from Charlotte's imposing obelisk. Still, Emma's faded sandstone marker was draped carefully, lovingly, with a few small pride flags laid there by modern visitors.

Marginalized identities of all kinds have always had a home in Gothic narratives, as have the questions of gender roles and restrictions. Sheridan Le Fanu's Gothic novella *Carmilla*, published in 1872, presents a fascinating, enigmatic, explicitly sapphic vampire in the titular character. Mina in *Dracula* chafes against the idea of the "New Woman" even as she embodies the concept of emancipation. She is more capable of defeating the vampire than any of the men trying to help her. Jonathan Harker is the ailing sweetheart while his new wife confronts the villain and survives. In a chapter celebrating a titan of the stage, I'd be remiss not to mention that Bram Stoker's writing career was simultaneous with his management of the Lyceum Theatre in London, where his actors were *well* aware of Charlotte Cushman and her otherworldly talents.

But what of Charlotte's *haunted* history?

Once we closed our *Let's Misbehave* run, I wandered the Omni Parker as directed, seeking Charlotte and her energy. I knew, thanks to Boston tour guide friends of mine, to go up the stairs to the second and the third floor, and to be mindful of the elevator and an incredible mirror along the way. As a professional actress trained in Shakespearean theater, I felt such a kinship with this ghostly subject. Researching Charlotte, her performance style and her roles hit hard. I played as many men as women during my contracts with the Cincinnati Shakespeare Festival and beyond. But New York City casting directors didn't know what to make of me. One director explained the disconnect after I auditioned, at age twenty-four, with a monologue from *Macbeth*. "Listen, you look like a young ingenue, but when you perform, some ancient force comes out. I don't have any paranormal creatures in my season. Come back to me when you're forty and I'll give you Lady Capulet." I was an enigma; a young woman who read as something *else*, energetically. Something otherworldly.

People didn't know what to make of Charlotte Cushman either, even while in awe of her. Critics and audiences often referred to her not as a person but as a *weather event*. A force of nature. Unable to carve out a niche like Charlotte did, I walked away from the stage and focused on my books. But at age forty-five, I'm returning to the stage again to play intense, energetically powerful characters. When I do get around to Lady Capulet, I'm going approach it like Charlotte would; with earnest, raw intensity. I'm presently writing a one-woman show about Victorian Spiritualism where I'll "channel" a few different women of history to tell their stories. Surely, I'll summon Charlotte.

In seeking this foremother's guidance, what was admittedly hard for me to stomach is that Charlotte has become virtually forgotten in the building where she died, barely a sidenote at the Omni Parker. There is only one mention of her name in the entire building, relegated to a lower-level historic area, on a plaque beside the door to the room where she died. The door, removed from its hinges and placed below as a historic relic, happens to have been the same one Charles Dickens would have used during his stay in 1867. Dickens gets the most credit as a historic resident of room 138-39. Cushman is noted as an afterthought, even though her fame actually outpaced his in America during her lifetime. The theaters where Charlotte performed no longer exist. She is a ghost light without a stage.

So, as was our aim with *A Haunted History of Invisible Women*, here I am telling a story of a woman who is underappreciated and nearly forgotten in our modern world. Here I am willing her heroine/hero ghost back to life. I hope Charlotte's spirit knew how much she was mourned after her passing. Perhaps the magnitude of her loss can be felt again in a spectral echo.

I was immediately offered an "Omni Parker House Ghost Encounters!" handout by hotel staff when I, dressed in my usual goth regalia, asked about the hotel's history. Of the several stories the hotel is happy to share, the most evocative is the enormous, arched mirror on the second floor and its mysterious history of spectral vapor. A bronze placard beside it notes that the towering, imposing mirror is the same one Charles Dickens faced when rehearsing his orations and lectures during his time in Boston. The hotel handout declares elevators are called to the third floor and mentions Dickens as having lived on that floor, but no mention of Charlotte, even though she took the same room. She may have spoken to that same mirror.

My friend Sam Baltrusis, author, Boston tour guide and frequent speaker on television shows about the paranormal, has had many experiences in the Omni Parker. From his book *Ghost Writers*:

"The elevator heading to the third floor and next to the Charles Dickens mirror had a mind of its own. It would open mysteriously while I was giving my tours, especially if I mentioned Charlotte Cushman. Out of respect for her spirit, I would always mention her by the elevator and I would always hear a *ding*."

Sam notes in *Ghost Writers* that when he brought guests to the mirror, odd occurrences generally happened. Once, when he stood in front of the mirror talking to a tour audience, a "photographer noticed as if there was inhaling and exhaling behind me . . . as if a spirit was actually breathing on the mirror."

Sam went on to tell me, when I asked him specifically about Charlotte, that as a tour guide, "I tried to talk about Charlotte as much as I could, because I seemed to get more response from the elevators when I told her story. It was as if Charlotte Cushman showed appreciation from beyond the veil."

The third floor doesn't have any special historical markers or notable architecture. It is simply lined with guest rooms, all of which were renovated after Charlotte's time there. But I went to sit on the floor nonetheless. I had gone to pray at her grave and to ask for her guidance, and I did the same on the floor where her spirit left her body. As I sat in a chair by the third-floor elevators, meditating on Charlotte and how frustrated I was that she was not more featured or mentioned in the hotel ephemera, an elevator opened onto the third floor without anyone in it, and closed again.

The *ding* of the elevator immediately brought to mind the chimes and bells utilized in every theater. A theater-wide buzzer or small bells or handheld xylophones are rung or struck by ushers to signal that the show is about to begin.

Perhaps the *ding* of an elevator bell opening onto her floor when no one is visibly there is Charlotte's ongoing way of reminding us that her curtain never fell. That the show never really closed. And that we should demand an encore from the greatest actress of the nineteenth century, so that she might tell us where we are, or remind us where we've been, asking the greatest question of all, as she once did to such thunderous applause:

To be, or not to be?

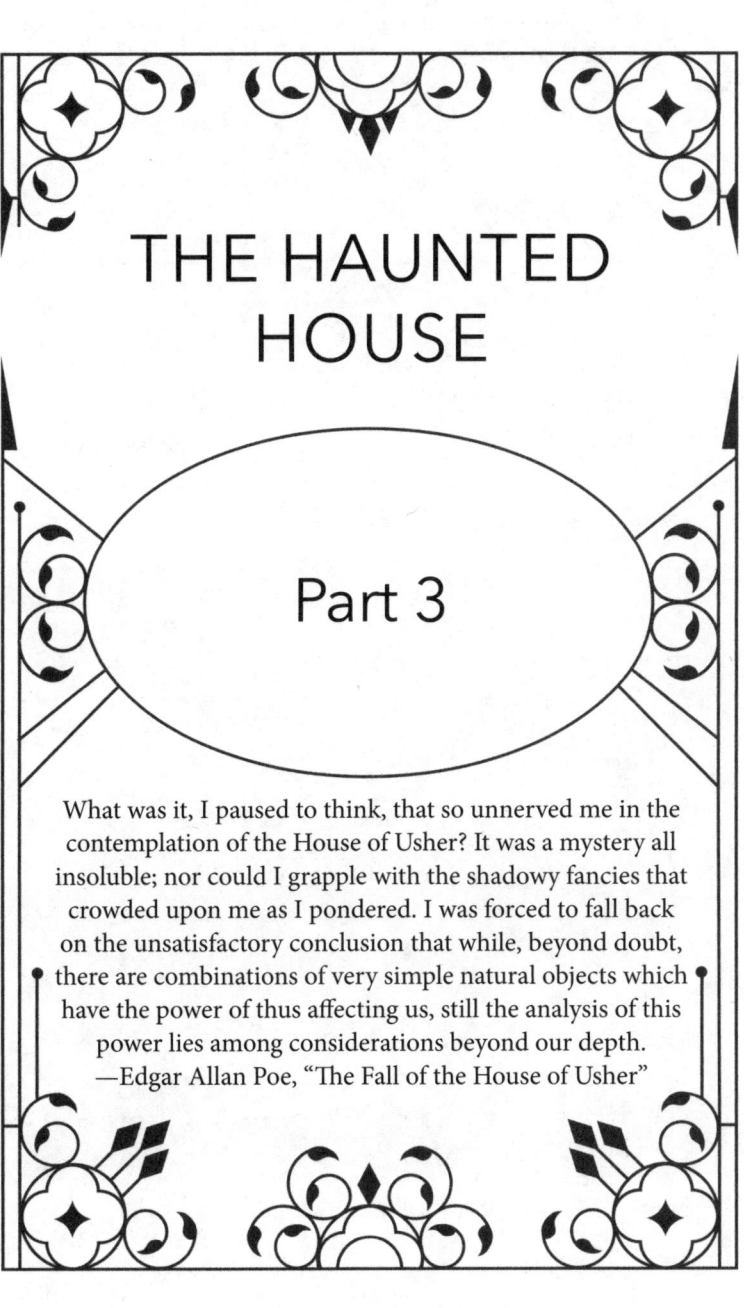

THE HAUNTED HOUSE

Part 3

What was it, I paused to think, that so unnerved me in the contemplation of the House of Usher? It was a mystery all insoluble; nor could I grapple with the shadowy fancies that crowded upon me as I pondered. I was forced to fall back on the unsatisfactory conclusion that while, beyond doubt, there are combinations of very simple natural objects which have the power of thus affecting us, still the analysis of this power lies among considerations beyond our depth.
—Edgar Allan Poe, "The Fall of the House of Usher"

The Octagon:
Washington, DC

Leanna

The Octagon is a perfect example of the complicated narrative of the Gothic house as character and setting, refuge and prison. It is both a structure of trauma and a vitally important building in US history. A place of entrapment at the same time it was trying to preserve certain freedoms. It is—like the Gothic itself—fraught with contradictions; "considerations beyond our depth" and remains home to ghosts.

Walking along a spate of modern office buildings in Washington, DC, past agencies and federal buildings that begin to showcase an array of architectural styles tracing the changes of the capital through time, within a block of the current White House and the President's Park, you come to the intersection of Eighteenth Street and the angle of New York Avenue. The building that sits along that sharp corner, angled and prominent, a curious building in a curiouser shape, demands you pause and take it in. Nothing else around it looks like it does, nothing else bears its particular weight of history. An inimitable building that *is* haunted. But sifting for the truth of that comes up against as many weird angles as the house itself.

This infamous edifice, a home that became the makeshift White House when the British burned the presidential mansion during the War of 1812, has collected wild myths that stubbornly persist.

Particular, distinct quirks of unusual architecture attract haunted accounts like moths to flame. Whether in the case of something like the Dakota apartments in Manhattan, where *Rosemary's Baby* cemented it as *the* look of a diabolical setting, or the Winchester Mystery House's endless, teeming eccentricities in San Jose lock in its haunted reputation as one of "madness" despite the fact Sarah Winchester was entirely sane, perhaps in the case of The Octagon, its tenacity and perseverance is what holds sway. It stands stoic: an old and oddly shaped building surrounded by twentieth-century office buildings. The Octagon faces off against modernism with strange angles and a looming appearance. It sits confidently in strangeness and its own discomfort. It challenges the viewer and the visitor, inviting and off-putting in equal measure.

The Octagon was built in 1799 for the wealthy Tayloe family. The architect of the building, William Thornton, was not formally trained. He was a fascinating jack-of-all-trades who possessed a remarkable intuition. He had "to plan a house for an eccentric site" and he created something wholly imaginative and original.[1]

When Washington was divided up and plotted as the new capital of the country by Pierre L'Enfant, with the hope of solidifying the capital city by 1800, it was laid in grid and diagonal street patterns that created oddly shaped land plots from pentagons to trapezoids, to wedges, meanders, triangles, and the occasional square. Thornton crafted the off-axis placement of the house with exacting intention, creating "a graceful effect of having avoided being plugged into this acute angle and impaled on its own geometry."

On some sort of subconscious level, for our modern era, an octagonal structure has the ability to process in our minds as a sign we see regularly, a reminder for caution. STOP. The Octagon is in red brick, even, playing into this moment of pause. Well, it would fully register if it were actually octagonal. Even its name is already a lie.

Standing before it, I had to trace the building's outline, wandering around the corners and angles, counting its sides, to note that it is, in fact, *six*-sided, not eight. It *should* be called the Hexagon. Perhaps not wanting to associate a hex with the government, and as "evidently the front pavilion got confused long ago with two more sides, and as far as the Tayloes were concerned the house was The Octagon; so it remains."[2]

The curiosities of this structure are myriad. So much of it at curves and angles, with thirteen paneled doors that slide and swell to fit curved walls, it has an unusual, unexpected feeling. The human mind seeks patterns it knows, and there isn't a homey familiarity in this space, which reads like a modern art project well over a hundred years before its time. Thornton's bold choices as an intuitive architect remain a clear reason this house is a particular treasure of the historic register. And its unique features factor into its ghostlore.

Considering The Octagon's vast collection of ghosts through the years, none of it appears to have been much questioned, which, in and of itself, begs the question: How did the myths run so wildly rampant? In part, because the tales conjure up a lot of dead women, and that has often simply gone without saying in many historic accounts. As if it's simply expected. But if there's one thing we hope to do in our work, it's to question *why* so many dead women?

The Tayloe family began living in The Octagon by 1801. Colonel John Tayloe III, famous for his racehorses and a close personal friend of George Washington, also owned a Virginia plantation and held enslaved people on all his properties, The Octagon included.

Important buildings in the nation's capital were erected with, and alongside, blood and trauma. There are so many uncomfortable truths we cannot look away from when examining these spaces. That discomfort in and of itself is what the Gothic asks of us; to understand the sins of predecessors as we seek to escape the wrongs clawing at us, looking for ways to escape toward a brighter, freer future. This house had people imprisoned in it, on every floor, through its early tenure. That leaves psychic residue that cannot be removed, a "damned spot" that Lady Macbeth would demand to blot out but could not. The still-extant brick walls around the outside were erected not to keep outsiders from climbing in, but to keep people who were enslaved from breaking out. The Gothic haunted house might be a shelter to some, a prison to others, entirely depending on one's lot in life, and Gothic literature takes note of these power dynamics and bids us take them to task.

While on The Octagon grounds, I noted the plaque outside naming Paul Jennings, a man enslaved from birth by James Madison when Jennings was born at Montpelier in 1799. Jennings lived at The Octagon with the Madisons during its time as the makeshift White House in 1815 and he went on to write what is considered to be the first White House memoir in 1865: *A Colored Man's Reminiscences of James Madison*. He remained enslaved by the Madisons until Massachusetts Senator Daniel Webster arranged for his freedom in 1846.

Amanda Ferrario, manager of The Octagon museum, with vibrant, amiable generosity, kindly took time with me to discuss the history of the building and to help sort fact from fiction in this complex place. Ghostlore about The Octagon began to run rampant as early as the 1870s with reports of bells that wouldn't stop ringing.

The very first spectral event noted by the Tayloe family itself remains one of the most credible. Not only does it carry the most direct tie to the original owners, but it has multiple different accounts and assertions, one by Virginia Tayloe Lewis, a granddaughter of Colonel Tayloe III, who recorded a family memorate noting that the servant bells of the house continuously rang after her grandfather's death and that everyone considered the house to be haunted, as the wires were cut and still the bells rang. Maria Monroe Gouverneur, daughter of President James Monroe, one of the original proponents of the legend, and her daughter-in-law Marian Gouverneur, both wrote about the bells in their diaries and memoirs.

By 1874 the bell legend had appeared in print: "It is an authenticated fact that every night at the same hour, all the bells would ring at once. One gentleman, dining with Col. Tayloe, when this mysterious ringing began, being an unbeliever in mysteries, and a very powerful man, jumped up and caught the bell wires in his hand, but only to be lifted bodily from the floor, while he was unsuccessful in stopping the ringing."[3] The bell legend appeared in print regularly nearly every year after that, with a few variations, going quiet around 1911 but then resurfacing again in 1952 when none other than Jacqueline Bouvier, before she was Jackie Kennedy, notes the mysteriously ringing bells in an unpublished manuscript titled "The Octagon House" that the museum holds in their archives.

The remaining, and in some cases the most famous ghost lore of The Octagon is much harder to trace. But the weight of history itself is indeed at work.

Visitors to the house, even those who know nothing of its history, do note an oppressive feeling in the basement in particular, the lower-level kitchens, where most labors were carried out. The cellars were a feature of the original construction and a half circle wine cellar beneath the vestibule, outfitted with vaulted brick cells, puts one in mind of crypts and catacombs, a structure that gives a full "Cask of Amontillado" feel. But really, if there's a weight here, the truth of it is because the work of those enslaved was corralled here. The bricks remember containment, imprisonment. The museum curators deliberately leave the basement bare and unadorned. They're not going to redress away the pain. In my discussion with Amanda, about her role in navigating hard truths, she said very plainly: "We don't need to re-create trauma, here."

We couldn't agree more, as Boroughs of the Dead, the ghost tour company Andrea founded, takes a similar approach with the ghost tours we lead in New York. The moral imperative remains for us not to sensationalize trauma, murder, dehumanization, or abuse. Tell the truth of it, yes; a great deal of history *is* traumatic without any embellishment. But not for show. Hard truths serve as cautionary tales; there to instruct and to guide. To scare us, like the spirits in *A Christmas Carol*, into doing better. Now, more than ever, the truth of difficult history, a subject that has been facing bans in many schools and institutions, must be grappled with and discussed, but without fetishizing pain.

An additional aspect of The Octagon that took on a sense of intrigue through the years is its tunnel; an underground chamber that is six feet wide, brick-vaulted and adjoining the basement kitchen, extending twenty-seven feet toward Eighteenth Street. The popular supposition had been Tayloe had a tunnel built all the way to the river for supplies, while other ideas about adjoining tunnels were posed in a more compassionate turn; that they were used for those escaping enslavement during the days of the Underground Railroad, as if turning the tables on what was once a prison. But when it comes to Washington's layout and architectural quirks, *especially* concerning tunnels, suppositions run wild as to border on conspiratorial lunacy. Tunnels always generate speculation and unease, going back to that primal human concern with subterranean spaces and ancient legends of underworlds. The reality is more mundane in that it likely served as a coal bin.

On August 24, 1814, when British forces marched into Washington, they promptly burned the White House, the Capitol building, and many other government buildings. President Madison was away, already with his militia, when his wife Dolley escaped just ahead of the invasion, gathering as much as she could carry into a carriage. She saved a few personal items, and with the help of Paul Jennings, a French cook, and another staff member, the frame of the famous portrait of George Washington, painted by Gilbert Stuart, was broken in order to rescue the canvas. It is the only surviving item from the former White House. Dolley, along with her pet parrot, were taken over to the residence of the French minister by her steward, also a Frenchman. This minister, Louis Serurier, was staying at The Octagon while the Tayloe family were not in residence.

The Octagon soon took up the mantle as the presidential residence of James and Dolley Madison (one of five mansions that served as presidential residences through the years). The Octagon is only one of three that remain standing. The Treaty of Ghent, ending the War of 1812, had been signed by the British in Belgium on December 24, 1814. James Madison signed it on February 14, 1815, at the distinct, circular mahogany table whose shape mirrors the circular walls of the second-floor study. That table still lives in The Octagon, in that study that was then renamed the Treaty of Ghent Room.

Dolley's ghost, in every account, from the nineteenth century on, becomes part of the house lore. But this *isn't* a place that she was fond of, as Amanda was quick to point out, finding it hard to believe she'd choose to haunt it. Not to mention *many* other DC buildings wish to claim Dolley as their own haunt. If she's really haunting all these places, she has quite the spectral dance card. It is true she did enjoy a good party.

Stories make her out to be a gracious, if not sometimes flirtatious hostess, forever holding court at the makeshift White House. Focusing on her reads like escapism, especially when there's no evidence she cared for the place enough to make it an eternal haunt; she was there out of necessity due to the war. For the period-drama fans, there's even a part of Dolley's ghostly legend that has her running to the back garden for a fond rendezvous with Aaron Burr. But Burr, who also features in the ghost stories of the Morris-Jumel Mansion (where he was ousted by the lady of the house, Eliza Jumel, once she realized he was only after her money), has just as many spectral engagements, his name and ghost relegated to eternal infamy after killing Alexander Hamilton in a duel.

Additional otherworldly accounts The Octagon has accrued include mysterious noises, sobbing, wailing, and thudding sounds, as if a body hit the floor. In 1888, twelve men were dubbed the "ghost watch" and their task was to either drive the ghosts out or prove the legends wrong.

"The hours wore quietly on. The party were dispersed from garret to cellar. At the hour of midnight, as I and two others were crossing the threshold of a room on the second floor, three feminine shrieks rose from the center of the room. Aghast we stood . . . After those screams our band was closely knit together . . . collectively we listened through the waning hours of night to the clanking of sabers and tramping of footfalls."[4]

The "feminine shrieks" bring us to the cluster of unnamed, dead women. A veritable staple of a haunted house.

Two Tayloe daughters are said to have fallen to their deaths on the dramatic, curved main stair. One was said to have taken her own life in distress, another fell after an argument with her father, both said to have arisen out of conflict involving suitors. Myriad stories describe these young women's bodies poetically falling onto the marble floor below, staining the stone with blood. The marble bit is repeated often in these retellings, as if the hardness of the stone leaves little room to doubt the immediate, crumpling deaths of young women foiled in love; there for dramatic effect. But, as Amanda noted, there *is* no marble there at the base of the stair, the only marble lies in the entryway. The *Evening Star* irreverently debunks the marble details in an October 18, 1956 article; "Octagon House; Mythical Place" as journalist Richard Rogers declares: "There was even a legend that her blood stained the floor's marble. Since the marble section was a good many feet distant from wherever she could have landed, this stain thing is not likely. Even in the early 1800s, girls didn't bounce that far."

Colonel John Tayloe III and his wife Ann had *fifteen* children, thirteen of which survived into adulthood, and none of their daughters died in The Octagon. They are all accounted for.

Jacqueline Bouvier got caught up in the legends too, repeating this same lovelorn suicide story in her unpublished "The Octagon House" in 1952. Bouvier's accounts are enclosed in *The Haunting of The Octagon*, a full, chronological collection of ghost stories compiled by Museum Studies student Alicia Clarke in 1982, a document I was given access to thanks to present-day museum manager Amanda Ferrario. Jacqueline Bouvier also mentioned the former first lady Dolley Madison and her ghost, associating Dolley with a clairolfactory haunting manifesting as an overpowering scent of lilacs. Completing the trifecta of the museum's most infamous legends, Jackie also notes the grisly tale of a murdered woman buried in the walls of the building itself. This gruesome finale marks the third of the "feminine shrieks."

Otherworldly sounds, particularly knocking, have been reported through the years. Several accounts point to the early days of twentieth-century renovations when the American Institute of Architects took over care of the building, legends claiming that crews discovered a skeleton of a young woman behind a wall whose finger bones were curled and raised against the wall. As if knocking to get out.

I admit, that one got a visceral reaction out of me when I first read it in *Ghosts!: Washington Revisited*, by John Alexander. But as I suspected, it has no basis in actual history. Amanda Ferrario confirmed no skeleton was ever found in the walls during any repairs or renovations. As author George McCue notes in his architectural treatise on The Octagon, the murderer would have had to have taken great pains to even *find* a hollow wall to put a body in the first place.

What's particularly upsetting is that this narrative posits the victim of this violence as either a mistress or an enslaved woman, a fabricated, exaggerated claim on top of the horrors of slavery as an institution. This is another case where a story is made up to offshore guilt from contemporary horrors. Much like how the stories of the sadistic tortures Madame Lalaurie enacted on enslaved people in her New Orleans home, her horrific extremes served to absolve white women of their own abuses, as if enabling the response of "Oh, we weren't *that* bad."

The legends pin this murder and cask-of-Amontillado-like fate onto a French diplomat or a British officer, depending on the version of the story. This further shifts the violence onto the other, to an outsider, a foreigner, a distraction, thus distancing from the horrors that were more mundane but no less dehumanizing and carried out daily before slavery was outlawed. The violence in this remains fetishized, but distanced to remain more palatable. And again, none of these women are named. None of them have actual identities or verifiable details. That's something storytellers should examine when driven to repeat these stories unquestioned. These fabricated women are reduced to props, sounds, and special effects, disembodied cries and crumpled forms hitting the floor or knocking to be set free.

A curious detail of the house caught my attention; the "Amity button," generally made of metal or ivory, inlaid at the center of the newel posts at the base of the staircase, indicates the house and its detailing was all made by experts and was fully paid for, a sort of seal of artisanal approval. It is an ironic addendum to a staircase that has such grim, violent ghostlore attached to it.

But that's not the only staircase in the building. There are the back stairs. The front stairs slope three floors of gentle curves. The back stairs ascend and descend at hard, dizzying triangles, hidden away from high society by clever tricks of doors shielding the Tayloe family so that those that were enslaved in their house would go unseen. Those stairs carry a different, and historically verified, weight.

Writer and artist Thom Truelove, as my partner, has seen me navigate historic spaces with care and intent for some while now. He and I both have certain energy sensitivities. Where I can feel, in an acutely tactile form, the weight of certain spaces, he can *see* it. He credits a lot of his connection to the "otherworld" as being a side effect of his epileptic condition and seizure disorder, generally triggered by visual stimulus and light sensitivity. He had his own experiences in The Octagon, particularly on the back staircase. Thom felt time widen across that entire set of stairs; a long, spectral form stretched out like a streak of light captured on film, but in a long, slow descent. The pressure of being stuck; endlessly. Not that there was one particular soul trapped in this gyre, but an oppression of time not being one's own; in being denied freedom, every step on that stair would be one not of their own choosing. The staircase bears that spectral residue in weightless, drawn-out steps.

Every year the museum hosts "Poltergeist and Pints," an annual debunking celebration where falsehoods are taken to task and course-corrected. But there's still *plenty* of spectral activity to focus on. And the foundation is very mindful that this was a place that people lived, were forced into, a place where people fled to during fire, and a place others chose to work, and that it remains an important building in our nation's history. They're very intentional in saying it is "home" to the Architecture Foundation; that's a vital framing.

Again, it *is* a haunted house. Startlingly, verifiably so. *Who* roams the second floor in the middle of the night can't be proven. But *something* sets off the motion-sensor alarm on the second floor so often that there's a protocol between the museum staff and the security company not to bother; that if the alarm went off on the second floor and that floor only, it had to be the ghost again.

In her role as manager, Amanda, like me, tries to be a levelheaded skeptic first, while still believing supernatural phenomena do occur. Her daily routine is to say good morning and good night to the house, and to any presences within. As a courtesy. Just to be on the safe side.

A temperature sensor on that same second floor has registered a moving change of temperature as if someone were walking by when no one is there. Seeing that palpable shift moving at the speed of a person but when no corporeal body was present, the change still captured by technology, remains startling. In concluding our discussion, Amanda said of that sensor that could track something unseen, but clearly moving: "It *follows* you . . . *that's* stranger than fiction."

Harbinger and Haven:
The Dakota

Leanna

Standing tall and ominously beautiful on the corner of Seventy-second and Central Park West, the Dakota reigns over its Manhattan surroundings as it has done since 1884. Its Gothic details, its brick and sandstone and wrought iron rails all combine to create an atmospheric picture; it is no wonder it was used as the exterior shots for *Rosemary's Baby*, a 1968 film where the heroine, played expertly by Mia Farrow, unwittingly gives birth to a child a cult has proclaimed as their Antichrist. The structure's beauty is bold and inimitable—no other building in the city looks quite like it. As a New York City tour guide, there are many beautiful nineteenth-century apartment buildings in the city to celebrate, but even if it wasn't so fitting for the theme of this book, the Dakota would remain my favorite; the one whose atmosphere and stories haunt me comprehensively.

So many Gothic tropes and ghost stories focus on the singular haunted house in an isolated setting. This, by its nature, elides urban environments. The Dakota is a *village* of haunted houses, joined in a common architecture, each with its own private, personal story. Many have filtered out to us through the years due to celebrity, or more morbidly, by way of sensational murder. Countless other eerie moments must assuredly float just behind the closed wooden shutters, shifting out of the corner of the eye like a bit of lace curtain in the breeze, mysteries lingering wistfully in the interior courtyard built for horse and carriage access that only residents can access. Secrets rumble in the shadows of the secondary service courtyard that lurks a story below the streets in an exact footprint of what's visible above. Or perhaps untold stories float out toward Seventy-third Street through the "undertaker's gate," a pass too narrow for any services but hearses.

Susan Blackhall's *Ghosts of New York* notes that the Dakota became "almost a self-contained world."[1] Dakota founder Edward Cabot Clark needed to offer incentives to wealthy Gilded Age New Yorkers to entertain the then uncommon idea that the upper class live in an attached building. Living *together*, elites felt at the time, was the purview of tenements, a designation only of lower classes. Even the word *apartment* was crafted as a bit of marketing to remind prospective tenants that they were still living *apart* from others. The Dakota boasted enormous suites, around sixty in original total, ranging from five- to twenty-room options, offering space for staff quarters, a restaurant only tenants could access, hydraulic elevators, in-house laundry—every possible nineteenth-century luxury. It was its own being and its character was meticulously crafted by its owner.

A supreme labor of love for the prestigious former lawyer, Clark poured money from his successful venture as cofounder of the Singer Sewing Machine company into the Dakota. Isaac Merritt Singer, a truly gifted inventor, had been in great need of someone like Clark's savvy in patents and legal matters, and through their partnership Clark came to own half of the Singer company, one that positively dominated the garment industry, of which New York City was the capital and foremost producer during the late nineteenth century.

The origin of the name of the grand edifice has taken on apocryphal details through the years. In my first days as a tour guide, I'd heard from several guides that the name "the Dakota" began as an aspersion, that a journalist had derisively commented in the press about the absurd construction of a building "in the middle of the Dakota territory" and poking fun at "Clark's folly." I'd been told that Clark took on this insult as a benefit, adding Native motifs to the building's sandstone flourishes, turning what was at first an offhanded aspersion into a selling point. But this seems to be a widely dispersed urban legend. While it may have been underdeveloped at the time, it wasn't as if the Upper West Side was pure wilderness. Clark was fond of the frontier state and so the north and west placement, relative to Manhattan's downtown, as a mirror to the territory, was named in its honor. The carved figures on the exterior do remain a mystery: Neither Clark nor the architect H.J. Hardenbergh made note of who they were mirrored after, though one looks just like Clark's business partner, Singer. Perhaps the most striking features of the building are the black, wrought iron creatures that face passersby every day. Double-dragon motifs and faces akin to medieval grotesques line the ground-floor railings, bordering the building in its entirety with an extra Gothic element to frame its gabled setting.

The view of the still-in-progress Central Park was inspiring to all who visited or called the Dakota home. It was fully booked with residents upon its completion. In turn, an 1880s photograph of ice-skaters on the boat pond in the park with the Dakota towering behind, well above the still-growing tree line, is stunning. The Dakota looks like a castle towering over its surroundings, brooding and grand. Famous composers, artists, actors, writers, and musicians quickly became part of the building's roster, enjoying its views and stately prominence in the ever-growing metropolis.

As the city grew in height, breadth, population, and twentieth-century architecture became sleeker, taller, slimmer, and more modernist thanks to designers like Le Corbusier, a building like the Dakota naturally felt like a portal to another time, with its interior carriage courtyard glimpsed briefly if you walked past the arched entryway. Any way you'd look at it, you were between worlds.

This is a structure that has always known what it was; who it was, even though it had always been designed as apartments, its look remained cohesive. The Dakota has always understood it was a grand, Victorian lady. If setting is character in the Gothic, the Dakota *is* a character that will revert to its original form if left to its own devices. This type of haunting is my favorite: when a building will appear as it originally had been built, even after renovations. One twentieth-century tenant reportedly gazed into the building from outside, looking up at his living room, noting with growing curiosity that a chandelier hung there. A chandelier that was not his. During later additional renovations, a nub and fixture of the sort he had seen in his apparition were found in his apartment, just as his rooms had remembered them.

I love the idea that if left to itself, the building will revert to being seen as it was first unveiled. Similarly, many reports of visible spirits appear as they would *like* to be seen. In their youth, in their prime; beautiful and unscarred by age or change. Speaking from my own personal experience, I've been told often by sensitives and psychics that my great-grandmother, my namesake, is often with me, but as a young woman in a period dress. I've felt her as a protective, guardian presence in my life since the day she died; the moment of her death corresponding with the breaking of my dangerously high fever that could have been deadly for a six-year-old. It wouldn't surprise me that she'd want to be seen as young and pain-free, not as the bent, curled figure racked by rheumatoid arthritis she had been in the end. So does the Dakota, it seems, want to be seen in the grandeur to which she was first accustomed. There is a certain sentience to the building. Not quite as harrowingly sinister as Shirley Jackson's Hill House, but it knows itself.

By the 1960s, reports of strange incidents began to be reported, especially once some of the apartments had begun to be additionally subdivided. Lights were known to go off and on of their own accord, along with the elevators stopping and starting erratically. Objects were said to levitate and there have been several instances of small fires without a known human cause. The Dakota is indeed her own world existing on her own time, with long-term residents across the planes of life and death. A group of painters, while renovating actress Judy Holliday's apartment, each experienced a haunting figure floating through or an unseen hand grabbing them; one unsettling figure that all three of them saw had the body of an adult in period clothing, but the face of a child.

Clark's nearly obsessive doting and fussing over the building where he devoted the remainder of his life—he passed away two years into its four-year construction—is eternal. He was one of the first ghosts to be seen, and one of the most frequent to appear. A bespectacled, small man wearing a toupee, his unassuming but fastidious presence is particularly interested and involved any time any maintenance is being done on his building. Workers have noted that the man who appeared out of nowhere to startle them, inspecting their work with scrutiny, matches Clark's picture and portrait. He has been "seen by so many that it is an accepted fact, a part of the Dakota's personality."[2]

The Dakota is a prime example of public perception creating a feedback loop; because it looks haunted and was utilized as a piece of horror as the exterior for *Rosemary's Baby* (the interiors were all shot elsewhere), it must *be* haunted. In every book of New York ghost stories, the Dakota and *Rosemary's Baby* are forever entwined. There were many other Hollywood stars and their reputations who would make their own impression on the building. Boris Karloff, to his extreme sadness, evidently couldn't give out candy on Halloween; kids were too afraid of the real Frankenstein's monster living in the basement to approach him. But there's a ghost whose appearance predates any Hollywood horrors, the style of her yellow taffeta dress suggesting she shares the building's Gilded Age origins.

A young girl and her saffron dress has been seen, on specific occasions, bouncing a ball along a corridor, purportedly stating that the day is her birthday. A lonely and sad figure, she has become a dreaded one through the years. "Her spirit is a vanguard for death. When she is seen in the Dakota, someone in the building has been marked for the grave."[3]

But there is grandeur here too. A building as immense and storied as this is never just one thing, its personality as complex as the denizens it has housed through the years; the grounds have continuously proven ripe for inspiration. *The King's Handbook of New York City 1892*, a comprehensive if not exhaustive guide noting everything about the city one might possibly want to know, touts the Dakota as one of the "handsomest apartment-houses" in the city. "It is a many-gabled building in the style of a French Chateau, and is elegant in all its appointments." Just the year prior to the King's *Handbook's* accolades, famous composer Tchaikovsky visited the Dakota when he was the opening draw for Carnegie Hall in 1891 and he wrote about enjoying views from the roof, taking in a splendid sunset across Central Park.

In 1961, actress and singer Judy Garland lived at the Dakota while she navigated many of her most notable and acclaimed New York engagements. A dazzling star, she embodied the most tragic tropes of a Gothic heroine who could not escape the controls of what she'd been subjected to; a stunning talent ground up by the demands of an entertainment industry that literally put her on drugs at an early age. Her time at the Dakota was a less tumultuous one than would prove later on in the decade.

Long before reports of his own ghost dominated the Dakota ghostlore, famous singer and songwriter and former Beatle John Lennon, along with wife Yoko Ono, had been interested in the spirits of the building, after several odd occurrences of their own, to the point where they held a séance to inquire about previous tenants, specifically, of their apartment, where Jessie Ryan, wife of actor Robert Ryan, had died. Jessie came through in the séance, distinctly noting she had no intention of leaving *her* home. Additionally, Lennon had reported seeing a sorrowful woman wandering the halls who he referred to as "crying lady ghost" and he evidently witnessed a UFO outside the window that made enough of an impression to be noted in his album *Walls and Bridges*.

Acclaimed actress Lauren Bacall, a Dakota resident of fifty-three years, was said to have had a premonition that no one heeded. Earlier on December 8, 1980, she'd evidently expressed that she had an uneasy feeling and shared this with a guard or doorman regarding the paparazzi gathered outside. Gathering of fans and the presence of paparazzi had become common with so many famous residents, accepted as a given. But true to Bacall's unease, and perhaps the Victorian-birthday-girl-as-harbinger was aware too, that was the day a deranged "fan" shot John Lennon fatally in the back multiple times as he tried to enter his building, clutching tapes of the day's recording session.

Ghost stories about Lennon began immediately, many purported psychic accounts of which appeared to be self-serving, capitalizing on the death that had made world headlines. The account that most bears telling, and holds the most credence, is a simple tale from Yoko Ono herself. She saw her husband, sitting at the white piano in their apartment. Turning to her, he told her, "Don't be afraid, I am still with you."

As someone who was interested in the spiritual and metaphysical in his music and personal life, it is no surprise that Lennon would be a figure one would associate with a haunting, especially due to the violence of his death, but in this case, his violent death became far secondary to his next form. He has generally been regarded as a liminal, transcendent, and transformational figure. Psychic reports tend to place him not in a category of a ghost, but more of a guide between the worlds, a keeper of the veil. Kind of like the Dakota herself.

Much like a loved one might tend a grave, Yoko Ono decided to build an entire garden in honor of her slain husband. She financed the revitalization of a section of Central Park (by 1980 having suffered from starvation of state and federal funding thanks to the 1970s vogue of leaving big cities essentially for dead) just across the street, naming the section around Seventy-second and Central Park West Strawberry Fields for the beloved Beatles song. A memorial gift from the city of Naples, Italy, the circular black-and-white *IMAGINE* mosaic serves as a gathering place where musicians strum guitars and riff with passersby and where tourists leave tokens, flowers, and gifts on the tiny tiles. Each day the *IMAGINE* mosaic is renewed, each day it is cleared away for another set of ritualistic offerings from a different set of devotees from around the world, gathering to honor Lennon's vision of a more peaceful planet. It is clear Ono didn't want a staid, sad, grave-like memorial for her husband—she wanted Strawberry Fields to carry his energy as if, as he'd said to her, he were still with us.

If the haunted house serves as a metaphor for the constraints of an autonomous self in the grip of societal fears in the realm of Gothic fiction, the Dakota is more complicated. There isn't any one underlying theme of the hauntings here, other than that they tell stories of the many people who have lived and died there, some named and others simply ideas and thought-forms, like the harbinger girl in the yellow dress, attached to the place in fondness, in warning, or in transcendence. Above all, the building has been and always will be a home that knows what it is; historic, grand, and imposing, making an impression, creating a draw and larger-than-life magnetism, boasting famous figures under its eaves.

When I devised my Magic and Mysticism of Central Park tour for Boroughs of the Dead, I knew it was only right and proper to begin at Central Park West and Seventy-second Street, on the park side, looking across at the Dakota; telling its stories as an anchor. I encourage my guests to then consider allowing the spirit—the thought—of John Lennon to guide them into the park as a transition; exchanging the bustle of traffic for a celebration of music and flowers laid around a mosaic that encourages higher mindedness.

Facing the open walls of the famous public park whose entrances and exits are not gated, we flee the haunted house and find ourselves not in isolation across a treacherous landscape, but instead in the vibrant community of a bustling metropolis. We escape toward the restorative beauty of Central Park, a sacred scrap of greenery in an otherwise concrete jungle, where Transcendentalist thought might just encourage us to *imagine*, indeed.

The Sacrifice: Mary Virginia Wade of Gettysburg

Leanna

Verdant, green hills roll away into the distance on a rural county road in eastern Pennsylvania, where bending curves pass old wooden fence rows that note as many property boundaries as they do monuments. Birdsong fills the peaceful brush. This is no longer farmland, as long rows of cannons coming into view soon prove. This is a vast graveyard. Underneath the lush grass, soil is steeped in blood and decay, the land still able to trace every scar that wounded it. Gettysburg, Pennsylvania, site of one of the bloodiest battles of the Civil War, where approximately 51,000 soldiers lost their lives over three days of intense fighting, remembers everything. I knew I was approaching not just a haunted house, but a haunted town of interconnected traumas.

I'm energy sensitive. In places with intense residual energy, whether positive or negative, I'll feel it resonate in one of two ways: I'll either hear it, like a buzz or an audible note of some kind, or it will manifest physically; a pressure leading to shortness of breath or a pain either in my chest or head. When I'd first turned down the Pennsylvania county road that would take me into the small town of Gettysburg, I realized I was driving along parts of the land that had only recently been added to the total acreage of Gettysburg National Park, noting the rolling landscape around me as what had been collectively added to the swaths of battlefield memorials. I braced myself, but I didn't brace hard enough. A shooting spike of pain went from the back of my skull up through my left eye, bad enough that I had to pull over for a moment and massage behind my ear until it lessened.

This didn't necessarily alarm me; I've become accustomed to it. My first spectral encounter happened when I was around six years old, and from that point on, the spirit world, as a force, has always been part of my lexicon. When visiting notably haunted sites like this battlefield and the town itself, I assumed I'd have to pace myself. But at the same time, I felt I owed the dead some sympathetic pains. What was my stab of agony when compared to all their suffering?

When I checked into my room in the Farnsworth House Inn (one of the most haunted inns, per volume of reports, in the East), from the moment I set my bag down inside the quaint room decorated in a 1970s version of Victorian décor, I felt suddenly seasick. Woozy, I had to steady myself on the doorframe. It wasn't pressure on my lungs or my heart this time; it was full-body nausea, my head spinning from a rush of energy and a feeling like my mind was simply static. As a general energy-sensitive rule, if I feel an abrupt shift or rush, I have a quiet dialogue with whatever state and place I find myself in, acknowledging the new stimuli. *Hello, spirit world, this place is very powerful and I am here to honor that fact, and learn as much as I can.*

I make a deal with the spirit world *and* with myself, as just as many hauntings can be chalked up to imagination as those I've determined are indeed unexplained phenomena. My imagination is *powerful*, but I don't need it to convince me of the realities of the spirit world. The spirits will find their way in if they're determined to. I balance healthy skepticism with an open belief; hand in hand. After acknowledgement of a force that physically unsettled my balance, I make a request of the spirits. *Just please don't startle me.*

That night, they didn't. The only noise I noticed was the footsteps of my upstairs neighbor one flight up as they paced their floor, my ceiling, between two and three a.m.

When I left the next morning for our group's bus tour of the battlefield, I looked back at the door to my room, which opened directly onto the exterior courtyard. There *was* no second story on this part of the property.

Oh . . .

As a historic parallel, Confederate sharpshooters took to upper floors and rooftops.

In later discussions with staff and glancing over accounts of other travelers written in a guest book, it would seem I've not been the only one to hear footsteps on the ceiling when there are no second stories. I had asked not to be startled; I didn't ask the spirits not to *move*. As a creature of momentum, I respect this. Gettysburg is restless. To visit the place is to be moved. The spirits certainly don't stand still. Many of the most common haunts of the town are clairaudient. Cannon fire can often be heard when no reenactment of any kind is taking place. The psychic residue, the place memory of the town, remains as thick as the heat and humidity was on the days of the bloody battles that left those marks.

Sitting on an outcropping of rock at one of the sites where it seemed as though Union forces would not be able to hold, I stare at our talented tour guide, Bill, who evokes every harrowing detail with passion and fervor. It's a sunny day and I'm chilled. Tears well up against the wind. All around me are participating members of the *Feminine Macabre* journal series, spearheaded by author and lecturer Amanda Woomer. I'm surrounded by talented essayists on ghosts, grieving, death, paranormal subjects, magic, witchcraft, and otherworldly matters. None of us, even those who were already seasoned Gettysburg visitors, can quite breathe or keep our eyes dry as Bill explains what it was like for the entire Confederate army to turn *every* single one of its cannons, approximately 230, onto the rocky hillside we were sitting upon, and fire all at once. The sound was so deafening it carried for a seemingly impossible number of miles. Civilian Sarah Broadhead wrote that it sounded "as if heaven and earth were crashing together." Bill, to truly drive the point home for us, shared snippets of letters soldiers wrote to comrades and loved ones, noting their brothers-in-arms whose entire bodies were reduced to a "red mist" by this cannon barrage.

I can't wrap my head fully around this. Even with those harrowing descriptors, I simply recoil. But this deeply haunted, blood-drenched area deserves our attention, and I open my heart ever-deeper for the reason why Spiritualism became so necessary during and after this war; the balm of imagining an unbroken, whole soul as sacred and sacrosanct. Contactable. A soul *separate* from the unspeakable horrors of vaporized bodies; remains that could never be held, laid out, dressed, or buried with ceremonial closure.

Gettysburg as a whole remains overwhelming to a point of dizziness. I decided to focus my mind and heart on the admirable work of one woman and the tragic loss of another.

I'm one of those people who has to have something to *do*, always. As I spent the weekend in this psychically scarred town, I put myself in the situation of a civilian woman at this critical juncture. What would I have done when an unexpected battle came into the town itself, descending on an unarmed civilian population? I'd like to think I'd be as hardy—and as undaunted—as Jennie Wade or Elizabeth Thorn, but I think it's too easy, and prideful, to think I'd automatically be so heroic. Still, focusing on them gives my mind a way to hold onto the horrors while admiring their resilience.

A dynamic statue in Evergreen Cemetery greets visitors at the crest of a rolling hill. The Women's Memorial depicts a beautifully sculpted Elizabeth Thorn in bronze, with a hand to her brow and a shovel under her other arm, a hand to her abdomen, showcasing her second-trimester pregnancy. Her husband Peter was the cemetery gatekeeper, but had been called away with his Union regiment, so it fell to Elizabeth and her father alone to begin burying the dead that had piled up along the cemetery perimeter. Two soldiers had been stationed to help her, but could not take the stench or the state of the corpses blackening in the July heat and left after two days. With only her aging father to help her, Elizabeth dug graves for, and interred, ninety-one soldiers. She did not change her dress for six weeks. Three months later she gave birth to a baby girl, Rose Meade, a child who remained forever frail and died at fourteen. Amid Elizabeth's arduous labors during the battle of Gettysburg, she heard that a civilian had been killed, a woman she knew, young Mary Virginia Wade.

Elizabeth Thorn became a picture of fortitude. Mary Virginia Wade became a picture of sacrifice. Each tended to what they felt were their duties without complaint, diligent and steadfast. If Elizabeth Thorn is the prologue, Mary Virginia Wade is the conflict. I wish I could say there's a resolution.

Mary Virginia Wade was born in Gettysburg, Pennsylvania, on May 21, 1843. "Ginny" was a nickname due to her middle name, but "Jennie" was a newspaper mistake that ended up persisting even with relatives. I'm making the choice to refer to her here by her full name, rather than the perpetuation of journalistic error, even though the museum that bears her name and honors the site where she died is the Jennie Wade House. Mary Virginia was the one civilian killed out of Gettysburg's 51,000 casualties. A number that boggles the mind when taking in the small, peaceful, lovely town it is now.

The Wade family had already undergone their fair share of troubles by the time of the Civil War, with a father deemed mentally unfit and remanded to a debtor's prison, the Wade women took on work as seamstresses to stay afloat. They did so generously when it came to the Union cause; New York soldiers from the 10th Cavalry regiment stationed to protect the Pennsylvania border from Southern intrusion, considered the family "kindly and hospitable."[1]

The citizens of Gettysburg were aware that they were close to the Maryland border and that Rebel forces could come raiding. They'd done so in 1862, and while no civilian was hurt at that point, everyone was scared and goods were seized and stolen. But for the most part, the residents of Gettysburg tried to go on about their daily life. Until an unplanned meeting of General Lee's 75,000 and Union Army General George C. Meade's 93,000 soldiers in June 1863 resulted in the largest-scale conflict of the war.

In *Jennie Wade of Gettysburg*, author Cindy L. Small, in a rather Gothic manner, sets the scene of the town, directly before the battle, in her introduction: "but there were people too who laughed at these so far unfounded fears and brushed off the rumors, and said there's work to be done and money to be made, so they ignored the whispers on the wind, and the ominous rumblings that rent the heavy summer air like black storm clouds rolling in from the west."[2]

By June 26, Confederate General Jubal A. Early's troops had entered Gettysburg via Chambersburg Street and began firing guns into the air and brandishing swords. Mary Virginia's nephew Lewis Kenneth was born one hour before this ominous arrival, so her mother was tending to Georgia McClellan, Mary Virginia's sister, leaving Mary Virginia responsible for her family's home northwards on Breckenridge Street, some three hundred yards closer to the heart of the village.

The citizens of Gettysburg were literally caught in the crossfire of advancing Confederate troops, who initially outnumbered what Union defense had managed to be mustered to the location. At certain points, Union soldiers rushed in retreat through the streets of the town and citizens were advised to stick to their cellars. Many vulnerable civilians pleaded with officers not to leave them to the Confederates that began taking sharpshooting positions in upper floors of Gettysburg buildings to pick off "the boys in blue." Volleys would continue for days. Shells and bullet-holes began pockmarking the entire town; scars that still score the brick to this day.

The Wade family had an eventful time at the outbreak of hostilities, to say the least. Mary Virginia's sister, Georgia McClellan, had given birth to a son about an hour before Confederate troops first arrived in Gettysburg. Mary Virginia deemed the McClellan house, a bit up the rise toward Cemetery Hill, a safer location than her own lodgings closer to the heart of the town.

In the beginning of the surging battles that lasted from July 1 through July 3, in addition to trying to plead for her younger brother's release from Confederate capture when he tried to ride one of the family's horses out of town to safety, Mary Virginia accomplished a great deal. She tailored and hemmed her seventeen-year-old brother John's uniform so he could join his regiment as a bugler. She cared for a disabled boarder and kept him sheltered, checked in on her sister and newborn nephew, and she prepared food and offered water to Union soldiers in need, making countless runs to the nearby well.

On July 1, the Confederates had scored an incomplete victory and with Union soldiers repelled toward the crest of Cemetery Hill. Confederate soldiers began taking sharpshooting positions in the upper stories of several buildings and Union soldiers fell wounded on the McClellans' lawn. By nightfall, as the shots were less frequent, soldiers reported seeing Mary Virginia, at great risk to herself, tending to those who had fallen on the McClellan lawn, bringing them food and water, and a cup to Orderly Sergeant Albert Brewer, which he treasured as a souvenir. This was commented on in press reports and soldiers' correspondences at the time; thought to be an angel doing what she could in the midst of hell.

One hundred and fifty bullets struck the house over the course of the three-day battle and as hostilities increased on July 2, the house became caught in a crossfire of larger artillery. A ten-pound Confederate "parrot" shell screamed down onto the McClellan house in a diagonal direction and lodged in the south side of the roof, but did not detonate. When she heard the crash of falling bricks and plaster raining down upstairs, Mary Virginia fainted. But as the day wore on and she roused, the reports of her generosity of bread and water caused more calls. Soldiers continued knocking on the door for sustenance and her and her mother had to start more yeast as flour supplies dwindled.

On the morning of July 3, Mary Virginia and her family ate meager meals, as they'd given most of what they had to the soldiers, without charge, and she then began reading from the Bible. As she read from Psalms that encouraged bravery and trust in the Lord in the face of fear, including lines like "Though war should rise against me, in this I will be confident . . . " and "be of good courage . . ." while the sentiments were fitting, the words were too much for her sister Georgia, who asked her mother to bid her sister stop the recitation.

Eerily, fatefully, prophetically, the last words Georgia heard her sister speak, as noted in John White Johnston's 1917 account *The True Story of "Jennie" Wade, A Gettysburg Maid*, (replete with what must have been a nickname for Georgia) were: "if there is anyone in this house that is to be killed today, I hope it is me as George has that little baby." And with that, she went into the kitchen to bake bread for Union soldiers.

At around eight o'clock, a stray .58 caliber Confederate sniper's bullet cleared the thick wooden front door, blasted through a second door ajar between the front and the parlor, piercing Mary Virginia from the back and up her body, passing directly through her heart, killing her instantly as she bent kneading dough over a wooden mixing trough in the kitchen of her sister's home. In her pocket was the key to her home and a picture of her beloved confidant, Union solider Jack Skelly, a dear childhood friend and possible future husband—had either survived the conflict. Mrs. Wade, Mary Virginia's mother, had been working to start the fire for the bread that had been promised to more soldiers, turning just in time to see her daughter fall, lifeless, to the floor. She calmly strode to the parlor where Georgia was reclining with her newborn and announced the tragedy. Georgia's scream alerted Federal soldiers and soon New York infantrymen stood in the kitchen, staring with sadness at the scene.

But there was no time for anyone to mourn. With all the windows shot out and the house under increased fire, soldiers urged the rest of the Wade and McClellan family to seek better safety, guiding them to their neighbor's cellar on the opposite side of the shared building. To do this without being picked off by sharpshooters, the soldiers helped the family up and over, using the hole the unexploded ten-pound parrot shell had cleared in the upper floors the day prior, relocating the family through the interior, without further exposure to gunfire on the exterior. Mary Virginia's body was wrapped in a quilt her sister Georgia had pieced together at age five. Gingerly, the soldiers, at Mrs. Wade's firm request, transported her daughter's body down to the cellar with the rest of the family and their disabled boarder, where they would all wait in an uncomfortable eighteen-hour vigil until the following afternoon, the Fourth of July, proved safe enough to emerge.

But before she rejoined her living and dead family in the cellar, Mrs. Wade, urged on by hungry soldiers, finished the loaves of bread her daughter had begun baking, trying not to think about her daughter's fresh bloodstains on the wood beneath her.

On the afternoon of July 4, with no embalming, washing, or dressing of the body, dough still on her hands, Mary Virginia was lowered into a simple casket, quilt still wrapped around her, and buried in the back yard of her sister's home, where she would remain until the next January, when it was removed to the cemetery of the nearby German Reformed Church. It became family legend that her body had, in the interim, mummified, but in their idiom, it was said that she had "turned to stone." Two years later, Georgia and her husband Louis, as well as their brother John, transfererred their sister's body to the family plot the veteran bugler John had bought in Evergreen Cemetery. She lies there to this day, with a statue erected on a newer monument, a stoic-looking Mary Virginia stands with a jug of water in one hand, canteens hanging over the other, a hand gathering her robes to her breast in a peaceful, supplicant pose like that of the biblical Mary. Another saintly portrayal stands outside of the home where she died, a commemorative bronze statue where Mary Virginia holds a loaf of bread as well as a jug of water.

But in the immediate aftermath of the war, in stories with clear agendas and personal bitterness, Mary Virginia as saintly figure wasn't as settled a story. The museum known as the Jennie Wade house, as noted here, was not, in fact, her house, but her sister's. Her death there transferred ownership in the public mind along with the variations in her name. Women losing control of their own names and stories is nothing new in accounts like these, but it should still be noted, as the power of the name, in terms of identity and self-actualization, not to mention precision, remains important.

Bafflingly, questions about Jennie's moral character seem to have come from survivor John Burns, a cantankerous old man who was himself another civilian hero, perhaps jealous of the fact he shared the spotlight with an unmarried young woman.

"As time went by, people began to embroil the simple saga as they knew it or thought it should be, into a mudslinging mess to achieve personal gain, mostly to trumpet their own acts of patriotism shown in one way or another."[3]

Burns may also have cast aspersions on the family because of her father having been a Southerner as well as imprisoned, though Mary Virginia's commitment to the Union cause, as well as her brother's, and her beloved Jack Skelly, had all been made consistently, abundantly clear. Her acts of providing water and food for Union soldiers, acts that proved fatal, speak louder than words.

Letters and timelines do reveal family tensions and drama, especially concerning a Dutch suitor who gave Mary Virginia a set of jewelry she chopped up with an axe; later she burned a love letter the same man had written for Mrs. Wade, her mother, who had physically assaulted Mary Virginia after the jewelry incident. Mary Virginia confessed these things in correspondences with Jack Skelly months before their respective deaths, her letters revealing a feisty young woman who felt deeply; a generous soul who treasured the man she considered her only true confidant.

Skelly, lying mortally wounded in a Confederate prisoner of war camp, did try to send a message through a family friend, words meant to be passed solely onto Mrs. Wade, perhaps concerning Mary Virginia, perhaps in hopes of securing their future. One that never panned out. The man carrying the message never made it back either. Regardless of any family drama, the fact that any of the Wade family character or personal life became subject to speculation rather than simply noting the tragedy of Mary Virginia's death alone, especially considering she died because she hadn't taken further cover, but instead was trying to provide food for her brethren, breaks my heart.

A woman can't win. Even in death. Evidently she didn't go into her "sacrifice" quietly enough for a man like John Burns's liking. Her martyrdom outshone him and he sought to undermine her legacy paid for with her own blood.

Another aspect of the museum itself, which tells the story of the Wade and McClellan family in those tense and grief-filled few days, disturbed me greatly as I stood in the room where Mary Virginia was killed.

Visitors can see the very same doors the bullets passed through, with the very same bullet holes, the tattered edges of the wood worn smooth by over a century and a half of touching. And to the side of the second bullet hole, the interior door that was ajar, is a laminated little post about an urban legend that grew up around that door. Legend says that if an unmarried woman places her ring finger through that second bullet hole, she will soon be married. Reading this, I recoiled.

The cognitive dissonance of putting a finger through the hole that was left from a *bullet*, an act that killed a woman, and then that penetrative gesture leading to a marriage proposal . . . Much like when I got into my Gettysburg room, I had to steady myself on my feet. I had to bite my tongue. It wasn't the tour guide's fault that this legend had cropped up. I turned my face away so the guide couldn't see my distress. It is a *weird* thing to correlate; the bullet hole and a proposal. This folkloric ritual is noted on a placard inside the house and is then repeated on the museum's website.

In my opinion, that physical act is disrespectful. By all means, do honor Mary Virginia's death by celebrating your own life and your partnership, something she did not get the chance to have. But this legend also sends a certain message that her death happened before she could somehow be *completed* by marriage. As if it were the be-all and end-all of unfinished business. This sits with me; raw and irritated, the opposite of the worn-smooth wood that showcases the trajectory of a death.

The Jennie Wade House is a haunted house in a haunted town that wears its ghosts like the bullet holes strewn across the facades of old buildings. The house museum that took on the nickname of the woman killed inside it, assuming her death as its mantle, isn't what you'd expect a haunted house to look like. It is a simple, modest cottage of a home, and that's one of the things that makes it the most jarring. The tour begins in the living spaces and ends in the kitchen and cellar, taking you first through the familiar places of love and community, where a picture of Mary Virginia, her mother, and sister stare out at the viewer with directness and fortitude. Then you are led to where the safety of a house failed: it could not provide shelter from the stray bullet, the familiar becomes strange, and you are left to consider sitting with the body in the basement. Author Leila Taylor drives the point home in *Sick Houses: Haunted Homes and the Architecture of Dread*, asking "what's more frightening than your own home turning against you?"

The Gothic bids us sit with the uncanny and the unexpected. As setting is always character, Gettysburg lives on as wholly haunted, constantly reliving the battle that well and truly defined the Civil War and our country's future. This town is an extrapolation of Gothic themes writ large. Between the reenactments that regularly take place and the sound of cannon fire that is regularly heard even when no one *corporeal* is firing, Gettysburg and its haunted locations are all hovering in that unsettled existential question of whether this country would continue whole or be carved up into pieces. It's a heart ready to break over and over again. The town remains the most liminal space of history I've ever visited and researched.

As for spectral accounts of Mary Virginia, her spirit has been reported as distinctly active through the years. The house museum has been featured on shows like *Ghost Adventures* and *Ghost Lab*, and numerous reports have noted Mary Virginia wandering through her house or the surrounding countryside. EVP (electronic voice phenomena) recordings have been taken that indicate activity and photos taken inside the house have repeatedly showcased a spectral presence.

But again, it's hard not to simply assume, with all the focus on this young woman's tragic death while engaged in a noble act, that a ghost story is inevitable. We've spoken before about the concept of place memory, that a particularly intense event will leave a sort of psychic imprint on a space. In my experience, never has any place been so prevalent with place memory than the entire town of Gettysburg and this house in particular.

Author of *"I Would Still Be Drowned in Tears"* and *Civil War Ghosts*, historian and director of the Mary Washington House, Michelle Hamilton has been moved by Mary Virginia Wade and her story throughout her entire career. Michelle was also taking part in the *Feminine Macabre* writers' group pilgrimage as we made our way through Gettysburg. As our group gathered to tour the house in which Mary Virginia died, I knew we felt compelled, as a group of women writers, to honor the woman who had become a sacrifice and icon, curious about understanding her story in particular, within the greater context of the battle itself. I knew Michelle was deeply familiar with the history, as well as the house and had more personal details to share about the site than we could glean solely from our tour. Michelle considers her interest in history and the paranormal as existing side by side, in an uneasy alliance. I asked Michelle if she could elaborate on her own experiences:

"My first visit to the Jennie Wade House occurred on Jennie's birthday. To celebrate her birthday, the staff had a birthday cake for the visitors to enjoy. One of the guides had even taken a slice into the museum and left it on the kitchen table for Jennie. The tour was wonderful, but while in the kitchen I became overwhelmed standing where Jennie was when she died. For a moment I felt I was in a vortex of energy, and it felt like time was blurring. It only lasted a few seconds, but it left me disorientated.

"Later in the day my mother was reviewing the pictures that she had taken in the Jennie Wade House, and we discovered that one of the images taken in the kitchen showed a strange mist that surrounded me. I was standing where Jennie had died, and I was examining the breadboard where Jennie was kneading dough to make biscuits when she was fatally shot."

Emotions of longing and sacrifice remained with Michelle, to the point that she'd tried to write her graduate thesis on Mary Virginia Wade, but was discouraged by an advisor thinking this casualty too limited a topic. Still, Michelle has found ways to write and talk about this important figure. In June 2022, Michelle, serving as the historical advisor for the Association of Paranormal Study, took part in the team's investigation into the house. What began as a quiet night shifted when the group went into the cellar.

"We settled down on the benches, and my back was against the interior wall. This is when one of the strangest things that has ever happened to me occurred. I have felt energy before, sometimes I will even see the person in my mind's eye. It is strange for me to describe, because I am always doubting myself and I am careful to try to not let my imagination run away with me. I can't let flights of fancy damage the career that I have so carefully constructed. But in that cellar on a damp night in June, I sensed the spirit of Jennie Wade with a young boy standing in the corner. She was standing in the corner with the boy, who I felt was one of her brothers, because she was afraid of her father, who was also in the cellar with us. At first, I did not say anything to the team, because it felt so unearthly. One of the team members also picked up that Jennie's father was in the room and that he was a bully. Feeling emboldened, I told my companions what I was sensing. The team member who had sensed Jennie's father began to challenge him. I sensed that Jennie appreciated being defended, as she was truly terrified being around her father.

"Then, I started talking in a voice and manner that was not my own. I could hear the words coming out, but they were not my own. First, I was giggling and playful, then suddenly I started crying. 'I just wanted to help. I'm a good girl,' I sobbed. Then as soon as it had washed over me it was gone, and I had control of my emotions again.

"I am still unsure about what happened that night. If it was really Jennie that was speaking through me, I felt honored that she was willing to show herself as so vulnerable. Not the spitfire that once chopped up a gift with a hatchet that was given to her by a suitor that she found to be repellant. History tells us what a person did; ghost stories allow us to feel the emotions behind the events."

The emotions behind the events of Gettysburg, for me, whether standing on those fields in view of all the cannons as tall as me, positioned on their last marks of bloodshed, or standing staring at the wooden trough Mary Virginia was kneading dough upon when she was killed, overwhelm me still. As a born Ohioan, then a Minnesotan, and now a New Yorker, I've long been cognizant of the various roles each state played in the Union fabric, and I've been very aware of the fact that New York lost more soldiers than any other Union state. That loss is palpable on those fields and it remains sharp and aching inside that small house caught in the crossfire of a big war. A young woman trying to do what she perceived to be the right thing; extending mercy and hospitality and taking care of people led to her death. Had she gone down to the cellar as so many other citizens had done, she'd likely have lived.

Channeling all that loss through this one young woman, a tragic heroine sacrificed to a bloody conflict that played out on the literal streets of a small town, while she can serve as a focal point, doesn't make anything easier. Not that it should be. These are the parts of history that are meant to be uncomfortable, the original sin of slavery causing wave after wave of additional violences and injustices this country hasn't ever fully healed from nor truly solved.

I always considered the character of Lucy Westenra in *Dracula* as a sacrificial figure. She is killed so that the rest of the protagonists may learn from her tragedy and live. A young, vibrant, vivacious young woman surrounded by suitors, her whole life ahead of her. Due to Victorian propriety, she can't immediately say what's begun happening to her; that she's been visited nightly by a force she can't describe. But an invading force sweeps in to steal her life, nonetheless. Lucy is made all the more tragic as she never gets to fulfill any of the promise she exhibited at the start of Stoker's masterpiece. Even still, there's a sort of victim-blaming to her character. She had several suitors . . . perhaps she was a bit of a flirt . . . perhaps she was asking for trouble. Adding insult to injury, Lucy was not allowed to rest in peace after her death. A stake is driven through her heart.

Can Mary Virginia ever rest in peace? Her spirit is as active as her death is told and retold in endless cycles, her whole life and death on display, wide open. Even just this year, one of Mary Virginia's letters to Jack Skelly was stolen from where it had been on display at the Jennie Wade House Museum. I pray that letter is returned, out of respect for the private thoughts of the woman who wrote it as a gesture of care for a soldier she never learned had fallen. This woman's heart, pierced through, has bled enough.

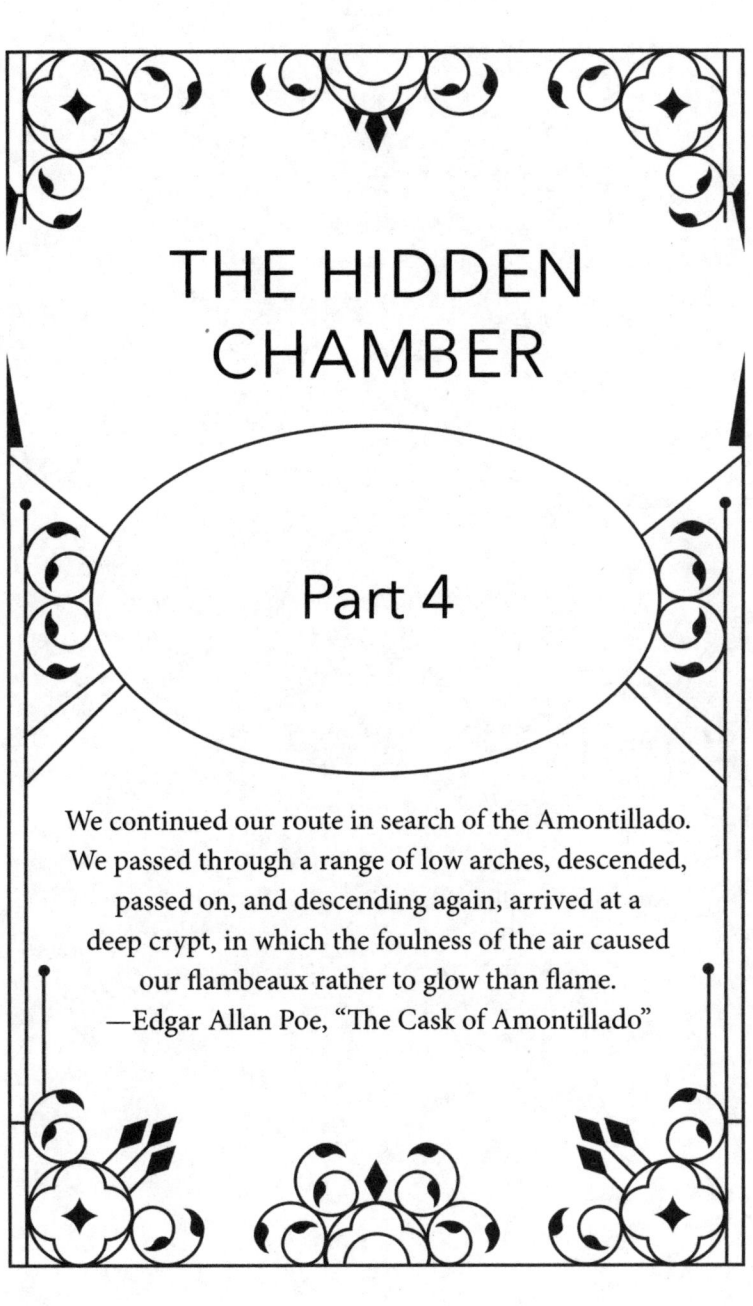

THE HIDDEN CHAMBER

Part 4

We continued our route in search of the Amontillado.
We passed through a range of low arches, descended,
passed on, and descending again, arrived at a
deep crypt, in which the foulness of the air caused
our flambeaux rather to glow than flame.
—Edgar Allan Poe, "The Cask of Amontillado"

The Nasty Blues: The Story of Melrose Hall

Andrea

In a hidden chamber in a labyrinthine mansion, a woman is locked away and starves to death. When her body is finally discovered, her nails are broken and bloody and there are scratch marks on the door. What must her final hours have been like? Who was she? Why was she there? And did it all really happen in Flatbush, Brooklyn?

This is a tale about a haunted house, torture chambers, a secret lover, and an actress. The story usually starts with the figure of Colonel William Axtell. He is the one character of whose history we can be sure, so let's start with him. We will return to the starving woman before too long. For now, let's leave her in the secret chamber, where in life she waited for him constantly.

Colonel Axtell was a "three-bottle man," a man who could drink copiously but still hold his liquor—a dangerous combination. A notorious figure of Revolutionary-era New York, Axtell was a roistering, hard-partying, possibly psychotic, colonel in the British army. He was known for his assorted, voracious appetites—hence his boozy sobriquet—and for his involvement in one of Brooklyn's most bizarre ghost stories.

Axtell was the owner of Melrose Hall, an estate now long gone, which once stood near the site of present-day Prospect

Park in the residential neighborhood of Flatbush, Brooklyn (near where Bedford Avenue is now, between Winthrop Street and Clarkson Avenue). Built in 1749, the hall was "the quaintest and queerest old place one could imagine," with "steep roofs slanted in all directions and gables projected here and there in the oddest sort of way." It was built by an Englishman named Lane (nobody seems sure of his first name, but it may have been John) whose carousing ways got him expelled from his homeland and banished to the colonies. The lavish home accommodated his lifestyle quite handily, with a spacious ballroom, well-stocked wine cellars, and a massive fireplace big enough to roast an ox. The house also contained "dark corridors, oddly shaped rooms, winding stairways, black holes, mysterious trap doors, and other unprecedented features," including hidden dungeons and a secret chamber.

Axtell, a Loyalist, bought the place on the eve of the Revolution and used it as his country house. He picked up seamlessly where Lane left off, filling the house with glamorous and glorious debauch. He financed the purchase with his wife's money, for he had married well. His wife was Margareta de Peyster, a wealthy woman from a fine old New York family. She was educated, graceful, and beautiful, but, according to lore, she was not the one Axtell loved—alas, he was in love with her sister, Alva. He simply couldn't bear to be without her, and so he did what any man would do: secreted his lover away in a hidden chamber above the ballroom. Alva spent all day in a locked room with only two high, narrow windows; at night Axtell would visit her and leave again in the morning. Only one other person knew Alva was there: a "slave woman," as she is called in these tales, named Miranda, who took care of her and brought her food. Alva would wait all day until the colonel could slip away and visit her clandestinely. One day, when the colonel was away on an extended journey, Miranda died. There was no one to bring Alva food or drink, and so she starved to death in her locked chamber.

When Axtell returned, so the ghost story goes, he was welcomed by his household with a lavish banquet. Troubled by a pervasive sense of unease, the colonel tried his best to enjoy the feasting and fêting, but as the night wore on, he became increasingly perturbed when he noticed the absence of the faithful Miranda. Upon inquiring of her whereabouts, he was told she died soon after his departure.

When he heard the news, the colonel leaped from his seat and sprang to the hidden chamber, whereupon he discovered the skeleton of his dear, starved Alva. Some versions of the story have him take his own life on the spot; others have him linger in delirious, tortured fever for three days before confessing and dying. In yet other versions, the ghost of Alva makes a splashy entrance at the dinner party, points a spectral finger at him and thunders, "Betrayer!" thus promptly scaring him to death in front of his guests. That version is my favorite because it's so dramatic. In real life, Axtell moved to England with his wife after the Revolution and died at a ripe old age.

The house was later purchased by Anna Cora Mowatt, a well-known writer and actress in her time, who wrote in her 1854 memoir, *Autobiography of an Actress* that "a young girl had been purposely starved to death in that chamber and that her ghost wandered at night around the house." Neighborhood whispers about the ghostly woman eventually found their way into local newspapers too. In the 1880s, the *Brooklyn Daily Eagle* took it a step further and embroidered the details about the lover and the secret chamber. In early articles the ghost is named Isabella, perhaps inspired by *The Castle of Otranto*; later, in the 1890s, the story is reprinted and she is called Alva.

Thanks to the malleable nature of oral tradition, and the un–fact-checked printing of spooky puff pieces in nineteenth-century newspapers around Halloween, there's the usual "broken telephone" aspect to this ghost story (astute readers will have noticed that Mowatt's version has Alva "purposely" being starved, while other versions have her starved accidentally). But surprisingly, unlike many such tales, quite a few details of the Melrose Hall ghost story can actually be substantiated.

William Axtell was a very real person, amply documented by historical record. You can see his portrait if you visit the website of the Metropolitan Museum of Art; he looks a bit rakish, painted by John Wollaston in a "sprightly, informal pose." We know that he was wealthy, he was born in Jamaica, he was a slaveholder. His grandfather was Daniel Axtell, a colonel in Cromwell's army, who was executed at the order of Charles II. His wife's family was one of New York State's most prominent families; she was a Van Cortlandt on her mother's side. Their images hang in galleries; their personal effects fill state archives. Axtell had no children of his own, but raised a niece, Elizabeth Shipton, as his daughter. You can see a transcript of his will on a website dedicated to the history of British slavery, and read the real thing if you go to the library at the New-York Historical Society. His activities during the Revolutionary War are extensively documented.

Melrose Hall was also a real place, substantiated by deeds of sale, numerous newspaper articles, books, and photographs. These articles mention the architectural quirks of the place, including chambers with no doors and stairways that lead nowhere. When the house was razed around the turn of the twentieth century, its owner at the time found human remains, and a dungeon with chains on the wall, again all documented by local newspapers, who noted that it was common practice at the time to bury soldiers there. (It is indeed true that this was actually fairly common practice in Brooklyn, and happened in locations throughout the borough, including Brooklyn Heights and elsewhere.)

Not only are Axtell's dungeons and secret chambers part of historical record, so is his penchant for sadism, mentioned in no less a source than Edwin G. Burrows and Mike Wallace's door-stopper history tome *Gotham*. According to Burrows and Wallace, Colonel Axtell of Flatbush commanded a troop called the Nassau Blues, who "entered local lore as the 'Nasty Blues' thanks to their thuggish abuse of the town's residents. Axtell himself allegedly tortured rebel prisoners in the secret chambers of his country house, Melrose Hall."

If the torture and secret chambers have made it into *Gotham*, a book considered one of the preeminent histories of New York, there must be some grain of truth to these claims. Even the New-York Historical Society, in their inventory of "Sundrys belonging to the kitchen & dairy, &c.&c." of William Axtell, dated September 11, 1795, notes that "in addition to rumors of the mansion being used as a place to torture American troops, there is a legend that Axtell kept his mistress hidden in a secret chamber where she eventually starved to death." All this in the *official* record!

His foil in this ghost story is less substantial; the spectral woman sometimes called Isabella, sometimes Alva, is of mysterious provenance and unproven existence. She is a rumor, a haunt, a whisper, a shade; she is legend and lore, and she may or may not have ever existed. Accompanying Alva (I will call her that, because she is most often called Alva) another spectral woman, the "slave woman" Miranda, also exists beyond the boundaries of historical record. Colonel Axtell did own slaves, this is known, but I did not find any records of an enslaved woman named Miranda among his household. Onto these spectral women, various observers, commentators, and storytellers have heaped their own details, anxieties, fantasies, and fears. These women are blank slates, to be formed and fashioned according to the whims of the storyteller.

Margareta de Peyster, Axtell's real wife, is also elided from this narrative. In most versions of the story, she is known only as "Mrs. Axtell" and various claims are made about the relationship between her and the colonel's mistress, who is said to be either her little sister or her niece. These claims are always made with the suggestion that there is literally *no way* to verify any of these things, as they are lost and shrouded in the mists of time. Which is really question-begging, because, as we have seen, the de Peyster family was extremely well known and well documented. It is very simple to determine that the real Margareta de Peyster did not have a sister named Alva or Isabella.

And yet I find myself willing to overlook this story's many, *many* errors and inconsistencies, because I love it so much. It is lush, romantic, perverse, gorgeous, and strange. As a history geek, I am thrilled to discover the real connections between an outlandish local legend and real people's actual lives. Even the mutable nature of Alva's identity seems fitting for a specter; the way her image changes with each teller is typical and emblematic of the nature of ghostlore. There's a poetry to her tale, symbolism straight out of Poe. The story of Melrose Hall is one of my favorite New York City ghost stories, tied with that of Elma Sands, the Ghost of the Girl in the Well, another haunting tale abundantly substantiated in historical record that took place in a similar time period. (For those who haven't taken my ghost tour, Elma Sands was allegedly murdered by Levi Weeks in 1799, and her body dumped in a well. Weeks was acquitted at trial, due in part to the savvy of his defense attorneys: Alexander Hamilton and Aaron Burr. Sands's ghost was said to haunt the location of the well at what is now 129 Spring Street. The remains of the old brick cistern are still visible in the basement of what is now a clothing store.) Do I love the ghost of Melrose Hall for the Gothic details, the many mirrorings, doublings, and symmetries? Do I find the image of a woman debasing herself and waiting for an asshole of a man eminently relatable? Is Alva the ghost of me in my early twenties?

I began to wonder about the person who wrote the 1880s *Eagle* article, which is the first written source to mention the secret lover angle. In this version, when "Isabella" starves in her hidden chamber, she is presented as a very willing accomplice to this whole affair. She will do anything to be with Axtell, willingly putting up with virtual imprisonment for the pleasure of his company. And all while betraying her own sister, no less! That's quite an erotic fantasy for a family newspaper.

But even the arguable appeal of a sexy ghost does not fully explain why Alva alone haunts the place while the dozens of male soldiers who perished on the spot rest in quiet graves. Well before the *Eagle* reporters tarted up her hungry wraith with pulpy sexploitation, she was the only one at Melrose Hall to ascend to the realm of official ghostlore. Axtell's ghost is never seen, and I only came across a single account that somewhat unconvincingly names John Lane as the resident ghost. I found no mentions of Miranda or Mrs. Axtell as a ghost. Why is Alva's story, however rife it is with fabrications and inconsistencies, the sole one that endures in the legend of Melrose Hall?

And what accounts for the profound undercurrent of genuine darkness to this tale? There was something so uncanny about Alva's precise placement at a Flatbush mansion during the period of the Revolutionary War, something that tugged at my mind. Something beyond the erotic Gothic madness of the story. Something I had read about Axtell that I just couldn't shake. Remember, Mowatt's 1854 account only says, "a young girl had been purposely starved to death in that chamber and that her ghost wandered at night around the house." Yet by the

1880s, that solitary female ghost had been transformed into a figure who was not only imprisoned and starved, but who was sexually subjugated as well. Why?

Let's get back to those Nasty Blues for a minute.

Like all of the environs around present-day New York City, Long Island, which Brooklyn is a part of, was occupied territory during the Revolution. The then-village of Flatbush was controlled by groups of British army regulars who stationed themselves in homes in the area and terrorized the local population. According to Burrows and Wallace, they were "given liberty to . . . ravage at will" and "satisfy their yearning to bayonet and torch." The Nassau Blues was one of many such regiments, and their nickname was a fitting one.

Women were especially apt to be leery of these soldiers; in nearby Staten Island it was said that "a girl cannot step into the bushes to pluck a rose without the most imminent risk of being ravished [by soldiers] as riotous as Satyrs." When I read this line, so casually tossed off by Burrows and Wallace, I shuddered. The use of rape as a war weapon is the real horror here, in my mind. Fear of rape is the subconscious terror that gives this story legs; the fact that the women in this story are imprisoned, starved, and enslaved only adds another layer to that feeling of dread. The women who were "ravished" by these "Satyrs" are unnamed. They may be Miranda, or Isabella, or Alva. We will not know all their stories, but that unspoken horror is, at least for me, the element that truly makes this story get under my skin.

Rape as a war weapon was a reality of the Revolution, as it is with any armed conflict. Historian Alexis Coe tells the story of Abigail Palmer, a thirteen-year-old girl in nearby Pennington, New Jersey. "British soldiers straying from a nearby camp took control of the premises," Coe reports. "For three days, several soldiers raped Abigail, her teenage friends, Elizabeth and Sarah

Cain, and her aunt, Mary Phillips." Another woman, Sarah Bishop of Long Island, was captured during a raid in 1778 and taken aboard the ship of British privateers; there, she was forced to cook, clean, and "become mistress" to the entire crew. Later, she would escape and flee to Connecticut, where she lived the rest of her life as a hermit in a mountain cave, as her experience was so traumatic it rendered her incapable of rejoining society.

We know that British soldiers billeted in the houses of Flatbush and basically trashed these homes, strewing garbage and broken glass everywhere and letting their horses and other animals use the places as a latrine. We know that they raped women and humiliated men whenever they felt the urge. We also know that whatever crops the retreating American army didn't burn, they consumed; whatever cattle hadn't been already slaughtered, they devoured. According to the testimony of a woman of Flatbush who was ten years old at the time: "Homes were burned to the ground, strewn with feathers and straw, furniture taken from the houses, and a pile of ashes marked the place where before a pleasant home once stood. Scattered about were the heads of hogs that had been killed and cattle with their horns still on them. Some of the stacks of grain were burned . . ." The people of occupied Flatbush faced famine during the war, and were helpless to do anything about it. They wrung their hands and starved, much like Alva. The specter of the famished, ravaged woman can be read as a symbol of Flatbush itself, whose people were suffering and starving.

Real events that happened in Brooklyn at the time this story takes place might have put these unconscious wheels in motion, leading to generations of Flatbush folk to whisper the tale of Melrose Hall's feminine ghost to one another. If myths are indeed public dreams, then the symbolic Alva might be the repressed subconscious horrors housed deep within the substrata of Old Brooklyn's buried memories. The real-life subtext that lies beneath this Gothic drama like so many subterranean torture dungeons is the story of the war itself.

Let's go back to Alva in that secret chamber now. Is she still waiting for Axtell, wondering when he will return? How does the hunger feel; does it gnaw at her, is it nauseating? Does it make her hallucinate? Is she regretting her choices? Does she wonder why Miranda has abandoned her? Does she scream for help to try to escape the chamber, or does she try to remain quiet out of fear of bringing shame to herself and her lover? In the end, does the madness of hunger force her to claw at the walls? Does Mrs. Axtell, in her own distant bedroom, hear Alva's cries and smile cruelly, ignoring them?

Honestly, it is possible that Colonel Axtell actually *did* have a mistress in a hidden chamber and, knowing what we know about him, this may actually be a probability. Stranger things have happened in grand old country houses. But because the identities of Miranda and Alva remain nearly impossible to prove, we will probably never know the truth. Regardless of the details, the spectral figure of the starving woman certainly reflects the reality of occupied Flatbush during the Revolution. But much like Alva's true identity, this history remains mostly unspoken and forgotten because, in this country, we have preferred to portray the Revolution as a noble cause, and have elided over the unsavory details. But, at least in Brooklyn, these perspectives are part of our shared history and deserve to be remembered. Which is why the real tragedy in this story may be the loss of Melrose Hall itself.

When Anna Cora Mowatt recorded the neighborhood gossip and transmuted legend into history back in the 1850s, she was one of the last links between Revolutionary Era Flatbush and our modern age. Mowatt was a romantic, without a doubt, and the idea of living in a haunted house appealed to her. She loved her large, old-fashioned mansion, writing that

> there were dark and spacious vaults beneath the kitchens, where it was said English prisoners had been confined, and there was a secret chamber above the great ballroom to which no access could be found, save by a small window. The neighbors confirmed that a young woman had been starved to death in that chamber and that her ghost wandered at night about the house. Indeed, the report had gained such credence that nothing could have induced many of the older inhabitants of the village to pass at night beneath the haunted roof.

It's been said that Mowatt was hard up for cash at one point, and knew that nothing would help sell a book like a good ghost story, so she included supernatural details in her *Autobiography of an Actress*. (She apparently even held tea parties where she dressed in period costume and reenacted the ghost story.) We have her to thank for the name too—it was she who dubbed the house Melrose Hall after the profusion of roses that grew on the property. According to the Brooklyn *Daily Eagle*:

> The young girl [Mowatt] took a fancy to the romantic place and it was bought for her soon after [her] marriage. The entire nature of the park was changed; the dismal chamber was closed, the vaults were locked and the grounds laid out in beautiful floral designs.

Remarkably, Mowatt was only sixteen when she became the mistress of such a grand house. Mr. Mowatt apparently pursued Anna Cora when she was a mere child of fifteen, persuading her to elope with him. She speaks frankly of how strange it was to be the mistress of a grand hall at such a young age.

If it sounds more and more like an Edgar Allan Poe story at this point, perhaps that's unsurprising. Poe actually lived in New York City at the same time as Anna Mowatt; he even attended one of her public readings in 1841, and praised her, saying, "a more radiantly beautiful smile is quite impossible to achieve." In his gossipy series of who's who sketches for *Godey's Lady's Book*, "The Literati of New York City," he described her admiringly:

> The great charm of her manner is its naturalness. She looks, speaks and moves with a well-controlled impulsiveness, as different as can be conceived from the customary rant and cant, the hack conventionality of the stage. Her voice is rich and voluminous, and although by no means powerful, is so well managed as to seem so . . . Her action is distinguished by an ease and self-possession which would do credit to a veteran. Her step is the perfection of grace . . .

Much like a Poe protagonist, Mowatt eventually dabbled in mesmerism; she would admit that her entire life she had been "occasionally addicted to natural somnambulism and had been repeatedly known to walk and talk in [her] sleep," demonstrating a willingness to engage with other states of consciousness. (She eventually became a Swedenborgian.) So perhaps Mowatt was predisposed to love all things ghostly; or maybe she was just a teenage girl excited to live in a haunted house.

Mowatt's fondness for old houses would bear out in her later adulthood as well, when she became a preservationist making efforts to preserve Mount Vernon and other old homes. That this imaginative, open-minded, romantic, fanciful, and prolific chronicler happened to be the one to live in Melrose Hall is a happy coincidence for all of us, as it's one of the few times a resident documented the house while they were living there. I found one other example of this, a local man called William Brown, who resided in a renovated version of Melrose Hall in the 1890s, and was passionate about its gardens. He regularly threw the conservatories open to the public for charity events to benefit places like the Home for Incurables. He was a neighborhood booster and president of the Flatbush Trust Company under whose auspices his history of Brooklyn, which included the ghost story of Melrose Hall, was published.

Another chronicler of Melrose Hall was a woman name Jane Stone, who wrote a play, *The Romance of Melrose Hall*, in 1908. It focused on the story of Axtell's adopted daughter, Elizabeth Shipton, and her romance with Aquila Giles, who fought against Axtell in the Continental army. Stone never lived in the mansion, but was a Flatbush resident and ardent local historian. Without their intervention, the old stories may have been entirely forgotten, and we have them to thank for the many chronicles, both written and visual, of the old mansion. One only wishes they could have saved Melrose Hall.

The house was demolished in 1912, an act bemoaned by local newspapers, who noted that we were losing an architectural treasure. Who knows what could have been if only the house were allowed to stand? Surely it would have been a sight worth visiting. It makes the heart ache to think that such an architectural treasure once stood here and was allowed to be destroyed, that the stories of those who lived through the Revolution have long since been forgotten, and that few people will ever know about all those who lived and died on this unprepossessing spot in Flatbush. When the mansion was razed, the land was then turned into a development of middle-class town houses called Melrose Park. Not too long after, in 1924, a writer from Providence moved into an elegant apartment on nearby Parkside Avenue with his new wife. That writer's name was H. P. Lovecraft. If he knew about Melrose Hall, he kept it to himself.

Today the block is a mix of prewar apartments and town houses, some of which actually date back to the Melrose Park development, providing one slender link to the past. (These town houses have since been landmarked.) A vintage advertisement for these homes, called W.A.A. Brown's Duplex Houses, gives us one final instance of doubling in this uncanny story. Beneath a picture of neat, trim row houses, the copy reads "the most perfect house ever built for two families."

Nowadays, the story of Melrose Hall is mainly kept alive through ghostlore. It has made appearances on podcasts, blogs, and in *Haunted New York City* guidebooks. Perhaps it is fitting. Like a ghost story, memory is an insubstantial, imperfect, and unreliable tool, and history itself is misquotable and malleable upon interpretation. Alva is essentially unknowable, and even those personages in the tale about whom much more can be known, such as Mrs. Axtell, remain ciphers to us: We have no idea how she really felt about her husband's reputation. The terror of occupied New York during the Revolution has also largely been written out of history. The accounts of the many women who suffered at the hands of war's "riotous satyrs" are also, for the most part, vanished, and the life stories of real people like Miranda and other enslaved Brooklynites were never properly recorded in the first place. I wish there was some way to know more about Miranda, but to date haven't found anything: no census records, no mention of her name in Axtell's holdings at the New-York Historical Society, nothing. This is likely because "Miranda" is also a cipher, a made-up story or some version of it, much like Alva and Isabella. There is a real version of someone like Miranda; a Long Island historian has written a book about an enslaved woman, Elizabeth, who went by the nickname "Liss," and who would have been Miranda's contemporary. Miranda's story may never be fully known, but reading about people like Liss and using our best scholarship and imaginations will have to fill the gap for now. In Flatbush there is currently an African Burial Ground, at the corner of Church and Bedford Avenue; a visit to this location, combined perhaps with a knock at the door of the nearby historic seventeenth-century farmhouse, the Wyckoff House Museum, would be a good place to start that scholarship.

What Alva in her secret chamber thinks of all this cannot be known either.

Maybe she was never literally there at all. During the demolition, some tales say that instead of the skeleton of a woman, "workers found hundreds of bodies of small birds, which had gotten trapped there." The noises emanating from that chamber were, they said, the flapping wings of the birds trying to escape.

The skeletal remains have been lost. Melrose Hall is demolished. All we have left is the slim, frustratingly vague story of an entity we call Alva. In the end, though, her ghost story has outlasted everything else.

In a way, she's outlived the house that killed her.

The Subterranean:
The Wabasha Street Caves
and Seattle Underground

Leanna

Air moist and cool, your first steps down into the catacombs are marked by unease. The drip of water is discordant and arrhythmic when compared to the rise of your heartbeat, which begins simply as an increase in pace, but then thumping pressure lifts from your throat to your ears; an ascent as you descend, the path narrowing and constricting with every step. Turning a corner below an archway of stone, you are confronted by bones; laid out on a grave shelf, an all-too real reminder of what lies underneath your layers of skin. The subterranean realm unnervingly reminds every single body of their own finality.

The concept of something eerie, otherworldly, and dangerous below the earth is as old as time and wholly cross-cultural. Whether posited as an epic journey to the underworld or the simple aversion to being enveloped by impenetrable darkness, anxieties of being lost or trapped underground are paired with the worry that things below will find their way to the surface.

Burial traditions between lands and peoples vary widely but burial, and concerns about the process, from being buried alive to being confronted by an unearthed corpse, are part and parcel of Gothic tales, famously, viscerally utilized by Poe but echoed across innumerable others. These tropes overlap with the fears that created vampires and other monsters, the horror of finding oneself confined in diminishing spaces with failing air; subject to one's surroundings and environment, swallowed whole, cut off from the safe, breathable surface.

Admittedly, when pairing subterranean narratives with the Gothic, my heart reaches for *The Phantom of the Opera*, a particular childhood obsession of mine. Floor plans of the Paris Opera House adorned the walls of my room and Gaston Leroux's original text remains one of my favorite and most formative novels. The story was an oversized influence on me as a young performer, author, and creative. It's for the best that I burned my thousand and some pages of *Phantom* fan fiction in a suitably Victorian fit of pique when I was a teen. But I find myself struck by its parallels as I navigate tales of otherworldly undergrounds.

The story of *Phantom*, regardless of the adaptation, generally remains the same: A disfigured musical genius lives in a lair far below the Paris Opera House and terrorizes the staff in a misguided attempt to lift the object of his affection (obsession) into the limelight. Tragedy (and at least one murder) ensues. There is an enduring allure to *Phantom* that remains exceedingly complicated. In most early adaptations of *Phantom*, Erik is very much a villain. But once he was made into a far more romantic figure by Andrew Lloyd Webber's phenomenally popular musical, there was no going back. Other literary adaptations took the romance of the tale even further. I'm still not sure what I think of Susan Kay's *Phantom* all these many years later.

Erik, the Phantom, can represent our own buried dark sides, our own tortured inner self that seeks control, coming up to the surface from our subconscious lairs. The half-mask the phantom wears in Webber's stage musical offers a visual metaphor of concise duality; half angel (of music), half demon. Christine as heroine and Raoul as typical romantic hero are caught in the crucible of a domineering force that lives outside of the bounds, boundaries, and laws of polite society. The original novel offers a far more nuanced and complicated Erik at the core, a polymath who endured pain and torture to only repeat those sins in a vengeful cycle that cannot be stopped or saved. He is a pitiable but ultimately irredeemable figure, his narrative cleverly crafted by Gaston Leroux to read as a true crime account (another Gothic staple), a tale told by a mysterious, unnamed man from the East who knew this tragic figure from his youth.

The Phantom of the Opera is a cautionary tale, perhaps, but he is also utilized as a force you can't ignore. You must deal with him. You must countenance him. You must acknowledge that there's something compelling in the shadows, but if you keep the lantern at the level of your eyes you might just survive your journey to his lair. His palace and prison. There remains an equal urge to free yourself from his grasp and free him from his exile. To free oneself of their dark sides and buried desires. As above, so below.

I came of age during the Ron Perlman and Linda Hamilton *Beauty and the Beast* television series and if I'm honest, that show is a core reason behind my inevitable move to NYC years later. The show was a treasure trove of Gothic tropes, where the Beast, Vincent, lives in a subterranean labyrinth below Central Park. A mysterious guardian who watches over the heroine, he leaves poetry for the heroine to discover later once he's vanished, all taken from classic texts and read by Perlman's rich voice. (Yes, I still have the cassette tape of Perlman reading Poe, Rilke, Shakespeare, and more with classical underscoring.) Much like the Phantom's more modern narratives, this television adaptation of *Beauty and the Beast* celebrated a forbidden love and angst-ridden romance, with various levels of power dynamics, questionable boundaries, and ongoing dualities of "normal" modern, surface life versus a vibrant underground community of orphans and exiles.

The Gothic hovers constantly over the thin line between beauty, terror, expression, and repression. We are forever at the edge of an abyss; a dangerous pendulum might start swinging across that pit and our footing isn't sure. As the engine of the Gothic is dread, the tension draws out a tightrope, readers and protagonists must walk carefully, not sure which side of the line anyone is on at any given moment. Any kind of relaxation could mean a dangerous stumble *or* a passionate encounter. As the thrill-seeking parts of human nature are drawn to these extremes, the Gothic allows us to explore them in relative safety. The entities of the underground must be navigated as carefully as the dark, subterranean spaces themselves.

In addition, and more tenderly, there is always the possibility of refuge; something that the *Beauty and the Beast* show illuminated clearly. Historically, "underground" scenes have served as safe havens for those who could not always live publicly as their authentic selves. Language has changed through time, and laws have limited any legal standing of same-sex or trans couples, not to mention the threats of "gross indecency" charges; the kind that put Oscar Wilde in prison and from which point on he would never recover. But people of every identity and orientation have always existed, many doing so "underground" for their safety or that of their loved ones. Leading lives of quiet duality or simple subversions. In the shadows.

But underground does not mean invisible. Hidden history doesn't have to be suppressed history. Often those underground scenes were full of joy and celebration rather than grave fears. The Gothic is never one note; it remains a dizzying lurch from terror to ecstasy with moments of softness made all the more meaningful against the backdrop of extremity. The only constant is the possibility of danger. And in this, one must remain mindful. Vigilant.

What goes on underground stays underground until you inevitably come face to face with it. If you don't descend, it will rise to meet you; haunted either way. So, mind your head. Let your eyes adjust. Try to remember your way back to the surface. You're in their underworld now, and the spirits have a lot of business to attend to.

The Wabasha Street Caves: Saint Paul, Minnesota

Faint jazz music kisses your ear. Dim lights flicker. Except . . . there is no band. And the music system remains unplugged. And the lights *had* been turned off, weren't they? A shadow moves, but you're the only one there and you're standing still. What time is it? What decade is it?

These were questions tour guides of the Wabasha Street Caves often asked themselves at work; myself included. My own personal ghost story as experienced in an old, illegal speakeasy profoundly affected how I interacted with haunted spaces from that point on.

It was 2004 and I was a struggling actress, playwright, and aspiring writer living in Saint Paul, Minnesota, a block from Summit Avenue, where a grand stretch of Victorian homes stood testament to the wealth accrued in the city's more industrial days. I couldn't afford to live on Summit, I scraped by in a small basement studio apartment around the corner and when I wasn't working on shows that would pay me a tiny, nonunion stipend, I was giving tours of a haunted cave just across the navigable headwaters of the Mississippi River.

The quieter of the Twin Cities these days, in the 1920s and 1930s, during the time when alcohol was outlawed in the United States by Prohibition, the capital city of Minnesota was anything but well-behaved. Turning a blind eye to crime and mob rule, the mayors and police chiefs of Saint Paul allowed the bootlegging business to flourish, provided crime did not happen within Saint Paul's city limits; as noted by a "layover agreement" of non-interference engineered by Police Chief John O'Connor in the early twentieth century. Saint Paul provided a perfect stop along the illegal rum-running route flowing from Canada, south through Saint Paul and east toward the hub of Chicago. But all that alcohol needed to be stored in a cool location between transports. What better place than a cave?

The Wabasha Street Caves are a man-made cave system; a series of hollowed, arched tunnels carved into the side of the sandstone cliff face that overlooks the Mississippi flowing below. Saint Paul's initial nineteenth-century wealth and settler growth came from industries setting up shop at the northernmost point steamships could travel before the river became too shallow for large boats. The lumber industry was king and grain mills and other manufacturing held court. The initial Wabasha Street Caves were hollowed out for agriculture, serving as mushroom farms into the early twentieth century. But when alcohol became illegal, the caves became far more valuable as a speakeasy and storage location for contraband spirits. It was an illegal nightclub, distillery and storage facility all in one, pretending it was still a mushroom farm.

Once Prohibition ended in 1933, the caves changed hands and purviews several times, but always remained a hub of activity. In the 1980s and 1990s it was a nonalcoholic teen club. But the site regained its old spirits, time and again. The Bremer family, the friendly owners during my tenure as a guide, ran a construction company as their main focus, but remained interested in the history of the caves themselves. They hired local artists, history buffs, and performers as guides and opened everything back up as an event facility for weddings, dances, concerts, and tours, with the back caves used as storage for some of their construction materials and equipment.

The setup and tours I led were very simple. The star of the show is the interior: 12,000 square feet of event space, with brick and tile laid in Art Deco patterns. Across connected cave hollows, arched ceilings had been finished in stucco around the widest caverns of the cave system. Where the stucco finishing was absent, sconces and lights shone upon open, raw rock like the vaulted ceiling of a cathedral, a mix of antique and modern lighting set at various intervals to create an entirely unique atmosphere that was transportive and immersive. A magnificent, historic wooden ballroom floor was expertly maintained and still had the nice, dance-friendly bounce it had always been prized for.

We'd begin at the bar, lead people onto the historic wooden ballroom dance floor, curve them around onto a carpeted dining landing, toward a large, historic fireplace where we'd point out specific evidence of violence, trail them into the back caves used for storage, then around to the bar again before escorting them back out to the big front doors set into the rock. Outside, a wide gravel landing was leveled as a parking lot before the land fell away sharply to the river far below. As has always been my practice, I'd lead with the history and then get to what they'd all come there to hear: the ghost stories.

About that violence. It was very specific and obvious. Bullet holes scarred the fireplace. Some actual holes were present with embedded bullets; other grazing marks, indicating an actual shoot-out, could be seen scoring the rock. With the direction of the bullets, and the fact that the victims would have been against the wall, it was clear there was no escape.

As the entire operation had already been illegal at the time of the shootings, it wasn't as though there were public records of this violence or these murders. The names of the dead were not known and their bodies were not divulged, especially since this would have violated the "layover agreement" that protected mob activity. It remained the owners and guides' consensus that victims' bodies would have likely been buried in the very back of the caves where sediment and rock had collapsed in more recent times.

In the couple of years I worked there, we learned the stories that had come before us and we began to add to them like a bar tab; one uncanny moment after another. As the entire parent company juggled different sources of income and focus at that time, ghosts were always a part of the overall allure, but not the only draw to the unique space. The most important financial momentum for the caves has remained renting out the whole facility, so bartenders were as much an important core part of the staff as the daytime guides. And no matter who was working when, every month another story of something moved, seen, heard, or felt would add to the tally. "The boys" were our coworkers, of sorts. They were a part of our setup and tear-down. They were part of everything we had to double-check. The ghosts of the caves.

It only made sense to connect "the boys" with the bullet holes; the spirits of those who didn't make it back from a night underground. They were quite active, sometimes exasperatingly so. Lights would go on after we'd turn them off. When tours were being given, we were the only staff members in the entire operation on call. No one was around to mess with the lights but us, and inevitably, the electrical weirdness became so common-place we didn't even mention the unpredictability anymore, just folded in ten extra minutes to keep turning lights off that we'd already turned off once or twice before.

While I never experienced the clairaudient hauntings of jazz music wafting out from the walls when no such sound could have been made (all the power to the bar and any sound system was always shut off when we gave tours), I believed the owner when he talked about hearing it; a man not prone to believing in any supernatural phenomena. Silhouettes were seen in mirrors, and footsteps sounded in distant recesses of the caves when one was working alone and standing still.

In each main cave section, tour guides set up easels showcasing large posterboard prints of period 1920s and 1930s photographs, some from the caves themselves, some from old Saint Paul, as visual aids to help tell the town's story. Inevitably, one of those large 2-by-3-foot posterboards would be on the floor, on its side, or upside down. We'd chuckle and say "Oh, boys," and pick them back up or set them right side up. While the caves were cool, there were no drafts through their sections, so there wasn't any way these could have been blown over, much less turned upside down. But much like the lights, the shifted photos happened so regularly we folded that into our tour too, unsure if any of our audiences believed us or not, but it was our near-daily reality regardless. Other small items would be maddeningly moved, discovered in odd places or disappearing, then reappearing. Glassware. Our coats and bags. My money.

I'd been having a particularly rough week when we landed a corporate client asking for a private tour for their company. Two of my freelance writing and performing jobs hadn't paid yet and I was struggling. I gave an extra-exuberant tour for the corporate folks, staying after my allotted time to answer some insightful questions and as the group headed for the hefty front door, the organizer tipped me a $50 bill. I was tearfully grateful as I folded the bill meticulously, thinking how many packs of ramen noodles I could stock up on, and tucked the bill in the back pocket of my dress slacks, buttoning the money in safely as I went to close everything up.

One of the back photographs was on its side again after I'd righted it, but I just shook my head as I gathered it up with all the other boards, then the easels, setting them all in the rear storage cave, out of the way. I turned off each set of lights in each separate cavern. While we all got very used to walking the spaces with only emergency exit lights guiding our way, it unnerved us every time, because we always felt like we were being watched; especially that last darkened walk from the rear storage caves to the front foyer space. No matter how many times we gave tours, no matter how used to the spaces we'd become, suddenly in the darkness, when the shadows drew claustrophobically close, all became foreign. I'd always make that last, dim pass at a clip. I darted to the coat check near the front door to gather my things and went to put that $50 in my wallet.

It was not in my pocket.

I panicked. I had made particular care to *button* it into the pocket. I hadn't made any kind of movement that could have launched it out from its spot, but I retraced my steps, heart pounding. I turned all the lights back on. I coursed the ballroom. The bar area. The dining area. The fireplace. The rear storage cave. Nothing. I made three full passes across every part of the venue I had moved through. Nothing. I didn't know what else to do but beg.

I'd been collecting ghost stories my whole life; always eager to talk with people about their own personal hauntings and my own, accruing points of commonality as I went, gathering empirical data about effective communication if a situation necessitated it. Generally, these exchanges would be about simple, almost mundane hauntings; or something privately meaningful like a loved one coming to say goodbye in a dream. Not the stuff of Hollywood movies, just random, small, odd things that would happen without any rational explanation, but didn't have a particular storyline. In the case of frequently active locations, it seemed to me that spirits wanted to be acknowledged and might prove more responsive if addressed. Having nothing else to lose, I just stood at the centermost part of the cavern system and blurted out, in a tumult of frazzled emotion: "Boys, I know money was part of your whole deal and you probably died because something went wrong with it, and for that, I'm sorry, but since you know how important it is, and that I am corporeal; this *living* body needs to be able to eat, buy groceries. Guys, please, I'm broke."

Tired, fighting back tears, I made one last dejected pass through the caverns.

Something pale caught my eye on the red carpet of the dining area. Over by the fireplace. Something that hadn't been there the last pass through. I approached slowly.

There it was.

My $50 bill. Lying crisp and flat as if it had never been folded.

Stretched out *right* below the bullet holes.

I clasped one hand on my heart to try to get it to stop racing, the other seized the money. This time I shoved it into my bra. In retrospect, I realize that might have been seen as an otherworldly act of flirtation, but I had to get to play rehearsal. I was already late and I wanted to feel the safety of that bill against my actual skin this time.

"Thank you, boys, you are gentlemen after all. I'll see you next week."

The boys never messed with my money again (to be fair, though, I never got that good of a tip again). But from that point on, I'd talk to them a bit more; say hello and goodbye, acknowledging verbally if they'd shifted something we'd put into a specific place. Tell them about my day. I'd be the only one there once the tour ended, so if it seemed like I was talking to myself, no one but me would know. Being relational to the spirits informed how I handled hauntings from then on, when I encounter them in other historic spaces across the country. It informed advice I give to others who seek out my opinion on handling prankster ghosts who love to make things disappear. The suggestion of exasperated but direct pleas has worked for other friends. Anecdotal evidences accrue. Ghosts want to be acknowledged. They might want company too; at least, some echo of that once-vibrant life; the sought and the seeking.

Isn't that relatable? Isn't that what one might have gone to a speakeasy for in the 1920s or 1930s? Connection? Camaraderie? Sure, a speakeasy centered around alcohol, but nightlife is relational. Community in the underground; where music, dancing, innovative fashion, artistic creativity, and socializing are all a critical part of the draw. Often, the cultures of underground, nightlife scenes throughout history may prove more welcoming and diverse, where relationships across gender, class, cultural, or racial delineations could more safely flourish in an arena that already had to take care and keep otherwise quiet.

But, as with everything, there are layers below the surface.

Prohibition was indeed a failed American experiment that created a great deal of unchecked mob violence in its wake, but I think it's very important to remember that many of those who supported banning alcohol didn't do so because they were prudes, they were doing it for their survival. The temperance movement became as popular as it was in the early twentieth century because women had little recourse against domestic violence.

Animal, child, and domestic or spousal abuse laws only went into effect in the 1860s once Henry Bergh and his American Society for the Prevention of Cruelty to Animals, after campaigning for decades, were able to statistically correlate and prove interconnected levels of animal abuse, child, and spousal abuse to court systems. Similarly to Bergh and his allies, the temperance movement correlated levels of substance abuse and domestic abuse, enlisting religious groups and suffragists into a wider holistic plea for temperance and human rights. The movement happened because of violence to begin with. It ended because folks just kept drinking anyway, finding ways around it, enabling mob control by proxy. There was always violence in the story somehow, and my sentimental, romantic heart wishes it didn't have to have played out that way.

While the bullet holes in that cave system were always the thing folks leaned in most closely to see, after I started talking to "the boys" I took more care with how I revealed the telltale signs of violence in the fireplace bricks. I reminded my guests that there was once a body sitting between where they stood and that stone mantel. These were someone's loved ones who didn't come back from a night underground. Who likely never got resolution. It didn't solve anything; my trying to humanize the story, but it did help me navigate the dizzying lurch of the Gothic, from a carefree speakeasy atmosphere to the terror of murder. We, as a species, are fascinated with violence. I saw it in every eye that widened as it approached the bullet holes. Every fingertip that reached out toward those breaches of the stone. And our ghostlore is steeped in violence, our country's past is steeped in it, and so we must wrestle with it layer by layer and be in community with victims, listening to those displaced and disenfranchised in hopes of understanding their needs, in hopes of breaking cycles of nightmares; to heed the cautionary tales. All too aware of the skeletons beneath all our skins. The only way out from the underground is through.

The Seattle Underground

Below the streets of downtown Seattle is another Seattle. A whole story's worth. Between twenty to thirty blocks of downtown have an entire level that was sunken deliberately by settler city planners who did not seem to understand anything about how tides or sea levels worked and clearly thought themselves above the steadfast expertise of the native Duwamish, who had not built on the Sound.

Arthur Denny, a "founding father" of the city, reportedly wrote, regarding setting some of Seattle's first settler foundations, that they would begin building in earnest "when it stops raining." This is how our Underground Tour guide, Clay, began the tour, and the international crowd all laughed heartily. He insisted that Seattle spirit means sticking with a terrible idea.

As a reset to poor initial planning, leaders of the struggling city, who took its name from the native leader but not his wisdom, advised everyone to rebuild after the Great Fire of 1889 (in which the entire downtown burned, but miraculously no one died) in such a way that would allow the first story of all downtown buildings to sink, pressing the ill-advised layers of sawdust fill further down; a sinking ship city leaders prayed would hit bottom. It has, mostly, they think, but I'll say that the extensive, shifting cracks across the cement that serves as a "floor" don't inspire confidence. While no one died in the great fire, as the city residents spent years getting in and out of buildings via ladders attached to the second floor while the first floor continued its steady descent, many men died trying to exit taverns while drunk, falling from second-floor ladders to their deaths. (The city marked these as "accidental suicides" in their records.)

The jokes really write themselves throughout the tour, because in addition to the city planners seemingly understanding nothing about tidal physics or about the near-constant levels of rainfall, their installation of plumbing wasn't faring any better. The scatological humor was on parade as we walked by examples of "crappers" that were left to sink below the city surface as long-lost relics, named for the engineer, inventor, and public sanitation advocate Thomas Crapper, who created some of the first toilets (I thought this was just another of our affable tour guide's jokes until I saw the words "the Venerable Crapper" delicately painted or stamped as factory marks on toilet bowls and wall-mounted water tanks). With the changing of the tides and pressures on the pipes, toilets could instead become fountains and city ordinances regulated when one could or could not flush their crappers.

In the 1960s, when Underground Tour founder Bill Speidel began clamoring for more historical awareness as downtown's nineteenth-century Pioneer Square stood on the brink of demolition, by 1965, he wasn't sure if anyone would be interested in exploring the city's odd, labyrinthine, underground secrets. The idea of a whole section of Seattle beneath the streets was thought to be myth and urban legend. But Speidel gained access points and began sharing his findings; that there were indeed countless interconnected passages available to wander, many of which could be navigated by daylight due to manganese-tinted glass set into sections of still-extant nineteenth-century sidewalk on the street level, from which small, unintentional terrariums of ferns had sprouted below. For his first tour on "Know Your Seattle Day," five hundred came out. Within the next few years, over 100,000 people petitioned the city for preservation of Pioneer Square as a historic district and by 1970, they had won. Speidel's Underground Tour company now rents out the sunken first floor walkways from the buildings above them and while only part of that near-thirty-block section is accessible, one gets a very uncanny, inimitable experience filing down below the ground. I noted, with great pride in my professions, that it took a storyteller and tour guide to preserve an entire swath of city history, a battle that held fast and prevailed against very powerful special interests that would have rather erected cement parking garages than preserve an inch of nineteenth-century brick.

As our tour guide led us down and through the meandering blocks of skids, narrow stairs, steel supports, cement bulkheads, old facings, and nineteenth-century columns, I was particularly struck by the inadvertent, entirely chaotic time-capsule nature of what's been left down there through the years. A whole city's basement of lost things. Earthquake damage; when antique decoration, cast-iron facades, and sandstone flourishes had simply fallen to the ground, they were then scrapped down below and forgotten. Beautiful details through centuries, from typewriters to Art Deco swirls and dissolving finials, to whole telephone booths to antique car parts, old electrical generators to antique baby prams (particularly unsettling) and tools of every kind and era, it just seemed to go on and on. With no order to the chaos. The haphazard and the once-useful was made useless but sat there still, as time and technology rolled on. Alleys of misfit ephemera not quite landfill, not quite trash, just set aside with no sense of ownership anymore; the Underground has claimed it as its own. The sunken-ship feeling all around me seemed almost cruel in nature, as every corridor and space we moved through was deliberately designated to be slowly buried and remain forgotten; damned from the start.

And yet, I couldn't help but feel there remained slips of life in all that scrap that had been left behind; an odd, static energy pulsing in the dim light and the dank air, a discordant hum that I couldn't quite get out of my ears.

Claustrophobia, unease with narrow descents, the clutter of everything around; there's a lot of ready-made phobias and discomforts that exist in this strange bit of history. As I turned corners and tried to think of what city block we might be under, I couldn't tell. I thought how terrifying it would be to get stuck down there. How easy it would be to get lost—to *remain* lost, I should say; I was lost the moment we turned our first underground tunnel corner. I hurried through the narrowest parts of the experience; looking reflexively into every shadow to see if something stared back. I wondered if anything was aware of our presence just as I was aware of the strange, decrepit immortality the whole labyrinthine amalgam took on. A catacomb of city bones. As I tend to think of places, spaces, cities, and buildings as having their own spirit, the feeling of morbid curiosity while still trying to be respectful in a graveyard felt like the same Gothically tinged tightrope-walk.

One of the most haunting visuals for me was all the antique windows; nineteenth- and early-twentieth-century open frames, some with broken glass, some with full panes, arched and full of faded beauty, stacked against various parts of the subterranean walls. If eyes are the windows to the soul, these eyes of buildings were all put out at one point or another, removed and now only skeletal scraps remained of what once would have been a lovely threshold by which to see the world. It made me ache to look at them; wide, unblinking eyes lying in wait for a restorative day that would never come.

It felt like we were walking the grooves of a cluttered, distracted mind, where memories had been swept into tangled piles. The soul longs for sense and order. One cannot find it down there. Often a Gothic protagonist becomes lost to a chaotic environment and must try to find their way toward abject reality again. I'm a nonlinear thinker and even this was too much for me to take on as a thought experiment because there wasn't one narrative here; we were walking through a whole city's disordered subconscious.

Halfway through, our guide paused at a section of Underground where a tall set of metal bars were bent and rent open like a screaming maw. A rusted vault space from a former bank could be glimpsed in the dim light beyond us; where a banker had been shot during the Prohibition era. His ghost still reportedly makes his final rounds, his spirit maintaining a cyclical loop of last moments. A luminous but shadowy figure flits in and out around bent and gnarled metal, his death a psychic imprint on the Underground landscape. And so we're back to violence again; echoing out from that particular, fraught, and often lawless Prohibition era of big business driven by secrecy and illicit goings-on, nightlife raging in the shadows. I thought of "the boys" back in Minnesota and yearned to know more about those souls than just the violences done to them and the echoes they've become, but that's all we have to go on; that they were shot.

Our guide went on to tell us that the Prohibition era also brought another concern into the tunnels: the plague. The *actual* bubonic plague, as carried by rats, surged in Seattle during the 1920s and early 1930s due to the number of speakeasies, brothels, and illegal liquor stills belowground. We were told to mind our step, that rats were still common, and that a previous guide had to pause for a relative parade ahead of his recent tour. The imprint of nightlife and its dangers, community and peril belowground, pleasure and pain, was a parallel to the work and history in Saint Paul. Full circle.

I began to fully understand why my dear friend Cherie Priest felt I needed to experience this place; and how it fed right into the kinds of narratives this book would cover. A talented, bestselling author of horror, suspense, historical fantasy, and Gothic-themed fiction, Cherie is as magnificent a host and guide to the city as she is a writer. We've talked for years about shared tropes in our fiction, about being "elder goths" navigating different cities through the years, and I wanted to know what the Seattle Underground meant to her, because while I knew it factored directly into books of hers like *Boneshaker*, it also seemed to mean more than just a stranger-than-fiction curiosity. She had this to say in response to my asking her about why the Underground remains dear to her, especially as a fellow goth:

"I ended up in Seattle, where I was assured the gothing was easier. In many ways, that's true—for nine months out of the year, the weather is pretty gross and perfect for bundling up in black and wearing boots. This was an adjustment for me. I still had some black and I still had some boots, but by the time I ended up out here I'd been living in Tennessee for years—and I didn't have enough to keep me dressed, dry, and warm for the whole year. It took some time to recalibrate.

"I won't lie: I had a hard time settling in. But there were a handful of places that really called to me—vintage theaters the Egyptian on Capitol Hill, and the Neptune in the U District. Volunteer Park and all its offerings, for I lived nearby. And then, of course, there was the Seattle Underground.

"These days I have a whole system for playing tour guide with out-of-town guests. I start at the old water tower in Volunteer Park, and show my guests the city from the top of a tower on top of a hill. And then I take them on the Underground Tour, to show them the city from the underside. To show them the roots.

"The Seattle Underground is about as far away from Tampa as you can get, but somehow, it still feels like it's become part of my DNA—as someone who's always plugged in to the darker side of genre, life, and days gone by.

"Some of the reasons are obvious. It's cool, dark, moist, and spooky—chock-full of regional history that's too weird to be made up. A city was inadvisably built on a low mud plain beside the ocean, in a land where it rains for most of the year. The city burned down, and when it was built again, people wanted flushing toilets and a drainage system that didn't leak raw sewage from overhead. They didn't want horses to drown in the streets (a real thing that happened, supposedly).

"But some of the reasons are less obvious, and more mythic. Think about it in archetypal terms: a sinking city that burns before it can drown, and when it rises again (unevenly, an unsteady phoenix), it stands atop a literal underworld beneath the streets. This particular underworld was as wonderful and terrible as any the Greeks ever conceived, with everything from high finance to child sex workers happening down there in the dark. No one knows how many people died under the sidewalks over the years—least of all during the time when it was officially sealed off and condemned in the early twentieth century . . . when it went Full Crime and became more like a simple hell than a tiered and nuanced Hades.

"But that's mythic too, isn't it? We inter our beloved dead; we bury our wicked sins and sinners underground, without a headstone or marker to remark them. We lose them entirely if we're able, and what better place to do that than within such catacombs? For ultimately, the Seattle Underground is a humid, chilly, subterranean dumping ground for a city's civic secrets and private sins. If you go, if you take the tour . . . you will follow your guide like Beatrice and Virgil. Even Christ was said to visit hell on one occasion, and in Matthew, chapter four, He called for believers to follow in His footsteps.

"So stay on the paths. Watch for rats. Laugh politely at the guide's punch lines (they're working for tips). How else can we be honest about where we came from?"

Hers was the lingering existential question that stuck with me throughout the tour. Energetically, I felt like there was still unfinished business. As Cherie and I exited out into a gallery space with scads of fascinating nineteenth-century ephemera that had been found in the Underground through the years, those notable enough to restore to museum-quality exhibition (including a whole printing press Terry Pratchett had been moved to write about), we chatted with our tour guide and perused odd, ghostly photographs taken in Underground corridors through the years where unmistakable forms were visible in misty, hazy light that was disconnected and unrelated to the shafts or casting of any natural illumination. But something was there nonetheless; floating amid the rubble and the lost treasures.

Exiting back up into the gray light of the Seattle afternoon, my eye fell across the street, drawn by the *1890* year prominently displayed on the signage of the Merchant's Cafe. Cherie was quick to note that it was famously haunted.

As we entered, I took in the general Victorian décor of the place, replete with amber stained-glass details and an enormous wooden bar. I ordered drinks right away. As our bartender served us, I was forthcoming: "So, I write about ghosts and I hear this place is haunted." Without missing a beat, she reached behind the bar and held out a well-worn three-ring binder as if she'd handed it over a thousand times.

Cherie and I took the compilation of what appears to be about ten years' worth of notes over to a table to sift through. Handwritten or typed accounts, pictures, bartender notes scrawled on lined paper, and personal anecdotes as printed out by the current owners, scrawled sketches from sensitives; it was just as chaotic a random, disorganized assortment as everything down in the Underground passages we'd just walked. What stood out most to me was a photograph of a host of broken liquor bottles, shattered on the cellar floor. The picture was taken by the owners who had arrived to open their bar only to find their entire stock broken across the floor when no one had been downstairs. The Merchant's Cafe's most consistent spectral account is of an unfriendly presence in the cellar, unseen hands pushing, shoving visitors or staff, exuding an oppressively unfriendly feeling, especially against women. The binder of ghost stories seemed to credit the unfriendly downstairs entity for this explosive act against their liquor stores. The owner said the entity seemed to calm down, in her experience, once she, after deigning to be a bit flirtatious while alone in the cellar, left out a shot of whiskey as a sort of peace offering.

The Merchant's Cafe cellar was part of the city's plan of sinking the first stories, the café founded just after the fire, and they utilize that sunken space as many businesses do, cordoning off their unconventionally designed basements, but one could see from certain vantage points how that cellar connected to the greater labyrinth of other former first floors beyond. Brick and antique wrought iron give the entire downstairs a historic look that I'm sure was meant to be atmospheric, but ended up feeling more like a prison cell.

Palpably, it was as if the past was at odds with the present as Cherie and I sat down there. It was *too* cold in that downstairs space; indeed unfriendly, unwelcoming, and unnerving. Not just a basement chill, but something more bone-deep. Cherie took a photo in the hallway going toward the restroom, where black walls and a trippy swirl of a scuffed floor led to a narrow door that felt particularly odd. Later, in going over the photos, she texted me her dark hallway shot. A strange green glow, captured mid-movement, can be seen along the wall, as if moving toward her, beside her. There were no reflective surfaces there, nothing in her phone or along the walls that could have created that green glitch. She and I were the only people downstairs. But *something* evidently noticed.

It waited down there just like those odd, misty swaths of light captured in photographs showcased at the end of the tour, hovering in the patchwork quilt of haunted space, all of it connected, all cold and dim and waiting. A purgatorial liminal space lost to time. A haphazard, forced solution born of poor planning and raging fires, a quirky, ongoing, elaborate oddity. In walking the bones, it felt like we were seeing a reflection of our own messy history; our own cluttered minds. All we've left behind and shoved below, unresolved, layered, and strange, inviting and yet repulsing. Stacks of things lined up, unused and unthought until we stumble over them again.

I believe it's a demonstrable public good that the Seattle Underground exists, not just as a unique bit of haunted, weird history but as a thought experiment, forcing us to descend into an immersive staging ground of our own anxieties, discombobulating us by turning a whole city on its head. The Gothic is always atmospheric, and both the haunted cave that's remained so dear to me through the years and this elaborate quirk of Seattle history are inescapable: They drag you under into another world. While you're there, these spaces remind you that it's sometimes been a very violent history, and let you go again if you can find your way back. Gothic atmosphere leaves the reader, viewer, and protagonist with a souvenir of unease that lingers long after emergence into the bright day; no longer able to ignore all the shadows still lurking below.

Water Cures and Electric Baths: Madwomen in the Attic

Andrea

The first American hospital dedicated exclusively to the treatment of the mentally ill was the Public Hospital of Williamsburg, Virginia. Also known as Eastern State Hospital or Eastern Lunatic Asylum, it opened its doors on October 12, 1773. Designed to humanely restore patients to "reason" and reorder their disordered minds, the hospital had a modern, forward-thinking quality much in line with current Enlightenment-era improvements in medical treatments for the insane, as it occurred to people that shackling, starving, beating, and entrapping sick people in dank, lightless cells might not be the healthiest or most humane thing in the world. The asylum's first superintendent was John Minson Galt, a sensitive and erudite man who by all accounts cared deeply about his patients.[1] In the nineteenth century, his son John Minson Galt II succeeded him as superintendent and continued in this vein, advocating for occupational therapy, music and bibliotherapy, and recreation. When the Civil War broke out, Galt II was prevented from entering his own hospital, which had been quartered for troops, and he died shortly thereafter. His official cause of death was "indigestion," possibly exacerbated by stress ("his anxiety about the patients was so great that he could neither eat nor sleep for several days and nights and it is thought that this caused his death").[2] Some accounts claim he took his own life, but there is nothing to substantiate this. All in all, the nation's first asylum doesn't seem to be a very frightening or haunted place. Also, it's still an active hospital with a solid 2.2 stars on Google.

So, no ghosts in the Public Hospital that we know of, but I did happen to find one very famous allegedly "insane" ghost in Colonial Williamsburg whose tale I find decidedly captivating. Lucy Ludwell was born in Virginia in 1752, the daughter of a wealthy and socially prominent citizen (they kept company with the likes of Thomas Jefferson). When Lucy was only five or six years old, her mother died, leaving her and her two sisters half-orphans. The girls were remanded to the care of an enslaved woman called Cress, who was apparently so devoted to the girls that she "sacrificed her life" for them in a frustratingly unspecified manner. While nobody is sure exactly what the "sacrifice" was, for the records are unclear, one thing we do know is that both her daughters were manumitted after Cress's death.

Sometime after this, around 1760, Lucy traveled to London with her father, and they lived there for years, riding out the American Revolution in England. They continued moving in the upper echelons of society there, and counted Samuel Johnson and other luminaries among their social circle. Lucy's father fell ill and passed away, and Lucy married a business associate of his, John Paradise, who was ten years her senior. She was only seventeen at the time.

We don't know much about the nature of their relationship, except that Mr. Paradise was apparently not very good with money, and that the family had continuous financial struggles because of it. Lucy lived abroad most of her adult life. She raised one daughter, also named Lucy, and did not return to the United States until around 1805, following the death of her husband. She was about fifty-two years old at the time.

When Lucy returned to Williamsburg, she took up residence in the family's house in town, a redbrick Georgian structure on a main thoroughfare. The house, which still stands, is an impressive structure, laid in Flemish bond, windows trimmed in merry red, and abutted by a capacious covered porch. It was called by the family, perhaps to distinguish it from their various plantations, the Brick House. The house technically belonged to Lucy's nieces, with whom she resided.

It was here that things took a turn for Lucy. Up until that point, she'd kept it all together admirably. She'd weathered the loss of her mother and of Cress, she'd weathered exile during wartime, extended separation from her family in the States, marriage to a man who wasn't very financially savvy, and return to Virginia from overseas when she was already well into what would have been considered a fairly old age back then (and starting over is a big leap of faith at any age). Now, cash poor, she relied on the charity of family and the good standing of their name to maintain appearances, and it seems that at some point she cracked under the strain of it all.

Lucy, who enjoyed being called "Madam" by her neighbors, held herself aloof while striding around town imperiously in borrowed finery—apparently, she had a tendency to "borrow" clothes and hats from her friends, possibly without them knowing—as if to remind everyone that she came from something quite above the usual common stock. When her few friends, or perhaps curiosity-seekers, came to visit her, it is said that she seated them beside her in a carriage she'd had reassembled on the rear porch, and while they conversed, she would have a servant hold the traces and jounce the carriage up and down, taking her visitor on an unnerving journey to nowhere.

Most notably, she was said to have been absolutely obsessed with cleanliness and took six to eight baths a day. Baths, you say? Yes. I can attest, as one of the 2 percent of women who has suffered postpartum OCD: the cleaning is real. Whether it's eight baths a day or scrubbing your bathroom ceiling with a Swiffer and bleach, the cliché is no joke. (Yes, you read that right: scrubbing *the ceiling.*)

Finally, in 1812, her nieces decided this cavalcade of eccentricities must come to an end, and after having her assessed by three aldermen, Lucy was committed to the state asylum. She died there in 1814.

The Brick House was one of the first landmarked historic houses in Colonial Williamsburg. It is a private residence now and not open to the public. During its restoration by John D. Rockefeller, Jr., who purchased and refurbished the property, it was inhabited by a caretaker, Rudolph Bares, and his wife Pauline. They are the origin point for most of the Lucy Ludwell ghost stories, for they are the ones who first claimed they heard the sound of water running and dripping in an unoccupied upstairs bathroom while they were downstairs and nowhere near the tub. They could hear water splashing, they said, but when they went upstairs to investigate, the tub was "bone dry." At first, they were confused and startled, but after a while they got used to their phantom bather. They soon learned to laugh it off, saying, "It must be Lucy pouring a bath for herself."

Lucy is one of those rare "substantial" ghosts, whose life has been documented and about whom we have a lot of detailed, fact-checkable information. While some of the details of her story are no doubt embroidered, the basic facts are her life are as I've described them. And it is irrefutable that she entered the asylum in 1812 and died there in 1814. (Ghost tours sometimes like to recount that she died by suicide there, but there is no proof to this claim.) When we write about ghost stories like this, nine times out of ten we find tales of "madness" to be greatly exaggerated, so it's interesting to have one that's verified. Interesting, but no less sad. It's impossible to read Lucy's story without a good dash of pathos. The poor girl was orphaned, then lost a woman she would likely have come to regard as a substitute mother, possibly in a violent or traumatic way. What Cress could have done that would've merited being called a "sacrifice" of her life we can only surmise, but it certainly couldn't have been pleasant. If this woman took a bullet for the little Ludwell girls, chances are Lucy saw it.

What Cress's daughters thought of it, we don't know: nobody documented their reaction to their mother's death either.

Lucy, still young, was then wrenched away from her girlhood home, passed into the care of a stranger when her father died, and then found herself married to her father's associate, a much older man, when she was still little more than a child herself. There's no evidence the marriage was forced upon her, but it has the hallmarks of a strategic or convenient alliance, or perhaps of a girl without parents trying to fill an emotional void. Either way, far more sad than romantic.

Then there was her personality. Lucy could sometimes be difficult. She was described as the "'beautiful and lively American' whose daring and high temper offended some but charmed many," as well as "eccentric, capricious, whimsical, odd" and—most telling of all—"unique."[3] Combined with the exaggerated hauteur of her manner, it is unsurprising that people whispered about her. Of course, all her posturing is so clearly a front for a high-strung, deeply insecure, frightened, aging woman alone in the world that it's utterly heartbreaking. I picture her toward the end, her face white with powder, looking a bit like Bette Davis in *What Ever Happened to Baby Jane*? It's the face I think all women secretly fear they will have one day, when our outsides catch up with our insides and all our years of secret, inner terror and anxiety creep into the cracks on our upper lips spidered by errant lipstick, or leak out the corners of our eyes, where mascara and eyeliner gather to mock our attempts to mimic youth. We will either become grotesque or invisible, a figure of horror in a bad indie movie, or simply a ghost out in the world. And if we lack money, then what? There's a label for that specific female fear: Bag Lady Syndrome. Will we become Eleanor Abernathy, aka the Crazy Cat Lady, from *The Simpsons*? Will we become Edie Bouvier Beale in *Grey Gardens*? (Though Big Edie and Little Edie Beale, with their rambling, ramshackle home, charmingly outlandish sartorial choices, and wistful eccentricities, *are* highly lovable.)

That Lucy was mentally unstable, there is no doubt. Even her most conscientious and sober biographers acknowledge this sad fact. But it's also worth noting that part of the gossip about her might have been chalked up to the fact that she practiced Eastern Orthodox Christianity, which was unusual at the time. (It may also have been why the family went to England prior to the Revolutionary War.) And she was very devout; an 1805 letter from her to a friend (Thomas Jefferson, no big deal) begins "I am well, thanks to the grace of God and the prayers of my spiritual father, the Reverend Jakov Smirnov." I imagine in a mostly Protestant society, this may have raised eyebrows, set tongues wagging, and been fodder for (ahem) jokes.

The volunteers at the nonprofit Ludwell Association have dedicated their time to keeping the memory of Lucy's father alive, and boosting the profile of this Eastern Orthodox family. They also address Lucy's story in philosophical, sympathetic, and clear-eyed terms, noting that it's important to keep her real story and the facts her life at the forefront in order to counteract the sensationalism of all the many ghost tours that gather before the Ludwell mansion most nights. They want her not to be reduced to a mere "Mad Lucy," but to have the fullness of her humanity acknowledged, writing on their blog, "it's much easier to perpetuate stories of 'Mad Lucy' than to look at her as a person and ask—what was her faith? What was her deep belief in salvation beyond the grave?" Meanwhile, a playwright has written a musical about her called *MADam LUCY, deceased*, which played at Virginia's College of William and Mary in October 2023. It's heartening to see that she is remembered. For my part, I find it fascinating that this high-spirited woman and her unusual, bath-taking ghost have a verifiable connection to our country's very first insane asylum, her ghost story interweaving itself into our real medical history.

The way we channel our anxieties about mental health into the world of ghostlore can be clarified by looking at it through a Gothic lens. Our intense fascination with hospitals and asylums as literally and figuratively haunted locations has a lot to do with the way we assign symbolism and stories to real lives and places, our human impulse to order a chaotic world.

The haunted asylum is one of the staples of American ghostlore, for good or for ill. Some think the whole idea atrocious, exploitative, ableist, and insulting. Others think there may be a place for ghost tours of former mental hospitals as a way to confront and metabolize our own fears. The famed Trans-Allegheny Lunatic Asylum in West Virginia threads the needle by offering both historic tours and haunted experiences, and disallowing any discussion of the paranormal on the history tours, out of respect. I can tell you with a fair amount of certainty that the haunted experiences float the historical ones financially. The maintenance of the asylum as a publicly accessible historic site would be virtually impossible without the revenue generated by paranormal tourism.

It's worth pointing out that, in keeping with the rest of American paranormal culture, the asylums offering ghost tours currently focus mostly on the experience of white Americans, probably in part because mental hospitals of the era were usually segregated. Former mental hospitals that historically served the Black population, like Crownsville Hospital Center, in Maryland, and Central State Hospital, in Virginia, are not yet, as of this writing, active participants in the paranormal tourism industry. At my own company, Boroughs of the Dead, I've made a choice to offer a tour of Roosevelt Island in New York City as a history tour instead of a ghost walk, yet many people take it mistakenly thinking it's exactly that, even though I explicitly label it as a history tour on my website. Roosevelt Island, with its smallpox hospital ruins and former insane asylum—now luxury condos—did not seem an appropriate place, to me, for a ghost tour. Nor does the former Willowbrook State School in Staten Island, though I have had many requests for it. Willowbrook was a horrible place, rife with abuses. The torture of mentally ill people and developmentally disabled children, and the forcible confinement of women, is just too much for me.

I'm reluctant to visit and be in these places. My own general dislike of institutional settings, particularly hospitals, has no basis in any specific life event—I'd never even stayed overnight in a hospital until I gave birth at the age of thirty-seven. It's probably just a common fear and I don't think too much about it, but crossing the threshold of a prison, asylum, or hospital always gives me a visceral reaction. It's probably related to my fairly severe claustrophobia and general hatred of authority; a person like me has strong reactions to any type of confinement and restriction. I'd rather walk in a thunderstorm than tolerate a slow-crawling subway train, climb six flights of stairs before I'd willingly enter an elevator. The idea of being trapped *anywhere* fills me with panic; the idea of being forcibly entrapped somewhere and dosed with Thorazine fills me, and probably everyone on earth, with genuine terror. Hence our obsession with revisiting these horror-haunted places.

The fact that the Trans-Allegheny Lunatic Asylum separates their ghost and history tours is very telling. There are plenty of other people like me who want to understand the history of these places and then get the hell out of there before dark. None of which is to say that there are no horrors on the history tour: One journalist wrote of a recent visit to Trans-Allegheny, "the image that haunts me most was found in the exhibit of patient art. It's a child's drawing done in marker depicting a stick-figure man with his hands around a child's neck and the stilted text: 'Father choking Shawn.'" This is heartbreaking and frankly makes me feel like ghosts are superfluous. But cultural historian Troy Rondinone felt that an overnight ghost hunt helped him process the experience: "We, as a society, created these horrors," he writes on the website *Atlas Obscura*, "in allowing the overcrowding and decline of places of healing, in the stigmatization of people with mental illness, in the mistreatment of even the staff. Something about spending the night in the facility let me trace this path of hope and despair for myself."

This impulse to tour asylums has been with us since the days of Bedlam. And since that time, the asylum has been fertile ground for art and fiction that help us process the fears and anxieties we all have concerning these spaces. The Gothic, which specializes in sounding the depths of the human soul, has always had a significant psychological component, and altered states, including madness and insanity, are staples of the genre.

Gothic grandaddy Edgar Allan Poe himself used to stroll up to Manhattan's Bloomingdale Insane Asylum, now the site of Columbia University, when he lived in New York City in the 1840s. He was friends with its superintendent, and they no doubt had many fascinating conversations on the latest in medical advancements, as Poe was always interested in that sort of thing. It's possible his visits to the asylum and his chats with its superintendent inspired his short story "The System of Doctor Tarr and Professor Fether," which was published in 1845. I won't spoil the story for you if you haven't read it, but I'll recommend it (and it was made into a pretty decent film adaptation with Ben Kingsley called *Stonehearst Asylum*, which I also recommend). It's a very humorous story overall, and it's interesting that Poe would take a topic that frightens most of us intensely and try to be breezy about it. Possibly he was preemptively staving off accusations of his own insanity.

Bloomingdale Insane Asylum was a fairly nice-looking place, actually, surrounded by a bucolic and pastoral landscape, approachable by wide, well-groomed roads, and sensibly Georgian in its architecture. None of that High Victorian Gothic Kirkbride stuff here, so well-intentioned, but unfortunate now that it evokes nothing so much as a haunted castle. In this context, neo-Gothic architecture did not age well. Bloomingdale no longer stands, though one of its buildings, Buell Hall, survives. It is the asylum's only surviving structure.[4] To be totally honest, just based off the etchings I've seen, Bloomingdale looks kind of . . . nice. There are plenty of days when I'm fighting for survival in New York City that I think, "Huh, that would be restful."

Rest from the relentless grind of capitalism is one thing, but enforced rest is another. Charlotte Perkins Gilman was famously told "never to touch pen, brush, or pencil again" during her experience of postpartum depression, and equally famously stated "I went home and obeyed those directions for some three months, and came so near the borderline of utter mental ruin that I could see over." As a self-employed person who had exactly zero days of maternity leave, I might have been into the idea of a little rest cure, but I take her point. Her classic weird tale "The Yellow Wallpaper" was born of this enforced ennui, cementing the link between female madness and oppressive or troubled domesticity. "The Yellow Wallpaper," with its nameless trapped narrator, is a cornerstone of the female Gothic and the genre's feminist treatment of mental illness in fiction. Along with *Jane Eyre* and that novel's legendary madwoman in the attic, Bertha Mason, we can see how forcible confinement was a major source of terror to Victorian women. And we all know how easily and capriciously such confinement could be induced: menstruation, masturbation, excessive horseback riding, talking too much, literally anything that popped into your husband's head could be considered grounds for institutionalization—or just chucking you in the nearest attic. Sometimes when I hear *Jane Eyre* stans defend Mr. Rochester's decision to keep Bertha Mason locked in the attic ("Because asylums back then were, like, terrible!") my mind drifts to Charlotte Perkins Gilman and I wonder what she would say. Hell, I wonder what Bertha Mason would say.

I'm not the only person to wonder about *that*, of course. Jean Rhys's 1966 prequel to *Jane Eyre*, *Wide Sargasso Sea*, is told from Bertha Mason's perspective before she becomes Mrs. Rochester, and I recommend it highly, if you haven't gotten around to it already. Having fully absorbed Bertha's story from both sides, both the original novel and the Jean Rhys follow-up, it's clear to me now that she is even more fundamentally significant to the American Gothic than I'd originally thought. Bertha's is a story of the Americas. The Gothic, as we've pointed out a lot in this book, emerged contemporaneously with the height of the transatlantic slave trade, and its legacy stains the shared history of Britain and America. The specter of this guilt—our shared colonial past, the mutual unspeakable secret that haunts the attic of our minds—is what gives the Gothic its horror and the power of ghostly menace.

Mr. Rochester's mansion, Thornfield Hall, is more than just the place of literal confinement for Bertha: It is a symbol of all the patriarchal restrictions that contain and oppress, a physical manifestation of capitalism and "signifier of misbegotten colonial wealth."[5] Bertha is imprisoned in colonialism's haunted house, and we're all hearing her scream. Her incendiary revenge is one of the most satisfying moments in the history of fiction.

While Lucy Ludwell was administering her own personal water cure, another "madwoman" in Ohio was about to be subjected to the real thing.

Harriet Martindale, known as Hattie, has long had a reputation in haunted lore as the "Veiled Lady" of Kirtland, Ohio. She was born in 1838 and lived a long, reclusive life at home with her mother and brother, then alone after their deaths, dying herself in 1919. She was quite wealthy and the enigmatic, eccentric spinster was known to keep to herself except for wildly generous acts of sudden charity, such as buying houses for destitute, elderly neighbors, and furnishing the local public school with a new library. She rarely went out, but when she did, she completely covered her face from forehead to chin with a thick, black veil. The origin story of the veil was, according to legend, this: On the eve of her wedding, Hattie caught her own sister in the arms of her fiancé and called off the ceremony, which was when she covered her weeping face with the long black veil, and swore never to let another man look at her again. She didn't take it off for the rest of her life.

Some ghost hunters claim her veiled spirit still haunts the Historic North Cemetery, where she is buried. A local blogger writes: "Through the years Kirtland locals and other paranormal visitors have reported seeing a veiled lady wander the cemetery at night near that grave site . . . Local lore has it that Hattie was jilted by her one true love, who may or may not have left her for her sister. Scared [scarred?] by this event, she never marries and lives a melancholy life till the end." The blogger, identified only as "Max," reports that "furniture is moved at night and

A Gothic mausoleum doorway in Mount Auburn Cemetery.
Photo by Leanna Renee Hieber

Wolfe's Neck Preserve on the coast
of Southern Maine.
Photo by Leanna Renee Hieber

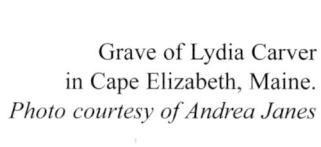

Grave of Lydia Carver
in Cape Elizabeth, Maine.
Photo courtesy of Andrea Janes

Vintage postcard of the Cruger-dePeyster Plantation, Volusia County, Florida, circa 1920.
Private collection of Tom Basket

The unnamed statue
at the grave of
Marian Hooper Adams
in Rock Creek Cemetery,
sculpted by Augustus
Saint-Gaudens in 1891.
Photo by
Leanna Renee Hieber

Miami University's
Peabody Hall
on Western Campus
where Helen Peabody
presided.
Photo by
Leanna Renee Hieber

Helen Peabody's infamous portrait in the main entrance of Peabody Hall, presiding over everyday business.
Photo by Leanna Renee Hieber

Charlotte Cushman's obelisk grave in Boston's Mount Auburn Cemetery.
Photo by Leanna Renee Hieber

Illustration of Charlotte and Susan Cushman as Romeo and Juliet, artist unknown.
Courtesy of the Houghton Library, Harvard Theatre Collection

Exterior of The Octagon.
Photo by Leanna Renee Hieber

The haunted mirror on the 2nd floor
of the Omni Parker Hotel, Boston.
Photo by Leanna Renee Hieber

Portrait of William Axtell
by John Wollaston
(Painted 1749–52).
Courtesy of The Metropol
Museum of Art

Portrait of Harriet "Hattie" Martindale,
circa 1861.
Courtesy of the Martindale Family Archives

Mary Virginia Wade's Grave in Gettysburg's Evergreen Cemetery.
Photo by Leanna Renee Hieber

Hammond Castle's interior atrium courtyard and pool. Gloucester, Massachusetts.
Photo by Leanna Renee Hieber

The Hoosac Tunnel in winter.
Photo by Leanna Renee Hieber

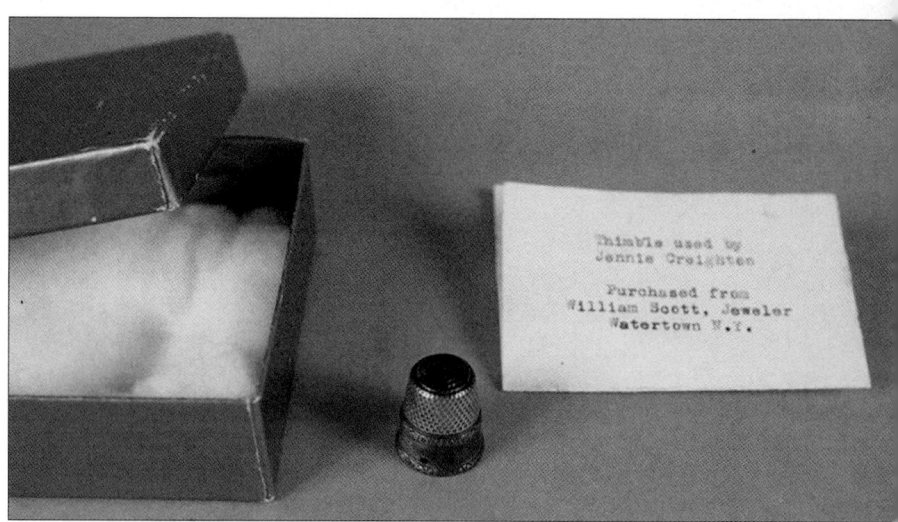

The Merchant's Café Basement, Seattle, WA.
Photo by Leanna Renee Hieber

Silver thimble used by Jennie Creighton, wife of F.W. Woolworth.
Photo courtesy of the Prince Edward County Museums Collection

Grave of Mercy Lena Brown,
n as America's Last Vampire,
in Exeter, Rhode Island.
Photo courtesy of Mike Lewi

Staircase at the former residence
of Mary Howe, now the
Clark Apartments in
Damariscotta, Maine.
Photo courtesy of Valerie Siebel

Lemp Mansion in St. Louis.
Photo courtesy of Stephen Walker

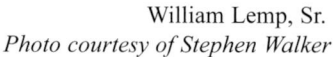

William Lemp, Sr.
Photo courtesy of Stephen Walker

Elsa Lemp.
Photo courtesy of Stephen Walker

Billy Lemp.
Photo courtesy of Stephen Walker

Edwin Lemp.
Photo courtesy of Stephen Walker

The Spirit of Life Statue
honoring Spencer Trask
in Saratoga Springs'
Congress Park.
*Photo by
Leanna Renee Hieber*

rumbling noises in the home have been heard." According to his profile, Max appears to be retired and an active civic volunteer, a friendly docent type. One comment, from Vicky, says only "I grew up in the Martindale house," but does not elaborate, and there is no reply. Max's last post was in 2016.

Others on the internet maintain Hattie haunts her old home, a blue colonial on Baldwin Road in Kirtland, where she tears up photographs of any man. According to the paranormal travel blog *Haunt Jaunts*, "Recent tenants have experienced the lights flickering for no reason at all, and Margaret Haller noticed something was tearing up all the pictures of her husband. Hattie also seems fussy on where things should be in the house. When Margaret moved some pewter candlesticks to another room, Hattie moved them back to the fireplace mantel." Predating the internet era, a 1970 "Things to Do" newspaper roundup of Halloween activities in the area noticed a house tour and included the following tidbit: "The existence of the ghost of a jilted Martindale daughter is rumored but not legally attested. She is said to peer from a second-story window, watching for her vanished lover and his new love, her sister." Then in 2000, a similar seasonal roundup "reveals another myth about the veiled lady reportedly seen floating down Chillicothe Road. The veiled lady was actually Hattie Martindale." The local historic society even offered themed cemetery tours featuring volunteers dressed as Hattie's ghost on Halloween. According to a cemetery tour guide, "for fifty-five years she wore a veil around her face everywhere she went. Turns out she was engaged to be married to, and, the night before her wedding, her fiancé eloped with her sister. She wore her wedding veil every day after that."

It's a decent ghost story and it ticks the usual boxes—Victorian-era figure draped in jet-black inverse-bridal veil; lonely/rich/eccentric/reclusive spinster; jilted lover; fussy female homeowner ghost, etc. Maybe it ticks a few *too* many boxes.

This ghost story is a little too tidy to be true, and sure enough, the facts don't match the fiction. How do we know this for sure? Hattie still has living descendants and they are not happy about this story still being perpetuated.

In an October 2022 article in *Belt* magazine, Hattie's own third great-grandnephew Paul Sturtevant set the record straight. Hattie, he strenuously insists, was merely a nice, normal girl from a good family of Presbyterians, abolitionists, and civic duty–doers. She attended Oberlin College, where she got top marks until she began to have trouble with her eyes. Letters to her sister—who most emphatically did *not* steal her beau—describe her attempts to get better while at the Cleveland Water Cure Establishment, but Hattie's love of peering at the small print in her French and German textbooks meant that the water cure was compromised (also, it just plain didn't work). Her sister admonished her not to study, but Hattie just had to have *something* to occupy her mind.

At the Cleveland clinic she also took something called "electric baths" for her eyes, which involved charging a patient with electricity and then leaving them "to sit with this charge, or [be] shocked by a doctor in an attempt to cure an illness." The clinic's "Electro-Chemical Bath" did not (shocker) actually do anything, and the practice was jettisoned by the medical community by the turn of the twentieth century.

Sturtevant is methodical in rebutting the myths surrounding Hattie point by point, calling the local ghostlore and the slew of salacious newspaper articles that fueled it "gossip" and "slander." He takes the *Cleveland Plain Dealer* to task for first covering Hattie's story in 1909, then subsequently reprinting and revisiting the story several times over the years.

Sturtevant backs up all his assertions with a wealth of letters, photographs, census records, and a blizzard of documentation. He quite literally has the receipts (specifically, the receipts for butter and milk Hattie purchased for a neighbor). Hattie was no stereotype, no stock figure out of a spooky story. She was, rather, "a brilliant, generous woman, deeply connected to her family and local community, who struggled with illness her entire life [and] due to a lifelong disability, became the subject of nasty local gossip that spread around the globe, and slanders her to this day."

Sturtevant blames a lot on Hattie's troubles with her eyesight. He wasn't the first to do so; in 1959, Hattie's sister's grandson, J. Morley Nutting, wrote a letter to the editor of the *Cleveland Plain Dealer*, stating that the veil she wore was, at first, to protect her sensitive eyes from the sunlight. Later, as she aged and became the subject of curious speculation, it also served as a protective layer against inquisitive and intrusive strangers. Nutting also refuted the claim that his grandmother eloped with Hattie's betrothed, and declared that she did not hate men: "I find that during her life Aunt Hattie had plenty of men friends. Only one was serious and she turned him down. Her only sister was my grandmother at whose wedding she was the bridesmaid . . . "

Sturtevant reveals that not only did Hattie have an eye disorder, she also struggled with mental illness and "encountered some of the worst of nineteenth-century women's mental health treatment." And this, reader, is the bombshell. An 1880 census lists her as "insane." In a marginal note, it appends the condition as "mania."

Sturtevant tells a story of Hattie disappearing one night, saddling a colt, and riding north, and alarming the whole county to the point where the lake was dragged: "But the girl was not drowned. She returned home while they were still patrolling the beach. She said she had gone away to be alone [and] no other explanation was made. When they saw her again the veil covered her face."

"Why make such a forty-year fuss over the fact that a woman wanted some alone time?" Sturtevant wonders. To me, it feels like a bit more like a cry for help than wanting some time alone. But then again, I am also very supportive of Hattie's decision to have some me time.

Sometime thereafter, Hattie was admitted to Newburgh Hospital for the Insane, where she said she experienced dizzy spells and a desire to weep but difficulty doing so. Sturtevant insists that these are merely symptoms of her eye trouble. He frames her condition as a disability misinterpreted as madness. "Research I have done in my family's archive has revealed the truth, that this original story was a lie, and the reason for Hattie's behavior was a lifelong struggle with a debilitating eye disability."

Hattie, after leaving Newburgh Asylum, lived quietly, performed numerous kind acts of charity, and died peaceably. Her obituary notes only that she was a lovely person, admired by all.

I'm glad for Hattie that she has living descendants willing to go to bat for her. It's a rare and lucky thing that the family happened to save so much intimate and archival family information. I always say that, when you tell a ghost story on a tour, you should always talk about the ghost as if they were your own grandmother: be respectful, not sensational, and give the fullest picture possible. I wish every ghost could have a relative like Sturtevant to advocate for them.

Incidentally, in response to the *Belt* article, the *Cleveland Plain Dealer* issued a lengthy apologia, wherein the editor, Chris Quinn, tries to set the record straight, noting that newspapers of 1909 had different standards than our own, writing:

Newspapers are reflections of their eras. Maybe readers loved a fanciful tale . . . Maybe the publishers sold a lot more papers—and a lot more advertising as a result—if they included pieces that built pseudo-mysteries around local gossip . . . That's why I feel it unfair to judge the reporters who wrote about Hattie or the many newspapers that carried the story. The reporters were operating within the requirements of their jobs at the time they were doing them.

Quinn is no less thorough than Sturtevant, and he corrects and contextualizes every *Plain Dealer* article about Hattie, and even appends the original 1909 article so that readers may see it and judge for themselves. It reveals a fascinating process of spooky mythmaking.

The original 1909 article truly is the stuff of Gothic fiction, and it is appropriately laid out with a moody inky-black illustration accompanying the piece. It is subtitled "For Forty Years No Man Has Seen the Face of This Feminine Recluse, Who in Her Youth Was Known as the Beauty of the Town" and begins: "In the house lives a spinster who was known in girlhood for her beauty. She has worn a heavy veil for more than forty years. In all that time, so far as people of the village know, no man has seen her face." A 1940 piece, written by a well-known columnist named Grace Goulder, who wrote a column called "Ohio Scenes and Citizens," also leans heavily into the romance: "So many of Ohio's old homesteads look like story-book houses with ghostly secrets and romance seeming to lurk in the set of the eaves, under the shadows, over worn steps; and here is a house with an authentic mystery, a real love story, and even a novel written around it."

After the correction was printed, a Victoria McWilliams of Twinsburg, Ohio, wrote a letter to the editor in response:

My parents bought the Martindale property from John Nutting in, I think, 1967 or 1968. They renovated the main house and we lived there as a family until 1971. Thank you for this fascinating article. As children, my brother and I were obsessed with Hattie. The house and property were the perfect play land for our childhood imaginations. We truly never experienced anything but a mysterious, walled-up doorway in the basement, which we were very curious about.

She doesn't elaborate on the mysterious door, but simply says, "Hattie has always been part of our family history also."[6] She is excellent at building suspense! This is probably the same Vicky who commented on Max's old 2014 blog post, I realized with some delight.

As for the novel locals claimed was inspired by Hattie, that was the 1906 *A Spinner in the Sun* by Myrtle Reed.

The novel, about a woman who wore a veil for twenty-five years, was written by the critically pilloried but commercially successful romance writer Myrtle Reed, whose own life story is so incredible I wish there was even the faintest hint of a ghost involved in it, so I'd have an excuse to write a whole chapter (or book!) about her. She was an incredibly intelligent, witty, hilarious woman whose lifelong struggles with her weight did a number on her self-esteem. Once she was rich and successful, she married an abusive ne'er-do-well clearly out for her money. They had fabulous parties for her many friends in her apartment, whimsically wallpapered in old rejection letters, where she was known to hold "husband pageants" where the skills portion of the event included lacing a corset and guessing the price of a hat. The winner was crowned the model husband.

Her model husband, however, drove her to overdose on sleeping powders at the age of thirty-six. "You have to marry a man to find out what he's really like," Reed intoned darkly before she died. "If you die, he's a toadstool; if you live, he's a mushroom." Reed, it should be noted, also suffered bouts of inertia followed by soaring periods of intense energy, creative output, and lavish expenditure. One feels a kinship of sorts, a lineage, between her and Hattie. In her 1911 novel, *A Weaver of Dreams*, Reed wrote:

> "Penetrate deeply into the secret existence of anyone about you, even of the man or woman whom you count happiest, and you will come upon things they spend all their efforts to hide. Fair as the exterior may be, if you go in, you will find bare places, heaps of rubbish that can never be taken away, cold hearths, desolate altars, and windows veiled with cobwebs."

I agree that all of us have these bare places and heaps of rubbish, and it's better to own them than to deny them.

"DEMENTED WIFE GETS ALL" howled the *New York Times* headline on April 15, 1919. One of the richest men in America, Frank W. Woolworth, had just died intestate, leaving his entire $35 million fortune to his "insane" wife Jennie. You may have heard of Woolworth, the man who built his eponymous emporia into a retail behemoth by introducing the concept of the five-and-dime—that is, affordable goods for everyday people. Others would follow his retail model, notably Sam Walton of Walmart notoriety, but it was really Frank Woolworth who pioneered the idea of a democratic department store experience for the working- and middle-class shopper. (Woolworth's lunch counters were decidedly less democratic; they were one of the Civil Rights era's staunchest holdouts against integration.)

Frank Woolworth came from a humble background and pulled himself up by his bootstraps using nothing but his guts, grit, whiteness, and the unpaid assistance of his perpetual help-meet, his wife Jennie Creighton. The two met in 1869, when she was a humble seamstress from Ontario, Canada, and he a simple store clerk from upstate New York. (I imagine they met while she was fabric shopping and they locked eyes over a bolt of cloth.) By 1876, they were married. Frank wasn't much of a biz whiz at this point; he apparently suffered from "nervous exhaustion" and got fired a lot. But in 1877, a year after he joined forces with Jennie, he suddenly became very successful. When a recession left his employer with a surplus of unsold goods, Frank suggested selling everything for a nickel, and voilà, everything sold out. He soon became his own storekeeper, still working on the 5-, 10-, and 15-cent model of cheap goods, and business was thriving. Jennie was right there with him, working in the stores side by side. Actually, a lot of Creightons were right there with him. Frank was way ahead of the nepo-baby trend and hired his relatives all the time. In fairness, the Creightons were all excellent workers. Jennie's sister Mary Ann apparently sold 50,000 items her first day at work. Jennie was no slouch herself, not only toiling alongside Frank but raising three daughters while she did it. She legendarily used to bring the girls with her to work when they were babies, and was said to have tucked them into dresser drawers for their naps.

As time wore on, Frank became increasingly successful and was away from home most of the time. Jennie became sad, withdrawn, and reclusive and began to sound like the Smiths song when she voiced the opinion that, in the days when Frank was hopelessly poor, she just liked him more. None of the opulence of being a Woolworth seemed to matter to her. They lived in a mansion on Fifth Avenue and had a palatial summer estate on Long Island's Gold Coast, but to no avail. Frank was even so very rich that when he built one of New York City's first skyscrapers in 1913, the Woolworth Building, he paid 13.5 million dollars for it ... *in cash.* (That's about $416 million today.) Dubbed "the cathedral of commerce," the Woolworth Building is the only Gothic Revival skyscraper in Manhattan. It has gargoyles and everything. (A truly appropriate touch for a story with so many Gothic elements.) Despite her wealth, Jennie was still sad. She ached for the family life and camaraderie of the old days, and missed her husband. Her sadness seems to have found its way to at least one of her daughters: Edna Woolworth died by suicide in 1917 (obituaries say the cause of death was a chronic ear infection, but this was a PR job by FW, who had hush money to spare). Edna's daughter Barbara Hutton was said to have discovered her own mother's body. Barbara was just four years old at the time. Barbara Hutton would grow up to become known as the "poor little rich girl," for all her millions couldn't buy her happiness. She married seven times and spent her entire fortune with a manic determination. Everyone's favorite of her husbands was the charming actor Cary Grant; the press dubbed them "Cash and Cary." (I had to look up the origin of the pun, by the way, since nobody says "cash and carry" anymore. Basically, it's a retail term that means buying items in-store with cash, not store credit, and taking them home with you, as opposed to, say, ordering and having them delivered from a catalogue.) By the time Barbara Hutton died in 1979, she'd managed to divest herself of almost all her cash, as if it were a curse and she couldn't rest until she got rid of it.

Jennie Creighton's depression and isolation were magnified by her own early-onset dementia, which set in around 1916. It's painful to compare that timeline to the date of her daughter's suicide, and heartbreaking to imagine that she may have been involuntarily unaware of her own child's, and grandchild's, deep need for her presence, or unable to process her grief through the veil of her dementia. To his credit, Frank did try to make her happy. According to one source, around this time he opened a Woolworth's in Picton, Ontario, where Jennie grew up, in the hopes that managing the store would buoy her spirits and give her something to re-tether her to the world from which she seemed to be slowly, tragically drifting away. The store was a money pit, of course, as the small town of Picton didn't have the population to sustain a place like that, and Frank knew it; he was just trying to make one last-ditch attempt to do something kind for his wife of three decades. At the same time, though, he was rushing to the courts to have Jennie legally declared non compos mentis, and essentially prevent her from having any ability to access or manage the family, or company, finances. In fact, it seems to have been his second-highest priority. His first was, understandably, little Barbara, for whom he cared after the death of her mother. I feel pity for him, imagining he must have been torn between the needs of his wife and his grandchild. Perhaps then it's also understandable that he never got around to finalizing his will, which was drafted in 1889, when Jennie was in full possession of her faculties (and, incidentally, when Frank wasn't quite worth $35 million yet).

When Woolworth died without a finalized will on April 8, 1919, and Jennie inherited everything, the usual stuff happened that always happens when rich families squabble, lots of money is at stake, and lawyers are involved. Fast-forward through all the dull litigation to 1924, when, at the age of seventy-four, Jennie Creighton left this mortal plane. Her body was interred next to Frank's in their ostentatious Egyptian revival mausoleum in Woodlawn Cemetery in the Bronx.

In the *New York Times* article with the notorious *Demented Wife* headline, the reporter goes on to say that Jennie was declared incompetent due to a "mental derangement," which gave rise to the many rumors that she was insane (the harsh word "demented" in this context may have simply been an old-fashioned way of saying she had dementia). People even began to say that Frank kept Jennie locked up in a secret room with a tapestry rolled over it . . . just like Rochester does to Bertha in *Jane Eyre. Exactly like it*, in fact! I've found that particular bit of trivia in a number of sources of varying degrees of reliability, both online and in print. Many of the sources claim that Jennie's ghost still haunts the Woolworths' lavish summer home in Long Island, Winfield Hall. It's also said that, the night Edna Woolworth died in 1917, a bolt of lightning struck the house and somehow slashed a line through the portrait of the three Woolworth daughters: right through Edna's face. The bolt of lightning, like the tapestry over the door, is also reminiscent of *Jane Eyre*; as usual, our ghostlore is informed by our cultural artifacts, in this case, the preeminent example of madness in our collective Gothic library.

A woman named Monica Randall, who later lived in Winfield Hall, claimed that its construction materials, namely Italian marble, are highly receptive conduits of spirit energy and have kept the spirits trapped on the site in a residual haunting. It's a sort of real-life version of the stone tape theory, which posits that residual energy can be imprinted on certain materials, like marble or stone, and be recorded there.

The house does exude a haunted air. I went up there recently with my assistant, who lives in Oyster Bay. We drove around to various macabre points of interest, including the cemetery where Little Edie Beale is buried, and the Woodward pool house, site of a notorious 1910 murder-suicide. When we got to Winfield, we were surprised to find the house wide open. It was a beautiful day in June, a single day of reprieve during a weeklong heat wave, and the sky was bright blue and nearly cloudless. The mansion's white marble gleamed in the sun and its front door was temptingly open, showing the breezy palazzo-style interior.

The house was currently in the process of renovation, and we were able to roam around the grounds fairly freely before the construction foreman got suspicious. Apparently, the ceiling restoration inside was exquisite to behold, but sadly I am averse to trespassing, and that foreman really had his eyes on us (if his boss is reading this right now: rest assured your employee follows his orders diligently). You can see the ceiling on Google street view, though. *Ornate* is an understatement.

I think of Jennie wandering these halls in a mental state that varied from sadness to incomprehension of exactly where she was and what she was doing there. How surreal it must have felt to her, how lonely, and how far away from her simple girlhood in rural Ontario. There's a touching article online from a (sadly) now-defunct Canadian magazine about Jennie, which notes that the Macaulay Heritage Museum in Picton still has some memorabilia of Mrs. Woolworth's. There on display in the small country museum, donated by her family, is a remnant of her humble beginnings as a seamstress: a single silver thimble.

Even though Jennie wasn't actually mentally ill, the Woolworth case is relevant, in that Frank's first impulse was to control an aspect of his sick wife's finances—or more accurately, to prevent her from having any control. Genuine concern for a woman's mental health and the caretaking of that woman can sometimes be nothing more than a ploy to control her (usually significant) finances. And, like Hattie and Lucy, Mrs. Woolworth's vulnerabilities marked her as an easy target for potshots by press, the tabloids, and the gossipmongers. As Paul Sturtevant wrote, the true horror "is not found in the ghost story itself, but in the story of how often and how casually our rumor mills and our media set up women and people with disabilities to be figures of public spectacle." Reading this, my mind turned to another contemporary example of a real woman trapped in her own Gothic story of madness.

In 2007, pop star Britney Spears began to exhibit erratic behavior in public. She shaved her head and attacked a paparazzo with an umbrella. She was mocked mercilessly by the public and by the media, and when her one defender went to bat for her on YouTube, they were mocked as well. Her career was floundering and she was flailing. She'd gone through a messy breakup and another messy divorce. She had two young children, born very close together. This twenty-six-year-old woman had grown up in the spotlight and was cracking under the pressure. In response, her father assumed total control over her, creating a conservatorship that made her a virtual prisoner in her own life. She was stripped of her money, her legal rights, and her personal agency and autonomy. Her sons were taken away from her and she was involuntarily hospitalized. I write this all, dear reader, not because I think it will be news to you, but because it is only when you put these stark facts on paper that their true horror emerges. Reread these sentences slowly, or listen to them again if you're reading the audiobook. Then close your eyes for a moment and remember that this all happened not in 1807 or 1907, but in *2007*.

It wasn't until 2019 that she finally faced her father in court to end her conservatorship. By this time, she'd regained the support of the public and she told her whole story in the memoir *The Woman in Me*. Reading it made me want to scream with frustration and rage. One anecdote that stays with me involves an incident in which Britney, who incidentally was sufficiently mentally stable to work like a donkey throughout most of her conservatorship, generating millions for her father with nightly shows at her Vegas residency, tried to take her staff and backup dancers out to dinner to thank them for their hard work. Because she was on such a tight leash financially, her credit card was declined. Elsewhere in the book, she notes that she was put on a strict diet of skinless chicken breast and steamed vegetables, and she was starving all the time. Nearly every chapter contains something enraging, and if I quoted everything that I'd underlined in my copy of the book, my publisher's legal department would have a heart attack. But one thing that struck me as particularly applicable was this comment of her friend, who said, "If someone took my baby away from me, I would have done a lot more than get a haircut. I would have burned the city to the ground."

Britney's conservatorship and the treatment of her public mental breakdown were allowable because of the way our society understands "madwomen." Without centuries of cultural influence, both real and fictional, Britney's narrative would have been received very differently, and her conservatorship might not even have been possible, or would at least have looked quite different. But as we are all collectively inculcated into this trope, we stood by and watched obligingly as she was mocked, ridiculed, and disempowered legally and financially. It took years for us to collectively notice and acknowledge that, maybe, just maybe, this was wrong.

One of the first things people say when they're telling a ghost story that happened to them is, "*You're going to think I'm crazy,* but . . ." Women, especially, use this phrasing. We are understandably hesitant to discuss our experiences, lest we fall on the wrong side of the line between normal and nutso. We have seen what the world does to women it deems insane. Society is so quick to let us know that our feelings, sensations, illnesses, and intuition are all in our heads. We're *crazy.* And sometimes, yeah, we do feel crazy. We're maxed out, burned out, overworked, underpaid, condescended to, and ignored, and when we dare to vocalize our sneaking suspicion that maybe we shouldn't be feeling the way we do, we're gaslit, as the kids say. Maybe our feelings of madness are an entirely justifiable response, possibly the only *sane* response, to the world we live in. Because you know what actually *is* crazy? Exploiting and enslaving, depleting the earth's resources, and destroying human happiness for the sake of relentless, excessive profits: *that's* crazy.

So I root for Bertha Mason as she burns Thornfield Hall to the ground. I root for them all. I root for Britney. For Lucy with her curative water, Hattie with her electric baths, Jennie with her silver thimble. A flash of a silver, a rush of water, lightning, electricity, heat and fire. Let it burn brightly.

The Great American Castle

Leanna

It lies in wait along the Massachusetts coast. Winding along a curving drive, the grounds of a great Gothic castle aren't immediately visible when the trees are in full foliage. It takes stepping down along irregular stone stairs to a lower plateau before the full effect comes into view. But when Hammond Castle reveals itself, one has to gasp in delight. Its impressive grounds and grand towers are set against a stunning view of the Atlantic Ocean beyond its cliffside perch. Replete with a facade built as a ready-made ruin, its built-in-progress stones reaching dramatically against a wide sky, Hammond is the perfect example of a curious historic trend: the Great American Castle.

The United States loves mythologizing itself; it remains one of the country's great pastimes. And all around the nation, particularly in the late nineteenth and early twentieth century, there was a penchant, usually among wealthy eccentrics, to build castles. These large, bold, romantic structures, in some vein of Gothic or Romanesque architecture, later became quirky local attractions and generally accrue ghostlore because—if *Hamlet* and the original Gothic *Castle of Otranto* taught us nothing else—one expects it of a castle. The Gothic literary genre too is a European import, and these castles all enjoyed accruing artifacts from various classical eras, all of which have their own place memory. Objects may carry their own ghosts with them, traveling across time and continents, the old brought into the new as curiosities and museum pieces, relics from fading European royalty.

The Gothic notion of a home mirrors the body, society, and the structure of existence; protagonists fight to define themselves from within that haunted house or to escape from it. Considering the American castle phenomenon adds an additional layer of complication to each one of those separate dialogues, because a castle is for shows of strength. Gothic literature contains elements of external politics and internal power dynamics in play at all times. In an American environment without a ruling aristocracy, the castle may become a new manifestation of personal identity. It is meant to make a statement and is, ostensibly, a place of defense.

In Shirley Jackson's *We Have Always Lived in the Castle*, the unreliable narrator protagonist presents the castle home she shared with her sister as a haven from the suspicious villagers outside. When the narrator seeks to protect her sister from outside influences further, the traumatized family retreats back into its disintegrating ruin by the end of the story. The castle is still a metaphor for a body, one that has been battered and the worse for wear, its ability to fend off an attack diminished, but it is still their place of identity and safety. Jackson herself had to balance the power dynamics of being a notable woman writer but someone also expected to also be mother, housekeeper, and caregiver. Her writing reflects societal changes in the twentieth century and the difficulties of protecting an autonomous self.

Gothic romanticism, as an art form, loves nothing more than a castle dotting a landscape. Plucked from the canvasses of romantic landscape painters, a castle against a dramatic rock was a core part of the vision for Central Park in Manhattan, a civil engineering marvel that was the first of its kind on such a large scale. Belvedere Castle was built in an amalgam of nineteenth-century Gothic architectural styles, a gray stone observatory outcropping on Vista Rock, at the highest point of elevation in the park. The castle still haunts the American mythos, staking a claim in a country that abandoned aristocracy but never got over fetishizing it.

I admit, I understand the appeal of the castle-dotted landscape. When I first visited Germany on book research, I enjoyed a slow boat cruise along the Rhine River, where every hilltop showcased a small, lovely castle. Visiting the land of my ancestors for the first time, I felt a sort of nostalgia attached to these lovely edifices, even though I didn't descend *from* them myself. My people were poor farmers and woodworkers who emigrated to Brooklyn, and later Ohio, in search of better prospects than the late nineteenth and early twentieth centuries afforded in the southern and central regions of Germanic countryside. But everyone likes to pretend, and that certainly included American entrepreneurs and eccentrics who wanted to carve out their own little fiefdom.

The history of Château Laroche is its own fairy tale of service. Also known as Loveland Castle, the classic, Medieval-style castle is built on the banks of the Little Miami River in Loveland, Ohio. Just outside Cincinnati, an industrial town that was indeed home to so many German immigrants in the nineteenth century, the castle is a testament to perseverance and care. Château Laroche is unique among the haunted castles of this chapter in that it wasn't a wealthy heir or notable industrialist who built this castle; it was simply one man's passion project, a charming and entirely unexpected hidden gem in a forested area along the riverbank. The immersive feeling of losing yourself in a place that has stepped out of time is easily achieved here. As a teen, when I first rounded a forested drive and the castle loomed up ahead, I gasped. Learning the building's history, I've become ever fonder of the place.

Harry Andrews had been a World War I medic in "the war to end all wars." Knighted after he saved an earl's life on the battlefront, Andrews's interest in classical ideals and medieval knighthood sharpened. After a terrible bout of meningitis, Andrews was presumed dead and his sweetheart back home married someone else. After making a full recovery, Harry shifted a broken heart toward architecture and knightly ideals instead. He spent time in Europe after the war, marveling at historic castles and immersing himself in studies of medieval architecture. Bringing that love home with him, he returned to Loveland, took a newspaper job, and began working with a local Boy Scout troop, buying a subscription to the *Cincinnati Enquirer* that came with promotional plots of land, upon which he began hosting troop camping retreats.

Beginning construction in 1927, the castle manifests Harry's romanticization of a time long before the bloody horrors of the gruesome war in which he'd treated so many patients. Château Laroche, translating to "castle of rock" in French, was named in honor of the military hospital where he had been stationed, a bastion of healing and survival. Wanting to provide more resilient campground shelters for the Scouts hosted on the grounds, Andrews built two stone tents that provided the core of what would become the castle structure. He founded the Knights of the Golden Trail Boy Scout troop, with Château Laroche as headquarters. The passion project took on a life of its own.

Made from some 56,000 pails full of stone pulled from the riverbed and completed with 32,000 cement bricks made in milk cartons, Andrews's layout of expenses was around $12,000. Other castles of its era were astronomically more expensive and more quickly built. It took Andrews nearly fifty years, and the Knights of the Golden Trail continued working on it after his passing in 1981, unfortunately due to a painful accident while either burning trash or cooking on the castle rooftop. He had

willed the castle to his order and the Knights of the Golden
Trail have continued his mission uninterrupted, maintaining
the unique, well-loved grounds where children can learn skills
like building fires, sword-fighting, and my favorite offering:
storytelling.

Tales of the castle being haunted by Andrews are *pervasive*, stories valiantly upheld by his volunteer Knights themselves. A shadow has been seen climbing the spiral staircase
to "Sir Harry's" old bedroom, safely presumed to be Harry's
spirit himself going about his daily routine. Staircases in particular maintain one of the most commonly reported locations
of a haunting, as the climbing of a stair was such a countlessly
repeated act, it is easy to wear a psychic groove on the paths
most commonly trod. The disembodied slamming of doors to
alert vigilant Scouts to a problem has averted at least one disaster of a septic problem, and the chandeliers have been known to
swing in time to the music of old medieval ballads, especially if
played on period instruments.

There's so much love and work there, so much of the founder's energy and care, his own hands on all those stones; his spirit
is perhaps his own place memory.

Hearst Castle, the ambitious palace that newspaper mag-
nate William Randolph Hearst commissioned, known officially
as La Cuesta Encantada, "the enchanted hill," bears significant
mention. Located in San Simeon, California, "Hearst's Spanish
gothic folly San Simeon"[1] took the meandering years between
1919 and 1947 to build. Hearst and his castle were inspirations
for Orson Welles's celebrated *Citizen Kane*, which showcased its
own vast castle, Xanadu, as the centerpiece.

Welles's expert biographer Simon Callow minces no words
when it comes to the progressive-turned-fascist Hearst, or
the castle where he kept his mistress Marion Davies: "built
as a temple to his love, the castle was a bizarre aberration of

the otherwise impeccably tasteful Beaux-Arts architect Julia Morgan, an extraordinary operatic creation, crammed with art works cheaply bought from impoverished European noblemen arranged in a sequence of enormous rooms without regard to period or style. An art lover's Disneyland, it is impressive only as a monument to its creator's will."

This sits in stark contrast to the layout and careful curation of other American castles of the period, each with distinct wings and carefully curated themes that sought to manifest historical accuracy, matching architecture and time period to the interior treasures collected.

Hearst's castle was most certainly built as a narcissistic show of strength, as opposed to Hammond's sense of whimsy, fun, and fancy, with an eye to a museum-quality experience. Hearst, who had become increasingly dictatorial in nature as he aged, used his castle purely to lord over others, particularly the only royalty we've ever really had: Hollywood stars.

As Hearst lacked the cohesion in his presentation of art and architecture that a house-turned-museum like Hammond Castle managed so expertly, it made Hearst's entire costly operation more like an exclusive theme park and selfish endeavor. Hollywood elites from Charlie Chaplin to Cary Grant wined and dined there, and anyone who wanted to *be* somebody sought an invitation. Across the vast grounds, one could take a tour through Hearst's private zoo, acres of ostentatious chaos in which silver-screen royalty mingled and tried to stay on Hearst's good side, lest they be torn to shreds in his newspapers. An ego-driven villain who started the Spanish-American War by lying in his papers that the battleship USS *Maine* had been attacked by Spain rather than victim to a tragic onboard accident, Hearst has all the hallmarks of the greedy, overbearing Gothic villain who thirsts for violence while lording over a woman.

In this case, Hearst's fixation was the iconic 1920s actress Marion Davies. A talented woman in her own right, Hearst constantly tried to make her into something she was not, by sponsoring and demanding projects that tried to shape her into an epic, tragic, dramatic heroine. As these films and productions proved underwhelming, Hearst undermined Davies's natural skill as a charming, witty star better suited for lighter fare. Though Davies was Hearst's mistress, the affair was entirely public, a fact that flew in the face of his increasingly conservative views, and his love for her seemed to know no bounds. In turn, Davies bailed out Hearst's media empire when he had fallen short, to the tune of a million dollars in liquidated bonds and jewelry, sold to shore up his debts. When tour guides tell this story, the castle, over a century later, reacts to it.

The ghost story remains fittingly reserved for the castle's Gothic study, a lavish room with pointed arches, rafters and walls fully painted with medieval-style motifs and wrought iron–faced cabinets and bookshelves. Hearst's portrait lords over a long table with high-backed chairs. Large, multi-paneled glass lanterns hang from the ceiling with beautiful filigree bases with metal tassels. Reports that whenever tour guides would discuss Davies using her own funds to help the man who built a temple in her honor, the lanterns would begin to sway. The present-day management evidently instructs guides not to mention ghosts anymore. Not since a patron first claimed a ghost followed her home from the premises and then tried to send the castle the bill for an exorcist.

After Hearst's death, he willed the entirety of the estate to Davies, who turned around and generously gave it back to the Hearst family for a dollar. This set the more open tone for the Hearst descendants to then offer the entire grounds and lavish structures to the State of California, a gift from the Hearst

Corporation in the 1950s. (The family does retain access to the still-private pools.)

Citizen Kane, a great, inimitable work of artistic cinema, proved to undo Orson Welles just as his genius star was ascending. A film that evokes many Gothic tropes, *Citizen Kane* pokes savagely at Hearst and his hubris, in addition to mirroring a disenchanted Marion Davies–like heroine isolated in the grand, chaotic Xanadu castle, to the point where Hearst sought to ruin Welles going forward. Hearst held enough sway to prohibit mention of the film in any of his papers and to block the release from every movie theater except one, Radio City Music Hall, for its 1941 premiere. But as can often be the case with authoritarian censorship, there was great curiosity in the film world about what Hearst wanted so desperately to bury. The film was nominated for nine Academy Awards. Herman Mankiewicz and Orson Welles won for best screenplay. The film surged in popularity upon its rerelease in 1956, thanks to the praise of French critics and in 1989 the Library of Congress selected the film as part of the inaugural National Film Registry, noting it as a work of cultural, aesthetic, and historical significance.

I find it particularly fascinating that Marion Davies's own biography, *The Times We Had: Life with William Randolph Hearst*, features a foreword by none other than Orson Welles, a fact I'm sure Hearst's ghost would *hate*.

Belcourt Castle in Newport, Rhode Island, a sixty-room villa built to mimic Louis XIII's hunting lodge, was created originally as a summer home for Oliver Hazard Perry Belmont, who wanted a place to showcase all his thirteenth-century stained glass and European antiquities he'd collected through the years as heir to a $60 million fortune (3.2 of these millions he poured into Belcourt).

Twenty-seven-thousand square feet of grandeur began construction in 1891 and would last until 1894, designed by famed architect Richard Morris Hunt. The first floor originally housed all of Belmont's prized racing horses, as Oliver was famously skilled in four-in-hand carriage racing. (The Belmont Stakes is named for Oliver's father, August Belmont Sr.)

Notable features of Belcourt include the French oak grand staircase, which took three years to carve. Some three hundred European-trained artisans would work on the interior details. The north wing showcased a French Renaissance design, while the other wings were half-timbered, sporting Elizabethan English, Norman, and Germanic styles. The Versailles dining room is colonnaded and mirrored, while the Italian banquet hall could seat up to 250 guests and features thirteenth-century glass depictions of saints. But it is the French Gothic ballroom that's particularly spectacular, with a breathtaking vaulted ceiling, more thirteenth-century stained glass in Gothic arches along the ballroom floor and a clerestory line of trefoil stained glass windows above. A vast hearth depicting a medieval-style castle anchors the room.

Into this grand space walked an icon of high society who would make it her own.

Alva Erskine Vanderbilt shocked the country when she divorced her reportedly unfaithful husband William Vanderbilt in 1895, the same year she'd seen her daughter Consuelo married off to the Duke of Marlborough. Divorces initiated by women at that time were *extremely* rare, particularly one as high-profile as a Vanderbilt. The next year, Alva married Oliver Belmont, a man with whom she'd long been familiar, whose summer home of Belcourt was near the famous Vanderbilt summer home the Breakers. Belmont had been friends and a business partner of her ex-husband, and had traveled extensively with the family on-board the Vanderbilt yacht, the *Alva*. Alva Belmont spent a happy twelve years summering with Oliver at Belcourt and making changes of her own. Oliver died of septic poisoning from a burst appendix in 1908 and Alva would continue living at Belcourt, throwing her attention, money, and considerable skills wholly into the women's suffrage movement.

After Alva's death in 1933, Belcourt survived a rather tumultuous set of circumstances before it would reach its former glory again. Utilized as a naval base during World War II, with subsequent periods of disrepair, the home had periods of being largely uninhabited for decades, save for a sole caretaker. Benny Collin did his best to keep people from breaking in or leaving graffiti. The first ghost stories of Belcourt were circulated because Collin pretended to be a ghost to scare off would-be troublemakers who had found their way inside. Word of the startling haunting in the deteriorating manor spread quickly. Belcourt would never live down the reputation for being haunted.

It wasn't until the Tinney family took over in 1956 and redubbed it Belcourt Castle, buying the fixer-upper for only $25,000, that it again began to live a life of grandeur. The Tinney family had their own lavish set of antiques to bring into Belcourt and they were skilled renovators and restorers, pouring time, care, and money into the building that would prove a multigenerational family home until 2009, when Harle Tinney put the mansion up for sale following the death of her husband. In 2012, Carolyn Rafaelian, founder of the jewelry company Alex and Ani, purchased the property and changed its official name to Belcourt of Newport. Restoration of the premises remains ongoing. Reopened in 2014 for tours, the building also serves as an art gallery and event space.

The Tinney era had been one that welcomed ghost stories, folding them into their tours. Harle Tinney credits her family's range of antiquities in her 2010 book *The Ghosts of Belcourt Castle* as the reason why it has been haunted. A figure of a monk, attached to a German wood carving of a cowled monastic figure that was part of the Tinney antique collection, showed up at the foot of her bed. His hooded figure was later seen wandering around the areas where his statue was placed. The second-floor gallery sometimes features a pleasant, spectral figure in a ball-gown thought to perhaps be Alva Belmont in happier days, surveying the grandeur she was so fond of.

In the French Gothic ballroom, girls in period dresses are said to dance about. Less pleasantly, a sixteenth-century Italian suit of armor turns its helmeted head to watch visitors warily. The Tinney family said they could sometimes hear the knight's screams, reliving a traumatic death when a spear was lodged through the visor of his helmet. Reinforcing the idea that a Gothic theme might increase the amount of haunting or expectations of haunting, the French Gothic ballroom is reportedly the most haunted room in the castle.

The Shelton McMurphey Johnson House, known as the Castle on the Hill in Eugene, Oregon, is the town's only nineteenth-century house museum. A beautiful, dramatic, sea-green Gothic fever dream of a structure with an enormous cast-iron spire soaring from the upmost cupola, the house reaches halfway up the butte behind it, striking against the backdrop of rock and forest. Built originally on a 320-acre tract for Dr. Thomas Shelton, later left to his daughter, its full completion was delayed until 1888, as the house burned in 1887 when an angry workman set fire to the building, confessing to arson on his deathbed. While the museum itself *insists* it isn't haunted, the local *Register-Guard* newspaper noted that it was the first building that came to mind when visualizing the *idea* of a local haunted house, again proving a willfulness about hauntings, because people think a place *looks* haunted, it may become so in popular imagination.

A dramatic work of Queen Anne revival architecture, with sharp corners and a mansard roof cantilevered at severe angles, the many windows of the building that look out onto a world far below make it seem like a dollhouse against the rock. In this vein, the home has a "doll room," itself an unsettling detail. A visitor reported one of the dolls turning and falling directly face down when they entered the room when no breeze or draft took place. Dolls, let alone a whole room of them, *are* unerringly creepy.

Doctors Eva and Curtis Johnson bought the house from the McMurphey family in 1950, Eva practicing psychology and Curtis a pediatrician. A World War II veteran, Curtis, according to the museum website, spent much of his time in Eugene unhappy and would keep to himself up in the attic turret, once having to cut a hole in the wall to let himself out. That the owner's psychological state factors into the discussion of the building's history is worth noting. With psychological focus at the heart of any Gothic narrative, a troubled mind in a house that people say "looks" haunted ends up condemning a place further to that fate.

Even the museum director, who has been quoted as saying the castle isn't haunted, heard footsteps above her on an upper-floor porch when no one else was there. I'm not trying to force a haunting on anything or anyone but . . . hearing footsteps when no one is there is a *defining* trait of a haunted house.

One castle that also bears a *presumably* haunted weight, even though there hasn't been any reported or documented activity, is the splendidly Gothic Revival style Lyndhurst mansion near Sleepy Hollow, New York, designed in 1838. Much like the Dakota building became infamous for *Rosemary's Baby*, Lyndhurst's interior and exteriors are utilized in the first two *Dark Shadows* movies. This fame begat paranormal assumptions; the films create their own feedback loop and Lyndhurst's proximity to Sleepy Hollow brings its own haunt-by-association. I admit, my own personal love for Lyndhurst had me hoping it was haunted, but nothing has stuck, despite plenty of time for a spirit to have lingered and made itself known. This mansion is certainly worth a visit, though, especially during one of their *Dark Shadows* themed weekends.

I'll end as I began, with my personal favorite of these castles: Hammond.

If there are to be villains or heroes here, then William Randolph Hearst appears the greedy, oft vindictive, pedantic former, while generous John Hammond; quirky, genius inventor and humorous prankster, holds court as the latter.

High atop a bluff in Gloucester, Massachusetts, sits Hammond Castle, with a stunning view of the Atlantic Ocean and a storied history. Gothic arches created in the style of a partial ruin trail away from the main drawbridge and turret feature that cuts a bold profile against the sky. A modern castle built to be a medieval treasure, this magnificent edifice was to be a playground and art gallery for its owners while they lived, a public gift of a museum after their passing. Hammond Castle was always meant to be more than just one man's fancy and it continues to hold an incredible court a century later.

Made manifest by gifted inventor and innovator John Hays Hammond. Jr. in the 1920s, the castle was the dream of a man "aptly described as a man of the future, but who chose to live in the past." His vision for his castle and its grounds, as implemented by the architectural firm of Allen & Collens of Boston, well known for Gothic Revival architecture, was to utilize a medieval style as a baseline but to incorporate many eras within it, matching antiquities to each respective section, ranging from the thirteenth to sixteenth centuries. The complex features four main architectural styles, Romanesque, medieval, French, and Gothic, with parts of each section brought in from Europe and reconstructed on site. These wings combine in a central courtyard with a rectangular pool and a glass atrium ceiling.

Hammond could create a foggy, misty, Gothic atmosphere just by adjusting the many steam pipes in this grand courtyard, where a stunning number of Italian sarcophagi and other decorative ephemera from historic graves adorn the walls and walkways. (Hammond used to use a small sarcophagus as a pedestal for diving into the pool.) A beautiful graveyard of art in a courtyard setting, Hammond brings his various eras from medieval to Tudor style together in this blended arena. Looking from one wall to the section opposite is to travel in architectural time.

Hammond Castle is perhaps most famous for its pipe organ, a grand, Gothic staple. Much like how Hammond Castle gathered and incorporated classical antiquities into an amalgam architecture, the construction of the pipe organ was managed by a collection of world-famous pipe organ builders Hammond gathered and hired over a decade to create an inimitable instrument within the walls of the building. The largest pipe organ in the world with 8,400 pipes, it incorporated nineteen different aspects of technology that Hammond himself had patented as a pipe organ innovator. When all the stops were out, it could be heard for miles, as ships in the harbor could attest to, trumpeting out into the sea beyond.

Interest in the supernatural gripped the castle from the moment it opened. By the 1950s Hammond and a coterie of gifted, acclaimed scientists and luminaries were conducting telepathic experiments in the castle. Hammond's interest in the science of psychic phenomena was keen, but his application of science as an inventor and his innovative mind led to the invention of remote control. To those who didn't understand the *science* of remote control and wireless technology, a remote-controlled object would have appeared to an outside observer as being moved by telepathy or telekinesis; something mysterious and magical.

Hammond is also responsible for early advances in television technology. He accrued over four hundred patents in his lifetime. Mentored by Thomas Edison, Hammond maintained a friendship with Nikola Tesla and worked closely with Alexander Graham Bell. Everyone who met him could attest to his keen mind.

Hammond was directly inspired by philanthropist and art collector Isabella Stewart Gardner, who left her museum of a home, and the stunning array of art and artifacts within, to the city of Boston. Hammond was in her social circle, attended her funeral, and because he wished to mirror her actions, was granted access to her will to see how she set about creating her foundation. Passing another torch, John D. Rockefeller was so impressed by what Hammond had done with collections, antiquities, and how he staged them all, Hammond Castle inspired Rockefeller to create the famed Cloisters in Manhattan. The importing of European classical objects carries that place memory with them, mixing then with a new landscape and creating a new blend of haunted atmospheres, old history with new intention.

Hammond's wife Irene Fenton Reynolds was married when she and Hammond met. She divorced her husband to marry Hammond, to the extreme disapproval of their families. Both were fascinated by psychic phenomena, Irene purportedly having some psychic gifts herself. She wrote a newspaper astrology column titled "What the Stars Say" from 1919 to 1921, writing as Madame Renée Lonquille.

There's a theme here between Belcourt and Hammond Castles, with scandals and divorces preceding high-profile romances. Another parallel between Belcourt and Hammond is the variance of classical styles from one space to the next; allowing for several styles to coexist but separated out into their own rooms or wings. This definitely creates a sense of character and setting from one place to the next, which ties into the Gothic idea of the house as having its own identity and often compartmentalized places, but that one home can be many worlds and changing moods.

Hammond was a known prankster. One lovely room features wallpapered doors that when closed, create a seamless space. He was known to quietly shut the doors once his guests were sleeping. Confused upon waking, unsure how to get out, they'd have to call for help out the window, concerned voices echoing into the courtyard and misty pool below. Host to a wide array of famous artists, actors, writers, and high-society types through the years, Hammond prided himself on giving visitors an immersive, inimitable experience. Actor Burgess Meredith wrote in the Castle guestbook: "Jack, *where* am I?"

Artist, performer, and tarot reader Lauren "Onça" O'Leary kindly shared some personal details about growing up near the castle and the coterie Hammond enjoyed hosting there. The man she describes as her "occult godfather-of-sorts," acclaimed poet Gerrit Lansing, who passed in 2018 at age ninety and whose funeral was held at the castle, told her vibrant stories of his time there, drawing back a curtain for her.

In Onça's experience, having grown up decades later in Gloucester, she recalls a time when Hammond Castle very much did *not* want to talk about any occult or metaphysical pursuits that most *certainly* happened there. But magic and séance culture had been unabashedly present in Hammond's days, and Lansing, a gay man, found support and camaraderie in a circle that certainly welcomed queer members as openly as they welcomed the practice of the metaphysical arts. Hammond himself was a bit of a bisexual icon, before that term even existed.

On the Hammond Castle website, a Pride Month blog post this year discusses that particular point:

While it is impossible to know how our Museum's founder would have specifically identified in the modern landscape of diverse Queer identities—ongoing research efforts at the Museum supports a clear acknowledgment that Hammond had intimate romantic relationships with both men and women throughout his life. Moreover, the inventor was but one individual thread in a fascinatingly vibrant tapestry of Queer contemporaries that stretched across the globe.[2]

Gerrit Lansing was one of them. As Onça recalls, Gerrit told her that Hammond and others used to do a lot of "Magickal workings of the harbor." She notes that the historic, deep, dark, and often dangerous body of water surrounding Gloucester was essential to the founding of the United States with its resources of the long-depleted Stellwagen Bank and the vast harbor area. Hammond's circle called down the spirits over these waters.

"It is the most amazing, glorious conceit ever that these men had the time, resources, and the inclination to work in this way. Gerrit told me that they would have séances in the great hall, where they hung a human-sized metal cage up high (no small feat in a room that epic) and charged it with electrical current . . . Famed New York medium Eileen Garrett would sit in it and channel scientific information that he used to fuel his research and his huge empire of patents. I have seen just such a cage there in a thou-shalt-not-go-here area of the castle about thirty years ago, but I do not know if it was a prop or the real thing; I never heard this story from anyone but Gerrit himself, so I do not know why else there *would* be such an item in storage there."

What Onça saw specifically tracks with scientific, extrasensory perception (ESP) trials described by historians as headed by the Parapsychology Foundation in 1951 and 1952, of which

Eileen Garret herself was president. Hammond placed Garret in a Faraday cage, designed to keep out electromagnetic waves in order to determine whether the carrier wave for ESP was on an electromagnetic frequency. Since Garrett was still able to telepathically communicate with the exterior science team through ESP tests while *inside* the Faraday cage, the team took this as proof that ESP *wasn't* being transmitted on frequencies that were electromagnetic in nature. The Parapsychology Foundation still exists and continues funding investigations into psychic phenomena using traditional scientific methods.

Hammond had been originally buried, per his final requests, in a mausoleum alongside several of his beloved mummified—or "pickled" in formaldehyde—cats. This crypt was unfortunately vandalized and had to be removed. Now visitors can pay their respects to the celebrated inventor at his simple, elegant headstone in the back of a beautiful, shaded public garden, where his remains are laid beside a peaceful fountain.

But Hammond's spirit hardly rests. Not only is the museum palpably vibrant with his positive, open, inviting, and often playful presence—a fact repeated by nearly every account of the place, and one I can attest to myself—his disembodied voice has been heard at different levels within the house, sometimes in the upstairs balcony looking down over the great hall, as if enjoying watching the visitors below as they wander through his treasures. Sometimes his distinctive footfalls can be heard echoing, as he had special shoes to help with issues with his feet. The beautiful circular library, with its own unique acoustics, remains eternally sparked by disembodied intellectual discussions, as if the inventor and his coterie of inquisitive minds had never stopped asking the greater questions of the universe. On an episode of the *Ghost Hunters* TV show, "Jack" was conversational and pulled out another favorite trick of his: swinging lights and chandeliers.

Irene turns up too, wandering through and holding court. When one visitor noticed that there was someone napping on a museum bed, she went to tell staff, returning to find the bed empty. But when the visitor saw a picture of Irene, she insisted *that's* who'd been lying in repose. The lady of the house still finds her castle comfortable and lounges in the grand, celebrated space that had been her sanctuary and great escape.

Appropriately, many of the supernatural encounters seem to happen in the Gothic Guestroom. During my visit, I spoke with tour guide Mary about her experiences and she described a specific shadow she noticed had been cast in the center of the Gothic guest room that moved in an intentional, curious direction. When she tried to imitate the same phenomenon with lights and angles, there was no way that person-shaped shadow could have been cast by any of the lights or furniture in the space. It remained inexplicable and unrepeatable.

A groundskeeper purportedly spectrally checks in on how the place is being maintained and other unknown and unidentified spirits wander through to examine the offerings; as if the spirit world appreciates the museum as much as the living. The castle opened a communicative portal to the dead during Hammond's lifetime and that door never shut. But thankfully, Hammond curated his company well, as the energy there is never negative, it is always appreciative, inquisitive, responsive, and fun. Dear friend and fellow Gothic enthusiast Perseus LePage, a dancer and creative soul, regaled me with delightful stories of how the castle once hosted the most lavish and immersive Halloween décor imaginable. It is such a well-loved and pleasant place, with a fascinating room devoted to Hammond's inventions and genius, I feel confident the ghosts are well-pleased that the legacy he'd taken great pains to leave wholly to the benefit of Massachusetts is so avidly appreciated.

In the end, the purposes of these grand homes and ambitious, distinctive, extraordinary structures is to transport those inside to another time and place. They are liminal spaces where setting is character, where place memory has been directly planted and residents and visitors are bid to create their own; summoning a moment-out-of-time through fancy, imagination, collection, curation, and a healthy dose of stagecraft.

Those who have lived in and visited these castles engage in the kind of time-slipping that a ghost itself does. The ability of these structures to let creativity and imagination run wild remains key to their lasting appeal. They are the perfectly adapted places in which to lose oneself. Or, perhaps, to be found anew in a fairy tale of one's own making. The great American castle disorients as it transports, blending reality and fiction, past, present, and future.

In the immortal words of Burgess Meredith as noted in the Hammond guest book; "Jack, *where am I?*"

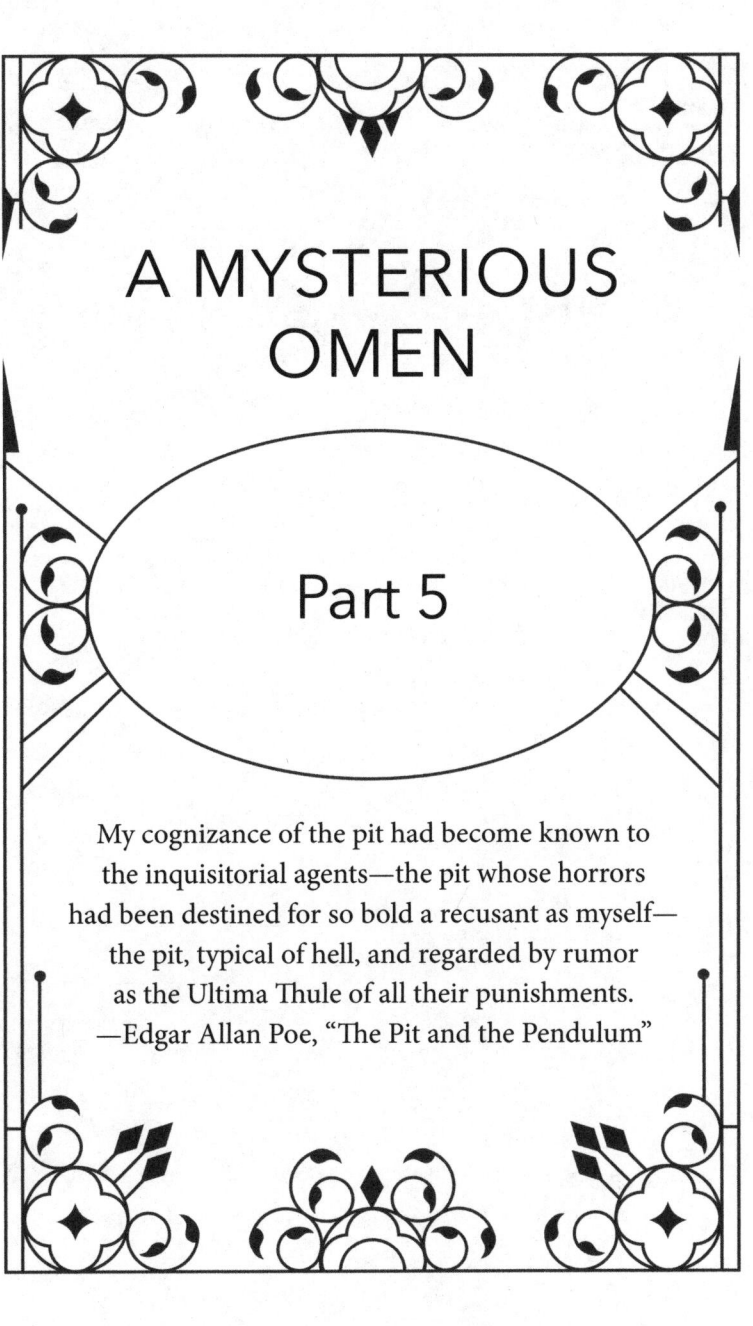

A MYSTERIOUS OMEN

Part 5

My cognizance of the pit had become known to
the inquisitorial agents—the pit whose horrors
had been destined for so bold a recusant as myself—
the pit, typical of hell, and regarded by rumor
as the Ultima Thule of all their punishments.
—Edgar Allan Poe, "The Pit and the Pendulum"

They Told You to Run:
Spirits of "The Bloody Pit"

Leanna

I've been on a narrow, icy mountain road in western Massachusetts for a while now where one slip along any of the hairpin turns would send me down a sheer drop some hundreds of feet. Turning in toward a sparse population getting sparser as I go, the land rises around me as if I've turned into a valley. The forest thickens. I've now lost cell phone service and have *not* arrived at my destination as GPS has claimed. Instead, I find myself on a narrow, residential, gravel, dead-end street and there are three large, barking, unleashed dogs surrounding my car. I hastily turn around at the *No Outlet* sign and retreat slowly so as not to hit any of the angry German shepherds, extremely mindful of the large *No Trespassing* signs.

This has quickly become unwise and unsafe. But I've come so far. I need to find this place. I want to honor the dead. I want to tell their story. So, I make the turn in the street, hoping not to get shot (a sick side effect of accidentally turning into the wrong driveway these days, a concern I never had growing up in rural Ohio, but something I fear no matter where I travel now), and turn back toward the county road I'd come in on.

I have no cell phone bars or orientation. Raised in the era of paper maps and AAA service cards gifted by relatives in little gold boxes, my father still insists my glove box carry those lovely foldout maps of every state I tend to travel—wise in a situation like this—but Massachusetts is missing from the stack, and since I have a vague notion that what I'm seeking must just be straight ahead, I continue further, away from the angry dogs, and toward a steep rise in the rocky environment. I cross railroad tracks; the promising indication I've neared the spot.

I glance back. There. Over my shoulder, over a curve in the rails, against the snow-covered backdrop, carved into the base of a ravine. An open, gaping black maw. An unlit tunnel, whose exterior face is set in dark stone, bears the year 1875.

I have arrived and only the spirits know it.

This end of the Hoosac Tunnel, still an active railway, is visible to passersby, and as I find a flat landing that serves as a parking spot next to a tall stack of decaying timber, I note that in the two inches of snow on the ground, there are relatively fresh footsteps in it that have gone ahead of me, curving around toward the tunnel. As a woman alone, a black pit ahead of me, noting small liquor bottles scattered to the sides of the weathered rail ties, I hang back. I'm curious but not stupid. I *am* driven by the need to see this mouth and sense its endless scream for myself and I've come a long way to do so.

Yes, there have been many accounts of spirits groaning from within this dread tunnel through the years, and it is easy to imagine. It rings true, supernatural or no, as cries are doubled by the landscape. A fierce wind has kicked up around me and it literally bellows, positively *howling* through the forest and across the ravine this tunnel is carved into. The trees groan like bodies twisting in pain. The acoustics of this place sound like effects taken from horror films. A channel, carved as a gutter to reroute runoff coming down the mountain to the side of the tunnel, roars water from melting snow.

The shape of the ravine is a steep V and even on a bright day, the sun would shine through the forest canopy for only a few moments. It is a place surrounded by shadow.

A faded, barely legible gray sign on a rusting metal tower to the side of the tracks reads *Danger, Active Rail Line, No Trespassing*. Past it, the rail line bends toward the wide, blackened arch of the tunnel entrance. To the side of the warning sign sits a little wooden bench on a stone dais with a dedication plaque honoring a local train club. This *is* a noted historical landmark, after all.

I do not cross the line of the sign I can barely read, because I think warnings from both sides of the veil should be heeded. I take a picture. I record the howling wind and the rushing water. I say a prayer for the dead; the heartbreaking number lost while building this nineteenth-century "feat of engineering," and I go. But every single sound, sensation, and image will haunt me long after I've gone back the way I've come and regained cell phone service.

"The Bloody Pit" is now the only thing I think of whenever the wind rises around me and I strain to hear its warning, all my senses heightened, much like Poe's imprisoned protagonist.

The Hoosac Tunnel was the first significant rock tunnel built in this country. Its harrowing nickname of the Bloody Pit seems plucked straight out of Poe's fiction, but it is well-earned: 135 confirmed deaths, 195 serious injuries occurred during construction. The bold, gray-black arched stone entrance to the tunnel at the base of a vast mountain looks like a portal to the underworld, contrasting with the verdant green around it in spring or the icy, eerie white snow-covered rocks in winter. Still in use by freight lines, trains rumble regularly through its storied corridor.

Marred by difficulties, a project that began in 1851 and finally opened in 1875 could easily be deemed a "cursed" work of civil engineering. Not even five miles long, the tunnel was built to provide rail service between upstate New York and the Boston metropolitan area. Its history is directly responsible for innovations in explosives, as well as the pneumatic tool industry, using compressed air as part of the drilling process, which then revolutionized the mining industry; another workplace full of ghost stories.

Herman Haupt headed the Hoosac Tunnel project in the beginning, but left after significant financial setbacks bankrupted him. Perhaps this should have been the first sign to turn back; for the project to quietly fold, never piercing the earth. Haupt took his skills instead to the Union Army as a railroad engineer, later becoming a general who played critical roles in key battles. The Canadian firm of W. & J. Shanley saw the Hoosac Tunnel through to completion.

This tunnel has the infamous distinction of being the first civil works project to use nitroglycerine as a blasting agent. Even this first blast was marked with death. And as a result, ghost stories.

On March 20, 1865, three explosive experts, Ned Brinkman, Ringo Kelley, and Billy Nash, had readied nitroglycerine, set the explosive, and were prepared to run to a safety bunker. But the charge itself was somehow set off prematurely by Kelley. Nash and Brinkman were buried alive beneath tons of falling rock. It wasn't long after the accident that Kelley himself disappeared. Work had continued in the tunnel regardless, without word on Kelley. His body wasn't discovered until almost precisely a year later, March 30 1866, found strangled to death at the very site of the explosion.

Deputy Sheriff Charles F. Gibson placed Kelley's death sometime between midnight and 3:30 in the morning. While a murder investigation was mounted, no suspects were ever named, found, or arrested. Superstitious workers were vocal, *certain* it was the vengeful spirits of those Kelley had buried under the blast. Kelley's estimated time of death fell exactly in the time frame spirits are noted, in the annals of "anecdata," as being the most active.

After this, workers balked at entering the tunnel. Who can blame them, considering these bad omens, the constantly dripping water, the all-encompassing darkness? Soon, workers began complaining they heard the sounds of men groaning in agony. While the foremen assured them it was just the wind, loud and strange through mountain passes, work stalled to the point where an engineer and manager had to conduct their own investigation into the noises. This resulted in a firsthand spectral encounter, relayed in September 1868.

Paul Travers, an engineer on the Hoosac project and noted Union cavalry officer, wrote a letter to his sister, relaying that he and Mr. Dunn had traveled into the tunnel at night to investigate the sounds:

"As we stood there in the cold silence, we both heard what truly sounded like a man groaning out in pain. As you know, I have heard this same sound many times during the war. Yet, when we turned up the wicks on our lamps, there were no other human beings in the shaft except Mr. Dunn and myself. I'll admit I haven't been this frightened since Shiloh. Mr. Dunn agreed that it wasn't the wind we heard, perhaps Nash or Brinkman—I wonder?"

The pervasive horrors of the Civil War, the first truly "industrialized" war, permeated further into this man's life experiences and that of so many others.

Perhaps these groans were the proverbial canary in the coal mine warning them all. Canaries were historically used in coal mines to detect gases dangerous to any living being. Small, colorful, innocent sacrifices in the cold, black depths. The ghosts were the canaries in this mine, warning the living about dangers;

their sacrifice having already gone before. But a warning has to be *heeded*. Only one month after Travers wrote that letter, the greatest single tragedy of the tunnel's ongoing woes unfolded in a sequence of horrific events.

On October 17, 1868, a naphtha gas explosion destroyed a surface pumping station. Men were working in a 538-foot shaft which, in an instant, became filled with debris, water, and deadly gas. Thirteen workers died. A man lowered by bucket and rope to check for any survivors was brought up half-conscious from fumes, murmuring that there was no hope.

With no operating pump and the shaft filling inevitably with water, some bodies eventually came to the surface. It was more than a year later that the remaining bodies were found on a makeshift raft, hastily crafted to try to escape the rising water, but the gas fumes suffocated them long before anything else could. During that year where bodies remained unaccounted for, folklore was rife with tales of luminous spectral workers roaming the steep, forested mountainside, leaving no tracks along their snowy trails and restless wandering. Reports of the marching, roaming dead only settled down once all bodies were found and given proper rites and burial.

I couldn't help but think of those floating bodies leaving no tracks as I was noting the fresh footsteps that *were* visible to me, curving toward the tunnel upon my own approach, giving me plenty of caution. The rushing water, the creaking trees, and the wind all made rumbling, wild sounds to amplify my own anxious thoughts.

Reports of strange noises from within the tunnel would continue for the next century.

An additional layer of tragedy haunts this tunnel; employees repeatedly tried to tell everyone they were in danger. Workers had gone on strike in 1865, the year of the nitroglycerine explosion, to demand safer conditions. But their collective action couldn't save the next victims once the strike was broken by management. Much like how the garment worker strike known as the "uprising of the 20,000" in 1909 predated the horrific Triangle Shirtwaist Factory fire of 1911, the protest and clear warning made the resulting fire—which killed 146 as young as fourteen years old—all the more infuriatingly tragic. In each of these cases, the workers *tried* to tell the world they were in danger. The Triangle and the Bloody Pit chewed up and spat out around the same number of victims, sacrificed for product, progress, and commercial output.

The Hoosac Tunnel marked many engineering and excavation firsts, but also served as a critical new section of the supply-chain connector of goods and products from the East Coast further into New York State, whose population was growing by leaps and bounds in the nineteenth century.

Further tales about the tunnel and its ghosts swirled throughout the 1870s as reported in local papers. There has never been a shortage of unnerved accounts and baffling sights of spectral forms, blue lights of eerie flame, odd noises and disembodied voices.

Even a century later, spectral voices were on hand to save a life. Not just once, but twice.

Joseph Impoco, formerly employed by the Boston and Maine Railroad whose services routed through the Hoosac Tunnel, began working for the company at age eighteen. In an interview featured in the *Berkshire Sampler* on October 30, 1977, he told his interviewer he was clearing ice off the tracks when he heard a voice exclaim:

"Run, Joe, run!" he explains: "I turned and sure enough there was No. 60 coming at me. Boy, did I jump back fast. When I looked, there was no one there."

Having heard the voice before hearing the train, he felt sure that call saved his life. Earlier in the day a man with a torch had passed by and waved; someone he hadn't recognized, but didn't seem threatening. Joseph hadn't thought anything of it until after the incident, wondering if the disembodied voice came from the unknown torchbearer.

Several weeks later, Joe was in the process of unblocking freight cars stalled on icy tracks, using an iron crowbar, when someone shouted, "Joe! Joe! Drop it, Joe!" Just as he dropped the crowbar, 11,000 volts of electricity surged from a short-circuited power line overhead, sending the crowbar flying against the wall of the tunnel. Had he still been holding the tool, he wouldn't have lived to tell the tale.

Even though Joseph Impoco left that job and moved away, he returned to the tunnel yearly to pay homage to the inexplicable presences that had saved his life, feeling sure tragedy would befall him otherwise. The month in which his interview appeared in the *Sampler*, his wife had asked him to stay with her while she was ill, rather than returning to the site in ritual fashion. She soon passed away.

The Gothic screams through this story like a train whistle, from the heaping tragedies to the warning for those who might be otherwise helpless to run from danger. The tunnel became a catacombs, an unwitting mausoleum, and while the project was hailed at the time as a "gateway" for the Northeast in terms of goods and services, it was also a gateway to the underworld; spirits and all.

There is an honor to these ghosts, a heroism, watchful eyes that intervene to prevent others from suffering. Researching this truly stirred me because I *always* gravitate toward stories of helpful ghosts. Don't be fooled by the Bloody Pit moniker; this isn't just a horror story. There is resilience at work here. Like Mister Rogers said, "look for the helpers" in times of tragedy. Here's ghosts doing just that, even when they were literally left for dead by exploitative practices and harrowing, increasingly dangerous conditions. Their ongoing sounds, presences, voices, are all warnings, and when taken quite literally, can prove lifesaving.

In 1975, the tunnel was named a historic civil engineering landmark.

Atlas Obscura, noted site of eerie things, has an entry about this tunnel by *The New England Grimpendium* author J. W. Ocker, focusing on the tragedy rather than any associated ghost stories. The article warns any potential visitors to stay off the still-active train tracks. Which should go without saying; my own experience outside the unlit site should serve as another example.

If a disembodied voice gives you an order, don't think, don't question it.

Just run.

The Crossroads:
Motorcycle Ghosts and
Resurrection Mary

Leanna

> By a route obscure and lonely,
> Haunted by ill angels only,
> Where an Eidolon, named NIGHT,
> On a black throne reigns upright,
> I have wandered home but newly
> From this ultimate dim Thule.
>
> —Edgar Allan Poe, "Dream-Land"

You walk alone down an overgrown path. You speed too close around a bend. A figure suddenly appears. Startled, you do not know which way to go and your heart races, pounding in your ears. In this screaming pause where two paths diverge in a wood, you have to think quickly; your fate may be decided by a hair's breadth. Will you journey forward with the dead or the living? Are you able to continue along the road or do you career off into some unfathomable distance?

In Poe's final stanza of his poem "Dream-Land," in the narrator's liminal state between the nightmare of day-to-day material existence and the yearning for the sublime, the narrator confronts an "Eidolon," a Greek term for a spectral look-alike of the human form, while wandering back from "Thule"—the northernmost part, the outer extremes, of Greek cartography; the edge of the world. The "Eidolon" specter confronts the wanderer on their path home.

Spirits at crossroads are common in folklore and indeed in Gothic literature, with a nod to all the classical Greek myths where ominous figures lurked at forks in the road, marking pivotal points in the protagonist's saga. Hecate, after all, is the Greek goddess of the crossroads and witchcraft. By the wayside spirits are icons, omens, warnings, and road signs personified. The historic fear of brigands and highwaymen lurking along carriage paths, a popular brand of ghostlore from the 1700s on, simply transformed and anthropomorphized with technology and its new concerns. Any spirit at a crossroads is meant to give us pause, no matter the era.

Washington Irving's famed Headless Horseman, gleaned from local, Dutch-infused Tarrytown ghostlore Irving heard during his youth, is himself a figure at a crossing; a spirit treading paths, seeking and searching, hoping to reunite with his head, pausing iconically over a bridge to strike fear into those who wronged him.

As horses gave way to automobiles, the narrative changed and the language adapted, but the core part of the storytelling continued unaltered. That sense of caution and minding your way across a bridge, a sharp turn, or across an intersection remains, as does the awareness of your surroundings. Are you now a stranger in a strange land?

I travel constantly, for conventions, lectures, presentations, research, and I drive thousands of miles each year. The growing predominance of roadside shrines noting the exact place where a life was lost is a widening development. Considering these markers are outside the prescribed boundaries of a cemetery, and seeing that there are no remains at these memorials, it's noting the act of loss, the psychic imprint. A marker of trauma. A reminder to those fellow travelers to take care and a plea to remember loved ones lost in one shattering moment at that specific spot. Whether ghost stories are attached to these road-side markers I can't yet say. I haven't yet seen or heard enough anecdotal data and these shrines are too fresh to have become longtime lore. Those stories may evolve with time. But every time I pass one, I am reminded that everything could change in the blink of an eye. I don't look too close; I can't. It isn't safe to turn and stare. As a driver, those markers are figures that remain only safe to engage with out of the corner of your eye as you remain focused on the road ahead. As a passenger, you can drink in their stories and wonder about the lives they lived.

An interaction with a spirit of the crossroads can change your life. It may very well *save* your life. One spirit's tragedy is a reminder for you to live and to take care around the bend. The 13 Curves in upstate New York bears a folkloric marker and as is very common with ghostlore, it is a dead young woman who bears that reminder; an everywoman of cautionary tales and the tragedy of youthful beauty whose cord was cut by the fates before her time.

The following stories are omens sharing a similar theme. Slow down and heed the warnings ahead.

Motorcycle Ghosts of Western Ohio

I honestly never thought I'd experience an urban legend that proved *true*. Generally speaking, while everyone loves to share a local urban legend, no one really, in their heart of hearts, thinks they could witness or be part of one. But three friends and I, one crisp night in the fall of 1996, went searching for one. It found us.

Terrified and fascinated, what happened that night changed my behavior to this day.

I say "urban legend" here first, rather than "ghost story," because when I first heard about the motorcycle ghost in school, the account was so generalized. It had all the abstractions of a folktale, not an account of one particular spirit. There was no name and no precise year in which the motorcyclist had died, and his tale followed so many of the generic patterns of this kind of story that I just assumed it was a tall tale, impossible to trace to a real person or anything verifiable. Certainly not something that could be experienced by the prompt of headlights flashed three times at a given spot. A sensible, well-balanced belief in the paranormal means one should be a skeptic about any given situation at first, lest overactive imaginations get the better of the proceedings.

I've been telling ghost stories since I could talk, making them up as I went along, folding in specific details if I knew any history to add in. I'm very familiar with the structure that's most effective. While I research extensively for books like this, and for my ghost-filled fiction too, I don't actually go *looking* for ghosts. I go looking for interesting history and if it happens to be haunted, even better. Going searching specifically for ghosts gets mixed results. Ghosts are like cats, hard to predict and don't often come when called.

At age six, I experienced my first ghost when the spirit of my great-grandmother, the woman I'm named for, made her presence known to me at the time of her passing, though we didn't learn of her death immediately. So my respect for spirits as either mine or someone's loved one influences how I saw and thought about ghosts from that moment forward. I don't use the term "ghost hunt" because ghosts are people and again, respect for the dead precludes me from "hunting" *people*. So when friends suggested we go searching for the motorcycle ghost along his usual route, for us, it felt more like a séance, asking a haunted place if someone was there, rather than trying to harangue anything or anyone. His ghost didn't haunt a house, it haunted a road. But I just didn't think we'd get a response. None of us did, really.

But I wasn't about to say no to a ride in the country on a bright, beautiful, moonlit night with my friends; I lived in the middle-of-nowhere north of Cincinnati some forty-five miles and there was frankly very little to do. We'd already spent plenty of time in the local graveyards. While they weren't gated and it was easy to park and wander around in them, we were obedient, respectful kids and we tried to be mindful that we didn't want to push our luck with a local police patrol.

Automobile and motorcycle ghosts are, of course, a uniquely twentieth-century invention, shaping new horrors to fit changing technology, but the stories trace older patterns of ghost riders, ghostly carriages, and ghosts furiously riding on horseback across treacherous terrain, each mode of transport coming with their pet dangers.

See, we all *know* this story; it follows the pattern of teenagers testing boundaries and engaging with the unexpected; wanting to be scared. A story similar to this continually crops up, with many variations across the country; high school kids drive to a certain bend in a road or the bottom of a hill and do something to prompt a response, often flashing headlights, sending a signal for a ghost to appear as if sending Morse code. A call-and-response. Séance by headlight.

Our local version was a motorcycle ghost who lost their life on one particularly steep, dangerous hill in an extremely rural area near the college town of Oxford, Ohio, home to Miami University.

The lore was that either he was driving to a girlfriend's house to propose or upset after being refused as a suitor. There was some sort of emotional tie that explained the reckless driving on an obviously difficult stretch of road. The time frame of his death vacillated between the eras of the 1940s and the 1970s. It seemed important that it wasn't recent.

The hills and curves of southern Ohio are steep, long, unpredictable, and dangerous.

My friend and fellow ghost-enthusiast Erin drove four of us in her red Jeep to the base of the enormous hill in question and pulled over onto the grassy berm. She flashed her lights three times. Sure enough, a single headlight appeared at the top of the hill half a mile ahead. All four of us gasped.

These moments seemed to take forever. We opened our eyes and closed our eyes, asking each other if we saw it. We all did. There was no *sound* of a motorcycle. All we saw was just the light. Uncanny and silent. Approaching slowly.

It floated down the hill, but where it should have dipped down with the landscape before coming back up level with our car, the light instead floated *over* the gully and then dissipated. But just when it would have passed our car, had it been a corporeal object maintaining speed, a LOUD CRASH pounded on our roof. Like something heavy struck overhead.

God, how we screamed.

All of us looked around out every window, frantic; we alternately shrieked and cursed up a storm as Erin *tore* away from the side of the road, tires spitting gravel and scraggly grass. Surely someone was out there pranking us with a big rock or some trick. But no.

As we whirled around, no one was there. The fields, visible all around us, silver in the bright moonlight, remained quiet and empty. Once we had put enough distance between us and that thunderous noise, we were miles away when we stopped in a brightly lit parking lot to catch our breath and assess the damage. A sound like that *had* to leave a mark. Getting out of the car tentatively, we held onto the car doors as we stood along the baseboards and checked the roof. No dent, no chipped paint. *What* and *how* were words we all just kept repeating. What *made* that noise?

We'll never know.

While our motorcycle ghost has his own page on a section of Miami University's website devoted to ghostlore, it isn't the only one on the western side of Ohio. All the way up north, one of Miami's rival universities, Bowling Green University, has its own motorcycle ghost too, in nearby Elmore, Ohio. This motorcyclist's story has a World War I vintage attached to it. In this case, the motorcyclist has returned from the war to visit his sweetheart, only to find that she has married another in his absence. He roars away from the scene of his heartbreak and his recklessness on a hairpin turn just before a bridge proves his demise. The Bowling Green account, as collected in Beth Scott and Michael Norman's *Haunted Heartland*, has an additionally gruesome additive, noting the biker was decapitated in the accident and the headlight was also wrested from his motorcycle. Perhaps the persistence of this particular tale is owed to it *also* fitting into the ready-made Headless Horseman trope.

While I never experienced *that* ghost, the instruction of anyone who "summons" him to flash headlights three times for the headlight to appear reads the same in both accounts, as does viewers' descriptions of the fading light as it passes.

In *Haunted Heartland*'s account dating March 1968, a group of Bowling Green students took a movie camera, a tape recorder, and a still camera to the bend in the road just before the bridge. As if on cue, after both flashing lights three times and honking the horn, a light, as if a solo headlight, appeared, careened around the bend, and disappeared halfway across the bridge. Reportedly, the young men then enacted further tests each time the light returned. First, the string they tied across the bridge to see if something had passed remained unbroken even though the light was again visible. A student who stood in the path of the motorcycle was flung to the ground and disoriented, with no memory of being struck or thrown. The students parked their car on the bridge, and the light passed right through it. The students, unnerved by these subsequent "tests," quickly left the scene. Checking later, their video footage was blank, the audiotape recorded gathered high-pitched noises, and there was some weird glowing on the photographs.

Maybe this was a story that simply spread as an urban legend from one school to another, from one dangerous hill to one sharp curve, a story meant to entertain and scare the kids, a function of all such tales. That I can understand. Floating ghost lights across roads, paths, and bodies of water, whether attached to a spirit itself or to a vessel or craft, have truly timeless and cross-cultural traditions attached. These motorcycle ghosts play into those patterns. They are meant to terrify teenagers.

That's exactly how the sorrowful ghost bride of the 13 Curves got started in central New York. The "woman in white" of the 13 Curves, a hairpin stretch of swerving road along Cedarvale Road in Marcellus, upstate and just outside of Syracuse, got started. The story, pinned to the first days of the automobile, has its own plaque, the story codified by the New York Folklore Society William Pomeroy Foundation, whose red metal placards with cream lettering note Legends and Lore of the state, erected beside various folkloric landmarks in the hopes of promoting historic preservation alongside cultural heritage tourism. The 13 Curves sign announces the legend:

Along this route a woman in white searches for her groom. Both died on their wedding night in the early 1900s while driving the 13 curves.

The 13 Curves entry on the Pomeroy Foundation website notes that this seeking woman fits into many different recurring themes: the vanishing hitchhiker or traveler, sorrowful La Llorona stories as well as the myriad "women in white" tales of a mysterious, spectral, white-clad woman floating along a site of caution or tragedy. An Onondaga Historical Society writer, Dick Chase, claims this ghost bride was just a story made up by a local woman wanting to scare children into behaving better, employing her daughter to be the ghost while she drove the meddlesome kids, hoping the sight of a phantom would do the trick. But the entry does note *just* how dangerous those curves are, and how many accidents have occurred on those turns, which is the point of the story to begin with; something that has more staying power.

It would be so easy to say that what my friends and I experienced outside of Oxford was all just pranks and overactive imaginations on twisting, steep, and isolated roads, but to this day I have *no* idea what to make of it. No idea what, if not for something spectral, could have made that light or thundering sound on that moonlit night. My friend Erin still remembers it as clearly as I do; we talk about it when she comes to my book signings back home. She knows that experience is part of the reason I can't help but keep writing about ghosts, because the inexplicable has had such an ongoing, profound effect.

Personally, I had to make that encounter at the base of that hill mean something; otherwise, it was just scary and my mind refuses not to transform fear into something useful. Thinking of that mother in upstate New York wanting to scare kids into taking better care, ghosts unerringly serve a purpose. Their deaths and their spirits then floating like a symbol, a buoy on the water, make us reflect on how to live.

That bright-then-fading light and then that harrowing, crashing thud . . . It was a warning. A chastisement. An exhausted *what are you doing, get off the road, this isn't safe, go away and leave me alone. Go live your life. But watch your damn speed.*

Flashing the lights along that road wasn't something we tried again. We were curious kids, but we weren't stupid. The crash on our roof was *quite* definitive.

So, I say this with the respect to the dead that I try to bring to every story: thank you, motorcycle ghost. It remains true that nearly thirty years later, I drive far more carefully on huge, sloping hills down dark country lanes because of you. I think of that light. I remember that terrifying sound and the memory makes me a far more mindful driver in the present moment, around every turn. Because of you.

Consider your warning well-heard and deeply valued. I hope that somewhere, somehow, you did end up making it to your sweetheart and that you're riding down some peaceful, elysian road with blessed company on an eternally nice day.

Resurrection Mary

With a name like Resurrection Mary, Chicago's most famous ghost, one simply has to lean into her story and go along for the ride, perhaps listening to various ballads that have been written about her through the years that tell her story in the vein of classical, epic poetry. A muse that has danced across various artistic mediums, she has fascinated storytellers for nearly a century.

Easily classified into the popular "vanishing hitchhiker" trope of folklore that has become relatively universal, cross-cultural, and adaptive through time and technology, she's more than just a mysterious passenger. Jan Harold Brunvand notes in the preface of *The Vanishing Hitchhiker: American Urban Legends and Their Meanings* that urban legends proliferate as "the storytellers assume that the true facts of each case lie just one or two informants back down the line with a reliable witness, or in a news media report."[1]

With Resurrection Mary, that's absolutely the case; there *are* facts and informants and media reports, which is why she has proved particularly resilient, surviving decades of reinvention. There are actual names associated with her and reports of a Mary or Marija who died in automobile crashes. She has accrued more details than the average vanishing hitchhiker, making hers a far more plausible, quite memorable, and much richer story to tell.

Legend has it that a beautiful, blue-eyed blond teenager named Mary died in an automobile accident in 1934 after dancing the night away in one of Chicago's ballrooms. Supposedly buried in a lovely dancing gown and favorite shoes, she was laid to rest in Resurrection Cemetery on the southwest side of Chicago. The cemetery christening her with a memorable new name, her spirit simply couldn't wait to get back to the dance floor.

Jerry Palus was famously the first to go on the record about dancing with Mary all night in 1939 at the Liberty Grove and Hall ballroom in the Brighton Park neighborhood, noticing she didn't seem to know anyone there. When he offered to drive her home, she accepted. When they drove by Resurrection Cemetery, she insisted she had to leave and that he could not follow her. She disappeared at the gate.

Mary's presence became further chronicled in the following years when motorists complained of a young woman dressed in an evening gown hopping onto the running boards of their cars, hitching a ride to or from the Oh Henry Ballroom (later the Willowbrook Ballroom) only to startlingly disappear. During its 1940s heyday, Willowbrook boasted around 10,000 dancers every week. It had been praised and sought-after for its truly wonderful wooden dance floor and the roster of famous musicians who played the hall, from Count Basie to Doris Day to Frank Sinatra. Into this lively mix, a ghost reportedly made her rounds and tried to get back to her favorite pastime. One dance partner even reported having kissed her.

A few particularly evocative, eerily poetic details about her that witnesses have described through the years really struck me as I sifted through the narratives. While reports of her were common through the 1940s, there was a subsequent lull, but tales of Mary resurfaced again in the 1970s, a decade in which she was far more noticeably out of place in both her period dress and antiquated movement, but it was again a cultural time when the idea of going out dancing was vibrantly rejuvenated by the disco era.

Night manager at the now long-closed Harlow's club, Bob Main saw her twice in the 1970s, describing a deathly, powdered-pale blonde in a pale dress who sat to the side of the dance floor, or would dance by herself in a more classical style, and would shake her head if anyone tried speaking with her. Main noted that everyone was carded at the door coming in but no one had checked her in. He had this eerie detail to say to the *Chicago Tribune*:

"She had this teardrop on her cheek that looked like nail polish. But when you got right up to her, it looked like her eye was bleeding." Just as no one carded or allowed her entry, no one saw her leave.

As manager of Chet's Melody Lounge, a bar that faced Resurrection Cemetery, Rich Prusinski would hear all about Mary sightings, the bar gaining additional traffic and curious visitors as a result. He told the *Chicago Tribune* that in 1973, a cab driver dropped off a woman at the bar who didn't pay her fare. He waited and finally came in to find her. Everyone searched the bar for the blonde he had described, but she was nowhere to be found. Rich shared a story about a police officer who thought he'd hit a woman in a pale dress who had been in the road, but whose body couldn't be found, a story the cop reportedly shared on the TV show *That's Incredible!* Unsure if he believed any of it or not, Rich would still leave a Bloody Mary at the end of the bar for her, just in case she was thirsty.

The 1940s reports of Mary were warmer, more conversational, and vibrant, it being closer to a world she knew. By the 1970s the reports of her personality were more aloof and non-verbal with the disco crowd, entirely out of her time and frame of reference, but still wanting to be in community. And then, suddenly, senses reel and confusion sets in when she disappears. A ghostly Cinderella, running away from a ball, her pumpkin carriage the necropolis itself, her ball resetting at another time, to begin the cycle anew. Perhaps that's why this story has such a power to it; she is assumed to be a living girl (albeit those who claimed to have touched her during a dance note cold hands and brittle-feeling skin). She is interactive.

But then, suddenly, Mary is something else; like the moment the green ribbon around the neck is undone in that terrifying children's tale and the girl's head falls off. Mary is startling because she vanishes, she is unsettling because she's cold and she can't tell people where she lives or invite anyone to follow, she is harrowing because she asks to be dropped of by a graveyard. But there's a fanciful, wistful, romantic sort of encounter that precedes the reveal of her crypt home. A classic Gothic tale will draw the reader and listener in with its promises of atmosphere, the possibility of ghosts, and the titillation of flirtation. One becomes further ensnared when it's clear that no one can trust their senses. She makes her dates into unreliable narrators.

Who *was* Mary? There are many plausible possibilities to choose from. A strong initial theory is that she was Mary Bregovy, whose death was chronicled in a brief *Chicago Tribune* report on March 11, 1934, stating that "Miss Marie Bregovy," a twenty-one-year-old passenger, was killed when the car she was riding in, per the driver's explanation, hit a part of the El (elevated rail) substructure along Wacker Drive that he didn't see. What doesn't quite connect this Mary to her dance halls is that if the driver hit the El along Wacker, that would place them downtown, not out by the roads and the southside ballrooms where Mary has been a fixture.

Mary Bregovy was buried in a term grave at Resurrection Cemetery. After a certain amount of time, without a renewal of terms, the land would be regraded, fresh bodies laid atop the old. Through the years, *that* Mary's grave has been lost, but she's not the only possibility.

Author and ghost tour guide Ursula Bielski was always drawn to Mary's story, a tale she'd been told as a child while sipping a Shirley Temple in Chet's Melody Lounge, compelled by a shared Eastern European connection. Most of Mary's stories have noted her as the child of Polish or Czech immigrants. As Bielski searched further for Mary's identity in the early 1990s, Bielski gained access to conversations and interviews with the congregants of St. Joseph's parish near Resurrection Cemetery, and several Marys were offered up, each noting a tragic girl that died too young, each storyteller bringing some sort of personal connection. One parishioner, Ray VanOrt, said that as a young man in 1936, he and his fiancée had been the first on the scene of a terrible car crash on Archer Avenue, where three of four young people in the car died, one of which was a young woman, and all were coming home from the Oh Henry Ballroom. He was convinced that was Mary's accident, the inciting incident of her infamy.

In a 2007 blog post that describes her further discoveries, Bielski posits that Resurrection Mary could have been Anna Marija Norkus, a thirteen-year-old Lithuanian immigrant who died in a car accident having just passed Resurrection Cemetery, when the car fell into an unmarked railroad cut and fell twenty-five feet, killing her instantly. She had been begging her father to take her out dancing and this was the day he finally relented. After her death he was told this was his punishment for letting a girl dance so young. Bielski theorizes that Anna Marija's body may have been temporarily buried in Resurrection Cemetery due to a gravediggers' strike. She would then have been unidentifiable and irretrievable when it came time to move her to her permanent family plot in a different cemetery, adding a "restless spirit at an improper grave" prompt into the ghostly mix.

The founder of Chicago's first ghost tour company, Richard Crowe, was an early propagator of Resurrection Mary tales in the 1970s. A picture of burned, gnarled iron bars along a section of cemetery fence pops up in the Wikipedia page about the ghost. Crowe folded the twisted iron immediately into Resurrection Mary's lore; that she tried rending the fence open herself in the middle of the night, the burn marks proof of raw, phantasmagorical energy. The cemetery itself, which has long denied that Resurrection Mary exists at all, explains that the damage was done by a truck hitting the gate and blowtorches trying to reshape the iron, not supernatural spectral strength. But the image of charred, crumpled iron imprinted with a worker's gloved handprint was stirring and evocative enough for the attribution to Mary to stick.

To this day, people are raised on stories of Resurrection Mary.

I love Chicago; it's enormous and completely overwhelming (and I say that as a New Yorker, the difference is Chicago is just so *wide* and *vast*) and just as full of thousands of vibrant little neighborhoods as any big city, each with their own character, evident as one drives through. Chicago was the first *big* city I ever visited as a kid growing up in rural Ohio; the metropolis felt magical. Earlier this year, attending a Chicago genre fiction convention as a guest of honor, my presentation on the importance of ghost stories led to a lively discussion with locals. When

I referenced Resurrection Mary and that she would factor into this book, attendees mentioned she was a regular part of their childhood folklore; that they'd grown up hearing about her. Even though the dance hall venues, focal points of her haunting, are long gone, her story remains; the person far outliving the places where she'd been so famously seen.

Two devastating fires hit the Willowbrook Ballroom over the course of its long tenure, and the 2016 fire saw it razed for good. Plans to rebuild the dance space eventually gave way to a housing developer and only the Willowbrook sign remained. The venue most often connected to Mary now too has become a lost entity, a ghost, a memory, a holdover from when cars had running boards a wayward spirit could hop up upon. But the cemetery that bequeathed such a stirring name still stands; that remains Mary's through line.

The word *resurrection* in a Gothic frame of reference inevitably brings up Mary Shelley's *Frankenstein*, the first real work of science fiction (written by a teenage girl in 1813, no less) in which a scientist cobbles a body together from various parts and reanimates it with electricity. Before legislation like "bone bills" were passed to cut down on the plundering of graves, lessons of anatomy and surgery were often practiced on dubiously sourced dead bodies. The people who procured those corpses for doctors and medical students were called *resurrectionists*. Resurrection Mary as a name creates such a lasting impact, whether you know that's the name of the cemetery or not is immaterial; her name reflexively makes the statement that this is a young woman who has come back to life. Her name is an assurance of an everlasting haunt.

Mary regularly stirs imagination, providing fuel for talented contemporary storytellers like Cynthia Pelayo. A Chicago native and the first Latina and Puerto Rican to win a Bram Stoker Award for her work in horror, Cynthia incorporates

Resurrection Mary alongside her own love of local history and lore into her recent 2025 fiction, *Vanishing Daughters.*

The Vanishing Hitchhiker: American Urban Legends and Their Meanings discusses the natural appeal of automobile-based folklore in a modern, highly mobile society:

> Earlier generations told more stories of haunted houses, hunting adventures, or witchcraft, but we prefer stories centering on the family automobile, pleasure trips and the open road. The role of the automobile in many well-known urban legends is significant. Access to a car allows youngsters to separate themselves from family, home, and even from the inhibiting company of peers (except for a date or a close friend) for a considerable period of time. For a lower- or middle-class family a car provides a temporary escape from the humdrum world of home, neighborhood or suburb.

And that's the crux of Mary; the appeal of a young woman out and about, celebrating her youth and freedom. She focuses on her dancing, on socializing, on being seen, not on her death. Who doesn't love the idea of an unobtrusive, party-girl spirit? This lovely young maiden forever trying to find a bit of community and happiness in a dance hall pulls on the Gothic heartstrings that Edgar Allan Poe evokes in so much of his work—yes, the death of a beautiful young woman indeed is a most poetical topic, but there's something to celebrate about Mary rather than mourn.

That Mary has sought out dance partners for momentary, chaste but distinct intimacies makes her almost like a siren—but in a far less dangerous capacity. She isn't luring men out to their deaths in cold water, she's simply haunting her activity that brought her joy. By asking to be returned to the cemetery it isn't that she's trying to avoid her fate, she's accepted it. She knows she is dead and that it may be unsettling to the living, hesitating to say exactly where she has to be dropped off and insisting that she can't be followed, or simply disappearing on cab drivers who thought they had a living fare. This cognizance of existing differently than her living peers also makes her rarer in ghostlore, an awareness not every ghost possesses. Perhaps that's the Chicagoan in her; existing with a certain pride of place and surety of self.

Keep dancing, Mary, no matter what year it is. I have a feeling the Windy City will keep resurrecting you.

AN OPEN CRYPT

Part 6

The boundaries which divide Life from Death,
are at best shadowy and vague.
—Edgar Allan Poe, "The Premature Burial"

We have put her living in the tomb!
—Edgar Allan Poe, "The Fall of the House of Usher"

"Bacteria with Fangs": Mercy Brown and the Vampires of Rhode Island

Andrea

Mercy Lena Brown is known as New England's "last vampire." She lived in Exeter, an isolated village in rural Rhode Island, and died in January 1892 at the age of nineteen. Mercy died of tuberculosis, or as it was more commonly known in the nineteenth century, consumption. Her mother and sister had perished of the same disease several years earlier; her brother Edwin was also gravely ill at the time she died. He'd been suffering from consumption for some time, and had been sent west to Colorado to recuperate in a sanitorium, but to no avail. Consumption was a widely feared disease at the time, and was one of the leading causes of death throughout most of the late eighteenth and nineteenth centuries in America. In New England, some people thought the dead were continuing to transmit the disease to their living relatives. Mercy Brown's neighbors thought this might be the case. And so, after her death, her body was exhumed by her family and neighbors in an effort to halt the contagion.

Mercy's mother and sister were also exhumed but, because both had attained a reasonable degree of bodily decomposition—that is, they were skeletal—they were dismissed as possible sources of continued sickness among the living. Mercy, however, had been lying in a receiving tomb for two months, having died in the depths of winter when the ground was frozen solid. Her corpse remained, unsurprisingly, fairly fresh and well-preserved, and her heart was still engorged with blood. Her father, George, was not present, but requested a physician be on the scene to conduct an autopsy. The physician affirmed that her lungs showed evidence of tuberculosis and declared that her body was in a normal state of decomposition for someone who had been only deceased about two months, and had lain in an icy cold receiving tomb during that time. The neighbors, however, were undeterred. To placate them, George Brown allowed the performance of a gruesome folk remedy, a last attempt of the desperate to stave off further death. Mercy's heart was burned and the ashes were placed in a tonic for her brother to drink (there is no evidence that he drank it). Edwin Brown died two months later.

Mercy lives on in folklore and hers is the first name most people reference when they talk about the thrillingly-named "Great New England Vampire Panic." Her grave is in Exeter Historical Cemetery number 22, where the cemetery records state: "This unfortunate girl, who probably died of tuberculosis, was accused of being a vampire. She was dug up and her heart was taken out and burned."[1] It is visited by hundreds of goths, ghost-hunters, and various curiosity-seekers every year.

Mercy Brown wasn't the only vampire in the history of New England, merely the most famous. She's not even the only vampire in the history of Rhode Island. Far from it, in fact.

In 1796 in Cumberland, some thirty-odd miles northeast of Exeter on the Massachusetts border, a man named Stephen Staples petitioned the town council for permission to disinter his deceased daughter Abigail in order to "try an experiment" on her corpse in an attempt to save her ailing sister Lavinia. According to the official request in Cumberland Town Council meeting minutes of February 8, 1796:

> Mr. Stephen Staples of Cumberland appeared before this council and prayed that he might have liberty granted unto him to dig up the body of his dofter [daughter] Abigail Staples late of Cumberland single woman deceased in order to try an experiment on Lavinia Chace wife of Stephen Chace which said Lavinia was sister to the said Abigail deceased which being duly considered it is voted and resolved that the said Stephen Staples have liberty to dig up the body of the said Abigail deceased and after try-ing the experiment as aforesaid that he bury the body of the said Abigail in a deasent [decent] manner.

Staples was granted permission to perform the "experiment." Abigail Staples is one of the earliest recorded examples of a Rhode Islander who was allegedly exhumed after death out of fear of contagion to the living. There is no record of what followed, what occurred during the actual exhumation—or if indeed it ever took place—or when and how Lavinia Chace died. (Stephen Staples lived until 1815.) We can probably assume, based on what we know of other similar cases, that Abigail's heart—and possibly other organs, likely her liver—was cut out and cremated before she was reinterred. Lavinia may have ingested the cremains in some form, but we don't have any details. The town council meeting minutes do not elaborate on these experiments, nor do they use the word "vampire."

This small but intriguing scrap of information raises more questions than it answers. What drove these Rhode Islanders to take such extreme measures, and by what process did they imagine their deceased loved ones were actually transmitting disease to their living relatives? Did these people actually believe in, and truly think they were dealing with "vampires," in the sense that we understand the word today? Did they see any element of magic in their folk medicine, or did they genuinely see it as just another type of home remedy, if a particularly ghoulish one? And how on earth did they get the idea to conduct these macabre rituals in the first place?

The answer to that last question is, nobody knows. And it only gets more complicated from there.

"How the tradition got to Rhode Island and planted itself firmly here cannot be said." *Providence Journal*, 1892

When the epidemic of consumption tore through the United States in the eighteenth and nineteenth centuries, there was little understanding of the disease or reliable treatment, and the cause of consumption was not widely understood. Some people thought it was hereditary, others assumed it was caused by bad behavior such as habitual drunkenness, or was divinely ordained predestination or punishment.[2]

In 1720, an English physician named Benjamin Marten published *A New Theory of Consumptions—More Especially of a Phthisis or Consumption of the Lungs*, where he identified consumption's cause as microscopic organisms, which he called, somewhat adorably, "wonderfully minute living creatures." Marten suggested that consumption was transmissible through close contact, and that it was airborne.[3] But Marten's theories about consumption's causes and methods of transmission were slow to gain wider acceptance. German scientist Robert Koch identified consumption as being caused by bacteria in 1882, ten years before the Mercy Brown case, but again, his ideas were slow to catch on in popular consciousness. There were apparently other reasons not to trust Robert Koch.

According to Rhode Island author Christa Carmen, with whom I spoke about the Mercy Brown story, "Koch was a man driven by ego, to the point where he made his claims of a cure without having conducted the proper tests to verify his hypothesis. Ultimately, his remedy was proven ineffective, but not before innumerable people had taken false hope from the announcement." [4]

Aside from that, Christa continued, Koch "cheated on his wife with a teenaged mistress, whom he then used as a human subject in TB antibody tests that he conducted too early in his research to be considered safe. He was impulsive and vain and was driven more by a longstanding rivalry with another German scientist than he was by any intense desire to help patients suffering from what was, at the time, the world's deadliest disease." Warming to her subject, Christa dropped even more insight:

> Plenty of men have been, and still are, extolled for their contributions to society while their less-than-moral characteristics go unacknowledged and undiscussed. In Berlin, Germany, the Robert Koch Institute is a federal government research agency that includes a museum to preserve both the work and the man behind it. Conversely, Mercy Brown, a young girl whose life was plagued by hardship and tragedy, is remembered today as . . . a vampire.
>
> History turns many undeserving men into heroes and even more undeserving women into monsters.

With folks like Dr. Koch not offering much help, nineteenth-century Americans were left to their best guesses about how consumption was transmitted, and they had *all* kinds of ideas about how it was ameliorated or cured, including warm sea air (which actually sounds pleasant), deep breathing, seaweed placed under the pillow, milk from a pregnant woman, and cold baths.[5] Other treatments included drinking brown sugar dissolved in water, and "bleeding, blistering, climatology, diet, drug regimens, exercise, leeching, open-air treatment, health resorts, opium, poultices, purgatives and emetics, rest cure, sanitoriums, [and] voyages for health."[6] Then there's everybody's favorite remedy: frequent horseback riding.[7] By the 1850s, the concept of the sanitorium was introduced and folks sought fresh air and dry climates for a cure. The sanitorium was the only resource that people had that even came close to ameliorating the scourge of consumption, and even that—as we have seen in the case of Edwin Brown—did not always work.

In the Western world, vampires have nearly always been associated with public health crises. In Europe in the 1720s, overcrowded cemeteries and outbreaks of disease gave rise to vampire legends and panics. These began mostly in Serbia, Hungary, and other regions of the lower Danube. The psychological origins of these vampire panics aren't hard to surmise. Obviously, people in eras that lacked our current scientific knowledge had to come up with ways to explain and understand sickness and contagion; what's more, when bodies behaved in aberrant ways, not decomposing as they should, spiritual explanations abounded. In seventeenth-century Serbia, good, religious people who didn't rot in normal ways became saints; drunkards and unpopular people became vampires. Depending on how they died, and what stage of decomposition they were exhumed in, even a perfectly normal body could look strange. A modern medical examiner could tell you that sometimes the heart is still engorged with fresh-seeming blood and that's not necessarily a medical anomaly; but a Serbian peasant who lived three hundred years ago did not have access to this knowledge.

These Eastern European vampires were "shaggy, bestial peasants" who were highly corporeal, extremely ensanguinated, and in general not at all sexy. Peasants staked them, urbanites

mocked them, poets were inspired by their metaphorical qualities. Voltaire wrote of them scathingly, and may be the first
modern writer to compare vampires to capitalism. Voltaire
says the only urban vampires are "stock-jobbers and men of
business" who suck the blood of people in broad daylight and,
though not dead, are corrupted. In 1819, Lord Byron and John
Polidori latched onto the vampire's life-draining qualities, and
in fact Byron's own status as what we might call an "energy vampire" today inspired Polidori to write *The Vampyre*, thus transforming our shaggy bestial peasant into the suave Continental
vampire we know and love today. The first vampire fiction
published in America, incidentally, was the short story "The
Black Vampyre: A Legend of Saint Domingo," also published in
1819. It was written in response to Polidori's *The Vampyre* and
designed to ride the wave of that novella's popularity. Written
pseudonymously, it is a "supernatural Gothic romance set in
America and Haiti."[8]

By the time Mercy Brown was exhumed in 1892, genuine vampire belief was already a curious throwback. Even earlier in the
century, it was an outlier: Thoreau wrote, on September 29, 1859:
"The savage in man is never quite eradicated. I have just read of
a family in Vermont who, several of the members having died
of consumption, just burned the lungs, heart and liver of the last
deceased, in order to prevent any more from having it." When I
read about the New England "cure" for consumption, I immediately wondered why nobody else, anywhere, was doing this. Yes,
there were a few isolated cases outside of New England—one in
Minnesota, one in Ontario, Canada—but this was mostly confined to a very limited region. How then, and from whom, did
New Englanders get the idea for this folk remedy?

An oft-cited 1784 article in the *Hartford Courant* warns of
a "certain Quack Doctor, a foreigner" telling New Englanders

that they could combat consumption through the act of exhumation and cremation. This foreign quack doctor claimed to have "a cure for consumption, where any of the same family had before that time died of the same disease: directing to have the bodies of such as had died to be dug up, and further . . . consumed in the fire, would be an effectual cure to the same family."[9] There appears to have been a divide between believers in (and users of) these remedies, and commentators who opined on them, usually unfavorably. The author of the *Courant* article disparages these quack doctors and warns people away from them. Clearly the people of New England didn't heed this warning: Almost a hundred years later, local Rhode Island historian Frederic Denison included in his book *Westerly and Its Witnesses* (1878) a chapter called "Swindles and Swindlers," where he also disparages this idea and warns that some "ignorant" persons still believe that "in some mysterious way the dead, or the diseases of the dead, may feed upon the living."

Quack doctors made the rounds of the medicine show circuit throughout all populated regions of nineteenth-century America, so it's hard to say exactly why this notion didn't spread south, or west, or really anywhere else. Maybe the doctor was run out of town, or died, or changed professions before he could spread his bizarre methods any further. Or maybe these practices did spread and we just don't know about it (yet).

Or maybe there is something unique to New England that allowed these ideas to take root and flourish.

> "New England's secret history of Puritan hypocrisy, persecution of Quakers and witches, and the long fall from grace is revealed in Hawthorne, King, and Lovecraft . . ."
>
> —*Faye Ringel, The Gothic History and Literature of New England*

New England is the first home of the Gothic in America. Author Faye Ringel locates the origins of the American Gothic not in the steamy decadence of the South, but in the prim wooden houses and plain churches of New England where the Puritans "transplanted Europe's nightmares to the New World." The American Gothic sprang from this rocky soil and was watered by "Puritan fears of the wilderness and of attacks by the native peoples . . . New England Gothic narratives [embody] the repression, anxieties, and hypocrisy of four centuries of New England's history and the literature that emerged from it of hauntings, immurement, repression, and revenge."[10] The terror of the Gothic has its source in a dreadful secret history, "the historical violence of dispossession and the blood soaked into the land."[11] In the Gothic, nothing stays buried for long. The past impinges upon and erupts into the present, the hidden becomes visible, and repressed secrets come to light. Here is New England's terrible colonial history, all the hanging of witches, flogging of Quakers, murder and expulsion of indigenous Americans, and pillaging of the land and water—all the hidden secrets becoming unburied.

The Puritans were indeed pathologically terrified of the wilderness and of the indigenous American people who dwelt in it. They had willfully destroyed the former and brutalized the latter, and they sought to sweep away their guilt by completely eradicating them—and all traces of the violence they had perpetrated against them—as swiftly and completely as possible. Their ecophobia was so intense, and New Englanders cleared their forests so furiously, that they actually lacked sufficient firewood by the early 1800s.[12] In fact, disputes over firewood were even in play as early as 1692, and they were a factor in the tensions between neighbors in Salem village in the run-up to the witch trials.[13] The settlers worked the land as hard as they could and New England "yielded in return a fine crop of stones."[14] The soil was barely arable and has been described as "rocks, rocks, and more rocks."[15]

Rhode Island began to lose population as early as the 1830s. After the Civil War further decimated the male population of rural Rhode Island, new rail lines opening up in the Midwest and West enticed the last young men who still remained out to literal greener pastures, and they abandoned their rock-strewn old farmsteads. By the time Mercy Brown died, a second wave of forest growth had encroached to cover up what had formerly been farms. Hauntingly, "the stone 'fences' that once separated neighbors' fields became mysterious artifacts in the second-growth woods."[16] The ruin, of course, is another hallmark of Gothic environments.

Decaying rural New England was fertile ground for vampire belief. Observers, such as a writer from the *Atlantic Monthly*, compared western Massachusetts to the Appalachians or the Ozarks—backwoods folks in a "decaying, superstitious backwater," as they put it.[17] Edith Wharton, who chose to summer in western Massachusetts, and set her chilling short story "Bewitched" there, described the "grim places [where] insanity, incest, and slow mental and moral starvation were hidden away behind the paintless wooden house-fronts of the long village street, or in the isolated farm-houses on the neighboring hills." And here is how H.P. Lovecraft described the village of Dunwich in "The Dunwich Horror":

> [The] natives are now repellently decadent, having gone far along that path of retrogression so common in many New England backwaters. They have come to form a race by themselves, with the well-defined mental and physical stigmata of degeneracy and inbreeding. The average of

their intelligence is woefully low, whilst their annals reek
of overt viciousness and of half-hidden murders, incests,
and deeds of almost unnamable violence and perversity.

Contemporary commenters on the Mercy Brown case, specifically the *Boston Globe*, also hinted darkly that rural Rhode
Islanders' superstitious nature had something to do with the
frequent intermarriages among family members.

Into this environment of decline and isolation stepped a
sophisticate from the big city of Providence, a reporter for the
Journal, sniffing out a juicy scoop about the backwoods rustics
and their ancient superstitions. He found the story of Mercy
Brown waiting for him, almost too good to be true. The urbanite
journeying into a "decayed, superstitious backwater" is a staple
of Gothic horror—picture *Dracula's* Jonathan Harker traveling
through Transylvania—where he discovers the persistence of
ancient rituals in isolated rural areas.[18] I was put in mind of one
of my favorite Sherlock Holmes stories, "The Adventure of the
Musgrave Ritual," wherein Holmes says, "I look at [these scattered houses] and the only thought which comes to me is a feeling of their isolation and the impunity with which crime may be
committed here." In the country, no one can hear you scream.

These rural spaces also feel strangely bypassed by time:
anachronistic, holding on to vestiges of an era most others
have forgotten. Anthropologist George Stetson remarked on
this quality in his 1896 article "The Anamistic Vampire in New
England." When I first read about Mercy Brown, I also thought
it was bizarre that such a thing should take place in the very
modern year of 1892. This was only three years before the first
movie was screened in Paris (*Workers Leaving the Factory*,
December 28, 1895) and one year before Charles Duryea and
J. Frank designed the first American gasoline automobile. The

people of Exeter seem completely out of step with modern times, which only adds to the mythlike, fantastical quality of Mercy's tale.

When Voltaire wrote in his *Philosophical Dictionary* in 1764 that "we never had word of vampires in London, or even at Paris," he cemented the link between vampires and remoteness, and makes village folklore the stuff of modern metaphor and satire.[19] Voltaire already expressed surprise at the old-fashioned nature of vampires—however long ago people are writing, it seems that they always believe vampires belong in an earlier age. The tensions between science versus superstition, urban versus rural, and modernity versus anachronism, what Roger Luckhurst calls the "disjunction in time between nature and culture," are "crucial to the Gothic sensibility."[20] Luckhurst notes that the powerful psychological effect of this dissonance is precisely the place that horror comes from:

> The shivery effect of Gothic tales comes from the slight hesitation we feel when we confront a story of uncertain status—where we cannot, at first, know if it is a true story, an old legend, folktale, or fiction . . . [The] same shivers [overcome] the city sophisticate when they enter the superstitious network of beliefs in a village community: 'What if these superstitions turned out to be true? What if the country bumpkins are right?' After all, shouldn't Jonathan Harker have listened to the peasants along the road to Dracula's castle?[21]

I certainly see Mercy's story as quintessentially Gothic, though not everybody agrees with me, or if they do, there are a few qualifiers. Christa Carmen, who writes contemporary Gothic fiction, says, "I do see hers as a Gothic story, though not one that ends the way traditional Gothic stories do. Ultimately,

Mercy would have triumphed over evil if hers was a Gothic tale penned by, say, Ann Radcliffe or Jane Austen."[22]

Folklorist Michael Bell told me he adheres to a fairly orthodox definition of the Gothic, in which stories contain a psychological element: "I don't see much of the Gothic psyche aspect in [the New England vampire] narratives, as they have been recorded," he said. "But I know that this aspect has developed in current oral [and] internet stories. I would say that the psyche development is an inevitable outcome, a trajectory that is part and parcel with the legend process in general. I believe there is an ingrained human need to create better and better stories, which often veers into the mind and mental states."[23]

H.P. Lovecraft described the mental state of the Gothic as one of dread arising from "a malign and particular suspension or defeat of those fixed laws of Nature which are our only safeguard against the assaults of chaos and unplumbed space." In the New England vampire tales, the horror comes from the suspension of one of the fundamental fixed laws of nature, that is, that the dead do not rise. Vampirism is a transgression, an inversion of the normal. Lovecraft was no stranger to the Mercy Brown legend, and integrated it into his 1924 novella *The Shunned House*.

The lines between fact and fiction are definitely blurred in *The Shunned House*, as Lovecraft freely mixes fictional characters with real historical personages. The narrator is a Providence man, and knows of vampire tradition only from the notebooks of an antiquarian uncle, which "revealed to me at length the darker, vaguer surmises which formed an undercurrent of folklore among old-time servants and humble folk." This characterization of the "darker, vaguer surmises" in the folklore as attributable to "old-time servants and humble folk" speaks to the city-country divide as well; he consistently refers to the rural characters in the story as the "Exeter rustics."

The Shunned House residents' "vitality was mysteriously sapped" by vampiric forces, and the characters of Mercy Dexter and the servant Ann White, of Exeter, overtly refer to the Mercy Brown event. (Other side characters who were also real people include Sidney Rider, who we will meet in a moment, and Pardon Tillinghast, who we will also meet soon.) Pardon was a trader in the "notorious triangle," importing slave-produced goods from the West Indies, including sugar, rum, and molasses. His nickname was "Molasses Pardon."[24] Lovecraft weaves in the real—Sidney Rider, Mercy Brown, Pardon Tillinghast, a house on Benefit Street—into the fantastic, just as the Gothic moves fluidly between fact and fiction.

What really grabs me about *The Shunned House*, though, is the way that the dream state figures into the narrative. Without giving away any spoilers, dreams are central to both the premise and climax of the story; early on in the backstory, various characters succumb to vampiric attacks while they sleep, much as many in the Rhode Island legends were said to. This is par for the course in the Gothic tradition, where dreams and nightmares often "direct the action."[25] In an oneiric state, the rational mind is loosed from its moorings and all manner of supernatural horrors come out to play. The nightmares that disrupt our sleep are part of the fog of dread that looms over the Gothic, where we confront the pervasive, intangible "anxieties and traumas of the human condition."[26] Many Rhode Island vampire stories involve nighttime visions of departed loved ones, and are suffused with archetypal symbols and imagery. Sidney Rider's account of the Sarah Tillinghast case is even more overt; it literally begins with a nightmare.

In 1799, Exeter resident Stuckley Tillinghast, known to his friends as "Snuffy," had a dream that half the apple trees in his orchard died. Later, half of his fourteen children would perish by consumption. In the midst of this crisis, he exhumed the bodies of his dead children to identify the vampire. The blame fell on a daughter, Sarah. When her coffin was opened it was discovered that Sarah's eyes were "open and fixed"[27] "her hair and nails had grown," and her "heart and arteries were filled with fresh red blood."[28] Like Mercy Brown, her family cut out her heart and burned it.

Incidentally, the Tillinghast family can be traced to many other vampire legends in Rhode Island, showing that they have an outsized influence on this particular branch of lore. Another family plagued by vampires was that of William Rose; his second wife was Mary G. Tillinghast, Snuffy's great-granddaughter. Rose disinterred his young daughter in 1874, in South Kingstown, Rhode Island, not too far from Exeter. William Rose was a member of the Exeter Grange, sort of akin to a town council, and so was George Brown, Mercy's father. They undoubtedly knew each other socially. The social links between these three families—the Tillinghasts, Roses, and Browns—reveals the Tillinghast family to be a sort of nucleus in this particular regional cluster of vampire phobia. [29]

The Tillinghast story appears in a work called *Book Notes* by a local historian and bookseller, a man named Sidney Rider— the same one who was name-checked back in Lovecraft's *Shunned House*.[30] Rider published his *Book Notes*, a collection of "literary gossip, criticisms of books, and local historical matters connected with Rhode Island" biweekly as a way of getting more business to his shop at 17 Westminster Street in Providence.[31] When I first encountered Rider's version of the tale, the dream of the fourteen apple trees immediately struck me as having a biblical flair; it also has a fairy-tale familiarity. It's a perfectly structured narrative . . . and a little too trope-y to be real. It relies heavily on what Lovecraft would have called "the common stock" of supernatural lore, and therefore beggars belief. Surely Rider embroidered and embellished this story. Or perhaps it's possible that Rider was just the messenger, and that his source was the embellisher, and Rider was just relaying what he heard. Perhaps the story had made the rounds in oral tradition for a while before Rider heard it, and it naturally got embroidered there, "attracting traditional motifs," which is a natural facet of how stories are remembered and retold.[32] Everyone adds a detail; that's how the transmission of folklore happens. It certainly feels like someone along the way definitely embellished this story . . . but who knows? Maybe Snuffy really did dream about losing half the trees in his orchard. Stranger things have happened.

Sarah's spirit supposedly appeared to her siblings and sat on their chests, haunting them, and telling them that they would be the next to die. In his 1896 article the "Animistic Vampire in New England," George Stetson writes that "It is believed that consumption is not a physical but a *spiritual disease, obsession, or visitation.*"[33] I emphasize the "obsession" part of this sentence, because that term had a very specific context in the late nineteenth century. Obsession was a bit like possession—it was the idea that a spirit could enter a living person and direct their actions. Its connotation is that the dead can return to influence the lives of the living through spiritistic means, and it has a negative connotation. The spirit obsesses, or inhabits, the mind and body of the living person, usually with unpleasant results. The New England vampire is a discarnate spirit, more like an angry ghost than a corporeal monster.

At some point in the course of my research, I noticed that the Rhode Island vampires I was going to talk about in this chapter were young, unmarried women. Innocence in peril is another standby theme of the Gothic. These innocent virgins accused of vampirism are violated after death, their bodies and graves desecrated. They evoke the character of Lucy in *Dracula*, who was turned into a vampire just at the cusp of her own marriage and thus also died a virgin (presumably). And yet, while innocent, they are lusty, faintly sexualized, living double lives at night and riding abroad secretly, doing as they please. Florella, in Amy Lowell's narrative poem "A Dracula of the Hills" is "passionate" and filled with lust for life.[34] The Mary E. Wilkins Freeman short story "Luella Miller" (1902) features a woman who drains those around her, energy-vampire-style, sucking the life out of everyone who gets close to her. The vampire is perhaps the most iconic Gothic monster, and the Gothic vampire is sexy, period, even as it repels.

As for Lucy, while there are connections between her and Mercy Brown, I do need to say she was *not* the inspiration for the character, no matter what you may have heard. The name and character "Lucy" was mentioned as early as February 1892, one month before Mercy Brown was exhumed, in Stoker's handwritten notes, and so could not have been based on her. The oft-cited observation that Lucy sounds like an amalgam of "Lena-Mercy" also strikes me as odd. To my ears, Mina—the main female character in Dracula—sounds far more like an amalgam of Mercy and Lena than Lucy does. Lucy's name, incidentally, was intentional: it means "light" or "light-bringer," and evokes Lucifer; according to the *Norton Critical Edition* of *Dracula*, Stoker intended to give her an allegorical name.[35]

In 1827, in a town called Foster, on the border of Connecticut and Rhode Island, a certain Captain Levi Young dug up the body of his daughter Nancy, whom he believed to be a vampire. The family burned her remains and inhaled the smoke. A contemporary account, underwhelmingly titled "Interesting notes of Foster in 1827," states that:

> There seemed to be a curious idea prevailing at the time in
> some localities, that by cremating or burning the remains

of a departed friend or relative while the living relatives stood around and inhaled the smoke from the burning remains, that it would eradicate the disease from the systems of the living and restore them to health.

A short time after the decease of Nancy, in the summer of 1827, the neighbors and friends, at Mr. Young's request, came together and exhumed the remains of Nancy, and had her body burned, while all the members of the family gathered around and inhaled the smoke from the burning remains . . . [36]

Smoking the ashes of Nancy Young did nothing to stop the spread of tuberculosis, naturally. The contemporary account, written by a local man named Casey Tyler, is pretty matter-of-fact about all this. Nowhere is the word "vampire" mentioned, and there's really very little spooky or salacious about it. It honestly seems rather . . . practical. A bit gory, but ultimately there's a certain logic to it—it's an intuitive kind of inoculation. Yet some modern residents of Foster have transmuted her story into a Hollywood-style tale of terror, and it is whispered that her ghost still rides abroad in the darkness of a rural Rhode Island night. They believe Nancy Young was, and is, truly a vampire, and "still roams the countryside looking for fresh victims."[37]

Many of the Rhode Islanders I spoke to while researching this chapter are only vaguely aware of Nancy Young, or don't know her at all. She isn't a household name like Mercy Brown. The cemetery where Nancy rests is a classic, tranquil New England family farm plot, and her grave looks to be in good condition, as though it is little-visited. It rests in a hidden spot behind a newish subdivision, and the current owner of the adjoining property seems only vaguely aware of who Nancy Young was. When a local TV crew once visited the grave site, she asked if they'd come to see "the witch." Upon being corrected, she said casually, "Oh right, vampire."[38] Spooky legends have a tendency to get muddled and misremembered.

In some cases, the legend actually "created" vampires, as in the case of Nellie Vaughn. An instance of mistaken identity created an entire mythos around this poor girl, leading to tales of vampirism *and* ghost stories.

Nellie Vaughn was a regular nineteen-year-old who died of natural causes, probably consumption, in 1889 in West Greenwich, Rhode Island. She is buried in a nondescript cemetery behind the Plain Meeting House church. There is no evidence to support any claim that her contemporaries ever suspected her of vampirism, or ever disinterred her or tampered with her corpse. Yet she is nearly as well-known as Mercy Brown. Her grave is repeatedly visited and vandalized to the extent that the church has had to remove her headstone to a safe space, and the same types of legends as Mercy Brown's—for example, that no grass grows on her gave—have been frequently repeated.

Nellie Vaughn's misidentification as a vampire is likely based on her proximity to Mercy Brown in age, death date, and burial location, and probably also due to the sinister-seeming inscription on her grave: "I am watching and waiting for you." This inscription is fairly innocuous if you're familiar with nineteenth-century cemetery monuments, and likely is a reference to the young deceased person waiting for the rest of the family to join them in heaven. But to someone unschooled in the ways of late-Victorian-era burial—say, a teenager—this inscription seems creepy.

Legend-trippers continue to visit Nellie's grave site. Stories of her ghost haunting the graveyard have circulated, and there is no going back . . . despite the fact that most of the trippers can't tell Nellie from Mercy. One group of folklorists wrote, while visiting the grave to study the ephemera left behind by visitors, that "many people appear to visit the cemetery in the course of looking for Mercy Brown's gravestone. Indeed, on one occasion a carload of teenagers approached us as we stood near Nellie's grave site and asked if we knew where Mercy Brown was buried." These visitors are generally disrespectful and destructive, not only vandalizing the grave but leaving "the remnants of parties and other clandestine activities [that] litter the cemetery [such as] pornographic magazines, black knit hats, guitar picks, scores of broken bottles, beer cans, and drug paraphernalia . . . Because of vandalism [spotlights] operate intermittently."[39] Opinions differ on the fine line between vigils and vandalism. Both Christa Carmen and Michael Bell have thoughts on what constitutes an appropriate offering. Christa says that she doesn't "really see much respect behind the leaving of Band-Aids and hair elastics."

> It's just…strange to me to leave such things. It's like the person leaving said items just wanted to be able to say they'd left something, regardless of whether any forethought or care was put into the offering. I feel like there's a difference between bringing something with intent and dumping the trash from your car's ashtray onto her grave site.[40]

Mercy Brown gets her fair share of folks who leave plastic fangs on her grave. I asked Michael Bell what he thought of that and he replied that "fangs are no worse than coins, beads, fake flowers (or even a tampon!), or other items that do not damage the grave site. Such items can be removed if necessary and there is no lasting damage." Bell has no problem with legend-trippers per se, as long as they're respectful:

> I'm fine with legend-trippers. Supernatural place legends have always attracted people and led them to actually

visit these sites in person. I do take issue with those who disrespect the sites they visit. Vandalism increases with such traffic, which is a shame. Leaving material items at the sites is marginally okay, in my view. But when there is physical damage, such as graffiti and breaking the material culture on these sites, then things have gone too far. Also, since the majority of the trips take place in darkness—and mind-altering substances (alcohol, weed, et al.) frequently are involved—there is danger for those who drive to and from these sites, many of which are in isolated areas accessible only via small and winding roads. That's a lethal combination in too many instances.[41]

Mercy Brown's descendants play it safe: they hold Halloween vigils on her grave to keep such legend-trippers away.[42]

And just as Nellie Vaughn attracts legend-trippers, she also attracts ghost hunters.

People have reported seeing a young woman dressed in Victorian clothing near Nellie's grave who disappears when approached. There is an oft-repeated story about an auditory manifestation, a soft, female voice plaintively protesting, "I am perfectly pleasant." A woman named Marlene, from Coventry, had several mysterious events occur when she went to Nellie's gravestone to do some rubbings. Her papers repeatedly became damp, despite the fact that it was not wet or rainy outside, and the gravestone was dry. Her charcoals repeatedly disappeared, and in photos of the rubbing, every letter was backwards. Later, her friend felt a disembodied spirit poking her arm, and on another visit, her husband heard the refrain, "I am perfectly pleasant," and was mysteriously scratched in the face by an invisible entity (counterpoint: that's not particularly pleasant). Marlene, who seems to have been a frequent visitor to the cemetery, also had an apparitional experience on another visit: She was walking among the tombstones when she encountered a young woman who she described as "attractive" and "chatty," though she can't recall any specifics about what she looked like. They stopped at Nellie's grave and the young woman became agitated when Marlene started talking about the vampire story. "Nellie was not a vampire," the young woman insisted, so vehemently that Marlene grew uncomfortable and returned to her car. When she looked back, the mysterious woman was nowhere in sight.[43] Another story holds that a local couple heard Nellie Vaughn's voice speaking to them through their answering machine. Nellie died in 1889 and the first stories of her vampirism didn't begin to circulate until the 1970s, so it's easy to believe the origin of her supernatural story rests merely on a case of mistaken identity.

But here's the funny thing: Nellie is buried in the West Greenwich Baptist Church cemetery. The church was also referred to as the Plain Meeting House, and its pastor from 1840 to 1878 was none other than the Reverend John Tillinghast, a second cousin of our good friend Snuffy.[44] Maybe an archivist or historian will unearth some primary sources one day that proves the teenage legend-trippers were right.

The relationship between fact and folklore in Nellie Vaughn's story is a really fascinating one. It reminds us that it's important to allow for and consider alternate possibilities, or if that feels too irrational for you, then to at least watch the process of folklore unfurling with a sort of open-minded, nonjudgmental detachment. Total skepticism is the last refuge of the genuinely frightened person, who ropes off deep fears they cannot face with the yellow tape of logic. Unqualified skepticism also keeps this story at a critical remove, something to be engaged with only on an intellectual level, denying the reader or listener the joy of "active, visceral participation" in the spooky story.[45] Isn't storytelling and myth as fundamental to the human experience as the collection of facts and data? Storytelling traditions exist for a reason; if we rely too heavily only on historic fact, we lose a huge facet of culture. Perhaps instead of choosing sides between skepticism and credulity, we should remain flexible and open to both knowledge and mystery. Some people, when discussing the New England vampire panic, opt for a purely rational viewpoint: they dismiss it as nothing more than sensationalistic, eye-catching headlines perpetuating a myth. The reality, they say, was just some poor farmers desperately trying anything they could to stop the spread of tuberculosis, just regular people struggling with a virulent epidemic in an era of premodern medicine, blown out of proportion by the media, nothing more than another chapter in the history of tuberculosis, albeit a macabre one. It's certainly valid to simply observe the enmeshing of medical history, archaeology, and folklore in the New England vampire stories with absolutely no spooky angle, and just be fascinated, in an empathetic way, by the extremes people would go to in the desperate search for their number one killer. That's definitely one approach, but it leaves something important out of the story.

In his landmark book *Food for the Dead*, Michael Bell, the foremost folklorist studying the New England vampires today, describes the tension between two parts of himself he calls "Dr. Rational" and "Mike." They are at war with each other, the first striving for historical accuracy at all costs, the latter finding himself charmed and enthralled by the magic and wonder of these tales. I've often felt that way, as someone who is both responsible for historic fact-checking *and* enthralling storytelling on my ghost tours. It's like I have a microscopic Mulder and Scully battling inside my brain. I emailed Dr. Bell to say how much I liked his book, and I asked him how Dr. Rational and Mike were doing. He responded wryly, "That is an ongoing struggle. But these two sides of one coin have always found ways to coexist peacefully. In my view, both of them—work and play—are necessary for living a complete, harmonious life. The boy inside has never died."[46]

Similarly, I prefer to simultaneously enjoy the deliciously Gothic folklore that has sprung up in the wake of the transmission of verifiable history. I don't believe the New England vampire was real, any more than I believe eighteenth-century Serbian peasant Peter Plogojowitz was actually a literal vampire. But to me, that doesn't really matter. It's the imaginative qualities of the New England vampire that intrigue me. As Paul Barber succinctly puts it in *Vampires, Burial, and Death*, a vampire "might be defined as a corpse that comes to the attention of the populace at a time of crisis and is taken for the cause of that crisis." In which case, yes, Virginia, Mercy Brown is a vampire.

The entire Gothic mode depends on this kind of thinking, of privileging the imaginative qualities of life over the strictly rational, a "penchant for the uncanny" and eagerness to engage with other realities.[47] From its beginnings, the Gothic has always accepted the possibility of the irrational and embraced "phenomena that were not easily explained by rational Enlightenment thinking."[48] Mercy Brown and the Rhode Island vampires tick pretty much every Gothic box: the weather and landscape are extreme, inhospitable, and isolating (cold, snow, rocks, desolation); the architecture is morbid or foreboding (the crypt where Mercy's body languished); the texts are fragmentary, unstable, ephemeral, and obscure (newspaper clippings, folklore, strange practices with an unknown origin); macabre occult rituals are performed; ghastly secrets unearthed; ghostly presences amid grave sites and overgrown ruins; and pervading it all is a psychological element of horror and dread (fear of contagion, and the vampire) within which dreams and visions figure significantly.

It is said that Nancy Young's ailing little sister Almira dreamed that Nancy came to her at night, looking "bright like an angel" and foretold that Almira's pain would soon be gone. These dreams were, in fact, part of Levi Young's motivation for exhuming Nancy, and they echo the motifs of the Tillinghast vampire a generation before. The angelic imagery is both beautiful and sad, and to naysay all these stories into oblivion robs us of an essential human element of grief and mourning. The angelic appearance of Nancy Young recalls Sarah Tillinghast's lovely face and bright blue eyes; the beautiful dead girl is, for better or worse, a hallmark of poetry. Without this haunting, uncanny imagery, would the vampire stories have so much staying power? There are processes in the human mind that are inherently intuitive and irrational, such as belief in the unknown, or the creation of art, and equally important as the search for empiric knowledge. This is the very essence of the Gothic.

Let nobody tell you unfounded tales without delving responsibly into their sources, and let nobody's skepticism rob you of your joy. When all is said and done, we need ghosts, and vampires, and all things supernatural.

Our scientific, progressive world nailed the last coffin lid shut not long after Mercy Brown's story took place, but we continue to, if not believe, to seek vestiges of our old beliefs, often filtered through culture, holding on to them in our collective memories and subconscious because we need them. They serve a purpose. Human beings cannot exist on a purely rational plane—as Shirley Jackson says, "No living organism can continue for long to exist sanely under conditions of absolute reality"—and if we ever try to make it so, spooky things will emerge like a vine from a graveyard, bursting through cracks in the walls, and unfurling itself around our minds. People often ask me why ghosts are so popular now, and of course the answer is: It is not a question of *now*. They have always been and always will be popular. As long as humans have souls, we will need our soul-food, and that soul-food is mystery and wonder.

Or as a wise man once said, the blood is the life.

Elena and the Count:
Key West, Florida

Leanna

Where do I start with this story? With a handcrafted airplane that would never fly, but was meant to cure tuberculosis in space? The painstaking construction of a mausoleum, only to later blow it to pieces? The reports of dancing with a dead body in a bridal gown? Installing a telephone into a crypt where a spirit would call to sing a song about death? A body's three trips to various funeral homes over the course of nine years? Or perhaps something altogether more disgusting.

No matter where one starts with the death and inescapable afterlife of young Elena Hoyos of Key West, Florida, the most puzzling thing is that it's all true.

In the 1930s, one man's obsessive love created one of the most disturbing spectacles imaginable in the hopes of defying death. While drafting this book, when friends asked what I was working on and I listed the mad details of this story, they thought I was talking about a villain I'd dreamed up in my fiction. *Wait,* they'd say, staring at me after I clarified, *this is for the nonfiction?!* Liz, editor of this book, who is also one of the editors of my fiction, would surely stop me after three of these improbable details, let alone the litany of them.

Let's start with the ghost story that started it all: a white woman in a castle in Germany. According to Karl Tanzler, born in Dresden in 1877, who took on the name Count von Cosel, he had been haunted for quite some time. The ghost of the castle he claimed he grew up in gifted him a vision of a beautiful, dark-haired woman who would become his bride in some future time and place. He would be visited by spectral visions of his bride-to-be at other points in his life, notably during his internment in a prisoner of war camp in Australia, presumably due to having served in the German military during World War I, a fact he never conclusively admitted. He was, however, industrious while interned. He carved an entire pipe organ out of wood. Playing and maintaining organs would be one of his ongoing passions. *The Phantom of the Opera* parallels remain rife.

Upon his return to his family "castle," he found life miserable and the country economically devastated, so he decided to emigrate. His years from 1920 to 1926 are unaccounted for in his memoirs. That he married Doris Tanzler and had two daughters was a minor detail he didn't think warranted a mention.

Tanzler's backstory, as he presented it in writing and to those he met in America, is entirely unreliable aggrandizement. For example, there was a Castle Cosel in Dresden, Germany, but the Tanzlers were not descended of it. But, upon traveling first to Cuba, then to the United States, he declared himself nobility, reinventing history, taking on the name of the local castle he'd likely romanticized as a child as his own. He carried it off well enough to be (mostly) believed, spoke excellent English, held himself as superior, and had a credible enough background and knowledge to land a job as an X-ray technician at the Marine Hospital in Key West, an island previously called Cayo Hueso; "Island of Bones" by the Spanish.

Claiming to have nine collegiate degrees that cannot be traced, he left the wife he'd brought with him and his two children behind in Zephyrhills, Florida, near his sister, who had already been established in the area. None of them were a part of "the count's" grander plan.

On April 22, 1930, he looked up at the patient whose blood he was drawing for testing at the Marine Hospital. Gazing at the twenty-one-year-old Elena Hoyos Mesa, his world turned upside down and his restless heart found the focus of his obsession. This, he was sure, was the vision from his childhood haunt come true; this was his intended bride. Never mind that she was already married and now diagnosed as dying of tuberculosis.

Nothing deterred Tanzler as he tried everything in his power to cure and save her. Ben Harrison, author of *Undying Love*, a book that chronicles the entire bizarre ordeal, titles the first chapter of his book "Stranger than Fiction" and the events unfold exactly as billed.

Evidently, from all accounts of those who knew her, Elena was a sweet, polite, kind woman who was an accomplished singer, a marvelous dancer, fluently bilingual, and a stunning beauty. A miscarriage in the first year of her marriage signaled a decline in her health and a telling cough began racking her form. Her husband entirely abandoned her when she became ill and there was never a finalized divorce.

Into that void eagerly stepped Tanzler. If Elena couldn't come into the hospital regularly for treatment, he would bring tons of equipment into the Hoyos home to treat her in person (without any authority or clearance from his employers). The Hoyos family were Cuban immigrants that had done well for themselves in Cuba but had fallen on harder times in Key West, where much of the Cuban population, including Elena's father, worked at the local cigar factory. Tanzler's offers of personalized care surpassed what they could easily have afforded, and in this Tanzler exerted a deterministic power and broad license.

The "count's" constant attention and affection was met with a certain amount of appreciation for the moments when his unusual range of treatments did help her, but also healthy amounts of skepticism regarding his intentions toward a far younger, technically still-married woman (the Hoyos family didn't know there also was already a Mrs. Tanzler, which didn't come out until the courts got involved), wondering if he was, as he claimed, entirely altruistic in his efforts.

It is true that Tanzler had the boundlessly creative mind of an inventor, and many of his elaborate, unorthodox electrical and radiation treatments did have a precedent and methodology, but the fact remained that tuberculosis was at that juncture untreatable. The disease would eventually claim the entire Hoyos family.

Toward the end of her life, during one of her treatments, Elena evidently translated a song for Tanzler, a ballad that she enjoyed, as it played on the radio. "*Boda Negra*," which translates to "Black Wedding," is a mournful bolero written by acclaimed and nationally beloved Cuban troubadour Alberto Villalón, with verses by Colombian poet Julio Flores. The song describes a heartbroken suitor who digs up the corpse of his dead love and holds her as he takes his own life.

Tanzler assumed their discussion of "*Boda Negra*" was blanket permission. He felt he had been "given" Elena as a bride, both by her father and by words he put in Elena's mouth.

Elena died on October 25, 1931, and Tanzler, who was brought to the house by Elena's brother-in-law Mario Medina, was furious that he hadn't been contacted sooner. Tanzler tried some of his devices on her in hopes of revivification, but an additional doctor confirmed her death. She was buried in the Key West Cemetery's Catholic section after a well-attended funeral service. Tanzler imagined the funeral procession as a wedding march for him and his departed bride.

There wasn't proper drainage in the Key West Cemetery in which Elena had been interred and the heavy rains worried Tanzler, who felt Elena's corpse was too vulnerable to decay. So, with the family's permission, Tanzler did properly obtain a disinterment permit from the state to move her body from the underground grave and into a lavish white mausoleum that he designed. This disinterment would mark Elena's second trip to a funeral home. There, she would receive more thorough care, in an unprecedented "re-bedding" as she was transferred into a sturdier metal casket. That Tanzler, after clearly bribing the mortician, spent three nights alone in the funeral home morgue to clean, detach fabric from skin, re-embalm and redress Elena's body himself was not made public. He created an "incubation" tank for her, filled with a custom antiseptic formula meant to revitalize cells, and soaked her in it, like a specimen might float in formaldehyde. Her body lay in wait for her mausoleum to be completed.

Built atop her original burial site, featuring an arched roof, decorative urns and flowerpots on the corners, with a Latin inscription that translated to "summoned by angels," the mausoleum Tanzler designed was tucked in among palm and pines; a peaceful and lovely place of rest. And Tanzler visited every day, unlocking the door and sitting inside, vigilant in a chair by her doubled casket with its interior and exterior metal shell.

He paid the Hoyos family rent to sleep in Elena's bedroom, on the large mahogany bed he'd bought for her comfort when she was alive, and he noted that he felt closer to her and her spirit in that place—and that the bed still smelled sweetly of her hair.

The antagonism between Tanzler and the Hoyos family eased some after Elena's passing, likely in an act of shared grief, perhaps in part because the family continued to be baffled by him. From all accounts, from all sides, the one thing that does seem to prove true about Tanzler is that his grief for Elena was genuine. But as was made clear by his actions, he felt his grief gave him a mandate that overrode anyone else's wishes, and increasingly escalatory acts of obsession flew in the face of custom, decency, and respect.

At some point, two years into visiting Elena's crypt every day, something changed. He was no longer content simply to keep company by her side while she was in her casket. According to Tanzler, she began singing to him from the crypt; verses of "*Boda Negra.*" He claimed her casket locks sprung open and fingernails scratched against metal, as if she were trying to get out. He took the song lyrics as a directive; to take her corpse out of the grave and to lie beside it in a romantic act of eternal love. In the song, the suitor commits suicide to be with his love, a concept Tanzler would have been very familiar with as a fan of Wagnerian opera, but he did not take his own life as the song showcased. Instead, he lived in a morbid world of his own making.

Meticulously planning how he would get the casket out of the mausoleum, onto a wagon, up and over the locked gates of the cemetery, then ferry his prize to a halfway point, he picked a moonless night and euphorically got to work. Thinking himself the Gothic hero heralded by a parade of the dead whose spirits rejoiced and whose hands reached up from the earth to help him along, he wasn't accounting for the casket falling on him as he tried to get it over the fence. Foul black liquid dripped onto the wedding tuxedo he'd worn for the occasion. Proving more the duplicitous Gothic villain instead, he managed to partially wash the putrefaction off with a bottle of whiskey at his midway-point storage shack. He secured the casket there for the rest of the night and had the audacity to creep back into the Hoyos family home during the witching hours, none of them the wiser.

Behind the Marine Hospital where he worked, in an abandoned area, Tanzler had been building an airplane fitted with enormous, hollow wheels that would supposedly roll on water to allow the craft an amphibious landing. The "airship" was never completed, but its main cabin was closed and secluded enough. As Tanzler had free rein of the area, it was into the cabin of this airship that he secured Elena's casket. When she was alive and visiting the hospital, he would take her for visits to the airplane and sit with her in the cockpit, dreaming up wild fantasies of flying to a South Sea Island with her for their "honeymoon." Even in his memoirs, he notes that she blushed and was modest, likely unsure exactly how to respond to the caregiver thirty years her senior. He named the ship for her, *Countess Elaine von Cosel C-3*, and went so far to say that he'd endeavor to take her into the atmosphere to cure her with radiation from outer space.

Much like when he tended to the body after the first disinterment, this time Tanzler meticulously bathed the body in Chinosol, a powerful germicide he had ordered from Germany, and did several "incubation tank" rounds, again with the hope of restoring tissue. He truly seemed to think he could bring her back to life, his thought process ranging from metaphysical sciences and various interfaith principles into the utterly delusional. Perhaps, if he got the plane working, the outer atmosphere could entirely revivify her. He spent many hours trying to dislodge fabric and mold from her skin without tearing it, moving her arm from folded to lying flat; the process he describes is gruesome and steadfast. Eventually, as his access to equipment, radiation, and electricity was limited, he began lining her body in silk and in time, the process of mummification began.

Years passed. Seven entire years.

Tanzler moved Elena twice. The first time after the "airship" was no longer welcome on hospital grounds, he had Elena's brother-in-law help tow the airplane to a large wooden shack along isolated Rest Beach, where Tanzler could set up a laboratory and continue his labors. Mario agreed to help Tanzler, never knowing that the airplane carried the slowly, inevitably desiccating corpse of his sister-in-law.

When Doris Tanzler wrote to her estranged husband to implore him for help, that his daughter Crystal was ill, she was ignored. When she wrote again to say that Crystal had died and asked him to come to the service, he did not answer and did not attend. He only had time and resources for Elena's corpse.

When the shack on Rest Beach was compromised by WPA renovations along the waterfront, he had everything moved again to a smaller, still-isolated, wooden structure off Flagler Avenue. A harrowing picture, presumably taken by Tanzler, looks like a silent-era horror film still, or a spirit-photo meant to trick an unsuspecting Victorian into thinking there's a ghost. His picture shows a sort of funereal bier with curtains drawn aside. Elena's body lies in partial shadow, but a woman's form is clearly visible. Gauzy layers of bridal veil over a crowned head and still face make her form glow, dressed in a voluminous white gown. A small Christmas tree sits to the side of the picture, with little gifts and offerings. He made her body into an unsanctioned reliquary and continued worshipping at her feet, restructuring her body where decay and rot had taken over, using wax, silk, and sterile cotton to rebuild her, trying to keep insects at bay through the whole process.

Eventually, in a relatively small town, even a laid-back and generally carefree one like Key West, an island that weathered the Great Depression in many ways better than most due to ample fresh food in the waters and on land, people will talk. Especially about eccentric behavior—and Tanzler was nothing if not that. Local shops began to wonder why on earth he was buying heaps of soaps, fragrances, and oils. It looked suspicious, but locals were loath to think it was all to mask something as unseemly as the stench of ongoing decay. Yet it was precisely that.

Supposedly, a local boy saw Tanzler dancing with what looked like a large, life-size doll in a bridal gown through a window. Whatever justified fears Florinda Hoyos Medina, Elena's older sister, had about the fate of her sister's body mounted. When the grounds of Elena's grand mausoleum had become overgrown and no longer fastidiously maintained, the remaining family could no longer ignore the probability that the "count" had absconded with Elena's body. Florinda, known as Nana, demanded that Tanzler open the crypt and show her proof that her sister lay in undisturbed rest and that she continued to be cared for.

Indignant and self-righteous, Tanzler insisted that Nana come see for herself *just* how well her sister had been taken care of. He invited her into his modest abode filled with heaps of random equipment, a large organ he was repairing, and the grotesquely reconstituted body of Elena Hoyos. Laid out like Tanzler's bride. He proudly crowed about all his painstaking efforts and how happy anyone should be to see such meticulous care.

Exactly what Nana said or thought in those moments isn't known and I'm not going to put words in any more of these women's mouths than has been done to them already. But just imagine it: You lost a loved one to a wasting disease, a disease that would continue to take other members of your family, and then a person who had promised to take care of a crypt to honor your little sister has her continuously decaying body laid out like a gruesome doll under layers of mosquito nets. The word *horror* doesn't do it justice.

When Nana left, Tanzler must have thought her satisfied. But that couldn't have been further from the truth. She went to the authorities. A few days later, the first week of October, 1940, there was a knock at Tanzler's door and a request for a certificate. When Tanzler produced Elena's death certificate without an additional disinterment certificate, he was taken into custody and charged with malicious and wanton disfigurement of a crypt and removing a body to his home, in defiance of state health laws. He spent a night in jail before local bar owners who he was relatively friendly with paid his bail.

Elena Hoyos's waxen, mummified, reconstituted body was laid out for a third time in a funeral home. This time, it wasn't a somber, pensive, mournful affair. This was an ungodly sideshow attraction under the unconvincing guise of "paying respects." That her grotesque, wax mannequin of a corpse became a carnival feature for what added up to nearly seven thousand gawkers and tourists alike . . . What a grievous injustice.

In an act of supreme courage, Doris Tanzler actually wrote to the authorities, saying that perhaps she could shed light on her estranged husband's troubled mind. She was never called upon to elaborate or testify, but the papers had a field day learning that there was already an abandoned wife and child in the mix.

Given the news coverage of Tanzler's arrest, reporters clamored to get inside the initial courtroom discussions that would decide whether a full trial was warranted; it was all an enormous spectacle. It was the biggest, and strangest, story to ever come out of Key West. Tanzler insisted in court that he did nothing wrong, that he had been trying to save her life and was still trying to preserve her. It was press coverage of the arrest and initial depositions that first floated the idea that Tanzler had a telephone installed in the crypt to talk to the dead body—one tall tale Tanzler did not admit to in his own writings. Elena's family did share their story, but their efforts, emotions, and testimony were not enough. By October 19, it had been determined that the statute of limitations on grave robbery and defilement were up, meaning the case could not go forward with a full trial, further sentencing or any jail time. Tanzler was free to go. But he could not, as he so ardently requested, have Elena's body returned to him.

The opinions of the time (according to newspapers, Harrison's biography, Tanzler's own memoirs, and online retellings of the dread tale) were that many people, women in particular, found all of this wildly romantic. Tanzler received letters, poetry, visitors, and loads of support. I suppose it shouldn't be a surprise; people do form fetishes around serial killers. I don't understand that either.

Doctors dePoo and Foraker examined Elena's remains during the arraignment process. They found that her body had indeed been sexually violated; an inserted tube reconstructed a vaginal interior and cotton inside bore traces of semen. The most startling (and prolonged) case of necrophilia any doctor could have imagined. And yet, for reasons entirely unknown, the doctors did not come forward with the truth of this evidence until over thirty years later.

Dr. Foraker, when he decided to talk about the case in the 1970s, "psychologically profiled the Count by paralleling his behavior with the notions of 1800s German Romanticism," noting the attachment to Wagnerian themes. In his 1976 paper "The Romantic Necrophiliac of Key West", Dr. Foraker went on to quote other experts who said that they'd never seen anything like this case in over half a century of sex crimes. While Foraker's discussion of nineteenth-century inspiration might explain a certain mindset, it takes a unique disposition—an obsessive, horrifying compulsion—to have gone to the ongoing lengths to fully actualize onto a dead body what should have remained purely in the realm of literary thought-form.

Perhaps if *all* the details of the kind of relationship Tanzler had with a dead body had come out at the trial—and they did *not*—people might not have been so ready to think him such an old-fashioned romantic or a perfect, lovelorn gentleman.

A classic Gothic villain will take an unsuspecting young woman and control her, shape and manipulate her into what they might wish her to be; the Phantom willing Christine to be his "angel of music" and muse, while dragging her to his lair and throwing her into a bridal gown without regard for a more reasoned or compassionate courtship. Hardly romance.

It's thought that, at the time of the trial, the most intimately disturbing parts of the already distressing case would have been too much for the Hoyos family to take or bear, not to mention the further disgraces to Tanzler's wife and daughter, regrettably bound to his name by association. There was also an air of things that *just weren't talked about*; a bridge too far, as it were, and as the matter wasn't going to a further trial, with both sides of each family wanting *nothing* to do with the morbid circus, it was let go.

The all-male panel tasked with assessing Tanzler's mental state found him sane, albeit obsessive. Doris Tanzler's experiences and information were never sought, nor brought to bear. Whether the physical evidence of Tanzler's necrophilia had actually been entered into the record or not at that point, a detail that *could* have proven a chargeable and punishable offense, was unclear. In any case, World War II loomed on the horizon, and judicial priorities were elsewhere.

The only thing that came out of the arrest that did align with the wishes of the Hoyos and Medina family was that Tanzler not be permitted anywhere near Elena's remains again. But unfortunately, they would go to their own graves never knowing Elena's final resting place; this secret died with the last of those involved.

Now the subject of international notice, Tanzler was turned celebrity. While that hadn't been his intention, he reveled in it. The attention continued to feed and reaffirm the idea that he had done nothing wrong; oblivious to the insult and injury done to others, his entitlement remained unchecked. His position at the hospital had already been eliminated by budget cuts by the time the trial broke, so to survive, he began charging tourists who would show up at his home out of morbid curiosity. There, he'd expound upon his whole story, show off some of his equipment and perhaps one of Elena's death masks. Thankfully, there was no longer an actual body to ogle. Tanzler was now consumed with his next great task: his memoirs. The trial and his admirers only emboldened his idea that he was the ultimate romantic hero.

Celebrity in Key West turned exhausting for Tanzler, and as the scrutiny on Germans living in the United States intensified due to World War II, Tanzler left the island for Zephyrhills, where he moved in with his ailing sister and devoted himself to tall tales. But first, he had something else to destroy.

Tanzler, as a last bon voyage to Key West, exploded Elena's former tomb, an edifice he'd spent such time and resources to construct. He blew the mausoleum apart using two sticks of dynamite left inside the door, set to go off once he'd safely escaped Key West for Zephyrhills. It wasn't speculation that Tanzler did it: He admitted it in his own words. The crypt ruins became overgrown and then were later cleared entirely for new plots.

After struggling to find a publisher for his memoirs (for good reason), some 70,000 words of his memoirs were reduced to under thirty-three and published as *The Secret of Elena's Tomb* in the pulp magazine *Fantastic Adventures* in 1947. His writing is pompous, overwrought, meandering, and wildly false. He makes himself out to be a hero in the eyes of God and the angels, as if he were acting on divine instruction, without self-reflection, humility, or shame. It is a narcissist's manifesto, interspersed with detailed descriptions of removing fabric from dead skin.

Throughout Tanzler's accounts, he always uses a possessive; always *my* Elena. He refers to an adult woman, who was a grieving mother and wife when they met, aged twenty-two by the time she died, repeatedly in childlike terms. Newspaper articles noted Elena as younger than she was when she died, keeping her perpetually a teenager.

Another disturbing trend in Tanzler's narrative is the revisionism of Elena's spirit, a force that he said visited and guided him repeatedly. He made her into another woman, literally and figuratively, while thinking he was actually preserving her. An alternate-universe delusion.

Tanzler's alteration of Elena Hoyos's entire personhood showcased his adoration of an ideal, not a real woman. The cultural dynamics, economics, and racial privileges in play add additional, insidious weight. Whether it was anglicizing her name to Countess Elaine von Cosel when naming the airship for her, as if she were his legal bride, or the sections written in his memoirs where he said her spirit began speaking German and her eyes changed from brown to blue. He would play Bach and Wagner on the organ, her husk as sole audience, saying that the harmonics would have a healing effect, insisting those Germanic classics were her favorites.

But they weren't. Her favorites had been the great Cuban boleros on her old radio in the Hoyos family home; the ones she used to sing to great acclaim in local theaters before she fell ill. Her eyes and hair were *brown*, not some Aryan fever dream. This bride to Tanzler's Frankenstein was just as much of an ill-advised idea as Mary Shelley imagined such an endeavor to be.

Tanzler died alone at age seventy-two in 1952, having moved out of his sister's house, needing isolation to continue another iteration of his grim work.

His body wasn't discovered until it was in a significant state of decomposition, lying near a bedecked mannequin in another fine gown, a form that he'd reconstructed as another Elena, using one of the several death masks he'd made of her as its face. Pictures, ephemera, and heaps of flowers created a shrine around her re-created body, an idyll at whose side he breathed his last.

The *Haunted History Chronicles* podcast first brought my attention to this story; I appreciate Michelle Fisher's range of subjects and her thoughtful interviews. She approached this narrative with a delicate touch rather than sheer sensationalism, even as the most lurid details were so trumpeted in newspaper headlines from the moment the story first broke. Even a Cuban *novela*; a serialized radio drama chronicling the events, with "*Boda Negra*" as a theme song, gained traction on Havana stations at the time the news was breaking. To this day, this story is hard to engage with in a way that I feel is sensitive to who deserves the empathy most: Elena.

Elena never got to be the narrator of her own story at any point in her life or death and in the end, she was just reduced, by others, to pieces.

Elena's augmented remains were dismembered, placed into a square metal box, and deposited in the ground in the dead of night, in secret.

Only three men knew the location of Elena's final resting place: Key West Police Chief Bienvenido Perez, Lopez Funeral Home undertaker Benjamin Sawyer, and cemetery sexton Otto Bethel. They went to their graves never revealing the location.

This beautiful young woman deserved so much more respect, volition, and autonomy at every stage of her life, early death, and involuntary afterlife. There's only one thing left to say:

May you *truly* rest in peace, Elena, remembered as you really were. You yourself were never trapped in that horror that man put you through, your lovely spirit was long gone, the shell discarded; traded for a glowing raiment. Your sweet, kind soul would have sung and danced, free and far from any of the cares and troubles of a broken world and those toiling in it.

It's time we give Elena Hoyos back some joy. Her role as a Gothic heroine can be one of transcendence; we can know her because she lived, not because of all that was made of her death. The name Elena means a bright and shining light; triumphant against any darkness foisted upon her.

An Unusually Warm December: The Mysterious Fate of Mary Howe

Andrea

They said she thought she could fly.

Fifty-year-old Mary Howe lived with her brother Edwin in an old inn called the Wayside in the remote Maine village of Damariscotta. Her father, Joel Howe, had built the structure after the War of 1812, when he retired following a distinguished army career and struck out on his own with his wife and large family, buying up a generous plot of land in the area near what is now Hodgon and Elm Streets. He built a large, square, white clapboard building, named it the Wayside Inn, though it became better known as Howe's Inn, and hung out his shingle. His wife assisted in the daily operations of the inn and tavern, while raising their nine children.

His children were ingenious, creative, and spirited; the youngest boys, Edwin and Lorenzo, loved to tinker with homemade contraptions. They created a "perpetual motion" machine, and devised an apparatus for the counterfeiting of half-dollars. Perhaps this tendency toward petty fakery and their natural engineering skills was a harbinger of things to come. Meanwhile, their sister Mary demonstrated a flair for theatricality and an eccentric spirituality that was definitely a foreshadowing of her future career. Once, as a child, she became convinced that she possessed the power of flight, and in a fit of faith, threw herself over the topmost railing of the main staircase in the family's home. When she merely snapped her ankle instead of ascending angel-bound into the ether, the family doctor, a Dr. Dixon, came and set her bones, warning her against any more such foolishness. Mary just frowned and wondered if her heavenward flights should take another, less corporeal form. Dr. Dixon may have had an odd feeling he hadn't seen the last of this one.

As the Howe children grew into adulthood and took over ownership of the inn, Mary discovered a penchant for the new craze of Spiritualism that was cresting over the country in the wake of the Civil War. She was drawn to séances, was convinced she had telepathic, spiritualistic, and clairvoyant powers, and claimed she had developed a method of trance-induced astral travel that enabled her spirit to roam beyond the limitations of her body. The depth of her trances was such that she would disappear inwardly for days at a time, barely breathing, with no discernible heartbeat and, somewhat oddly, a markedly lowered body temperature. Her brother Edwin, her staunchest supporter, kept her warm during her trances by placing rocks he'd heated in the fireplace near her bedside. When Mary emerged, in her own good time, from these trances, she bore news and revelations from the Other Side.

Mary had audiences eager to see and pay for her celestial insights. Curious villagers and travelers passing through town were invited to come and see Mary and receive their own messages from the beyond—for a reasonable fee, naturally. The family business was extremely convenient in this regard, for Howe's Inn had a steady flow of fresh clientele. The inn quickly became the talk of Damariscotta, and a sought-after establishment for those looking for food and lodgings with a side of thrills. The Howes, you might say, were at the vanguard of paranormal tourism in this country.

Though her trances were intermittent and came and went unbidden, and audiences never knew what to expect with Mary, that was all part of her appeal. She was wildly idiosyncratic, eccentric, unpredictable, and always dramatic. When she held séances, they were lively affairs, with disembodied voices and tipping tables, and all manner of spirit presences roving about the room. She was charismatic and convincing, notorious and novel.

Mary's séances were highly variable—sometimes you'd get an incredible performance or a stunning prediction; other times she'd just pop off into a trance and you'd get to watch her sleep. Either way, I can easily picture the *No refunds* sign they surely had somewhere on the premises. In one of her more dramatic predictions, a village resident once asked about a man she knew who had gone to New York City on a short trip. Would he be coming back soon? The man, predicted Mary, was never going to come home at all. She saw him perishing in spectacular fashion amid a blaze of light. Sure enough, he died of a heart attack soon thereafter, during the illumination of the Brooklyn Bridge.

At some point, Mary and Edwin moved out of the inn and took up residence in a private home on Hodgon Street. Well, nearly private. They continued to hold public séances and allowed visitors to view Mary when she was in her trance states.

Then, one night in early December 1882, Mary went into a trance from which she never awoke.

As with all of her deep trances, this one affected her physical body: her heart rate slowed to imperceptibility, her breathing ceased to be detectable, and her body necessitated warming by hot stones, with Edwin at the ready. She remained in this state for a week, and then two weeks. Inquisitive spectators gathered by her bedside, watching this middle-aged woman hover in a state that was not quite life, not quite death, not quite sleep. I wonder what she looked like. Was she peaceful in repose, or was she slack-jawed, drooling, double-chinned? Did her bedroom have the close, sour-breathed odor of a sleeping chamber in winter, or were the windows opened to let in the fresh air? It was warm that December, records show, unseasonably warm. One villager complained in her diary that the Christmas season felt as "hot as July" that year. How often were Mary's bedclothes changed? What did she wear to sleep? Did she scratch or move or stretch, did she kick off the covers, or was she absolutely immobile the entire time? One imagines she was, or there would have been no doubt whether she was dead or alive. As it was, one onlooker softly wondered out loud if she was still living. The room murmured; the town began to talk.

One afternoon there was a soft knock at the front door. A man was admitted; he removed his hat, set down his doctor's bag, and asked to see Mary. It was none other than their family physician, Dr. Dixon, the very same man who had set Mary's ankle when she was a little girl who believed she could fly.

The doctor was let into Mary's bedchamber. He felt for a pulse, he held a mirror to her face to check for respiration—he could ascertain neither. She did not breathe, her heart did not beat—by all laws of medicine and science, she was dead.

Edwin maintained that it was just a trance. A long one, albeit, longer than usual, but nothing they hadn't seen before.

The doctor noted that her body was cold.

It always is, when in such trances, Edwin insisted. Their method of warming her with hot rocks had been done dozens of times before.

The doctor slowly shook his head as he rose from Mary's bedside. This was a difficult case. The woman's body wasn't stiff, she had no odor of putrefaction. And yet she did not seem to breathe! He would need a second opinion before he could declare her dead.

He consulted with two other physicians and they all declared she was medically dead.

The body would have to be moved, they said. A corpse lying around in a private home would pose a health hazard. Edwin refused. He had the support of many villagers who were familiar with Mary's trances. Even the sexton at Hillside Cemetery, where the Howes were always laid to rest, believed she was merely in a trance and refused to bury her.

Dr. Dixon fretted. He was *almost* completely sure that Mary was no longer alive. Her claims of trance states and clairvoyance didn't hold much water with him. He knew her. The odds that her body was merely in stasis while her spirit was roaming mystical regions were . . . remote. She hadn't moved, breathed, eaten, or had a heartbeat in two weeks. Her body was cold. She was dead, plain and simple. And she was a public health hazard.

He signed her death certificate.

She would have to be removed from the Howe home and properly buried. This was no small task, given her brother's obstinate insistence that she yet lived. Dr. Dixon actually came to the Howe home in the night, accompanied by two city officials, and took Mary. They put her in a wooden coffin, nailed it shut, and smuggled her away in the darkness. Two out-of-town gravediggers had been hired; they were either unaware of her case or unaware of whose corpse they were interring that night.

The cemetery they took her to was undisclosed.

About halfway through digging the grave, the two men they'd hired somehow learned who Mary was, and refused to dig any more. They walked off the job and the city officials had to finish it. At some point, Dr. Dixon apparently became impatient, rolled up his shirtsleeves, and joined in the effort. One can imagine him mopping sweat from his brow as the sun threatened to rise and disclose everything. The threat of an angry mob must be highly motivating, because shortly before dawn, the men finished their work. They left the site unmarked, not wishing anyone to disturb the grave, and went home with aching bones and nagging doubts that they kept to themselves. It had been done. To do otherwise would be to undermine the physician's authority, a tacit admission of the triumph of Spiritualism over science. Nobody could ever know where Mary Howe's unmarked grave was located, nor would they ever know if she woke up screaming in terror, clawing at her coffin, when she found herself interred.

To this day, Mary's legend still floats around the small town of Damariscotta. Locals have theories about where she may be buried, and teens enjoy legend-tripping at these sites, swearing they've heard groans, whispered moans, and eerie sounds in the wind when they stand in certain areas that might possibly indicate the site of Mary's grave. Author Greg Latimer, who has written extensively about the Mary Howe case, has narrowed down the possibilities to three graveyards: Pine Knoll, Glidden Cemetery, and Glidden Street Cemetery (two different places, despite the similar names). Latimer has spent hours diligently searching these cemeteries for any signs of an unmarked grave that might be hers. He declared once that if her grave is ever found, he will raise funds for a marker, but assures the public there are "no plans for an exhumation."

The former building that once housed the Wayside Inn is now called the Clark Apartments, and some of the rooms inside can be rented on Airbnb—including the "Mystical Mary Howe" room, which Latimer says is definitely haunted, though maybe not by Mary. The building, he tells me, used to be a hospital and a morgue after it was the Wayside Inn, and residents in the Clark Apartments have many strange reports of unusual—and frightening—occurences there. Some have reported "levitations and visitations," and other disturbing phenomena that Latimer says "seem to be negative." One resident, he told me, had a collection of beach stones in their apartment. They went out for a walk one day and when they returned, the stones were arranged on their bed . . . in the shape of a body. Latimer attests that these residents aren't superstitious or actively looking for spooky experiences, and in most cases know nothing about the history of the building. These people aren't woo, he says: these are "hardcore Maine fishermen."

These experiences make Latimer tend toward belief rather than skepticism when it comes to Mary Howe. He's also on Edwin's side in the question of whether Mary was buried alive. "All the signs indicate she was alive in one form or another," he says. I ask him if that's why he's so dedicated to locating her burial place. It's partly to redress a potential injustice, he told me, but he's also just fascinated by the story of Mary herself, and thinks she deserves more respect and recognition. "She was an interesting and independent-minded woman," he says. She was unmarried and earned her own money, and seemed perfectly content to live life on her own terms even if some villagers considered her an oddity. She deserves to be remembered as much for the risks she took in life as for the bizarre circumstances of her death: "The notoriety she's gotten in her death has superseded the reality of her life." For a nineteenth-century woman to be so independent, Latimer reminded me, would take a lot of strength.[1]

Though Mary's was a remarkable, unusual case, she was not alone in her zest for deep trances. Throughout the nineteenth century, there were other American women who would exhibit similar states, some of whom Mary may have been aware of. One prominent case was that of Lucy Cooke of Montpelier, Vermont. Also known as "Sleeping Lucy," she was a remarkable healer who often went into a "mesmeric sleep" in order to determine a diagnosis. Though some accused her of quackery, others declared that she was a skilled healer and her clairvoyance was just part of her process. An intuitive, empathic physician with an arsenal of herbal remedies and a solid track record? She'd have a five-year wait-list if she were working in Brooklyn today.

Lucy Cooke worked from the 1840s to the 1880s, in both Vermont and Boston, and was a prominent, respected healer who not only advertised, but also received widespread media coverage. It's possible that Mary Howe had heard of her, and would probably have found her inspiring. It's a shame Lucy Cooke wasn't the attending physician at her bedside that fateful day in December—perhaps things would have ended differently for Mary Howe. But, as with all tragedies, a specific series of events has to happen just so, falling into place like dominoes, in order for things to go the way they did. If the weather, for instance, had been a few degrees colder, the ground would have been too frozen to inter her so swiftly, and she may have lain safely in a receiving tomb for a few months, and perhaps awakened . . . or not. Either way, things would have been more definitive.

Another nineteenth-century American woman prone to prolonged clairvoyant trances was Mollie Fancher, also known as "the Brooklyn Enigma."

In 1864, sixteen-year-old Mollie was horseback riding in Prospect Park when she was thrown from her horse, resulting in a severe head injury. She began to experience headaches and fainting spells, and exhibit other symptoms of concussion. Just as she was beginning to recover, another disaster struck. Her skirts got caught in a streetcar door; she fell and, still attached to the vehicle, was dragged by the trolley for nearly half a mile. According to journalist Herbert Asbury, she suffered a spinal injury that left her nervous system "completely deranged." Asbury writes:

On February 3, 1866, she suddenly shrieked, stood on her toes, and spun around like a top. Then she bent forward, clasped her feet in both hands, and began rolling about the kitchen floor like a hoop. She was carried to her bed, and didn't leave it for fifty years and eight days, until she died, on February 11, 1916.[2]

While confined to her bed, Mollie developed highly sensitive psychical abilities, and her "supernatural powers, clairvoyant gifts, and uncanny exploits" made her home on Gates Avenue a tourist attraction. Baffling physicians, astounding spectators, and providing newspapermen with endless fodder, Mollie Fancher grew so famous that P.T. Barnum reportedly begged her to tour with him under his management (despite his offer of a swan's-down mattress and gold-plated bed, she refused). Some of her remarkable feats included finding mislaid articles, describing the "dress and doings" of friends and relatives fifty miles away, predicting thunderstorms several hours before they happened, and reading the contents and letters of unopened books merely by running her hands over them. She could also identify callers at the door before they entered the house. Some attributed her clairvoyant powers to repeated conversations with the dead, or with angels, and some claimed she had been to heaven and back several times.

Throughout her life, Mollie went in and out of trances, some of which lasted only a few hours, some of which continued for days, weeks, and even months. Notably, she hardly ate anything during these altered states. Asbury describes her this way:

Throughout the nine years her eyes remained closed, and for six years her body was cold and rigid, there was no evidence of respiration, her physicians could detect only a slight pulse, and she never spoke. Occasionally she was fed by force, but for some months at a time she was given no nourishment except a little water... During the last three years of the long trance, Miss Fancher's body relaxed to some extent, she spoke once in a while, and she was able to move her left arm with considerable freedom. In that time, she wrote 6,500 letters, a score of poems and lyric prayers, made a satin waist and pleated lining for her coffin, did a great deal of fine embroidery, and fashioned many designs in wax flowers.[3]

The longest trance lasted nine years. Three years after she woke up from this extended nap, she also developed five distinct personalities called Idol, Sunbeam, Ruby, Pearl, and Rosebud. My personal favorite of these is Ruby, who is described as being "dashing and vivacious, even hoydenish, and very gifted in repartee."

Notably, both Mollie and Mary were described as being "cold and rigid" during their trances. Again, had Dr. Dixon known this, perhaps he wouldn't have been so hasty to consign Mary to her grave.

However, it's also worth noting that there are more than a few holes in Mary Howe's story and her claims of clairvoyance. For one thing, when the Wayside Inn was later sold and partially dismantled for renovations, workers found a series of tubes, wires, bells, and other contraptions with no discernible purpose hidden behind the walls. These were surely products of her ingenious brothers' tinkering—remember Edwin and Lorenzo's perpetual motion machine and half-dollar forgery apparatus? They were surely capable of engineering and installing these marvels and undoubtedly not above a little sly trickery to make a half-dollar. Such devices would have been a boon to anyone with an urgent need to make walls knock, tables tip, and ectoplasmic entities echo from the topmost corners of their rooms on a regular basis. A spirit medium, say, with a steady stream of cash customers. Like the best Gothic stories, there are gaps and fissures in Mary's tale, because veracity isn't the point. As the character Jonathan Harker declares at the end of *Dracula*, "We want no proofs, we ask none to believe us."

Another American "premature burial" story I found while researching this book was that of Octavia Hatcher of Kentucky. She apparently fell into a deep depression following the death of her newborn son, Jacob, and died in 1891. Not long after she was buried, a sleeping sickness took hold of the town, in which several people fell into deathlike trances. Her husband James Hatcher, a respectable and wealthy businessman and hotelier, became alarmed and feared the worst. He ordered her body to be disinterred. To his horror, there were signs of a struggle—her hands and fingernails were bloody and broken, as though she had tried to crawl out of her coffin. Thereafter, Hatcher became obsessed with his own potential premature burial, and invested in a safety coffin for himself.

Safety coffins came into vogue beginning in the 1790s, and their popularity peaked in the mid-nineteenth century. It is entirely understandable why people were concerned about premature burial in an era of waves of epidemics, hasty burials, and even isolated cases of real-life premature burials coming to light. These coffins were ingeniously designed and outfitted with contraptions Edwin and Lorenzo Howe would have admired, from bells attached to a string that wound round the finger that could be pulled and sound an alarm bell in the event of a premature burial, to coffins outfitted with glass openings that looked a little like a ship's porthole. Eventually, the fashionable thing to do, for those who could afford it, became building an aboveground mausoleum and just avoiding the whole unpleasantness of being in the ground at all. One legacy of the safety coffin, with its strings and alarm bells, is a couple of false etymologies for common phrases, notably "dead ringer" and "saved by the bell." Dead ringer is a horse-racing term that refers to swapping out one horse for another. A ringer is an exact double, and "dead" in this context is an intensifier signaling the best or the most of something (as in "dead sexy"). While the term originated in horse racing, it is used to signify anyone who looks uncannily like another person. Hence, the David Cronenberg film *Dead Ringers*, which is about identical twins and not premature burial. And "saved by the bell" refers not to a safety coffin, but to a referee in the boxing ring signaling the end of a round. If a boxer was just about to lose, but then the bell was rung, he could advance to the next round and redeem himself, and was hence saved by the bell.

While we do know that James Hatcher bought a safety coffin (which, incidentally, he never used, so one can assume he was not buried before his time) many other aspects of Octavia Hatcher's story aren't all that well-documented. Birth and death records, newspaper articles—all are conspicuously absent. It's just a . . . big blank. Possibly because everyone was down with sleeping sickness? Who knows. But while it's frustrating to not be able to fact-check a story, it's also kind of nice to just let a bit of lore wash over you from time to time. Particularly when there are as many imaginative possibilities as there are in Octavia Hatcher's story: a sleeping sickness immediately evokes images of a fairy tale, and I picture hedges of sharp thorns unfurling over Pikeville, Kentucky.

Also worth noting? Records do disappear from time to time, especially those from the era of paper and frequent fires. Things burn, in other words. Things get lost. That doesn't mean they never existed. And though it does seem a little suspicious that none of the three potential cemeteries where Mary Howe might rest have any burial records from the (relatively recent) year of 1882, without evidence, things can only remain conjecture. One wonders how many legends have sprung up in the wake of missing records, as we humans imaginatively fill in the blanks. Sometimes records get lost. Sometimes December is as warm as July. Sometimes a fanciful young girl launches herself down the stairs, convinced she is an otherworldly, ethereal seraph, who, unlike the rest of us mundane mortals, can unmoor herself from this earth and fly.

A FAMILY CURSED

Part 7

Father, I firmly do believe—
I know—for Death who comes for me
From regions of the blest afar,
Where there is nothing to deceive,
Hath left his iron gate ajar,
And rays of truth you cannot see
Are flashing thro' Eternity—
—Edgar Allan Poe, "Tamerlane"

Trouble Brewing: The Cursed Lemp Family of St. Louis

Andrea

The story of the Lemp family is a Midwestern Gothic set against the backdrop of the famed beer brewing industry in St. Louis, Missouri. At the height of the Gilded Age, a German immigrant family built a vast empire, becoming outrageously wealthy and powerful, and then lost everything in a series of misfortunes, financial reversals, and shockingly violent deaths.

Their story begins in the 1840s, with a bootstrappy immigrant from Eschwege, Germany: Johan Lemp. Upon arriving in America, Johan promptly changed his name to Adam and opened a grocery in St. Louis, selling beer and vinegar. Beer sales quickly outpaced vinegar sales, and soon Adam was in the full-time suds business. His brewery, Western Brewing, was a roaring success. Lemp was at the vanguard of introducing the lager-style beer to America, and everybody loved it. He had the stroke of genius of purchasing a plot of land atop a series of underground limestone caves that ran beneath the city, which made for perfect natural lagering of his beer. Half a millennium ago, medieval monks discovered that subterranean caves were ideal for the lagering process, a technique that was perfected in the German brewing trade, and which Adam Lemp took with him to the New World. Beer is brewed and then rests for a while, coolly and quietly in a dark, subterranean place, mellowing out as the water, hops, yeast, and barley work their *Reinheitsgebot* magic.[1] This light, refreshing beverage was an instant hit with Americans, who prior to that had only had dark, warm cask ale to drink (which, in fairness, can also be lovely when the time is right. . . ask your local Cicerone). The caves are a prime factor in St. Louis's outsized role in American brewing history. Fellow German immigrant Adolphus Busch set up his brewery nearby as well; you may have heard of the Anheuser-Busch brewing company.

When Adam's son William joined the family business, he grew their modest local enterprise into a nationwide empire, utilizing the latest technology to expand their business, including refrigerated train cars for transporting beer throughout the country. William Lemp married Julia Feickert, the daughter of a wealthy saloon keeper, in the 1860s, and the family built a stately home across the street from the brewery. They had eight children together. They were a large, prosperous, by all accounts happy, family. Until they weren't.

In 1901, Frederick Lemp, William's fourth (and favorite) son died tragically of heart failure at the age of only twenty-eight. His poignant obituary states that the family wished to keep the funeral a private affair, but that Frederick's many friends had already sent a bouquet to the house of five dozen pink American Beauty roses tied with a silk ribbon. He left behind a widow and a young daughter. Frederick, it seems, was universally beloved. He died in California, where he had gone for his health, but his body was brought home to St. Louis for burial. In a macabre bit of irony, he was likely brought home on a train car cooled with the same refrigeration technology that made his father's beer distribution possible.

William Lemp grieved hard. He was a changed, and much diminished, man, brought low by the loss of his adored child. He became increasingly unkempt, abstracted, and haggard. Employees at the brewery commented on his altered demeanor. Today we might identify this as clinical depression. Another great blow befell William Lemp in 1904.

Fellow fermenter Frederick Pabst, of Blue Ribbon fame, was William's best friend. William and Frederick had a lot in common. They were both born in Germany in 1836, and both immigrated to America at the age of twelve, and they were both in the suds biz. They shared a common language and clearly a deep bond: William named his son after Frederick Pabst; later his daughter Hilda married Pabst's son. William Lemp seems to have felt that Frederick Pabst really knew him and understood him, better than anyone else.

The loss of his two beloved Fredericks in such close succession would push William Lemp over the edge.

Following the death of his friend on January 1, 1904, from pulmonary edema, William Lemp simply got up from the breakfast table, declared he was feeling under the weather and going to lie down for a rest, and then went to his bedroom and fatally shot himself.

When William Lemp died, the brewery then passed into the hands of his son, William Lemp Jr., known as Billy, who—to hear most people tell it—basically ran the business into the ground. It's said he was apparently less interested in doing his job than he was in running through the family fortune, aided by his spendy wife Lillian, nicknamed the Lavender Lady for her predilection for wearing the light purple shade constantly, even dyeing her horses' bridles to match (she apparently had a different one for every day of the week). Others deny that Billy was an inept businessman, noting that he invested one million dollars into new equipment, and created the most famous Lemp imprint of all time: Falstaff Beer.

But fate wasn't finished with the Lemps.

The youngest Lemp daughter, Elsa, also died by gunshot wound, at her home across town on Hortense Place (number 13, aptly enough) on March 20, 1920. She'd recently been through a hellish time herself, losing her infant child, suffering apparent spousal abuse, and divorcing, then remarrying, her spouse. Her death occurred soon after they "reconciled" and remarried. Though some speculate the cause of her death may have been murder at the hands of her spouse, others believe she too ended her life in keeping with family tradition. When Billy Lemp heard about Elsa's death, he ironically remarked, "Well, that's the Lemp family for you."

Billy and Lillian's marriage, meanwhile, was under strain. Between his alleged philandering and allegations of physical and emotional abuse, and her spendthrift habits, the marriage eventually imploded. The ugly and messy divorce trial that ensued devolved into a media circus, airing everything out in public for all to see. As though Billy didn't have enough going on, the unthinkable soon happened: Prohibition. Billy was well and truly screwed. The brewery shut down and was auctioned off piecemeal for pennies on the dollar. After the acrimonious divorce and this brutal blow to the family fortune, Billy Jr. decided to follow in his father's footsteps in another way: he too died by suicide, shooting himself in the chest in his office in the Lemp mansion.

As if the death of a father and two siblings by gun violence wasn't enough, the Lemp family had one more tragedy in store.

In 1949, another son, Charles—the last Lemp to inhabit the family home—shot his dog, then turned the gun on himself.

He was the only one to leave a note ("If I am found dead, blame no one but myself"). The family name became infamous in the annals of St. Louis history. Small wonder, then, that folks began to refer to the "curse" of the Lemps.

After the death of Charles, the Lemp mansion became a boarding house. Then, in 1975, it was purchased and refurbished by the Pointer family, who operate a hotel and restaurant there to this day (it is noted for its Sunday chicken lunch and mystery dinner theater). Today, the Lemp mansion is considered one of the most haunted houses in America, still home to the family's unquiet spirits.

The Lemps constitute one of St. Louis's most enduring and outsized ghostly legends; it is hard to meet a person from St. Louis who hasn't heard of them. There are obvious reasons why the story is so powerful—all that violent death in the family in two generations is unarguably jaw-dropping. The rise-and-fall arc of the wealthy family is narratively satisfying, and the realness of the Lemps lends heft to a ghostly story in a refreshing contrast to so much ghostlore that is often disappointingly thin and flimsy. You can see their photos and read about them in old newspapers, collect Lemp beer memorabilia, and visit their home. The brewery is still there, right across the street from the mansion. You can visit their mausoleum in Bellefontaine Cemetery. The recency of their story puts them not too far beyond the reach of living memory. I can see the appeal and I've felt the thrill myself: As soon as I started researching the family, I realized how accessible and well documented they were (as many wealthy and socially significant families often are) and it puts a ghost researcher in delightful touch with the past.

Like many people, I first came to the Lemp family through the story of their ghosts and their "curse." Yet the more I learned about them, the less fascinating the ghost stories became in comparison to their real lives. That's not to say the ghost stories aren't fascinating. It certainly stands to reason that a family so cursed would continue to haunt the site of so many of their troubles, and the Pointers have opened the home to ghost hunters, tour guides, and guests curious to see for themselves. The hauntings vary widely in terms of fright and intensity. Some tales are curiously inoffensive (one ghost encounter involved ice being removed from an ice bucket and . . . placed into a sink). Others are classic, like the ghostly man in a black suit who sits at the same table every day but disappears when spoken to, and the piano that plays in an empty room. Some hauntings sound like garden-variety pareidolia—ascribing meaning and pattern to random shapes and sounds—such as shadowy figures and strange noises that are seen and heard in the large 150-year-old house. One genuinely delightful urban legend holds that Vincent Price was a family friend and often spent the night there. It seems Price *was* friends with Charles Lemp, the last surviving family member to live—and die—in the house.

But the more I dug in, the more I found that each new detail of their story reveals another deliciously Gothic layer, but by the time you dig deep enough to peel it back, you find yourself so caught up in the pathos of it all that you can no longer enjoy it as spectacle. An ineffable, unplaceable, unnamable feeling overtook me several times throughout my research as I found myself becoming more and more enmeshed in the world of Lemp. I never felt eager to debunk the ghost stories, as I am sure the house is certainly on some level haunted by their history, their weird energy, their pain. I wasn't becoming obsessed by them per se, but my fascination wasn't academic: Something about this family spoke to me deeply on a level I couldn't quite parse. Yes, I was haunted by the Lemps. But in a different way. I couldn't name what I was feeling. I'm sure the Germans have a word for it.

Poke far enough into any family tree and you'll find dozens of stories, struggles, triumphs, scandals, disasters, and divorces. In terms of pure fact, the Lemps are not that remarkable, outside of being very rich, and the few dramatic outliers (notably Elsa, Billy, and Charles) that are probably not statistically unlikely given the size of their family. What most ghostlore conveniently elides is that four other Lemp siblings lived relatively normal lives: these children, named Hilda, Annie, Louis, and Edwin, all lived well and died peaceful, natural deaths. "To me the Lemps don't stand out," agrees St. Louis historian Amanda Clark. "They just happen to have all the ingredients for a good story."

A vast amount of the Lemps' appeal is the way they conform to the logic of the Gothic. It's as if they'd sat around the kitchen table one night with a list of tropes, checking off each one they planned to embody. Whether because the real facts of their story miraculously align with the archetypes, or because we have retroactively molded them to fit (spoiler: it's a bit of both), everything about the House of Lemp is so hauntingly Gothic, it's hard to decide where to start.

The ancestral or family curse clearly frames everything about the Lemps. Like any good stereotypically Gothic family, the Lemps outwardly flaunt the excesses of their wealth, exhibiting the "moral decay at the height of power" so fundamental to these stories. The decadence at the heart of the Lemp family usually centers on Billy and the outrageously profligate Lillian. Their very excesses mark them from the start as doomed, just as their mansion conforms to the generic conventions of the ancestral home, the rarified environment that typifies Gothic settings—a Midwestern House of Usher.

It's hard to imagine any family that could withstand the kind of public scrutiny that was visited on the Lemps. The inevitable rumors got mixed in with facts, leading to urban legends that still get trotted out to this day, including one that involves Billy's putative illegitimate son hidden away in an attic in the Lemp mansion. Which would be an odd choice, since Billy and Lillian actually lived in the Adam Lemp villa nearby, and not in the Lemp mansion itself, which had ben converted to offices at the time. But that doesn't stop some paranormal investigators from claiming they see this mysterious son named, improbably, "Zeke."

Like most historic ghost stories, the Lemps' actually gets richer the further you get from the ghosts: the history of the family itself is fascinating enough, and honestly, even more Gothic. Bigamy, suicide, a possible murder mystery. The allure of wealth and power so vast it must be cursed, must have some occult source. Plus, let's not forget those underground caves. Part of me is tempted to go with an Ann Radcliffe explanation for the mansion's supposed paranormal activity: could it be some emanation from the underground caves making people feel the strange sensations we attribute to a haunting? Some sort of ether or vapor, as they may have said a hundred years ago. The Lemps used to have a theater down there: "In later years, when beer production began to rely on machine refrigeration, the Lemp family, rather famously, used the caves as a source of entertainment. The remains of the theatre, used for family theatricals, lie under Cherokee Street and a once heated pool is now filled mostly with mud."[2]

There is an undeniable satisfaction in watching life unfurl itself before you like art, and we get enjoyable schadenfreude as the Lemps' fall from grace mirrors our own subconscious fears, secret disappointments, and unresolved intergenerational trauma. Of course they weren't getting the help and support they needed, but this is precisely why they serve a purpose to us now. How boring would it be to hear a story about a happy, successful, therapized, functioning family? Nobody wants to read about that. No, the Lemps became the sacrificial symbolic family, utterly divorced from the reality of their actual lives, in order to serve some kind of cathartic purpose for the rest of us. Into the heart of this wealthy family brimming with dark secrets, we have a landslide of calamities heaped upon them, a "succession of horrors" including suicide, possibly murder, spousal abuse, killing of animals, and cruelty to children. Most of these stories revolve around Billy, who was cruel to Lillian, abusing her and flagrantly visiting sex workers throughout their marriage, shot neighborhood cats for fun ("only the ones who keep me awake," he declared), and terrorized his young son by brandishing pistols in his sight and forcing him to tearfully declare that he didn't believe in God while his mother Lillian tried to raise the boy as a Catholic (Billy would force the child to eat meat on Fridays). Billy goes far beyond a brooding hero; he's sociopathic. Not quite at the level of Manfred in *Otranto*, but still, he comes closest to being the quintessential Gothic male figure: dark, cruel, a terrible father.

Like the Lemp family, the entire concept of the Gothic has its roots in Germany, literally and figuratively, from Germanic tribes sacking Rome in the fifth century to the novels of the late 1700s. Despite the fact that many Gothic romances were set in Italy, Spain, or even France, it is Germany with its dark forests, stone-walled castles, and foreboding fairy tales that bears the stamp of ultimate Gothic-ness. Poe himself, when accused of "Germanism" (code for Gothicism, already retrograde by the 1830s and 1840s when he was writing), retorted that his was not the "terror of Germany but the terror of the soul." All of which is to say, German is the ultimate *Gothik* nationality. And if the sins of the past erupting into the present are another key component of the Gothic mode (and they are), then it is worth remembering that the original sin, as it were, of the Lemp family began in the Fatherland.

According to St. Louis historian Chris Naffziger, Adam Lemp fled Germany because he was bankrupt and owed huge debts. He was an erratic man who often exhibited odd behavior and was likely an alcoholic (he ultimately died of cirrhosis). His German brewery failed and so he came to America, leaving his second wife and his son, a young William Lemp, behind. Upon coming to America, somewhere along the line, he picked up a third wife, but there is no evidence he ever divorced his second wife, William's mother, back in Germany.

Eventually, after Adam succeeded in the New World where he had failed in Germany, and become a successful brewer, he sent an employee of his back to Hessen, near Frankfurt, to pick up his son, but his wife refused to let William go. Upon returning to America, the employee demanded the promised payment for his trip and Adam tried to stiff him; the employee took him to court. In 1848, Adam was forced to return to Germany himself and wrest William away from his real mother. He brought his son to America where he would live in a state of cold, tense resentment with his father and new stepmother. William did agree to live with them and run the new family brewing business, but he was loyal to his birth mother and went back to Germany at least once that we know of to visit her. He never brought her back to America with him, though. His birth mother died in Germany, having lost so many precious, irreplaceable years with her son—not to mention her grandchildren.

There is strong evidence that William Lemp hated, or at least disliked, both his father and his stepmother, the most unequivocal being the fact that, when he built the large Lemp family vault in Bellefontaine Cemetery and had all his family, including his in-laws interred there, he moved neither his father nor his stepmother to the family mausoleum. That's an eternal "fuck you" if there ever was one. And yet William Lemp was a dutiful son when it came to running the brewery. He threw himself into the work and was enormously successful. I wonder about that. Why did he work for his father? Why not defy him and strike out on his own? Was he just very pragmatic, sensing an ideal business opportunity that was too good to pass up? Did he see a chance to best his father, to really show him what he could do? Was filial duty really that strong despite his dislike of his dad? Or was it the pressure of the immigrant child to succeed at all costs? It's difficult for people to understand that kind of pressure if they are not immigrants or first-generation children of immigrants. There is no downtime for us. "You should work from the moment you wake up until the moment you pass out at night," is a direct quote from my mother. You're raised knowing that your parents sacrificed everything and are working their fingers to the bone so you could have a better life but, hey, no pressure. Just be sure to never stop working and succeed no matter what. Leisure is not a luxury you can afford. Was it this drive, this sense of urgency and pressure that made William Lemp work as hard as he did?

Work is also a great way to avoid your home life, if you want to. It's even better than alcohol that way. Of course, if you can combine the two, say, by working in your brewery across the street from your house, there's plenty you can avoid thinking about. And make no mistake about it: William was good at his job. He was at the forefront of mechanical refrigeration technology, soon obviating the need for his father's caves. He used up-to-date refrigeration not only in the brewhouse but also, as we have seen, on the trains that would ship Lemp beer nationwide. In William's hands, Western Brewing became a behemoth, and William became one of the richest men in St. Louis. After Adam died, William officially renamed it the William Lemp Brewery.

These days, some ghost hunting shows declare that William Lemp was a "patriarch" who "ruled his family with an iron fist" and still haunts the Lemp mansion; others assert confidently that his spirit has moved on to the other side. When I look at photographs of William, he doesn't look much like an iron-fisted patriarch. He looks sad, almost wounded, his eyes look like he's about to cry, his beard looks like it's hiding a trembling lip. William was a patriarch in one sense though: he fathered eight children. What kind of father was he? How did he learn to be a father, what lessons did he pick up from his slippery, lawbreaking, debt-avoiding bigamist of a dad? Clearly, he was devoted enough to at least one of his sons that the loss of the child drove him into a deep depression. What about the others? I wonder if he ever talked about fatherhood with his dear friend Frederick Pabst, who was by all accounts a doting, loving, expressive father, known to get down on the floor to play with his five children, and signing his letters to them "Your loving Papa." To be a parent is to relive, often with astonishing impact, your own childhood. You pass through every moment of your own life all over again as your children enter and leave the developmental stages at which you were particularly loved, or particularly devastated.

It seems as though William carried some of Adam's darkness with him, and then passed it down to his son Billy. I wonder if Billy ever felt he lived up to William's standards, to first generation expectations. Try as Billy might, he could not break free from this strain of familial gloom. That Billy should mimic his father's mode of self-destruction, and even carry his name, also speaks to the tropes of doubling so commonly found in the Gothic.

Doubling and duality play out here in many ways; the subterranean caves are a mirror of the terrestrial brewery. The two Williams double each other. Even youngest siblings Edwin and Elsa have a twin-like quality; in childhood they apparently shared a symbiotic closeness. Adam Lemp had a wife in

Germany and a wife in America. The two Fredericks. At all times the past echoes through the present and the horrors visited on this family seem to come in multiples. The dead continuously revive themselves and revisit the living family, and anyone who stays in or near the House of Lemp seems doomed to repeat the past.

Some take umbrage at treating this family's story like a soap opera or a ghost hunt; it's the worst kind of voyeurism, they say, exploiting a family with an obvious history of mental illness and depression. The Lemps aren't a sideshow, they argue. They are a family whose intergenerational trauma is on full display.

"People go to [the Lemp Mansion] to have a fun, creepy experience, but not really look at the tragedy behind it. It's a fun weekend thing to do. No one really talks about the family and the suicides—it's communicated as a fun adrenaline rush," says St. Louis local Mariah Pugliese.[3] They don't talk about the "the women [who] experienced abuse, [whose] mental health was destroyed." Historian Amanda Clark agrees, adding, "The voyeuristic element feeds into something."[4]

Lemp descendant William Byrnes spoke to me about his feelings on the subject. Famously reticent, he only agreed to speak with me after Lemp historian Stephen Walker vouched for me, and I don't blame him. "I don't particularly like the fact that when most people hear the name Lemp they think of the family suicides," he said. "Unfortunately, I understand that's what makes them intriguing. Overall, I think it's a shame that tragedy overshadows the integrity, and the things they achieved. It really tarnishes the reputation and legacy of a great family."[5]

For St. Louisans, the Lemps represent what they could have been—very successful before they crashed and burned. The Lemps lived at the peak of St. Louis and are tied to this "Gilded Age last gasp moment," as Clark characterizes it. In 1904, when the city hosted the World's Fair, St. Louis was considered the crown jewel of the West. But by the mid-twentieth century the city was in decline, reaching a nadir in the 1970s era of "urban renewal," epitomized by the disastrous Pruitt-Igoe housing project, which was eventually demolished on live television.[6] Downtown St. Louis has arguably never recovered, and the city remains suburbanized, segregated, and consistently ranked one of America's most dangerous. Clark notes that the mansion is also in a part of town where "a lot of people used to live and now they don't," noting how it is connected to a physical history of their own family's past. "We hang onto the things from that particular moment in time."

We feel safe projecting ourselves onto the Lemps. Because they have faded into obscurity and most of the main players in their story are deceased, it feels okay to do that. The poet Ted Hughes once wrote, "I hope each of us owns the facts of his or her own life." Critic Janet Malcolm responded: "But, of course, as everyone knows who has ever heard a piece of gossip, we do not 'own' the facts of our lives at all. After we are dead," Malcolm writes, "the pretense that we may somehow be protected against the world's careless malice is abandoned. The branch of the law that putatively protects our good name against libel and slander withdraws from us indifferently. The dead cannot be libeled or slandered. They are without legal recourse."

In the Lemp mansion gift shop, there is a life-sized cardboard cutout of William Lemp Sr. I have questions about this cutout, questions about many things at the Lemp mansion, and I understand the impulse to bust out a Ouija board for answers that history alone cannot provide. We have very few primary sources from the Lemps themselves; most of what we know about them comes from other people: newspapers, trial transcripts. One box at the Missouri Historical Society contains correspondence from Adam Lemp, but it is business correspondence. Like many wealthy families, when it comes to guarding their secrets, they close ranks.

Though this is rarely mentioned in stories about the Lemps, William's wife Julia also fell ill around the time of his suicide, with cancer. She died quietly in her bed in 1906.

Julia is a mystery. She apparently was very private, rarely appearing in public, getting her "greatest joy" from her home and children. She seems like a shadow. When I spoke to historian Stephen Walker he commented, admittedly somewhat speculatively, "We all know someone like that, the person who doesn't come downstairs for the party." "Anhedonia" is the clinical term for it. Speculation aside, there is little said about Julia in the official records, whatever the reason. We do know that Billy was apparently extremely close to his mother, and felt her death terribly.

In the Gothic tradition, the absent mother is a classic trope. According to scholar Choo Li Lin, "The typical Gothic mother is absent or dead. The repression of the mother allows the progression of the narrative in the Gothic mode. The missing mother also serves as a social commentary in which her absence and silence highlight the repression of women within an overwhelming and stifling patriarchal regime."[7] Think of Madame St. Aubert, who dies at the beginning of *The Mysteries of Udolpho*, or the dead mother in *Jane Eyre*, *Jamaica Inn*, or pretty much any other Gothic novel you can think of. Even the living mothers are suppressed in the Gothic—think of the way Manfred treats poor Hippolita in *The Castle of Otranto*. I can only imagine how William Lemp missed his mother after his father fetched him to America and to business, how he wished he could see her again, or hear the sound of her voice.

If I could ask Billy Lemp anything, I would probably ask him what it felt like to know that his brother Frederick was his father's favorite. Frederick, though the fourth son, stood to inherit his father's business; he was the golden child, the favorite, and everybody knew it. I wonder how it made his older brothers—Billy, Louis, and Charles—feel to know that their father loved Frederick best. I wonder how the other children felt when Frederick's death destroyed their father. Everything I read about Billy Lemp makes him sound like a psychopath: he allegedly abused his wife, his son, and his staff. I wonder if Billy's off-putting personality was already present in his youth and if that's why Frederick was the favorite instead of him, the oldest son. The mundane answer I got when I spoke to three different St. Louis historians is that Frederick simply showed the right combination of business sense and personality, and while the other sons participated in the business in their own way, it was mutually understood they all had their role to play. Yet another son, Louis, went to Germany to study brewing and sent his father back a 159-page handwritten report. Somehow this wasn't enough to convince his dad he should be in charge of the brewery. Louis, incidentally, absented himself from the Lemp family after his father's suicide and lived the rest of his days in New York City and other places. According to biographers, the Louis Lemps never returned to St. Louis to participate in family social events, and they shunned the Billy Lemps completely. I have a lot of questions about this family dynamic.

But cardboard cutouts rarely answer direct questions, and the ghosts have not, so far, revealed such nuanced details. We are left to divine what we can with dowsing rods and footsteps, quick apparitions, and the usual spectral mischief, like futzing with ice buckets. According to those in the paranormal world, Charles's ghost often appears in séances and communicates readily via Ouija board, but for the most part, provides only enigmatic, sometimes irrelevant answers. His ghost has communicated that apparently, like most rich people of his era, he disliked Franklin Roosevelt. Which seems a bit strange for a brewer's son to say, since it was FDR who repealed Prohibition. But then, Charles seems to harbor such a permanent grudge over Prohibition that perhaps even a repeal was too little too late. It may be worth noting here that Charles named his dog "Cerva," after the near-beer Billy Lemp introduced during Prohibition (it failed to save the business). And, yes, that would be Cerva, *the dog he shot*. So Charles is signaling a lot of *feelings* here. (Oddly, vis-à-vis the ice bucket ghost, Charles apparently loathed ice.) When not making his political opinions known, he communicates monosyllabically, dropping the words "help," "death," and "rest."

In German, incidentally, the word *lager* literally means "to store," but its connotation signifies something else that is best translated as "to lie down," or "to rest."

Billy Lemp wasn't the only beer baron in St. Louis to commit suicide when Prohibition hit. Brewers P.H. Nolan, Otto Stifel, and August Busch all also committed the "Dutch Act," as suicide was referred to in St. Louis at the time, because it was so tragically common among the ruined and heartbroken German brewers of the city. ("Dutch" was a corruption of the word "Deutsch," or German, which was apparently too much for the St. Louis police force to pronounce.) I got a pristine copy of *Family Reins*, the memoir by Billy Busch, out of the Brooklyn Public Library, wondering if he'd talk about his grandfather's suicide and how it might be framed differently than Billy Lemp's. Sure enough, it was related in a drama-free, matter-of-fact, and simply very sad way. I'm pretty sure I'm the first person to ever crack the spine of that book, and funnily enough it immediately fell open to the exact page I was looking for. Billy Busch simply related the story of his grandfather's medical and business troubles. "We all know now, pain does things to your brain," he writes. He sensibly attributes August's death to stress caused by the enormous pressures of running the business. Amid this epidemic of broken men, it comes to seem that beer was both the lifeblood and the curse of the German immigrant.

It's interesting that Billy chose to commit the "Dutch Act" in the Lemp mansion, which was by that time offices, and not in his home. It seems there is a message to his father in there somewhere.

Intergenerational trauma filters through parents in diverse ways, and traumatized parents have different ways of showing love.

Stephen Walker jokes that the Lemps "make your family look normal," but could any family withstand the scrutiny the Lemps received? My own family history involves World War II, the incarceration of my grandmother in a German work camp, then the imprisonment of my grandfather in a Communist reeducation camp, and, ultimately, my mother fleeing to Switzerland, then Canada, as a refugee. And that's just the stuff I can tell you about. The rest is, as my mother says, "Too much. It's just too much." And that's *just one branch* of my family tree—and every family has its traumas.

Imagine how our lives—your life, my life—might have been monetized if our trauma was packaged with a little more wealth and glamour, a higher profile? If we were famous already, if we were billionaires or royals—or if we were dead and unable to respond—would all the unspoken things that feel like too much to share become fair game for public consumption?

Trauma lives in the body, according to Dutch psychologist Bessel van der Kolk who, like my family, is still metabolizing the war. Bodily trauma can be expressed in many ways, including heart disease, insomnia, and hypertension. Frederick Lemp and Billy's son, William Lemp III, died respectively of heart disease and cerebral hemorrhage, like the kind a stroke can bring on. William Lemp suffered terribly from insomnia in the months before he died. Another cause of heart disease and hypertension is alcoholism.

It has been remarked that German immigrants couldn't seem to get together socially without a lager or two, and in this they were "different from other settlers in regard to social life." Stephen Walker quotes a president of a local German singing society as saying that they "did not come together to have a good time by eating ice cream and drinking soda [and found it difficult to] have a social time without drinking beer." The German word for the feeling of comfortable camaraderie and Falstaffian friendliness is "gemütlichkeit."[8] There is a high percentage of German immigrants' descendants in St. Louis still today, and beer remains the link between the past and the present.

Traumatized children react to their parents in diverse ways, too. Some cling, others grow distant. Fight, flight, fawn. My mother enjoyed flight, literally (she became a stewardess, as they called it in the days when they weighed you before your shift). There is a photo of her in *National Geographic* magazine from 1968, in an article about Communist Czechoslovakia. She is wearing a miniskirt; the caption reads, "Hemlines rise in the east." Her head is down, she is counting money in her change purse intently, like she's saving up to get the fuck out of there, which is exactly what she did. She left Czechoslovakia that August and never looked back.

Traumatized parents have different ways of showing love. My grandmother was an intimidatingly forthright woman, vocally critical and intolerant of fools, but she sewed beautifully, and my mother and aunt were the best-dressed girls in school. You can both lose and express yourself in work. Immigrants like my mother tend to do this often, to labor so intensively not only because they are reaching for the "American dream," but also because sometimes it is the only way to get through the days when you cannot fathom how to find the words to express all your love and grief over the life you left behind.

We all project ourselves onto the Lemps.

I gain no pleasure from poking holes in ghost stories; it is not my mission, my aim, my profession, or my purpose to bludgeon away the charm and fascination of these tales with the blunt force of logic. To dismantle a ghostly legend fact by fact is, to my mind, an unimaginably dull enterprise. The ghost story exists, like any imaginative object as a "thing-in-itself," and needs no proving or disproving.

In my mind, the Lemp family exerts their endless fascination because of the way they have burst out of the boundaries of real life and real history and become symbolic figures. They are the unconscious manifest and made flesh. In literally re-creating the tropes of the Gothic mode, they have entrenched themselves in popular imagination; some of it was an unconscious process of creation and mythologizing, as happens with all ghost stories; some was deliberate ghost tour industrial-complex humbug; and some of it was, uncannily enough, pretty close to the way it really happened.

Did any Lemp children escape the curse? Like a horror movie villain, it seemed capable of following the Lemps even after they left home.

There was at least one child who escaped, though. Edwin, the youngest brother, seems to have evaded the Lemp family curse entirely, living until age ninety as a colorful figure in St. Louis society, enjoying the bachelor life surrounded by his confidantes, his butler, and a bevy of gentlemen friends. He was high-spirited and had a sense of humor and joie de vivre. As a youth, he entered a beauty contest in drag and won. Once he was kicked out of a private club for showing up in a business suit at 4:00 am instead of the required black tie. He said, "Who dresses like that in the middle of the night?" before promptly resigning his membership. And, trust me, Edwin cared about clothes; he owned two hundred sports coats and dozens of pairs of shoes, and once gave away a brand-new camel hair coat when he saw another man wearing an identical one. He lived far away from the Lemp mansion, in a gorgeous home called Cragmore, far out in the country, where he enjoyed the fruits of his father's labor. This son of a captain of industry turned his back on the very economic system that filled St. Louis with sulfurous smoke for so many decades. In the countryside, he ate well, surrounded himself with art acquired on his travels, and generally enjoyed himself. Would he have traded it all for more time with his father, sister, and brothers?

Before Edwin died, he allegedly requested that all Lemp family heirlooms be burned upon his death. When Edwin requested his stuff be burned, was he trying to break the curse, or merely hide a century's worth of correspondence that he didn't want outsiders reading? Can you ever break the curse of intergenerational trauma? Will people ever stop grasping for more money despite the cautionary nature of tales such as the Lemps?

Edwin Lemp alone seemed to understand innately how bound up his family's troubles were with the fraudulent promises of capitalism. When he retired in 1913 at the age of thirty-three, he said that he had enough money, more than he needed to last him the rest of his life, and that he saw no need to make more. "Everyone is always making more money," he mused. "It seems to me that this is the curse of America."

The Trask Family and Yaddo Artist Colony

Leanna

"There are those who have seen ghosts. And those who have not seen ghosts yet." What a prosaically Gothic binary. That's how writer Allan Gurganus opens his essay on "The Ghosts of Yaddo: What They Taught" included in *Yaddo: Making American Culture.*

Those who gather in Yaddo's public gardens may knowingly or unwittingly fall into these categories, lounging in beautifully landscaped surroundings with a looming, Gothic-inspired manor lurking within view; unmistakable and storied. Those appreciating the lush gardens aren't focused on any of the myriad ghosts that lurk in the storied house. But they're there; for those who have not seen ghosts yet. Yaddo makes a promise of storytelling.

Yaddo is an artist colony founded by a family in seemingly endless mourning. The weight of rolling, ongoing, unrelenting loss is staggering to contemplate. And yet the gift to art and artists, born from that grief, is incalculable. There is their loss and then there is their gift.

Spencer and Katrina Trask first came to Saratoga Springs in 1881, escaping New York City while mourning the loss of their firstborn son before his fifth birthday. Their surviving child, four-year-old Christina, named the mansion they rented on the outskirts of Saratoga, noting that Yaddo "sounds like shadow but it's not going to be shadow."[1] Christina, like her parents, wanted to subvert the shadows of their grief and instead welcome something new into their lives. And they picked a particularly mystical, healing place in which to do it.

Saratoga Springs, New York, is a picturesque nineteenth-century spa town in northeast New York State that at one point, famous nineteenth-century female journalist Nellie Bly noted as "one of the most wicked cities in the nation." A destination location in many ways, from the spas that founded it as a site of healing, rejuvenating waters, Saratoga Springs boasted other pastimes like gambling and racing. The city continues to host a popular derby to this day.

During my collegiate years, I spent a summer at Saratoga's Skidmore College—which in Nellie Bly's time period, was a women's college. I undertook a graduate-level theater intensive focusing on performance, writing, and directing. The verdant Skidmore campus sits at the end of a long drive of grand, Victorian homes owing to the town's moneyed past. Not only a meaningful and formative time in my life, that historically grand place was critical in my understanding of storytelling. That summer, our intensive with the Saratoga International Theater Institute focused on the life of Orson Welles, who had a cursed, Gothic career in his own right; a brilliant man rising and falling by taking on one of the most controversial figures in twentieth-century media, William Randolph Hearst, thinly veiled in *Citizen Kane*. With these larger-than-life figures in my foreground, Saratoga's history proved the rich, fascinating background. When Andrea and I, along with the encouragement of our editor and publisher, settled on the topic of this book, I could feel Saratoga Springs calling out for my return. There was far more to its story and I wasn't done storytelling. It lured me back like a siren.

And the Trask family, who made Saratoga Springs their home and left the town a sacred gift, struck me to the core. That's how we choose the chapters we include in these pages; what literally calls to us, in an ineffable, ghostly way. Much like Manhattan's New York Public Library houses all of the Trask papers, including phonograph recordings of Spencer Trask and his family, and one can listen to his and his children's voices as if traveling in time to their grand estate, so has their family history called to me as if I were receiving a phantom telegram from another age.

The first Yaddo was situated on the grounds of a former tavern operated by a veteran of the Revolutionary War, Jacobus Barhyte, and it's said Edgar Allan Poe once visited and worked on some of his poetry at that location. Saratoga Springs lore likes to lay claim to "The Raven," but as a New York City tour guide, I must point out that Poe was working on "The Raven" while staying at a farm on Manhattan's Upper West Side. But Poe was always thinking, dreaming, and writing, so while it's very probable he visited the tavern, it's also very possible he left an imprint on the land of any number of his tales of sorrow and intrigue, of loss and of the specter of death. Connecting one of our most celebrated Gothic authors to this plot of land, who wrote at length about loss, is an exercise in foreshadowing.

If one visits the vibrant website of Yaddo, you'll see gorgeous vistas and stirring testimonies of art and creativity. In the historical section of the website, there is the mention that Yaddo was conceived as an artist colony because the Trasks had been "left without immediate heirs." That's a delicate way to describe utter devastation.

The Trask family summered in Saratoga Springs from 1881 on, but regularly returned to Brooklyn Heights. In March 1888, in the wake of the "Great White Hurricane," one of the severest blizzards ever recorded in United States history, Katrina Trask contracted diphtheria. Thinking her on her deathbed at the age of thirty-five, Katrina's attending doctor allowed her remaining two children, Spencer Jr. and Christina, to give their mother a goodbye kiss.

Katrina recovered. But the children were dead from the disease by mid-April.

I try to wrap my head around the idea of Katrina Trask, resigned to exiting this world, preparing her last goodbyes to those she cherished most in the world, only to outlive them while they perished from the disease contracted by kissing her farewell. If this book is about things stranger than fiction, this simply feels *sadder* than anything I, as an author of fiction and nonfiction, could have conjured on my own.

Katrina managed, in time, to turn grief into creativity, encouraged by friends and family, and privately printed a commemorative book of fonder family memories she called *The Chronicles of Yaddo*. But the family was not done with loss. In 1889, the Trasks' fourth and last child was born, a daughter they named Katrina. She did not live beyond two weeks.

And *still*, this unimaginable pain, the loss of every single one of their children, was hardly the last of their woes. In 1891, while Spencer Trask was severely ill with pneumonia in Brooklyn Heights, the couple received word that Yaddo had caught fire and burned to the ground entirely. Spencer Trask rallied in health and in mission; he demanded a new Yaddo. Clearing of the old structure and construction on the new began promptly. Commissioning William Halsey Wood as designer, a new fifty-five-room Gothic-inspired mansion was finished by 1893.

The Trasks sought sanity and recovery at Yaddo, immersing themselves in art and intellect. They hosted diverse, vital intellectuals like Booker T. Washington, who sought to elevate

Black voices. Famed painters Eastman Johnson and John Singer Sargent painted new works in Yaddo's halls; Katrina's portrait, along with their deceased children, among them. Spencer Trask became critical to the founding of New York City's National Arts Club as well as numerous Saratoga Springs artistic concerns. Additionally, through the 1890s, Trask was responsible for what some later called one of the first international human rights movements when he helped found the National Armenian Relief Committee in response to the Hamidian Massacres, known as the Armenian genocide. New York City was a critical landing point for refugees, from the nineteenth century onwards. I first learned about the Armenian genocide by researching a plaque I'd seen in Union Square when first learning the city's details as a tour guide. I was heartbroken I hadn't known of those horrors before; it felt like something everyone should know and guard against. Then and now. But I remain glad New York proves ready to educate, and has such a long history of sheltering refugees.

In 1899, Katrina had a quite literally spiritual vision for the future. As she and her husband strolled through their wooded land, she said that she felt an "unseen hand laid upon me, an unheard voice calling to me"[2] Katrina goes on to describe this certainty of her vision; exclaiming that Yaddo was meant to be a place of inspiration rather than instruction.

> Those who are city-weary, who are thirsting for the country and for beauty, who are hemmed in by circumstance and have no opportunity to make for themselves a harmonious environment, shall seek it here. At Yaddo they will find the inspiration they need: some of them will see the Muses—some of them will drink of the Fountain of Hippocrene, and all of them will find the Sacred Fire and light their torches at its flame.

She ecstatically explained to her husband that she could *see* artists creating on their grounds.

This grand, rejuvenating idea swept both of them up into something blissful and motivating in the wake of their staggering losses. One of the first things the Trasks did was to put in Yaddo's formal rose garden that would later inspire famous poets like Sylvia Plath. By 1900, Pine Garde was created, a trust to ensure that Yaddo, after their own deaths, would make Katrina's powerful, prophetic vision manifest as truth.

But Fate was not done tormenting Katrina Trask.

On New Year's Eve, 1909, after having campaigned against governmental and institutional corruption, Spencer Trask died in a railcar accident when his car was rammed from behind by another. A distrustful (sometimes misanthropic) part of me wonders if he was deliberately murdered for trying to clean up both the city he was born in and the spa town he adopted as his own.

An evocative statue in downtown Saratoga Springs honors Spencer Trask, his accomplishments, his devotion to the arts, and his ongoing influence as a reformer, philanthropist, and businessman. *Spirit of Life* is the gorgeous statue who reigns over Congress Park, an expansive setting that features some of the town's bubbling springs housed under little gazebos, representing Hygeia, goddess of health, she raises her arms with a shallow bowl in one hand, a pine bough representing the towering pines of Yaddo in the other, as if raising a victorious flame. Water pours from a rock she steps upon (much like Emma Stebbins's *Angel of the Waters* in Central Park, representing fresh water coming to Manhattan), and into a large, meditative reflecting pool below. Nineteenth-century "it girl" Audrey Munson, who author James Bone calls "America's first supermodel" modeled for this stunning sculpture crafted by none other than the man who carved the dynamic, seated Lincoln for his memorial in DC, David Chester French. But even Munson, "Miss Manhattan," has a sad tale to tell, from being the foremost inspiration for some of the most famous sculptures of the nineteenth century, utilized on three-fifths of the Panama-Pacific International Exposition sculpture, from being one of the first actresses to appear nude in a film to being the named reason a man murdered his wife. Dr. Walter Wilkins owned the boarding house Munson and her mother rented rooms in. In 1919, Wilkins killed his wife Julia to be available for Audrey, who, after questioning, said she was never in a relationship with the man. The murder, however, ended her career. Struggling for the next decade, in 1931 Audrey's mother petitioned to have her committed to the St. Lawrence State Hospital in upstate New York, where she was treated for depression and schizophrenia for the next sixty-five years. After her mother's death, she had no visitors for over twenty-five years until a half-niece discovered her. Only one local paper reported her death at the age of 104. It's almost as if the pain and difficulty of the Trask family spread outwards like a plague. But Audrey Munson, as the "spirit of life" is lovely, eternal, and celebrated in a fine park; remembered in better days. Much like how a ghost would likely wish to be seen and remembered; full of youthful grace, rather than struggling or seemingly broken.

Similarly, through their lives, the Trasks wouldn't let any of their tragedies define them. In death, their spirits persist. They are defiant. Yaddo lives on, so do their tributes in sculpture and written word, and so do their ideals.

Katrina Trask was an author and poet. Her office and meditative workspace in Yaddo was known as "the Tower Room" and it is fully appointed in Gothic tracery, a hideaway found up a narrow staircase, with arches and lavish detailing reminiscent of a cathedral. Her workspace was adorned as a chapel and it carries the spiritual weight of one.

A 1948 *Life* magazine spread about Yaddo's legacy as an artist colony featured many images, including a young Truman Capote at a grand desk, working on his debut novel in Katrina's Tower Room, sitting at her Gothic-arched chair, noting her as "Lady Katrina" and that the Tower Room was her "secret hideaway." The architecture, framed with this language, is Gothic trope and visual embodied.

Eventually, after thirteen years had passed after Spencer Trask's death, Katrina remarried close family friend George Foster Peabody in 1921. He had asked for her hand many times but she did not feel she could agree. In her biography, she noted that in that thirteenth year, a unique, inimitable blue light in her room increased in brightness until at long last, it disappeared. Feeling this was a sign that Spencer's spirit had made his departure from this world, she agreed to marry her dear friend. Within a year, on January 8, 1922, Katrina passed away and the town of Saratoga Springs closed down for the day in her honor. Peabody would go on to ensure her wishes were granted; that Yaddo be given wholly to the arts; to shelter and foster writers, artists, and musicians.

The same 1948 *Life* spread also featured a somber picture of the Trask burial plot on the highest hill on the grounds. Katrina's memorial is center, a beautiful carved ledger stone with a stone laurel wreath. Her husbands, featured in two smaller stones, face her. Included in this inner sanctum of a family plot is also the children's governess, Miss Pardee, who was kept on as staff even after the childrens' deaths. Her stone bears the phrase "ever in the circle," a bit of found family honored and retained, even though she long outlived the children she was meant to shepherd. At the core of the plot, Katrina Trask reigns as queen, even in repose, the nucleus, the heart, for all eternity.

The family plot, especially in a secluded, peaceful place, is a staple in many Gothic tales, an "ashes to ashes, dust to dust" reminder. A memento mori of the central characters. So too, in this setting, does Katrina become the long-suffering Gothic heroine of a tragedy. Finding peace at last, she remains centered and celebrated in this familial sepulcher. A reversal of the Gothic trope of absent mother, she was the only one left standing.

When researching this chapter, when I read about the Trask's graves on Yaddo's grounds, I was put in mind of *The Others*, one of my very favorite films, a masterpiece of spectral points of view via unreliable narrators. A transcendent ghost story that changes the viewer's understanding the moment a family plot is revealed and the very life of the characters at the center is called into question.

The Castle of Otronto, deemed by literary history to be the first Gothic novel, centers a family curse right out of the gate and its protagonists must grapple with its realities and consequences. Structurally, a curse presents an automatic conflict the story must tackle and try to resolve, or in some cases, it remains that particularly Gothic engine of dread that readers and audiences watch unfold in a tragedy, helpless to overcome. In these cases, some audiences may be drawn to a cursed narrative as a reminder that their own lot could be worse; "at least I don't have it that bad." An unavoidable curse could serve as a catharsis for readers or perhaps a warning. A curse immediately presents a threat and begs the question: What did those cursed do to deserve it?

In the case of the Trasks, it seems to be a prime example of bad things happening to good people. And still, they managed something generous out of that constantly unfolding tragedy. They still never lost sight of the fact that they did have a life of privilege that others did not have, and it factored into their wanting to offer a place of respite and refuge to struggling artists; seeing art as the way life could triumph over death. Tragic poetry, the lot of it.

Allan Gurganus describes his haunting when he was one of the writers in residence at the colony. He begins by regaling the reader with his first day at Yaddo, when he walked along a lane of tall pines near to the Trask family grave site and a barn owl dropped a bone onto his head. "I knew I had just left the realm of the literal. Anything merely actual, consolingly suburban, was now lost to me. A set of rules reigned gothic here. A bone had struck my cranium roughly sixty feet from the very grave of the lady whose own contagion had, alas, claimed her beloved children. There were rules in force here. But such inverse laws could not be taught. Only learned."

Initially a staunch disbeliever, an experience in his room at Yaddo changed his mind about the existence of spirits.

Between my own dark corner and the late light a figure stood. Five feet tall, it looked smoothed and faceless. Somehow "human," it resembled a dressmaker's dummy. No inverted V of light showed between its legs, so it seemed to wear a floor-length skirt. I knew I was on its front side, its observing side . . . I could see right into it but only as far as into some frosted-pane translucence. Through glass, if darkly. I somehow knew, as I held the three last pages of my story, this guardian spirit had some long proprietary claim on this, her room. She had come back from an unfamiliar storage time, returned to see if her space was being well used.[3]

Some research into the room he had chosen to stay in brought him to Miss Pardee, the children's maid who stayed on with the family, as family, until the literal end. It was her room that he'd found himself in, and he felt sure the ghost was hers, checking in to see that he was doing what he was supposed to. And he had; he'd just finished a manuscript he was particularly proud of. This seemed to draw her out of the ether.

The spirits seem to manifest at these times of artistic triumph, as if the act of creation is a séance drawing them forth.

Katrina Trask's spirit has been seen and reported often on the grounds. Recognizable. Iconic. Interestingly, she seems to always be moving; walking up the grand stairs or wandering the halls. The children too purportedly move freely about; memories still enjoying their home. They are a family together, reunited, in a breath, in a glimpse, from one plane to the next, shades seeking light, forever lending theirs to the transcendent power of the arts so that we may continue to celebrate and contextualize our world. Yaddo is a living, breathing entity for all the art it has nurtured, works that will live on indefinitely, immortal. Proving a curse can be redefined when one doesn't let tragedy be the last word.

The presence of a curse presents the equal and opposite opportunity to break it. The Gothic setting allows for transformation. A Gothic framework is a crucible of survival from which something stronger, albeit transformed, emerges. The Trasks offer unending life to all who create on their grounds. A spectral transaction from one realm to the next.

Above the mantel in the great hall, a mosaic by nineteenth-century décor titan Louis Comfort Tiffany showcases an iridescent blue phoenix rising from licking, golden flames and the Latin inscription below the fire translates to "Unconquered by flame, I, Yaddo, am reborn for peace." So too are the ghosts, eagerly awaiting chapters yet to be written in their midst.

CONCLUSION:
THE ESCAPE . . .

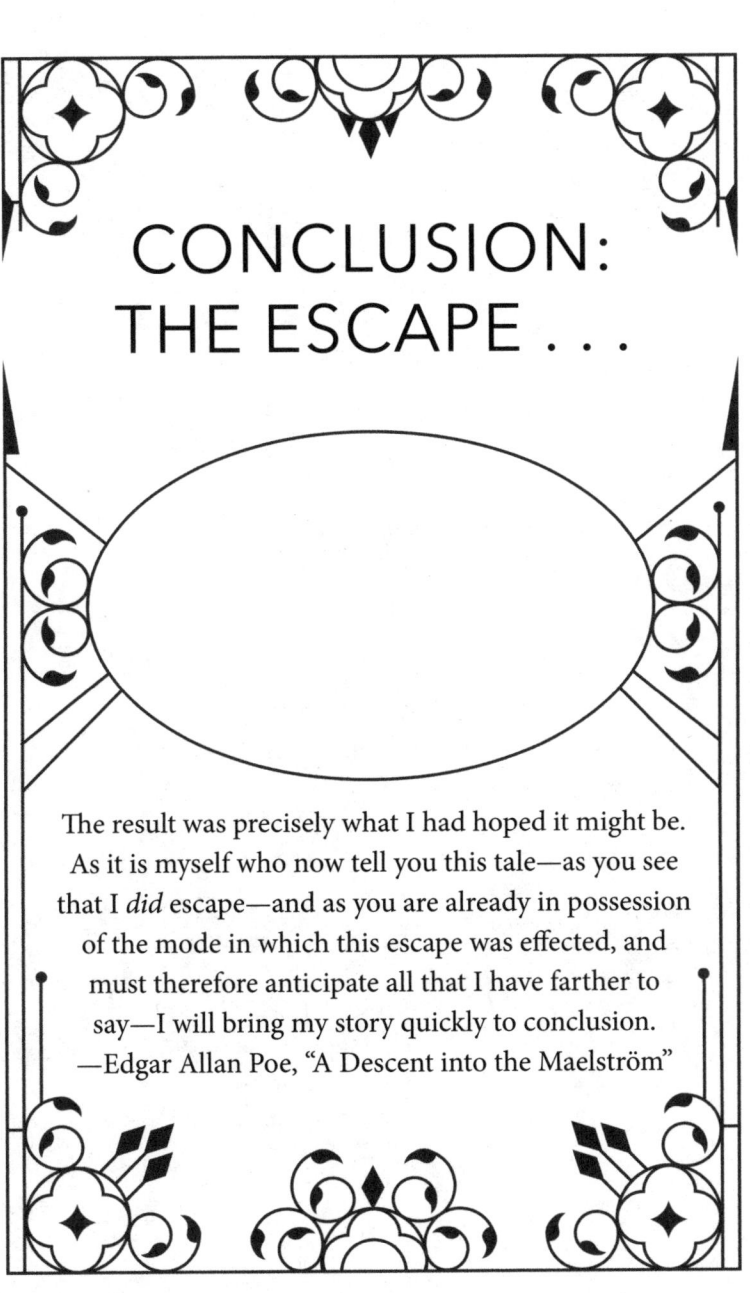

The result was precisely what I had hoped it might be.
As it is myself who now tell you this tale—as you see
that I *did* escape—and as you are already in possession
of the mode in which this escape was effected, and
must therefore anticipate all that I have farther to
say—I will bring my story quickly to conclusion.
—Edgar Allan Poe, "A Descent into the Maelström"

The Escape . . .

Leanna

The Gothic presses its finger on the pulse of the anxieties of the age in which it is written. The story proceeds through twists, turns, and tropes, leaving the reader on the other side of a cathartic, exorcising experience. The protagonist hopefully has been able to flee the house of dread and difficulty and find their way onto a different, safer path.

But what about the ghosts that do not flee, tied to their respective houses or settings? We can look at them as part of our journey; figures from another time reminding us of our own mortality, warning us of present danger through their complicated pasts. They are a part of the ongoing human grappling with mortality. They may be of the past, but their presence is a present concern. The ghost remains a critical part of America's ongoing dialogue with the Gothic, an emblem of our communal discomforts and unanswered questions.

And then, someday, the ghosts whose stories we tell might leave the home they haunted or fade from the setting to which they'd been so tied. Sometimes recurring ghost stories simply stop being reported. Perhaps the ghost managed to run from the house too.

We're asked in our work why there are so many nineteenth-century ghosts that factor into our books and tours.

While there's no consensus in the field, it's thought that perhaps the energy of a spirit has a limited run, both in popular imagination and in its own momentum. The nineteenth century saw us as a society, in art, fiction, film, and photography, begin to conceptualize the ghost as a complex human form rather than an abstract, one-dimensional omen. But as time goes on, perhaps the eighteenth- and nineteenth-century spirits whose stories are regaled across this country in local ghost tours will be replaced by more modern tales; told and retold because they withstand the test of time. I was deeply struck by a comment thread I saw online about how haunted the internet is; full of last posts on social media, seas of discarded forums for services or places no longer in business, old blogs like pages of diaries laid out for all to see, but the trails of any further life has gone cold. Ghosts of the future will be curious indeed.

As ghost tour guides, while we are viewed as both education and entertainment, we're also placing our fingers on the pulse of our audiences' anxieties and curiosities. We are walking through the zeitgeist and seeing what drives people to seek us, and the paranormal, out. We are part of escapism, but inevitably, discussions of spirits make people return to their own.

We're all a Gothic protagonist wandering through an often strange and foreboding world, but we've so many templates to follow and stories to tell about the ways in which we can, personally and societally, all make it to the last page, and beyond.

Acknowledgments

Leanna

Firstly, thank you to editors Liz May, Sarah Selim and the entire Kensington team for seeing this project through. Thanks to Ann Pryor for steadfast publicity support and to agents extraordinaire Sara Megibow and Chelsea Hensley for paving the way. Sara, your ongoing support is so dearly appreciated. Thank you to the Hieber clan as always, I couldn't do what I do without the best family and support system a lady could ever ask for.

Endless thanks to Andrea Janes, whose profound insights and commitment to these subjects continues to prove inspiring. This work would be a ghost of itself without your perspective and irreplaceable voice.

Thanks to Agatha Andrews of the She Wore Black Podcast, not only for talking with us early on in the process, but also for such amazing episode resources, and the material support of cover-reveals and signal-boosting.

Thank you to those in Massachusetts who hosted me and regaled me with stories. Thank you to the LePages for wonderful insights about Hammond Castle and much more. Thanks again to Sebastian Crane for his tour guide instincts, magnificent photos and expert adventuring skills. Thanks to Lawrence Gullo for the world premiere of *Let's Misbehave* that fit so beautifully into the need to tell Charlotte's story. Here's to another drink at the Omni. Thank you, Hannah Kates, for facilitating my time in Cambridge, here's to all *your* magic in the coming years!

Thanks to everyone I interviewed for this book, from Michelle Hamilton's great personal experiences to the Hammond Castle staff, each of you has contributed something really special, a particular thank you to Cynthia Walker for being such a great colleague for so many years and maintaining such a fantastic local resource in the Brick Store Museum. I truly couldn't have written The Octagon chapter without Amanda Ferrario's help, I am so glad that important building is in such kind and expert hands.

Thanks Erin Bryant-Durbin for driving that beloved red Jeep that terrifying night, hope you enjoy seeing that our group freak-out made its way to print!

Thanks to hosts and fellow spiritual travelers Daniel and Mary Holzman-Tweed, you've become such a important part of how my artistic life continues to unfold, Thank you to Molly Van Pelt for being a critical part of my DC experience, I'm so grateful to have shared that research time with such a special soul. Huge thanks to the magical Shveta Thakrar for all the solidarity and sound-boarding.

Thank you, Thom Truelove, for not only sharing your insights and energies but for all the material support, care and magic you've brought with you, physically and spiritually, you're such a treasure and I'm just so blessed by your presence and companionship.

And to Jason Ferrell, I am so sorry that we can't share this story corporeally together, but I raise a glass to your spirit for all we shared. May the cemetery lights forever flicker in your memory.

Andrea

Nothing gives lie to the myth of the solitary writer more than creating a work of nonfiction. This project would have been impossible without the insight, support, and feedback of the many archivists, librarians, historians, fellow writers, family, friends, and colleagues who generously assisted me throughout the writing of this book. I am humbled by your kindness, and truly grateful to you all.

Especially robust thanks are due to my friends in St. Louis, without whom my chapter on the Lemp family would have been a ghost of itself. Stephen P. Walker, thank you for your enormously invaluable assistance. Your tireless research and devotion to the Lemp family helped me to understand this complex clan in all their richness. They are lucky to have you as their champion. To William Byrnes, descendant of the Lemps, thank you for sharing your perspective, and for trusting me. To Amanda Clark, St. Louis historian and tour guide extraordinaire, thank you for sharing your time and resources, and being a fun interview. To Mariah Pugliese, thank you for perspective on St. Louis ghosts, and for being that greatest of modern superheroes: a librarian. To Rebecca Pittman, I am grateful for your generous assistance. And finally, to Chris Naffziger, thank you for making time to speak with me and sharing your encyclopedic knowledge of the Lemp family and St. Louis history.

To Chris Palmer, Jessica Chase, Janice Hubbs, and Liz Fennell at the Prince Edward County Museum in Picton, Ontario, thank you for your assistance with Jennie Creighton's thimble! Thank you to Chris Woodyard, who knows more about Ohio ghosts than anyone alive, for sending me an article about Harriet Martindale at just the right time. To Paul Sturtevant, I am deeply appreciative of you, and I know Hattie is, too. Thank you for sharing your family's story, and for providing us with wonderful photographs.

Thank you to the reference librarians at the New-York Historical Society, for helping me find the Axtell family documents in your archives. It was a thrill to hold original eighteenth century documents in my own two hands and swoon over Elizabeth Shipton's love letters to Aquila Giles.

Great thanks to Rita Leduc, Marie Carter, Silas Costello, and to the horror book club crew (Leila Taylor, Jane Rose, Spencer Lamm, Allison Meier, and Mike Lewi) for reading my shaky rough drafts. And a huge, haunted thank you to Liz Cousins, for driving me around the Gold Coast of Long Island and lunching with me at the Haunted House of Hamburgers. The cats of Long Island are lucky to have you!

Thank you to Michael Bell for your assistance with all things related to New England vampires. I'm glad Dr. Rational and Mike are learning to live in harmony. And to Christa Carmen, thank you for your insights about Dr. Koch and Mercy Brown.

To Ashlie Pounds and Tom Baskett, thank you for your help with some very difficult research, and for teaching me about a side of Florida I'd never imagined.

Greg Latimer, thank you so much for speaking with me about Mary Howe, and for caring so deeply about her. I hope you find her one day. If you do, I'll chip in for that memorial.

A heap of thanks to everyone who took the time to speak with me about the Gothic in the early days of this project as I was trying to get a handle on what I wanted to say: Agatha Andrews, Anna Biller, Laura Westengard, and Emily Alford, you all helped me clarify my thoughts and get the wheels turning, and everything I wrote was enriched by our conversations. Emily, your hand-drawn rubric for Gothic novels remains an endless source of joy and delight.

Thank you to Liz May, Sarah Selim, Rebecca Cremonese, and Ann Pryor at Kensington, to agent Sara Megibow, and to my co-author Leanna Renee Hieber.

To my family, thank you for your kindness and patience with me, as always. Thank you to my mother, Dani Cornell, for driving all over Florida and watching my kid while I meandered off in search of ghosts and ruins. To my dad, Robert Janes, thank you for instilling me with pride in our Newfie heritage. I am so excited that the Isle of Demons is my ancestral home, and I have never felt prouder to be a Canadian than I do right now.

To my dear father-in-law, Thomas Sweeney, who transitioned to Summerland during the writing of this book, I love you and miss you.

To my husband Rob Sweeney, who's put up with my spooky nonsense for seventeen years and still buys me (haunted) souvenir Lemp ashtrays. You're still my Belinski.

To my dearest, loveliest Alice. Your sharp wit and sick burns show me that you're already a stronger, swifter wordsmith than I, and a thousand times smarter and cooler than I ever was or ever will be. I hope you enjoy the Gravity Falls Easter egg I hid in this manuscript for you. I love you!

And finally, to my sister Dr. Daniela Janes, you are my absolute hero and this book would not exist without you. You helped me when I was spiraling, you read every word I wrote and provided incredible, insightful, manuscript-salvaging feedback. Thank you for bearing with me through all the panicked texts and frantic phone calls, for talking me down off the ledge, saving me from myself, and for being the best reader, editor, and big sister in the whole wide world. Thank you thank you thank you!

Further Reading

Obviously, all the classic Gothic novels we've mentioned directly in the text are starters, but a well-rounded understanding of the Gothic should also take into account the host of modern, diverse authors doing innovative, transformative things with the genre. Here are just a few examples. For an expert, ongoing conversation, follow the *She Wore Black* podcast for regular reviews and interviews with Gothic novelists working in the genre today.

Fiction:

Mexican Gothic—Sylvia Morena-Garcia
The Hacienda—Isabel Cañas
The Reformatory—Tananarive Due
Maplecroft / The Family Plot—Cherie Priest
The Ballad of Black Tom/The Changeling—Victor LaValle
Beloved—Toni Morrison
Daughters of Block Island—Christa Carmen
The Little Stranger—Sarah Waters
Weyward—Emilia Hart
The Silent Companions—Laura Purcell
Vanishing Daughters—Cynthia Pelayo

Nonfiction:

Sick Houses: Haunted Homes and the Architecture of Dread—Leila Taylor

Darkly: Black History and America's Gothic Soul—Leila Taylor

Folk Gothic—Dawn Keetley

Gothic: An Illustrated History—Roger Luckhurst

The Gothic: A Very Short Introduction—Nick Groom

Feral & Hysterical: Mother Horror's Ultimate Reading Guide to Dark and Disturbing Fiction by Women—Sadie Hartmann

Works Cited

A Wild and Foreboding Landscape

Canadian Gothic: Bear Woman

Boyer, Elizabeth. *A Colony of One: The Story of a Brave Woman*. Novelty, OH: Veritie Press, 1983.

Gilbert, Sandra M. and Susan Gubar. *The Madwoman in the Attic: The Woman Writer and the Nineteenth-Century Literary Imagination*. New Haven, CT: Yale University Press, 2020.

Luckhurst, Roger. *Gothic: An Illustrated History*. Princeton, NJ: Princeton University Press, 2021.

Ramqvist, Karolina. *The Bear Woman*. Toronto, ON: Coach House Books, 2022.

Thevet, André. *Cosmographie Universelle*. Paris: Chez P. Huilier, 1575. (Reprint.)

Hawthorn, Ainsley. "This phantom island was once believed to lie in the Strait of Belle Isle." CBC.com, July 2, 2023. https://www.cbc.ca/news/canada/newfoundland-labrador/isle-of-demons-1.6888832

Leperqc, Edmee. "Navigating the Silences of Women's History: On Karolina Ramqvist's *The Bear Woman*." *Los Angeles Review of Books*, April 21, 2022. Accessed November 2024. https://lareviewofbooks.org/article/navigating-the-silences-of-womens-history-on-karolina-ramqvists-the-bear-woman/

de Navarre, Marguerite. *The Heptameron of Margaret, Queen of Navarre*. Leopold Flameng, ill. (London: Publisher unknown,

1880), 509–512. Accessed July 2024. https://encyclopediavirginia.org/primary-documents/the-story-of-marguerite-de-la-roque-an-excerpt-from-the-heptameron-of-margaret-queen-of-navarre-by-marguerite-de-navarre-1558/

Parks, Soshi. "The Phantom Island That Haunted 16th-Century Newfoundland." *Atlas Obscura*, December 7, 2023. https://www.atlasobscura.com/articles/phantom-island-isle-of-demons-quirpon-island-newfoundland

Sasseen, Rhian. "She Wants to be Alone." *Aeon*, February 18, 2015. https://aeon.co/essays/is-becoming-a-hermit-the-ultimate-feminist-statement

Smith, Cynthia. "The Elusive Isle of Demons Revealed." Library of Congress, October 26, 2022. https://blogs.loc.gov/maps/2022/10/the-elusive-isle-of-demons/

Dead Ships and Dark Dreams

Smith, Sam. "The Ghost Ship of Harpswell" Sam Smith Archives, September 10, 2012. https://samsmitharchives.wordpress.com/2012/09/10/the-ghost-ship-of-harpswell

Brick Store Museum Script for their "All Souls Walk," courtesy of managing director Cynthia Walker and the Brick Store Museum Archives.

Scott, Beth and Michael Norman. *Historic Haunted America*. New York: Tor Books, 1995.

Bangor Daily Whig and Courier, December 5, 1842.

"Lines Composed on the Loss of the Barque Isidore of Kennebunk, 1842"—Unattributed 1842 Broadside courtesy of the Brick Store Museum Archives, Kennebunk, Maine.

Swamp Goth: Southern Gothic in the Sunshine State

Groom, Nick. *The Gothic: A Very Short Introduction*. New York: Oxford University Press, 2012.

Taylor, Leila. *Darkly: Black History and America's Gothic Soul.* London: Repeater Books, 2019.

Online Sources
Dummett Plantation blog, https://www.ormondhistory.org/dummett
"Dummett Sugar Mill Ruins," *Atlas Obscura*, Accessed July 2024. https://www.atlasobscura.com/places/dummett-sugar-mill-ruins
"Sugar Mill Ruins," Volusia Country website, https://www.volusia.org/services/community-services/parks-recreation-and-culture/parks-and-trails/park-facilities-and-locations/historical-parks/sugar-mill-ruins.stml
Dunlawton Sugar Mill website, https://www.dunlawtonsugarmill gardens.org/index.html

Articles
Solis, Steph. "Tananarive Due's Parents Left Her Civil Rights Lessons," *USA Today*, August 19, 2013.

A Woman on a Journey

Portrait of a Lady: Marian "Clover" Adams

Dykstra, Natalie. *Clover Adams: A Gilded and Heartbreaking Life.* Boston/New York: Houghton Mifflin Harcourt, 2012, p. 206.
Hieber, Leanna Renee. "An Unnamed Sorrow where Marian Adams Should Be" from *The Feminine Macabre, Vol. IV.* New York: Spook-Eats Publishing, 2022, p. 5.
James, Henry (introduction by Geoffrey Moore). *The Portrait of a Lady.* New York: Penguin Classics (reprint), 1986 (introduction copyright 1984).
Alexander, John. *Ghosts! Washington's Most Famous Ghost Stories.* Washington, DC: Washingtonian Books, 1975.

Online Sources

"The Haunted Hay-Adams Hotel" Ghost City Tours.com https://ghostcitytours.com/washington-dc/haunted-places/the-hay-adams-hotel/

Ghost Brides

Janega, Eleanor. *Once and Future Sex: Going Medieval on Women's Roles in Society*. New York: W.W. Norton, 2023.

Winthrop, Theodore. *Cecil Dreeme: A Novel*. New York: NYU Press, 2016.

Zwicker, Roxie J. *Haunted Portland: From Pirates to Ghost Brides*. Charleston, SC: History Press, 2007.

"Lydia Carver, Ghost Bride of Richmond Island." *Courier Gazette*, October 21, 2021. Accessed June 2024. https://knox.villagesoup.com/columnists/half-seas-over/lydia-carver-ghost-bride-of-richmond-island/article_19c17207-fbc2-5b83-86b7-d9298b7329d8.html

The Eternal Headmistress: Helen Peabody and Western College for Women

Walter Havighurst Special Collections Library—Notes from Helen Peabody to Bobbe Burk for a class presentation, assorted recollections from students on Helen Peabody, transcripts of board meetings, notes and ephemera from Helen Peabody, selections from a privately printed book about Western held in archive.

Costa, David J. *As Long as the Earth Endures: Annotated Miami-Illinois Texts*. Lincoln: University of Nebraska Press, 2022.

Online Sources

"Miami Tribe Relations" https://miamioh.edu/miami-tribe-relations/index.html

Mitchell, Madeline. "Calling All Ghost Hunters: New Play at Miami University Brings Back Displaced Spirits" *Cincinnati Enquirer*, October 12, 2018. https://www.cincinnati.com/story /entertainment/theater/2018/10/12/echoes-miami-new -play-miami-university-brings-back-spirits/1605200002 https://miamioh.edu/University_Advancement/MiamiAlum /history_tradition/mysteries/peabody-hall-ghost.html r/NoSleep—"Miami University, Oxford Ohio: The Ghost of Helen Peabody" August 14, 2011. https://www.reddit.com/r/nosleep /comments/jik06/miami_university_oxford_ohio_installment _2_the/

The Heroine Hero: Charlotte Cushman

Stebbins, Emma. *Charlotte Cushman: Her Letters and Memories of Her Life*. Boston: Houghton, Osgood and Company: The Riverside Press, 1878.

Wojczuk, Tana. *Lady Romeo: The Radical and Revolutionary Life of Charlotte Cushman, America's First Celebrity*. New York: Avid Reader Press, 2020.

Baltrusis, Sam. *Ghost Writers: The Hallowed Haunts of Unforgettable Literary Icons*. Maryland: Rowman & Littlefield, 2019.

Online Sources

Green-Wood Cemetery Events: "Gay Gothic: Love, Loss and the Hereafter" October 5, 2024. https://www.green-wood.com /event/gay-gothic-love-loss-and-the-hereafter-3

Wojczuk, Tana. "Charlotte Cushman Broke Barriers on Her Way to Becoming the A-List Actress of the 1800s." *Smithsonian* magazine, June 30, 2020. https://www.smithsonianmag.com /arts-culture/charlotte-cushman-broke-barriers-her-way -becoming-list-actress-1800s-180975221

The Haunted House

The Octagon: Washington, DC

McCue, George. *The Octagon: Being an Account of a Famous Washington Residence, Its Great Years, Decline and Restoration.* Washington, DC: The American Institute of Architects Foundation, 1976, pp. 26, 36.

Ames, Mary Clemmer. *Ten Years in Washington.* Hartford: A.D. Worthington & Co., 1874.

"The Tayloe Mansion," source unknown, printed June 12, 1892, compiled in *The Haunting of The Octagon,* Collected by Alicia Clarke, 1982, GWU Museum Studies Program, Architecture Foundation archives, p. 9.

Rogers, Richard. "Octagon House: Mythical Place." *Evening Star,* October 18, 1956.

Harbinger and Haven: The Dakota

Blackhall, Susan. *Ghosts of New York.* San Diego: Thunder Bay Press, 2005, p. 94.

Farnsworth, Cheri. *The Big Book of New York Ghost Stories.* Lanham: MD: Globe Pequot, 2009 (source, not quoted).

King, Moses. *The King's Handbook of New York City.* Boston: Moses King, 1892 (source, not quoted).

Online Sources

"The Top 10 Secrets of NYCs Iconic Dakota Apartments." *Untapped Cities,* October 14, 2015. https://untappedcities .com/2015/10/14/the-top-10-secrets-of-nycs-iconic-dakota -apartments/9 (source, not quoted)

The Sacrifice: Mary Virginia Wade

Small, Cindy L. *Jennie Wade of Gettysburg.* Gettysburg, PA: Gettysburg Publishing, p. 14.

D'Alessandro, Enrica. *"My Country Needs Me": The Story of Corporal Johnston Hastings Skelly Jr.* Lynchburg, VA: Schroeder Publications, 2012.

Taylor, Leila. *Sick Houses: Haunted Homes and the Architecture of Dread.* London: Repeater Books, 2025.

Interviews
Interview with Michelle Hamilton, June 2024.

The Hidden Chamber

The Nasty Blues: The Story of Melrose Hall

Burrows, Edwin G. and Mike Wallace. *Gotham: A History of New York City to 1898.* New York: Oxford University Press, 2000.

Grant De Pauw, Linda. *Seafaring Women.* New York: Houghton Mifflin Company, 1982.

Hoock, Holger. *Scars of Independence: America's Violent Birth.* New York: Crown Publishing, 2017.

McKito, Valerie H. *From Loyalists to Loyal Citizens: The DePeyster Family of New York.* Albany: State University of New York Press, 2015.

Brooklyn Public Library. "Haunted Brooklyn." Blog, October 24, 2011. https://www.bklynlibrary.org/blog/2011/10/24/haunted-brooklyn

Cutrale, Cheryl. "Pirate Women Storm into Museum of Early Trades." *Patch*, June 6, 2011. https://patch.com/new-jersey/madison/pirate-women-storm-into-museum-of-early-trades

Grose. "How Rape Was Used as a Weapon During the Revolutionary War." *Lenny Letter*, March 2, 2018. Accessed January 2023. https://www.lennyletter.com/story/how-rape-was-used-as-a-weapon-during-the-revolutionary-war

Poe, Edgar Allan. "The Literati of New York City." *Godey's Lady's Book*, 1846. Reprint. Accessed January 2023. https://www.eapoe.org/works/info/pmlny.htm

Ritchie, Anna Cora Ogden Mowatt. *Autobiography of an actress; or, Eight years on the stage.* Boston: Ticknor and Fields, 1859. Accessed January 2023. https://www.loc.gov/item/sd19000145

Spellen, Suzanne. "Walkabout: The History and Legend of Melrose Park." *Brownstoner,* June 25, 2013. Accessed January 2023. https://www.brownstoner.com/history/walkabout-the-history -and-legend-of-melrose-park-part-1/

Archival and Primary Sources

New-York Historical Society. "William Axtell Will and Inventory," September 11, 1795. MS 2958.379. https://researchworks.oclc .org/archivegrid/collection/data/892573841

William Axtell by John Wollaston, Metropolitan Museum of Art, ca. 1749–52. Accessed January 2023. https://www.metmuseum .org/art/collection/search/13338

"A Flatbush Legend." *Brooklyn Daily Eagle,* June 22, 1884.

"The Ghost of Melrose Hall." *Brooklyn Daily Eagle,* October 13, 1895.

"Historic Melrose Hall to be Sold at Auction." *Brooklyn Daily Eagle,* March 27, 1901.

The Subterranean: The Wabasha Street Caves and Seattle Underground

Interviews

Interview with author Cherie Priest, February 2024

Online Sources

"The Underground Tour." http://www.undergroundtour.com/about /history.html

"The Wabasha Street Cave Tours." https://www.wabashacaves.com /tours

Water Cures and Electric Baths: Madwomen in the Attic

Gilbert, Sandra M. and Susan Gubar. *The Madwoman in the Attic: The Woman Writer and the Nineteenth-Century Literary Imagination.* New Haven, CT: Yale University Press, 2020.

McKissack, Patricia C. *The Dark-Thirty: Southern Tales of the Supernatural.* New York: Yearling Press, 1992.

Moore, Kate. *The Woman They Could Not Silence: The Shocking Story of a Woman who Dared to Fight Back.* Naperville, IL: Sourcebooks, 2021.

Randall, Monica. *Winfield: Living in the Shadow of the Woolworths.* New York: Thomas Dunne Books, 2003.

Pratt, Misty. *All in Her Head: How Gender Bias Harms Women's Mental Health.* Vancouver, BC: Greystone Books, 2024.

Reiss, Benjamin. *Theaters of Madness: Insane Asylums & Nineteenth-Century American Culture.* Chicago: University of Chicago Press, 2008.

Rich, Adrienne. *On Lies, Secrets, and Silence. Selected Prose 1966-1978.* New York: W. W. Norton, 1995.

Wang, Esme Weijun. *The Collected Schizophrenias: Essays.* Minneapolis, MN: Graywolf Press, 2019.

Lockyer, Peter. "The Remarkable Life of Jennie Creighton Woolworth." *County & Quinte Living,* November 28, 2020. Accessed June 2024. https://countyandquinteliving.com/the-remarkable-life-of-jennie-creighton-woolworth/

The Great American Castle

Callow, Simon. *Orson Welles: The Road to Xanadu.* New York: Penguin Books, 1995, p. 473.

Online Sources:

"About Hammond Castle Museum." https://www.hammondcastle.org/about/hammond-castle-museum/ and "Hammond Castle

2024 Pride Month." https://www.hammondcastle.org/2024
-pride-month

Brooks, Rebecca Beatrice "John Hammond, Jr.'s Telepathic
Experiments at Hammond Castle." History of Massachusetts
Blog. April 16, 2012. https://historyofmassachusetts.org/john
-hammond-jr-conducted-telepathic-experiments-at-hammond
-castle/

"Cincinnati, Ohio: Loveland Castle." https://hauntedhouses.com
/ohio/loveland-castle/

Griffin, Melanie Ryan. "Best Places for a Ghost Encounter." Eugene
Cascades and Coast. September 27, 2024. https://www.eugene
cascadescoast.org/blog/post/haunted-places/

Denis, Matthew. "Café 541: A Survey of the Region's Scary
Places." *Register Guard*, October 30, 2019. https://www
.registerguard.com/story/entertainment/2019/10/30/cafe-541
-survey-region-s/2409400007/

Damon, Laura. "Ghosts of Belcourt Castle." *Newport Daily News*,
October 23, 2017. https://www.newportri.com/story/news
/2017/10/23/ghosts-belcourt-castle/12757001007/

"The History of the Shelton McMurphey Johnson House." https://
smjhouse.org/about/history/

"Movie Stars of the 1920s Favorite Getaway: Hearst Castle." *She Wore
Stars*. https://www.sheworestars.com/blog/hearst-castle-ghost

A Mysterious Omen

They Told You to Run: Spirits of "The Bloody Pit"

Scott, Beth and Michael Norman. *Historic Haunted America*. New
York: Tor Books, 1995, pp. 216, 220.

"The Hoosac Tunnel." *Brittanica*—https://www.britannica.com
/topic/Hoosac-Tunnel

Ocker, J. W. "Hoosac Tunnel—North Adams, Massachusetts."*Atlas
Obscura and the New England Grimpendium*, May 28, 2012.
https://www.atlasobscura.com/places/hoosac-tunnel

The Crossroads: Motorcycle Ghosts and Resurrection Mary

Brunvand, Jan Harold. *The Vanishing Hitchhiker: American Urban Legends and their Meanings.* New York: W. W. Norton, revised ed. 2003, pp. 13, 19.
Scott, Beth and Michael Norman. *Haunted Heartland.* New York: Warner Books, 1985.
Scott, Beth and Michael Norman. *Historic Haunted America.* New York: Tor Books, 1995.

Online Sources
"Ghost Biker." Miami Alumni Association. https://www.miam ialum.org/s/916/22/Interior.aspx?sid=916&gid=1&pgid=415
Raven, Rory. "13 Curves Haunted Legend of New York." *Magically.* https://www.magickally.com/pin/thirteen-curves-haunted -legend-new-york/
"Historic Marker: Thirteen Curves." William G. Pomeroy Foundation. https://www.wgpfoundation.org/historic-markers/thirteen -curves/
"Deathly Dancer." *Chicago Tribune,* October 25, 1992. https:// www.chicagotribune.com/1992/10/25/deathly-dancer/
Bielski, Ursula. "Marija: The half-life of Resurrection Mary." *Ghost Village,* March 23, 2007. https://www.ghostvillage.com /resources/2007/features_03232007.shtml

An Open Crypt

"Bacteria with Fangs": Mercy Brown and the Vampires of Rhode Island

Barber, Paul. *Vampires, Burial, and Death: Folklore and Reality.* New Haven, CT: Yale University Press, 2010.
Bell, Michael. *Food for the Dead: On the Trail of New England's Vampires.* Middletown, CT: Wesleyan University Press, 2001.

D'Agostino, Thomas. *A History of Vampires in New England*. Charleston, SC: The History Press, 2010.

Groom, Nick. *The Vampire: A New History*. New Haven, CT: Yale University Press, 2018.

Luckhurst, Roger. *Gothic: An Illustrated History*. Princeton, NJ: Princeton University Press, 2021.

Ringel, Faye. *The Gothic Literature and History of New England: Secrets of the Restless Dead*. New York: Anthem Press, 2022.

Skal, David J. *Something in the Blood: The Untold Story of Bram Stoker, the Man Who Wrote* Dracula. New York: W.W. Norton, 2016.

Stoker, Bram. *Dracula*. Auerbach, Nina and David J. Skal, eds. New York: W.W. Norton, 1997.

Wharton, Edith. *Ghosts*. New York: New York Review Books, 2021.

Articles

Holly, Donald H. and Casey E. Cordy. "What's in a Coin? Reading the Material Culture of Legend Tripping and Other Activities." *The Journal of American Folklore*, vol. 120, no. 477, 2007, pp. 335–54. JSTOR, https://doi.org/10.2307/20487558. Accessed May 6, 2024.

Sledzik, Paul S. and Nicholas Bellantoni. "Bioarcheological and Biocultural Evidence for the New England Vampire Folk Belief." *American Journal of Physical Anthropology*, 1994, 94(2):269-74.

Stetson, George. "The Animistic Vampire in New England." *American Anthropologist*, January, 1896, vol. 9, no. 1 (Jan. 1896), pp. 1–13.

Primary Sources

"Testing a Horrible Superstition in the Town of Exeter." *Providence Journal*, March 19, 1892.

"Vampires in Rhode Island." *Boston Evening Transcript*, January 28, 1896, p. 16.

Interviews
Interview with Michael Bell, June 26, 2024.
Interview with Christa Carmen, July 1, 2024.

Online Sources
Lovecraft, H.P. *The Shunned House.* Accessed online May 20, 2024.
https://www.hplovecraft.com/writings/texts/fiction/sh.aspx

Elena and the Count: Key West, Florida

Harrison, Ben. *Undying Love: The True Story of a Passion that Defied Death.* Key West, FL: The New Atlantean Library, 1999, p. 221.

Online and Podcast Sources:
"Karl Tanzler and His Corpse Bride: A Love that Would Not Die with Ben Harrison." *The Haunted History Chronicles* podcast, June 16, 2023.
https://podcasters.spotify.com/pod/show/hauntedchronicles/episodes/Karl-Tanzler-And-His-Corpse-Bride-A-Love-That-Would-Not-Die-with-Ben-Harrison-e25q65n/a-aa0pol7?utm_source=substack&utm_medium=email
Museo Nacional de la Música. "La ausencia de Alberto Villalón" *Medium.* June 12, 2021
https://medium.com/museomusicacuba/la-ausencia-de-alberto-villalón-25967ade9b38.

An Unusually Warm December: The Mysterious Fate of Mary Howe

Latimer, Greg. *Haunted Damariscotta: Ghosts of the Twin Villages and Beyond.* Charleston, SC: The History Press, 2014.

Online Sources

Bradley, Buzz. "Maine Hauntings: The Mystery of Mary Howe." https://b985.fm/maine-hauntings-the-mystery-of-mary-howe/?utm_source=tsmclip&utm_medium=referral

Caron, Sarah Walker. "A Mysterious Death in Damariscotta." *WGME.com*, October 26, 2017. https://wgme.com/news/local/a-mysterious-death-in-damariscotta

Stephens, Kay. "Buried Alive: The Damariscotta Medium Whose 'Death' Still Haunts the Living." *Penobscot Bay Pilot*, October 10, 2014.

A Family Cursed

Trouble Brewing: The Cursed Lemp Family of St. Louis

Busch, Billy. *Family Reins: The Extraordinary Rise and Epic Fall of an American Dynasty*. Ashland, OR : Blackstone Publishing, 2023.

Dickey, Colin. *Ghostland: An American History in Haunted Places*. New York: Penguin Books, 2016.

Johnson, Walter. *The Broken Heart of America: St. Louis and the Violent History of the United States*. New York: Basic Books, 2020.

Pittman, Rebecca F. *The History and Haunting of Lemp Mansion*. Loveland, CO: Wonderland Productions, 2015.

Walker, Stephen P. *Lemp: The Haunting History: The Chilling True Story of One of St. Louis' Most Mysterious Families, and their Ghostly Legacy*. St. Louis, MO: Paranormal Press, 2019.

Online Sources

Eastberg, John. "Captain Frederick Pabst: A Surprisingly Modern Father." June 14, 2018. Accessed March 2024. https://www.pabstmansion.com/2018/06/captain-frederick-pabst-a-surprisingly-modern-fa/

The Trask Family and Yaddo Artist Colony

Gurganus, Allan. "The Ghosts of Yaddo" in McGee, Micki, ed. *Yaddo: Making American Culture*. New York: New York Public Library, Columbia University Press, p. 62.

Trask, Katrina. *The Chronicles of Yaddo*. Privately Printed. (Also noted in the *New York Times*, November 12, 1898.)

Haedrich, Joe. *Haunted Saratoga*. Chestertown, NY: Joe Haedrich, 2019.

Endnotes

CANADIAN GOTHIC: BEAR WOMAN

1 Ramqvist, p. 102
2 *A Colony of One*, p. 2
3 Ramqvist, p. 31
4 Ramqvist, p. 102
5 Lepercq, Edmée. "Navigating the Silences of Women's History: On Karolina Ramqvist's 'The Bear Woman.'" *Los Angeles Review of Books*, April 21, 2022.
6 Ramqvist, p. 137
7 Luckhurst, p. 9
8 Cooper, 2004
9 https://benjaminlefebvre.com/the-dark-side-of-lm-montgomery
10 Ramqvist, p. 228
11 Luckhurst, p. 117
12 Sasseen, 2015

DEAD SHIPS AND DARK DREAMS

1 https://samsmitharchives.wordpress.com/2012/09/10/the-ghost-ship-of-harpswell/
2 All Souls' Walk Script, Courtesy of the Brick Store Museum, Kennebunk, ME

SWAMP GOTH

1 Author interview with Ashlie Pounds, January 2025.

2 https://www.daytonabeach.com/blog/post/the-dummett
-sugar-mill-ruins-sweeten-your-daytona-beach-vacation
-with-some-local-history/)

3 In fact, if the tourist website for the city is to be believed, Jacksonville seems to give lie to a lot of misconceptions about Florida, as it encourages tourists to explore the entirety of its history, including Black history. This is appropriate, considering the city was the home of James Weldon Johnson and John Rosamond Johnson, lyricist and composer of the song "Lift Every Voice and Sing," otherwise known as the Black National Anthem.

4 Taylor, Leila. *Darkly: Black History and America's Gothic Soul.* London: Repeater Books, 2019, pp. 26–7.

5 Leslie Fiedler, *Love and Death in the American Novel.* New York: Delta, 1966, p. 29.

6 Groom, Nick. *The Gothic: A Very Short Introduction.* New York: Oxford University Press, 2012 p. 101.

7 https://www.atlasobscura.com/places/dummett-sug-
ar-mill-ruins

GHOST BRIDES

1 Kim M. Phillips, quoted in Janega, pp. 59-60

2 Janega, Eleanor. *Once and Future Sex: Going Medieval on Women's Roles in Society.* New York: W.W. Norton, 2023, p. 60.

3 Janega, Eleanor. *Once and Future Sex: Going Medieval on Women's Roles in Society.* New York: W.W. Norton, 2023, pp. 61,63.

4 https://www.kxan.com/business/press-releases/ein-presswire
/662249066/grand-galvez-honors-its-resident-ghosts-with-a

-costumed-ghost-bride-ball-and-tours-by-the-ghostess-of
-galveston/

5 https://www.yellowstonepark.com/park/history/yellowstone
-old-faithful-inn-ghost/

6 https://www.cbc.ca/news/canada/calgary/banff-s-ghost
-bride-haunts-new-canadian-coin-1.2662400

7 https://www.health.harvard.edu/mens-health/marriage-and
-men-health

8 https://thegepi.org/the-free-time-gender-gap/

THE HEROINE HERO

1 *Lady Romeo*, p. 22
2 *Lady Romeo*, p. 83
3 Stebbins, Emma. *Charlotte Cushman: Her Letters and Memories of Her Life*, Boston: Houghton, Osgood and Company, The Riverside Press, Cambridge, 1878.

THE OCTAGON

1 McCue, George. *The Octagon: Being an Account of a Famous Washington Residence, Its Great Years, Decline and Restoration.* Washington, DC: The American Institute of Architects Foundation, 1976, p. 26.
2 p. 36
3 Ames, Mary Clemmer. *Ten Years in Washington.* Hartford: A.D. Worthington & Co., 1874.
4 "The Tayloe Mansion", source unknown, printed June 12, 1892, compiled in *The Haunting of The Octagon,* collected by Alicia Clarke, 1982, GWU Museum Studies Program, Architecture Foundation archives, p. 9.

THE DAKOTA

1   Blackhall, Susan. *Ghosts of New York*. San Diego: Thunder Bay Press, 2005, p. 94.
2   *Ghosts of New York*, p. 94.
3   *Ghosts of New York*, p. 94.

THE SACRIFICE

1   Small, Cindy L. *Jennie Wade of Gettysburg*, p. 14.
2   *Jennie Wade of Gettysburg*, p. 9.
3   *Jennie Wade of Gettysburg*, p. 53.

WATER CURES AND ELECTRIC BATHS

1   https://hekint.org/2017/02/22/colonial-madness-he-public -hospital-of-williamsburg-virginia/
2   https://scrc-kb.libraries.wm.edu/john-minson-galt-1819 -1862
3   Taylor, L.B. *Haunted Virginia: Ghosts and Strange Phenomena of the Old Dominion*. Mechanicsburg: Stackpole Books, 2009. See also https://research.colonialwilliamsburg.org/DigitalLibrary /view/index.cfm?doc=ResearchReports%5CRR1409 .xml&highlight=
4   https://www.westsidespirit.com/news/a-building-at -columbia-university-used-to-be-part-of-a-19th-century -insane-asylum-KE2565185
5   https://victorianweb.org/authors/bronte/cbronte/munjal3 .html
6   https://www.cleveland.com/letters/2022/11/i-lived-in-hattie -martindales-old-house-as-a-child-but-its-only-mystery -was-a-walled-up-door.html

THE GREAT AMERICAN CASTLE

1   Callow, Simon. *Orson Welles: The Road to Xanadu.* New York: Penguin Books, 1995, p. 473.

2   https://www.hammondcastle.org/2024-pride-month/

THE CROSSROADS

1   Brunvand, Jan Harold. *The Vanishing Hitchhiker: American Urban Legends and their Meanings.* New York: W. W. Norton, revised ed. 2003, p. 13.

"BACTERIA WITH FANGS"

1   D'Agostino, Thomas. *A History of Vampires in New England.* Charleston, SC: The History Press, 2010, p. 124.

2   https://www.smithsonianmag.com/history/the-great-new -england-vampire-panic-36482878/

3   Marten, Benjamin. *A New Theory of Consumptions—More Es- pecially a Phthisis or Consumption of the Lungs.* London: 1720.

4   Author interview with Christa Carmen, July 2024.

5   Author interview with Christa Carmen, July 2024.

6   Bell, Michael. Food for the Dead: On the Trail of New En- gland's Vampires. Middletown, CT: Wesleyan University Press, 2001.

7   https://www.smithsonianmag.com/history/the-great-new -england-vampire-panic-36482878/

8   Ringel, Faye. *The Gothic Literature and History of New En- gland: Secrets of the Restless Dead.* New York, NY: Anthem Press, 2022, pp. 7-8.

9 Bell, Michael. *Food for the Dead: On the Trail of New England's Vampires.* Middletown, CT: Wesleyan University Press, 2001.

10 Ringel, Faye. *The Gothic Literature and History of New England: Secrets of the Restless Dead.* New York, NY: Anthem Press, 2022, p. 2.

11 (Luckhurst, 88)

12 Ringel, Faye. *The Gothic Literature and History of New England: Secrets of the Restless Dead.* New York, NY: Anthem Press, 2022, p. 6.

13 https://www.denverpost.com/2015/10/29/book-review-the-witches-salem-1692-by-stacy-schiff/

14 Ringel, Faye. *The Gothic Literature and History of New England: Secrets of the Restless Dead.* New York, NY: Anthem Press, 2022, p. 60.

15 https://www.smithsonianmag.com/history/the-great-new-england-vampire-panic-36482878/

16 Ringel, Faye. *The Gothic Literature and History of New England: Secrets of the Restless Dead.* New York, NY: Anthem Press, 2022, p. 60.

17 Ringel, Faye. *The Gothic Literature and History of New England: Secrets of the Restless Dead.* New York, NY: Anthem Press, 2022, p. 264.

18 Ringel, Faye. *The Gothic Literature and History of New England: Secrets of the Restless Dead.* New York, NY: Anthem Press, 2022, p. 62.

19 Luckhurst, Roger. *Gothic: An Illustrated History.* Princeton, NJ: Princeton University Press, 2021, 92.

20 Luckhurst, Roger. *Gothic: An Illustrated History.* Princeton, NJ: Princeton University Press, 2021, p. 80.

21 Luckhurst, Roger. *Gothic: An Illustrated History.* Princeton, NJ: Princeton University Press, 2021, p. 83.

22 Author interview with Christa Carmen, July 2024.

23 Author interview with Michael Bell, June 2024.

24 Bell, Michael. Food for the Dead: On the Trail of New England's Vampires. Middletown, CT: Wesleyan University Press, 2001, p. 72.

25 Groom, Nick. *The Vampire: A New History*. New Haven, CT: Yale University Press, 2018, p. 71.

26 Groom, Nick. *The Vampire: A New History*. New Haven, CT: Yale University Press, 2018, p. 72.

27 Bell 2001:67; Kinder 1970:167

28 Rider 1888; quoted in Bell 2001:67.

29 Bell, Michael. Food for the Dead: On the Trail of New England's Vampires. Middletown, CT: Wesleyan University Press, 2001, pp. 76, 77 and 80.

30 Sidney S. Rider, "The Belief in Vampires in Rhode Island," 1888

31 D'Agostino, Thomas. *A History of Vampires in New England*. Charleston, SC: The History Press, 201056

32 Bell, Michael. Food for the Dead: On the Trail of New England's Vampires. Middletown, CT: Wesleyan University Press, 2001, p. 69.

33 Stetson, *The Animistic Vampire in New England*

34 Ringel, Faye. *The Gothic Literature and History of New England: Secrets of the Restless Dead*. New York, NY: Anthem Press, 2022, p. 63.

35 Stoker, Bram. *Dracula*. Auerbach, Nina and Skal, David J., eds. New York, NY: W.W. Norton & Company, Inc., 1997, p. 56.

36 Tyler, Casey. "Interesting Notes of Foster in 1827." *Pawtuxet Valley Gleaner*, 14 October, 18, 1827.

37 Bell, Michael. Food for the Dead: On the Trail of New England's Vampires. Middletown, CT: Wesleyan University Press, 2001.

38 D'Agostino, Thomas. *A History of Vampires in New England.* Charleston, SC: The History Press, 2010, and Bell, Michael. Food for the Dead: On the Trail of New England's Vampires. Middletown, CT: Wesleyan University Press, 2001.

39 Holly and Cordy. "What's in a Coin? Reading the Material Culture of Legend Tripping and Other Activities." *The Journal of American Folklore*, p. 343).]

40 Author interview with Christa Carmen, July 2024.

41 Author interview with Michael Bell, June 2024.

42 Bell, Michael. Food for the Dead: On the Trail of New England's Vampires. Middletown, CT: Wesleyan University Press, 2001, p. 345.

43 Robinson, Charles. *The New England Ghost Files.* North Attleborough, MA: Covered Bridged Press, 1994.

44 Bell, Michael. Food for the Dead: On the Trail of New England's Vampires. Middletown, CT: Wesleyan University Press, 2001, p. 108.

45 Bell, Michael. Food for the Dead: On the Trail of New England's Vampires. Middletown, CT: Wesleyan University Press, 2001, p. 150.

46 Author interview with Michael Bell, June 2024.

47 Source: Holly and Cordy. "What's in a Coin? Reading the Material Culture of Legend Tripping and Other Activities." *The Journal of American Folklore*, p. 344.)

48 (Young, 1999:88, quoted in Cordy)

AN UNUSUALLY WARM DECEMBER

1 Author interview with Greg Latimer, September 18, 2024

2 Asbury, Herbert, *All Around the Town: Murder, Scandal, Riot, and Mayhem in Old New York.* New York: Alfred A. Knopf, 1929, p. 34.

3   Asbury, Herbert. *All Around the Town: Murder, Scandal, Riot, and Mayhem in Old New York.* New York: Alfred A. Knopf, 1929, p. 39.

TROUBLE BREWING

1   The *Reinheitsgebot* is the famed Bavarian Purity Law of 1516, that stipulated only three ingredients could be used in brewing beer: water, hops, and barley. Some also consider yeast part of this list of ingredients, which is created naturally during the fermentation process.
2   https://www.demenil.org/cherokee-cave
3   Author interview with Mariah Pugliese, March 2024.
4   Author interview with Amanda Clark, April, 2024.
5   Author interview with William P. Byrnes
6   https://www.theguardian.com/cities/2015/apr/22/pruitt-igoe-high-rise-urban-america-history-cities

7   https://epublications.marquette.edu/gothic_motherhood/)
8   Walker, Stephen. *Lemp: The Haunting History.* St. Louis: Paranormal Press, 2019, p. 5.

THE TRASK FAMILY

1   From Katrina Trask's Yaddo, privately printed, also noted in the *New York Times*, Nov. 12, 1898.
2   Trask, Katrina. *Yaddo.* Saratoga Springs, NY, Privately Printed, 1923, p. 193.
3   Gurganus, Allan. "The Ghosts of Yaddo" in McGee, Micki, ed. *Yaddo: Making American Culture.* New York: New York Public Library, Columbia University Press, p. 62.